Introduction

KB046673

수능 1등급에 이르는 가장 과학적 · 경제적 · 효과적인 **길**

이 책은 《뜯어먹는 수능 1등급 기본 영단어 1800》과 더불어 수능 필수 영어 단어를
가장 과학적 · 경제적 · 효과적으로 학습 · 암기할 수 있도록 고안된 표준 매뉴얼입니다.
이 책에 제시된 단어들과 학습법에 따라 자기 주도 학습을 실천해 나간다면
누구나 수능 영어 1등급이라는 목표에 이를 수 있습니다.
(기본 단어가 부족하다면 《뜯어먹는 수능 1등급 기본 영단어 1800》을 먼저 학습하기 바랍니다.)

왜 과학적인가?

영어 단어장도 많고 영단어 학습[암기]법도 가지가지입니다.
고교 수준의 영단어를 어원 중심이나 연상법 등으로 암기하는 것은 적합하지 않습니다.
우리는 정통 기억 · 학습 이론을 바탕으로 우리나라 학습자의 특성과 학습 환경에 맞추어
실제로 단어가 외워질 수밖에 없는 독보적인 장치들을 개발해 이를 정교히 학습 과정화했습니다.
품사별 · 주제별로 범주화하고 최적의 관계망을 구축해 총체적 · 체계적 학습 · 암기를 이끌었습니다.
이는 기억 간섭[방해]을 최소화하고 기억 강화를 최대화하는 가장 과학적인 암기 방법입니다.
또한 능동적 사고 활동인 테스트를 통해 가장 확실한 장기 기억화를 이루도록 했습니다.

왜 경제적인가?

영어에 들일 수 있는 시간과 에너지는 한정될 수밖에 없습니다,
따라서 최소의 단어 암기로 최대의 효과를 거둘 수 있도록 철저히 경제적일 필요가 있습니다.
지난 20여 년 동안 모든 고교 교과서와 수능의 컴퓨터 분석과 가치 평가 작업을 통해
수능 필수 단어들을 엄선했습니다.
이 책에 실린 표제어들과 파생어 · 관련어들은 고교 중상-최상 수준의 단어들을 총망라한 것입니다.
그러므로 이 책을 마스터하기만 하면, 수능 1등급이라는 물고기가 절대 빠져나가지 못할
잔인하리만치 촘촘하고 튼튼한 그물을 갖추게 될 것입니다.

왜 효과적인가?

가장 과학적인 방법 · 과정으로 가장 경제적인 단어들을 학습하니 가장 효과적일 수밖에 없습니다.
이는 그동안 역대 수능에서 거의 100%에 이르는 적중률이 증명해 주듯이 결코 우연이 아닙니다.
표제어와 함께 부각시킨 파생어 · 관련어들에 더욱 주목한다면 학습 · 암기 효과는 극대화될 것입니다.
품사별 컬러화는 영문법의 기초인 영어 품사를 단어와 동시에 직관적으로 습득하게 해줄 것입니다.

세상에 가치 있는 것치고 노력과 정성 없이 이루어지는 것은 아무것도 없습니다.
부디 이 책을 길동무 삼아 수능 영어 1등급으로 가는 여정을 즐겁고 보람차게 끝내기 바랍니다.
이 책이 빛날 수 있도록 도와준 우성희 학형, 출판사 관계자 등 여러분께 깊이 감사드립니다.

김승영 · 고지영

수능 1등급에 이르는 가장 과학적 · 경제적 · 효과적인

11 가지 장치

1 고교 전 교과서+수능 단어 선정

현행 고교 교과서 전부와 그동안 치러졌던 수능을 비롯한 모의고사 · 학평 등 각종 시험 자료 전체를 컴퓨터로 처리한 결과를 바탕으로 엄밀한 가치 평가 작업을 통해 선정한 수능 필수 단어들 중 중상-최상 수준의 단어 1800개를 엄선한 것이다.

2 품사별 · 주제별 분류

품사별 · 주제별로 나누어 단어들 간 최적의 의미망을 짰다.

• Part 1 명사편(DAY 01~DAY 30)

주제별로 30일분으로 나누어 하루 30개씩 900개를 외운다.

• Part 2 동사편(DAY 31~DAY 52)

의미별로 22일분으로 나누어 하루 30개씩 660개를 외운다.

• Part 3 형용사편(DAY 53~DAY 60)

의미별로 8일분으로 나누어 하루 30개씩 240개를 외운다.

3 파생어 · 관련어의 강조

1800개 표제어의 가치 있는 모든 파생어(같은 어원의 다른 (품사) 단어)와 비교어(혼동하기 쉬운 단어)와 기타 관련어(합성어, 관용어 등)를 강조해 제시했다.

4 품사별 체계적 컬러화

색깔	품사	상징	기능
파랑	명사	하늘	사람 · 사물의 이름을 나타내는 중심 단어
빨강	동사	불(에너지)	동작 · 상태를 나타내는 중심 단어
초록	형용사	초목	상태 · 성질을 나타내고 명사를 꾸며주는 단어

영어 단어의 품사는 영어 문법의 기초이자 출발점이다. 가장 강력한 감각인 시각을 활용한 기능성 컬러화로 영단어 품사의 직관적 습득이 가능하다.

5 최신 활용 예구[예문]의 빈칸 문제화

자칫 무시하고 지나치기 쉬운 예구나 예문을 전부 빈칸 문제화했다.

단어를 외운 후 최신 영영 사전과 현행 고교 교과서와 수능 시험 지문 등에서 뽑은 생생한 예구[예문]를 통해 곧바로 능동적인 확인 학습을 할 수 있다.

6 Test를 통한 심화 암기

모든 표제어에 대해 즐겁게 문제를 풀면서 자기 주도 학습을 실천한다.
연어(collocation), 관련어(동의어 · 반의어 · 파생어), 영영사전 뜻풀이, 표준 예문 빈칸 넣기 등 살아있는 어구와 문장으로 이루어진 문제를 풀면서 단어의 뉘앙스와 전형적인 용례까지 확실히 소화할 수 있다.

7 수능 필수 어원(Word Origin) 초고속 완전정복

현대 영단어에서 다르게 변형되고 그 의미도 나뉘고 바뀐 어근(Root)을 통해 기본 단어들을 억지로 외우려는 건 단어 암기보다 어원 학습 부담이 더 커지는 nonsense다.
어원을 통한 단어 학습의 핵심은, 이미 익힌 기본 단어의 확장에 도움이 되는 어원의 꽃인 접두사(Prefix)와 품사를 만드는 접미사(Suffix)다.
수능 필수 접두사 · 접미사를 초고속으로 완전 정복할 수 있도록 총정리 도표화했다.
아울러 꼭 필요한 어근(Root)은 관련어들을 묶어 전부 문제화함으로써 확실하게 비교 암기할 수 있도록 했다.

8 수능 적중 다의어 · 혼동어

수능 빈출 대표적 다의어(여러 뜻의 단어)와 혼동어(형태는 유사한데 의미 · 용법이 상이한 단어)를 엄선해, 빈칸 문제화한 정선된 예구[예문]와 함께 제시했다.
늘 헷갈려 괴롭히던 단어들을 생생한 문장의 Quiz를 풀며 재밌게 잡는다.

9 일일 · 누적 테스트

순서가 바뀌어 제시된 그날의 단어 30개(앞면)와, 그 전 3일 간 누적된 중요 단어 30개(뒷면)로 확인 테스트를 하면서 확실하게 마무리한다.

10 미니 영어 사전

고교 교과서와 수능 문제 전부를 검색해 실제로 자주 쓰이는 단어의 의미만 추려 실은, 수능 영단어의 기준과 표준이 되는 작지만 강한 사전이다.

11 별책 부록 – 일일 암기장

1일 30개씩 정리된 암기장으로, 영단어와 우리말 뜻을 접어서 외울 수 있도록 되어 있다.
본책과 따로 지니고 다니며 언제 어디서든 편리하게 사용할 수 있다.

Contents

DAY별 주제

DAY 01 People & Life	DAY 31 Putting/Carrying
DAY 02 Food & Clothes	DAY 32 Holding/Hitting
DAY 03 Housing	DAY 33 Motion
DAY 04 The Body	DAY 34 The Body
DAY 05 Illness	DAY 35 Creation
DAY 06 Medicine & Health	DAY 36 Removing/Destroying
DAY 07 Feelings	DAY 37 Combining/Separating
DAY 08 Education	DAY 38 Change of Possession
DAY 09 Work	DAY 39 Helping
DAY 10 Transportation	DAY 40 Prevention and Harm
DAY 11 Leisure & Entertainment	DAY 41 Social Interaction
DAY 12 The Arts	DAY 42 Communication 1
DAY 13 Language	DAY 43 Communication 2
DAY 14 The Media	DAY 44 Feelings 1
DAY 15 History & Culture	DAY 45 Feelings 2
DAY 16 Religion & Philosophy	DAY 46 Existence
DAY 17 Society & Social Issues	DAY 47 Appearance/Disappearance
DAY 18 Law & Crime	DAY 48 Emission
DAY 19 Agriculture & Industry	DAY 49 Change of State 1
DAY 20 Economy	DAY 50 Change of State 2
DAY 21 Politics	DAY 51 Thinking/Studying
DAY 22 War & Peace	DAY 52 Judgment
DAY 23 Animals & Plants	DAY 53 Time & Space
DAY 24 The Environment	DAY 54 Degree & Power
DAY 25 The Weather & Disasters	DAY 55 Character & Attitude
DAY 26 The Earth & The Universe	DAY 56 Characteristics
DAY 27 Science	DAY 57 Reality
DAY 28 Technology	DAY 58 Excellence & Importance
DAY 29 Numbers, Quantities & Shapes	DAY 59 Similarity & Difference
DAY 30 Miscellaneous Nouns	DAY 60 Miscellaneous Adjectives

1. 품사별 컬러 표

색깔	품사
파랑	명사
빨강	동사
초록	형용사
갈색	부사

2. 약호(품사 표시)

명 명사   대 대명사

동 동사   접 접속사

형 형용사   전 전치사

부 부사

3. 기호

= 동의어   ▶ 파생어 · 관련어 · 숙어 · 관용어

↔ 반의어   / 공동 적용 어구

비교 비교어   ( ) 생략 가능 어구 · 보충 설명

[ ] 대체 가능 어구

권 장 학 습 법

1. 표제어 30개와 낯을 익힌다.(5분)
먼저 30개 표제어를 순서대로 쭉 훑어보면서 아는 것과는 반갑게 인사하고, 모르는 것과는 첫인사를 나눕니다.

2. 표제어 30개를 파생어 · 관련어와 함께 외운다.(20분)
모르는 단어를 중심으로 본격적으로 집중해서 외웁니다.
쓰거나 듣기 자료를 들으면서 따라할 수도 있습니다.
이때 뜻풀이 오른쪽 파생어 · 관련어 · 비교어 · 관용어 등도 반드시 함께 익힙니다.

3. 빈칸 문제화된 표준 예구[예문]를 푼다.(10분)
주어진 우리말 뜻에 알맞은 영단어를 빈칸에 넣어 예구[예문]를 완성한 후, 이를 통째로 암기합니다.
'오늘의 Dessert'를 맛있게 음미하며 끝냅니다.
※ 학습자의 취향에 따라 2와 3의 과정은 통합해서 할 수도 있습니다.

4. Test의 문제를 즐겁게 푼다.(10분)
답을 직접 써 보는 게 좋지만, 이동 중일 때는 머릿속으로 써 보아도 됩니다.

5. 채점해 보고 틀린 것을 골라내어 다시 학습한다.(5분)
▶총 소요 시간: 약 50분

6. 일일 · 누적 테스트를 통해 확인 암기한다.
부록으로 제공된 일일 테스트와 누적 테스트를 한 후, 틀린 것은 다시 학습 · 암기합니다.

7. 별책 부록 일일 암기장을 지니고 다니며 수시로 본다.
일일 암기장을 평소 수시로 꺼내 보면서 개별 단어의 형태 · 의미와 함께 전체 단어의 관계망을 시각적으로 익혀 장기 기억의 영역에 확실히 각인시킵니다.
※ 단어는 책상 앞에서보다 이동 중일 때 더 잘 외워집니다.

01 ancestor
[ǽnsestər]

조상[선조](=forefather) ▶ancestry (집합적) 조상[선조]

조상들의 나라를 모국이라고 부른다.

You call the land of your _____ s your motherland.

02 descendant
[diséndənt]

자손[후손] ▶descend 동 내려가다, ~의 자손이다
▶descent 하강, 가계

그는 자신이 세종대왕의 직계 후손이라고 주장한다.

He claims to be a direct _____ of King Sejong.

03 offspring
[ɔ́(ː)fsprìŋ]

자식[새끼](들)

그 질병이 있는 부모가 자식에게 옮기는 것 같다.

Parents with the disease are likely to pass it on to their _____.

04 sibling
[síbliŋ]

(한 명의) 형제자매[동기]

그는 형제자매가 없다.

He has no _____ s.

05 orphan
[ɔ́ːrfən]

고아 동 고아로 만들다 ▶orphanage 고아원

고아 소년들/소녀들 _____ boys/girls

그녀는 전쟁 중에 고아가 되었다. She was _____ ed in the war.

06 companion
[kəmpǽnjən]

❶ 동반자 ❷ 친구[벗] ▶companionship 동료애[우정]
▶company 회사, 함께 있음, 친구들

내 어린 시절의 벗 a _____ of my childhood

07 acquaintance
[əkwéintəns]

❶ 아는 사람[지인] ▶acquainted 형 아는[아는 사이인]
❷ 면식 ❸ 지식 (↔ unacquainted)

그는 친구가 아니라 아는 사람이다.

He is not a friend, but an _____.

08 infant
[ínfənt]

유아[아기] 형 유아용의 ▶infancy 유아기
▶infantile 형 유치한(=childish), 유아의

여성은 생리적으로 아기를 낳고 기르게 되어 있다.

Women are physiologically designed to bear and rear _____ s.

09 adolescent
[æ̀dəlésnt]

청소년(=teenage(r)) ▶adolescence 청소년기
형 ❶ 청소년의 ❷ 유치한

혼란스러운 청소년 a confused _____

10 juvenile
[dʒúːvənl]

청소년 형 ❶ 청소년의 ❷ 유치한

청소년들에 의해 저질러지는 범죄들 crimes committed by _____ s

청소년 소설 _____ fiction

11 puberty
[pjúːbərti]

사춘기

다양한 신체적·정서적 변화들이 사춘기에 일어난다.

A variety of physical and emotional changes take place during _____.

12 lifespan
[láifspæn]

수명(= life expectancy)　　　▶ span 기간, 길이

남성은 여성보다 수명이 더 짧다.

Men have a shorter _____ than women.

13 pregnancy
[prégnənsi]

임신　　　▶ pregnant 형 임신한

10대 임신　teenage _____ies

14 abortion
[əbɔ́ːrʃən]

낙태　　　▶ abort 동 낙태하다

낙태 반대 운동　an anti-_____ campaign

15 embryo
[émbriòu]

(임신 8주까지의) 태아[배아]

일부 과학자들이 인간 배아를 복제하려고 시도해왔다.

Some scientists have tried to clone a human _____.

16 fetus
[fíːtəs]

(임신 9주 이후의) 태아　　　▶ fetal 형 태아의

6개월 된 태아　the 6-month-old _____

17 cradle
[kréidl]

요람

아기가 요람에서 잠자고 있다.

A baby is sleeping in the _____.

18 gender
[dʒéndər]

(사회적) 성(= sex)

성차(性差)　_____ difference

19 spouse
[spaus]

배우자

배우자의 선택　the choice of a _____

20 engagement
[ingéidʒmənt]

❶ 약혼 ❷ 약속 ❸ 교전 ❹ 관여　▶ engage 동 ❶ 참여[관여]하다
　　　　　　　　　　　　　　　　　　　❷ 주의를 끌다 ❸ 고용하다
　　　　　　　　　　　　　　　　　　　❹ 교전하다

그들의 약혼이 발표되었다/깨졌다.

Their _____ was announced/broken off.

21 divorce
[divɔ́ːrs]

이혼　동 이혼하다

이혼율의 증가　the rise in the _____ rate

22 euthanasia
[jùːθənéiʒə]

안락사(= mercy killing)

많은 사람들이 죽기를 원하는 말기 환자의 안락사를 지지한다.

Many people support _____ for terminally-ill patients who wish to die.

23 corpse
[kɔːrps]

시체(= body)

▶비교 corps 군단[부대], 단체[집단]

전쟁터의 시체들 _____s on the battlefield

24 coffin
[kɔ́(ː)fin]

관

관이 무덤 속에 안치되었다.

The _____ was placed in the grave.

25 condolence
[kəndóuləns]

애도[조의]

▶ condole 동 조문하다[조의를 표하다]

나는 그의 미망인에게 조의를 표했다.

I expressed my _____ to his widow.

26 funeral
[fjúːnərəl]

장례(식)

많은 조문객이 그의 장례식에 참석했다.

Many mourners attended his _____.

27 cremation
[kriméiʃən]

화장(火葬)

▶비교 burial 매장
▶ cremate 동 화장하다

어떤 나라들에서는 화장이 매장보다 더 흔하다.

_____ is more common than burial in some countries.

28 grave
[greiv]

무덤(= tomb)
형 심각한

▶ graveyard 묘지
▶ gravestone 묘비
▶ gravity ❶ 중력 ❷ 심각성

요람에서 무덤까지 from cradle to _____

29 cemetery
[sémətèri]

(교회에 속하지 않은) 공동묘지

그는 국립묘지에 묻혀 있다.

He is buried at the National C_____.

30 widow
↔ widower
[wídou] ↔ [wídouər]

과부[미망인] ↔ 홀아비

그는 미망인과 3명의 자식을 남기고 죽었다.

He left a _____ and three children.

Today's Dessert

When you were born, you cried and the world rejoiced. Live your life in such a manner that when you die the world cries and you rejoice.

네가 태어날 때 너는 울었고 세상은 기뻐했다. 네가 죽을 때 세상은 울고 너는 기뻐할 수 있는 삶을 살아라.

사람들 · 인생

Part 1

TEST 01

A 영어는 우리말로, 우리말은 영어로!

1	a direct descendant		8	고아 소년	an o_____ boy
2	a business acquaintance		9	청소년 범죄	j_____ crime
3	adolescents aged 12 to 18		10	평균 수명	an average l_____
4	the age of puberty		11	불법 낙태	an illegal a_____
5	human embryos		12	성 역할	g_____ roles
6	the 6-month-old fetus		13	이혼 서류	d_____ papers
7	a decaying corpse		14	장례 행렬	a f_____ procession

B 영영사전 뜻풀이에 알맞은 단어 찾기

보기	ancestor cremation euthanasia offspring

1 _____ : a person's child or an animal's young

2 _____ : the burning of a corpse until only ashes are left

3 _____ : a member of your family who lived a long time ago

4 _____ : the painless killing of people who are very ill or old

C 관련된 것끼리 연결하기

1 companion ·   a. baby

2 infant ·   b. friend

3 sibling ·   c. husband or wife

4 spouse ·   d. brother or sister

D 빈칸에 가장 적절한 단어 넣기

보기	cemetery condolence coffin cradle grave pregnancy widow

1 He was buried in the National _____. 그는 국립묘지에 묻혔다.

2 It's harmful to drink alcohol during _____. 임신 중의 음주는 해롭다.

3 I expressed my _____ to his _____. 나는 그의 미망인에게 조의를 표했다.

4 The _____ was lowered into the _____. 관이 무덤 속으로 내려졌다.

5 She rocked the _____ to lull the baby to sleep. 그녀는 아기를 재우려고 요람을 흔들었다.

ANSWER

A 1. 직계 후손 2. 사업상 아는 사람 3. 12세에서 18세의 청소년 4. 사춘기 5. 인간 배아 6. 6개월 된 태아 7. 썩어 가는 시체 8. orphan 9. juvenile 10. lifespan 11. abortion 12. gender 13. divorce 14. funeral **B** 1. offspring 2. cremation 3. ancestor 4. euthanasia **C** 1. b 2. a 3. d 4. c **D** 1. Cemetery 2. pregnancy 3. condolence, widow 4. coffin, grave 5. cradle

사람들 · 인생

Part 1

01 **beverage**
[bévəridʒ]

마실 것[음료](=drink)

알코올/탄산음료 alcoholic/carbonated _____s

02 **refreshment**
[rifréʃmənt]

❶ (-s) 다과 ❷ (가벼운) 음식물 ▶refresh 동 생기를 되찾게 하다
❸ 원기 회복

휴식 시간에 간단한 다과가 제공될 것입니다.
Light _____s will be served during the break.

03 **liquor**
[líkər]

독한 술

그는 포도주와 맥주는 마시지만 독한 술은 마시지 않는다.
He drinks wine and beer but no _____.

04 **dairy**
[déəri]

낙농장, 유제품 회사   비교 diary 일기(장)
형 유제품[낙농]의

유제품 _____ products
낙농업 the _____ industry

05 **veal/mutton**
[viːl]/[mʌ́tn]

송아지 고기/양 고기   비교 beef/pork 쇠고기/돼지고기

구운 송아지 고기 roast _____
양 고기 스튜 _____ stew

06 **vegetarian**
[vèdʒətéəriən]

채식주의자 형 채식의

난 채식주의자가 될까 생각 중이다.
I'm thinking about becoming a _____.

07 **gourmet**
[guərméi]

미식가[식도락가] 형 (미식가용) 고급의

(미식가용) 고급 식당/식사 a _____ restaurant/meal

08 **cuisine**
[kwizíːn]

(독특한) 요리(법)   비교 recipe 요리[조리]법

한국 전통 요리(법) the Korean traditional _____

09 **ingredient**
[ingríːdiənt]

(요리의) 재료[성분], 요소

대접에 모든 재료를 섞어라.
Mix all the _____s in a bowl.

10 **dough**
[dou]

가루 반죽   비교 paste 반죽, 풀
                  pastry 페이스트리 (반죽)
                  ▶doughnut 도넛

빵 반죽 bread _____

11 spice
[spais]

(가루·씨앗) 양념   ▶spicy 휑 맛이 강한[매운](=hot)

양념한 음식은 맛이 좋다.
Foods with _____s taste good.

12 seasoning
[síːzəniŋ]

양념   ▶seasoned 휑 ❶ 양념한 ❷ 경험 많은

소금과 후추는 가장 흔한 두 가지 양념이다.
Salt and pepper are the two most common _____s.

13 flavor
[fléivər]

맛(=taste)   동 맛을 내다

초콜릿이나 바닐라 중 어떤 맛을 원하니?
Which _____ do you want – chocolate or vanilla?

14 appetite
[ǽpətàit]

❶ 식욕 ❷ 욕구[욕망]   ▶appetizer 식욕을 돋우는 음식[전채]

전채는 식욕을 돋우는 간단한 요리이다.
An appetizer is a small dish to get your _____ going.

15 leftover
[léftòuvər]

(-s) 먹다 남은 음식   휑 남은

먹다 남은 음식을 개에게 줘라.
Give the _____s to the dog.

16 nutrition
[njuːtríʃən]

영양 (섭취)   ▶malnutrition 영양실조
                   ▶nutrient 영양소[영양분]
                   ▶nutritious 휑 영양분이 풍부한

좋은 영양 섭취는 건강을 위해 필수 불가결하다.
Good _____ is essential for good health.

17 nourishment
[nə́ːriʃmənt]

영양분[자양분]   ▶nourish 동 영양분을 공급하다

아이는 적절한 영양분이 필요하다.
A child needs proper _____.

18 carbohydrate
[kὰːrbouháidreit]

탄수화물

탄수화물은 빠르게 에너지를 낸다.
_____s give you quick energy.

19 protein
[próutiːn]

단백질

콩은 좋은 식물성 단백질원이다.
Beans are a good source of vegetable _____.

20 intake
[íntèik]

❶ 섭취량 ❷ 흡입[주입]구

지방 섭취량을 줄이려고 노력해라.
Try to reduce your _____ of fat.

21 fiber
[fáibər]

섬유(질)   ▶dietary fiber 식이 섬유

과일과 야채는 섬유질 함량이 높다.
Fruit and vegetables are high in _____ content.

음식·옷

Part 1

22 fabric
[fǽbrik]

❶ 직물 ❷ 구조
면/견/모직물 cotton/silk/woolen _____ s

23 textile
[tékstail]

직물
직물 제조업 _____ manufacture

24 garment
[gá:rmənt]

옷[의류]
겉옷 outer _____ s
의류 산업 the _____ industry

25 outfit
[áutfit]

❶ (특수복 한 벌) 옷[복장] ❷ 팀[그룹/회사]
스키복/결혼 예복/슈퍼맨 복장
a ski/wedding/Superman _____

26 costume
[kástʃu:m]

(무대·시대·지방) 의상
연극에서 나는 왕의 의상을 입었다.
In our play I wore a king's _____.

27 cosmetic
[kɑzmétik]

(-s) 화장품(=make-up)   ▶cosmetic surgery 성형 수술
혱 화장[성형]의
가장 잘 팔리는 화장품 상표
the best-selling _____ s brand

28 gem
[dʒem]

보석(=jewel)
그 왕관에는 보석들이 박혀 있었다.
The crown was set with _____ s.

29 vogue
[voug]

유행(=fashion)
미니스커트가 다시 유행이다.
Miniskirts are in _____ again.

30 fad
[fæd]

일시적 유행
찢어진 청바지를 입는 것이 일시적 유행이었다.
There was a _____ for wearing ripped jeans.

Today's
Dessert If you have food in the refrigerator, clothes on your back, and a roof overhead, you are richer than 75% of this world.
냉장고에 먹을 음식이 있고, 몸뚱이에 걸칠 옷이 있고, 머리 위에 지붕이 있다면, 넌 이 세상의 75%보다 더 부자다.

Food & Clothes

TEST 02

A 영어는 우리말로, 우리말은 영어로!

1 gourmet foods
2 a delicate flavor
3 a high intake of salt
4 textile design
5 cotton fabrics
6 the cosmetics industry

7 유제품   d_____ products
8 (요리) 재료 목록   a list of i_____s
9 식욕 부진   loss of a_____
10 적절한 영양 섭취   adequate n_____
11 의류 산업   the g_____ industry
12 전통 의상   a traditional c_____

B 영영사전 뜻풀이에 알맞은 단어 찾기

> 보기   cuisine   fad   liquor   outfit   vegetarian

1 _____ : strong alcoholic drink
2 _____ : a particular style of cooking
3 _____ : a person who does not eat meat or fish
4 _____ : something that is fashionable for a short time
5 _____ : a set of clothes worn for a particular occasion or activity

C 관련된 것끼리 연결하기

1 beverage   •
2 gem   •
3 nutrient   •
4 seasoning   •

a. diamond, emerald, ruby
b. coffee, tea, mineral water, soda
c. salt, pepper, herb, spice, soybean paste
d. carbohydrate, protein, fat, mineral, vitamin

D 빈칸에 가장 적절한 단어 넣기

> 보기   fiber   leftover   nourishment   refreshment   vogue

1 Put the _____ s in the fridge. 먹다 남은 음식을 냉장고에 넣어라.
2 Most vegetables contain _____. 대부분의 채소에는 섬유질이 들어 있다.
3 Long boots are in _____ this winter. 긴 부츠가 올겨울에 유행이다.
4 _____ s will be served after the meeting. 회의 후에 다과가 제공될 것이다.
5 The fetus gets _____ via the mother's blood supply.
　 태아는 어머니의 혈액 공급을 통해 영양분을 얻는다.

ANSWER

A 1. 고급 음식들 2. 부드러운 맛 3. 염분 과다 섭취 4. 직물 디자인 5. 면직물 6. 화장품 산업 7. dairy 8. ingredient 9. appetite 10. nutrition
11. garment 12. costume   B 1. liquor 2. cuisine 3. vegetarian 4. fad 5. outfit   C 1. b 2. a 3. d 4. c   D 1. leftover 2. fiber
3. vogue 4. Refreshment 5. nourishment

음식 · 옷

Part 1

Housing

01 shelter
[ʃéltər]

주거지, 피신처[대피소/보호소] **동** 보호하다[피신처를 제공하다]
인간은 의식주가 필요하다.
Human beings need food, clothing and _____.

02 dwelling
[dwéliŋ]

주거지[주택]
▶ dwell **동** 살다[거주하다]
▶ dweller 거주자[주민]

전통 주택이 고층 콘크리트 건물로 바뀌고 있다.
The traditional _____s are replaced by multi-storied concrete buildings.

03 residence
[rézədəns]

❶ 주거지[주택/저택]
❷ 거주
❸ 거주 허가[거주권](=residency)

▶ reside **동** 살다[거주하다]
▶ resident 거주자 **형** 거주하는
▶ residential **형** 주거의

관저 an official _____   거주지 a place of _____

04 real estate [realty]

부동산
▶ realtor 부동산 중개업자
(=real estate agent)

부동산 가치의 하락 a fall in the value of _____

05 cottage
[kátidʒ]

작은 별장
난 시골 작은 별장에서 살고 싶다.
I want to live in a country _____.

06 cabin
[kǽbin]

❶ 오두막집 ❷ (배·비행기의) 선실[객실]
숲 속 통나무 오두막집 a log _____ in the wood

07 hut
[hʌt]

오두막[막사]
오두막이 폭풍우로부터 피신처가 되어 주었다.
A _____ gave shelter from the storm.

08 skyscraper
[skáiskrèipər]

마천루[초고층 빌딩]
마천루들이 도시 상공으로 우뚝 솟아 있다.
_____s tower over the city.

09 landlord/ landlady
[lǽndlɔ̀ːrd] / [lǽndlèidi]

남자 집주인/여자 집주인
집주인이 지붕을 고쳐주겠다고 약속했다.
The _____ promised to repair the roof.

10 tenant
[ténənt]

세입자[소작인]
그 세입자들은 어김없이 집세를 낸다.
The _____s are punctual in paying the rent.

11 suburb
[sʌ́bəːrb]

교외[근교]　　　　　　　▶suburban 혱 교외[근교]의

그는 서울 근교에서 살고 있다.

He lives in the _____ s of Seoul.

12 outskirts
[áutskə̀ːrts]

(the ~) (도시의) 변두리[교외]

그녀는 도시 변두리에 산다.

She lives on the _____ of the city.

13 province
[prɑ́vins]

❶ (행정 구역의) 도(道)
❷ (the provinces) 지방[시골]
❸ 분야

강원도　Gangwon　P_____

14 chamber
[tʃéimbər]

❶ 방[실]　❷ 상원[하원]

회의실　a council _____

15 suite
[swiːt]

(호텔의) 스위트룸

호텔의 신혼부부용 스위트룸　a bridal[honeymoon] _____

16 attic
[ǽtik]

다락(방)

집 꼭대기의 다락 침실　an _____ bedroom at the top of the house

17 cellar
[sélər]

지하 저장실(=basement)

그는 포도주를 지하 저장실에 저장해 두었다.

He has stored wine in the _____.

18 closet
[klɑ́zit]

벽장　　　　　　　　▶water closet[WC] 화장실(=toilet)

벽장은 내게 맞지 않은 옷들로 가득 차 있다.

The _____ is full of clothes that don't fit me.

19 ceiling
[síːliŋ]

천장

천장에 매달린 전등　a light hanging from the _____

20 pillar
[pílər]

기둥(=column)

거대한 돌기둥들이 지붕을 떠받쳤다.

Massive stone _____s supported the roof.

21 porch
[pɔːrtʃ]

현관

엄마가 현관에서 날 배웅해주셨다.

My mom saw me off at the _____.

22 hearth
[hɑ:rθ]

벽난로 주변[노변]　　　　　　　▶fireplace 벽난로

그녀는 벽난로 주변 의자에 앉았다.

She sat down in a chair by the _____.

23 hedge
[hedʒ]

❶ 산울타리　　　　　　　비교 fence 울타리
❷ (손실에 대한) 방비책

산울타리가 두 정원을 가르고 있다.

A _____ separates the two gardens.

24 faucet
[fɔ́:sit]

수도꼭지(=tap)

수도꼭지에서 물이 새고/똑똑 떨어지고 있다.

The _____ is leaking/dripping.

25 outlet
[áutlet]

❶ 발산[배출] 수단　❷ 아웃렛[할인점]
❸ 콘센트　　　　　　❹ 배출구

전기 콘센트에 플러그를 꽂아라.

Put a plug in the electrical _____.

26 plumbing
[plʌ́miŋ]

배관 (공사)　　　　　　　▶plumber 배관공

그는 배관 공사, 목수일, 지붕 일 등을 할 수 있다.

He can do _____, carpentry and roofing.

27 appliance
[əpláiəns]

가전제품　　　　　　　비교 application 적용, 신청
　　　　　　　　　　　▶apply 동 적용하다, 신청하다

세탁기와 식기세척기 같은 가전제품들

electrical _____s such as washing machines and dishwashers

28 utensil
[ju:ténsəl]

주방용품[요리기구]　　　　비교 tool 도구[공구]
　　　　　　　　　　　　　implement (옥외 활동) 기구[도구]

부엌/조리 기구　kitchen/cooking _____s

29 broom
[bru(:)m]

비[빗자루]　　　　　　　비교 mop 대걸레
　　　　　　　　　　　▶broomstick 대가 긴 빗자루

나는 빗자루로 방을 쓸었다.

I swept the room with the _____.

30 chore
[tʃɔ:r]

❶ (정기적으로 하는) (집안)일(=housework)
❷ 따분한 일

집안일　the household[domestic] _____s

Today's Dessert

It is better to dwell in a corner of the roof, than with a nagging wife[violent husband] in a wide house. – the Old Testament

넓은 집에서 바가지 긁는 아내[폭력적인 남편]과 함께 사는 것보다 지붕 모퉁이에서 혼자 사는 게 더 낫다. – 구약

추가

TEST 03

A 영어는 우리말로, 우리말은 영어로!

1 a homeless shelter
2 permanent residence
3 a real estate agent
4 a country cottage
5 a wooden hut
6 the outskirts of the city
7 a sewage outlet
8 domestic appliances
9 kitchen utensils

10 통나무 오두막집   a log c_____
11 충청도   Chungcheong P_____
12 고문실   a torture c_____
13 작은 다락방   a small a_____ room
14 포도주 지하 저장실   a wine c_____
15 침실 벽장   a bedroom c_____
16 대리석 기둥   a marble p_____
17 배관 누수   p_____ leaks
18 집안일   the household c_____s

B 영영사전 뜻풀이에 알맞은 단어 찾기

보기   broom   dwelling   hearth   porch   skyscraper

1 _____ : the area around a fireplace
2 _____ : a house or place to live in
3 _____ : a very tall modern city building
4 _____ : a brush with a long handle, used for sweeping floors
5 _____ : a covered structure in front of the entrance to a building

C 빈칸에 가장 적절한 단어 넣기

보기   ceiling   faucet   hedge   landlord   suburb   tenant

1 She turned off the _____. 그녀는 수도꼭지를 잠갔다.
2 He hit his head on the low _____. 그는 낮은 천장에 머리를 부딪쳤다.
3 I work downtown, but I live in the _____s. 나는 도심지에서 일하지만 교외에 산다.
4 Buying a house will be a _____ against inflation.
집을 사는 것은 인플레이션에 대한 방비책이 될 것이다.
5 The _____ evicted the _____ who didn't pay the rent.
집주인이 집세를 내지 않은 세입자를 쫓아냈다.

ANSWER
A 1. 노숙자 보호소[쉼터] 2. 영구 거주(권)[영주(권)] 3. 부동산 중개인 4. 시골 작은 별장 5. 나무 오두막 6. 도시 변두리 7. 하수 배출구 8. 가전제품 9. 조리 기구 10. cabin 11. Province 12. chamber 13. attic 14. cellar 15. closet 16. pillar 17. plumbing 18. chore B 1. hearth 2. dwelling 3. skyscraper 4. broom 5. porch C 1. faucet 2. ceiling 3. suburb 4. hedge 5. landlord, tenant

주거

Part 1

01 organ
[ɔ́:rɡən]

장기[기관]

▶organism 유기체[생물]
▶organic 혱 유기농[유기체]의

내장[내부 기관] the internal _____s
장기 이식 an _____ transplant

02 forehead
[fɔ́(:)rid]

이마
그는 집중하느라 이마에 주름을 잡았다.
He wrinkled his _____ in concentration.

03 retina
[rétənə]

(눈의) 망막

▶retinal 혱 망막의

영상들이 눈의 망막에 비친다.
Images are projected onto the _____ of the eye.

04 wrist
[rist]

손목

▶wristwatch 손목시계

그는 그녀의 손목을 잡았다.
He took her by the _____.

05 thumb
[θʌm]

엄지손가락

비교 forefinger 집게손가락(=index finger)

엄지손가락을 빠는 아기 a baby sucking its _____

06 thigh
[θai]

넓적다리[대퇴]
넓적다리는 사람 다리의 윗부분이다.
_____ is the upper part of a person's leg.

07 lap
[læp]

(앉아 허리에서 무릎까지) 무릎

비교 knee 무릎 (관절)

우리는 무릎에 냅킨을 놓았다.
We put the napkin on our _____s.

08 breast
[brest]

여성의 젖[유방], 가슴

▶chest 가슴[흉부]

여성의 유방은 임신 중에 부풀어 오른다.
The _____s swell during pregnancy.

09 bosom
[bú(:)zəm]

여성의 젖(가슴), 가슴
그녀는 그를 가슴에 꼭 껴안았다.
She held him tightly to her _____.

10 abdomen
[ǽbdəmən]

배[복부]

▶abdominal 혱 배[복부]의

숨을 들이쉴 때 복부를 완전히 팽창시켜라.
Expand your _____ fully as you breathe in.

11 **belly**
[béli]

❶ 위(=stomach) ❷ 배[복부]

나는 공복 상태로 잠자리에 들었다.

I went to bed with an empty _____.

12 **kidney**
[kídni]

신장[콩팥]

신장은 혈액에서 노폐물을 걸러낸다.

_____s separate waste products from the blood.

13 **liver**
[lívər]

간

간은 피를 맑게 하는 기능을 한다.

The _____ serves to clean the blood.

14 **womb**
[wu:m]

자궁

자궁 속의 태아 the embryo in the _____

15 **skeleton**
[skélətn]

뼈대[골격]

골격 엑스레이 사진 an x-ray picture of the _____

16 **skull**
[skʌl]

두개골

두개골이란 머리의 뼈대다.

_____ is a bony framework of the head.

17 **spine**
[spain]

❶ 등뼈[척추](=backbone) ❷ 기개[용기]

그녀의 척추는 휘었다.

Her _____ twisted.

18 **rib**
[rib]

갈비뼈[늑골], (고기의) 갈비 ▶rib cage 흉곽

그의 갈비뼈가 부러졌다.

His _____s were broken.

19 **flesh**
[fleʃ]

❶ 살[고기] ❷ (과일의) 과육 ▶flesh and blood (평범한) 인간
▶your (own) flesh and blood 육친

가시가 내 손의 살 속에 박혔다.

The thorn went into the _____ of my hand.

20 **tissue**
[tíʃu:]

❶ (세포) 조직 ❷ 화장지

지방/근육/신경 조직 fatty/muscular/nervous _____s

21 **nerve**
[nə:rv]

❶ 신경 ❷ 불안[초조] ▶nervous 휑 불안한[초조한], 신경의
❸ 용기, 뻔뻔스러움 ▶nervousness 불안[초조]

뇌신경 세포 brain _____ cells

22 vein
[vein]

정맥

많은 정맥은 피부 바로 밑에서 볼 수 있다.
Many _____ s are found just under the skin.

23 artery
[áːrtəri]

동맥

여성보다 더 많은 남성이 동맥 경화에 걸린다.
More men than women suffer from hardening of the _____ ies.

24 pulse
[pʌls]

맥박

비교 heartbeat 심장 박동

의사가 환자의 맥박을 잰다.
A doctor takes[feels] a patient's _____ .

25 circulation
[sə̀ːrkjuléiʃən]

❶ 혈액 순환 ❷ 유통

▶circulate 图 순환하다, 유포되다
▶circular 图 원형의, 순환[순회]의

몸을 문지르는 것은 혈액 순환을 활발하게 한다.
Rubbing the body stimulates the _____ .

26 respiration
[rèspəréiʃən]

호흡(=breathing)

▶respiratory 图 호흡의

인공호흡 artificial _____

27 metabolism
[mətǽbəlìzm]

물질대사[신진대사]

▶metabolic 图 물질대사의
▶metabolize 图 신진대사시키다

운동은 신진대사의 속도를 빠르게 한다.
Exercise speeds up your _____ .

28 complexion
[kəmplékʃən]

얼굴빛[안색]

그녀는 안색이 좋다/나쁘다.
She has a good/bad _____ .

29 mustache
[mʌ́stæʃ]

콧수염

비교 beard (턱)수염
비교 whisker ❶ 구레나룻
　　　　　　❷ (고양이 · 쥐의) 수염

그는 콧수염을 깎았다.
He shaved off his _____ .

30 mole
[moul]

❶ (진갈색) 점 ❷ 두더지

비교 birthmark 모반(母斑)

거의 모두가 적어도 점 하나는 가지고 있다.
Almost everyone has at least one _____ .

Today's Dessert

When the belly is full, the bones would be at rest.
배부르면 뼈들이 쉬고 싶어 한다[눕고 싶다].

The Body

A 영어는 우리말로, 우리말은 영어로!

1 the embryo in the womb
2 flesh and blood
3 a brain tissue
4 a nerve cell
5 carbohydrate metabolism
6 a pale complexion

7 넓은/좁은 이마   a high/low f_____
8 망막 질환   r_____ disease
9 가느다란 손목   slender w_____s
10 부러진 갈비뼈   a broken r_____
11 맥박 수   a p_____ rate
12 인공호흡   artificial r_____

B 표 완성하기

보기   artery   kidney   liver   skeleton   vein

	Organ	Function
1		to support the body and protect the internal organs
2		to clean your blood and play a major role in metabolism
3		to separate waste products from your blood and make urine
4		to carry blood from your heart to the rest of your body
5		to carry blood to your heart from other parts of your body

C 관련된 것끼리 연결하기

1 belly   •
2 bosom   •
3 mustache   •
4 skull   •
5 thigh   •

a. a woman's breasts
b. the bones of the head
c. the stomach or abdomen
d. hair that grows above a man's upper lip
e. the part of a person's leg above the knee

D 빈칸에 가장 적절한 단어 넣기

보기   circulation   spine   thumb   lap

1 Exercise improves the _____. 운동은 혈액 순환을 개선시킨다.
2 She sat on her mother's _____. 그녀는 어머니 무릎에 앉았다.
3 The posture puts stress on the _____. 그 자세는 척추에 압박을 가한다.
4 He clicked his finger and _____ together.
그는 손가락과 엄지손가락을 맞부딪쳐 딱 하고 소리를 냈다.

ANSWER_____

A 1. 자궁 속 태아 2. 살과 피(평범한 인간) 3. 뇌 조직 4. 신경 세포 5. 탄수화물 대사 6. 창백한 안색 7. forehead 8. retinal 9. wrist 10. rib 11. pulse 12. respiration   **B** 1. skeleton 2. liver 3. kidney 4. artery 5. vein   **C** 1. c 2. a 3. d 4. b 5. e   **D** 1. circulation 2. lap 3. spine 4. thumb

몸

Part 1

01 ailment
[éilmənt]

(가벼운) 병 　▶ailing 혱 병든

작은 병은 스스로 치료해라.

Treat minor _____s yourself.

02 disorder
[disɔ́ːrdər]

❶ (심신의) 장애 ❷ 엉망, 난동

위/폐/심장/간 장애 a stomach/lung/heart/liver _____

03 disability
[dìsəbíləti]

(심신) 장애 　▶disabled 혱 장애가 있는(=challenged)
　▶disable 동 장애가 있게 하다

신체적/정신적 장애 physical/mental _____ies

04 deformity
[difɔ́ːrməti]

기형(=malformation) 　▶deformed[malformed] 혱 기형의

약물은 기형의 원인이 될 수 있다.

Drugs can cause _____.

05 syndrome
[síndroum]

증후군

다운/빌딩 질환 증후군 Down's/sick building _____

06 infection
[infékʃən]

감염증[전염병], 감염[전염] 　▶infect 동 감염[전염]시키다
　▶infectious 혱 전염성의

귀 감염증 an ear _____

감염의 위험 the risk of _____

07 plague
[pleig]

역병[악성 전염병], 페스트 동 괴롭히다

에이즈 전염병 the _____ of AIDS

역병과 기근 _____s and famines

08 epidemic
[èpədémik]

(병의) 유행

독감 유행 a flu _____

콜레라의 유행 an _____ of cholera

09 germ
[dʒəːrm]

❶ 세균[병균] ❷ 싹[배아] 　비교 gem 보석

많은 병균이 손에서 입으로 옮겨간다.

Many of the _____s pass from our hands into our mouths.

10 immunity
[imjúːnəti]

❶ 면역(력) ❷ 면제[면책] 　▶immune 혱 면역(성)의
　▶immunize 동 면역하다(=vaccinate)

감염에 대한 면역 _____ to infection

면역 체계 _____ system

11 measles
[míːzlz]

홍역

비교 smallpox 천연두
polio 소아마비

홍역은 아이들에게 흔한 병이다.
_____ is a common disease in children.

12 pneumonia
[njuː(ː)móunjə]

폐렴

비교 asthma 천식

그녀의 독감이 폐렴으로 발전했다.
Her flu developed into _____.

13 diabetes
[dàiəbíːtiːz]

당뇨병

▶diabetic 형 당뇨병의

당뇨병의 흔한 증상은 체중 감소와 피로다.
Common symptoms of _____ are weight loss and fatigue.

14 arthritis
[ɑːrθráitis]

관절염

비교 osteoporosis 골다공증

난 무릎에 관절염 기미가 있다.
I have a touch of _____ in the knee.

**15 heatstroke/
sunstroke**
[híːtstròuk] / [sánstròuk]

열사병/일사병

▶stroke ❶ 뇌졸중 ❷ 치기, (수)영법
동 쓰다듬다

열사병에 걸리지 않으려면 물을 충분히 마셔야 한다.
You should take enough water to keep yourself from getting
_____.

16 allergy
[ǽlərdʒi]

알레르기

▶allergic 형 알레르기의

난 꽃가루 알레르기가 있다.
I have an _____ to pollen.

17 addiction
[ədíkʃən]

(욕구) 중독

▶addict 중독자
▶addicted 형 중독된
▶addictive 형 중독성의

알코올/마약/인터넷 중독 alcohol/drug/Internet _____

18 poisoning
[pɔ́izəniŋ]

(독극물) 중독

▶poison 독 동 독살하다, 중독시키다
▶poisonous 형 유독한(=toxic)

식중독/납 중독/수은 중독 food/lead/mercury _____

19 symptom
[símptəm]

증상, 징후

그 병의 증상은 구토와 고열이다.
The _____s of the disease are vomiting and a high fever.

20 diarrhea
[dàiərí(ː)ə]

설사

증상은 설사와 구토를 포함한다.
Symptoms include _____ and vomiting.

21 fatigue
[fətíːg]

피로(= exhaustion)

그는 육체적·정신적 피로로 고통을 겪고 있다.
He's suffering from physical and mental _____.

22 insomnia
[insámniə]

불면증

고양이가 불면증으로 고통을 겪는다는 말을 들어 본 적이 있니?

Have you heard of a cat who suffered from _____?

23 itch
[itʃ]

가려움
동 가렵다

▶itchy 형 가려운[가렵게 하는]

내 등 좀 긁어줘. 나 가려워.

Scratch my back – I have an _____.

24 lump
[lʌmp]

덩어리, 혹

넌 가슴의 혹을 절대 무시해서는 안 된다.

You should never ignore a breast _____.

25 blister
[blístər]

물집[수포]

데어서 손에 물집이 생겼다.

A _____ rose from the burn on my hand.

26 bruise
[bruːz]

멍[타박상]
동 멍들다

가볍게 베인 상처와 멍 minor cuts and _____s

27 scratch
[skrætʃ]

긁힌[할퀸] 자국[찰과상]
동 긁다[할퀴다]

비교 scrape 긁힌 자국[찰과상]
동 긁다[긁어내다]

깊은 긁힌[할퀸] 자국 deep _____es

28 scar
[skɑːr]

흉터

그는 이마에 흉터가 있다.

He has a _____ on his forehead.

29 coma
[kóumə]

혼수상태

비교 unconsciousness 의식 불명

그는 혼수상태에 빠졌다.

He went into a _____.

30 nearsightedness
[niərsáitidnis]

근시

▶nearsighted 형 근시의
▶far-sightedness 원시[선견지명]
▶eyesight 시력

그는 근시가 있다. He suffers from _____.

Today's Dessert

A *disease* known, is half *cured*.

병을 알면 그 병은 반은 나은 것이다.

24

TEST 05

A 영어는 우리말로, 우리말은 영어로!

1 an eating disorder

2 learning disabilities

3 a virus infection

4 an AIDS epidemic

5 immunity from smallpox

6 symptoms of diabetes

7 severe diarrhea

8 chronic fatigue syndrome

9 작은 병   a minor a_____

10 역병 발병   an outbreak of p_____

11 홍역 백신   a m_____ vaccine

12 급성 폐렴   acute p_____

13 식품 알레르기   a food a_____

14 알코올 중독   alcohol a_____

15 식중독   food p_____

16 흉한 상처   an ugly s_____

B 영영사전 뜻풀이에 알맞은 단어 찾기

보기   deformity   germ   heatstroke   insomnia   unconsciousness

1 _____ : inability to sleep, over a period of time

2 _____ : a very small organism that causes disease

3 _____ : a state like sleep caused by injury or illness

4 _____ : a disease caused by being too long in a very hot place

5 _____ : a condition in which a part of the body is not the normal shape

C 빈칸에 가장 적절한 단어 넣기

보기   arthritis   blister   bruise   itch   lump   nearsighted   scratch

1 She was crippled with _____. 그녀는 관절염으로 다리를 절었다.

2 She found a _____ in her breast. 그녀는 가슴에서 혹을 발견했다.

3 Scratch my back – I have an _____. 내 등 좀 긁어줘. 나 가려워.

4 New shoes always give me _____(e)s. 난 새 신발을 신으면 언제나 물집이 생긴다.

5 He wears glasses because he's _____. 그는 근시라서 안경을 쓴다.

6 His legs are covered in _____(e)s and _____(e)s.
그의 다리는 할퀸 상처와 멍투성이다.

질병

Part 1

Medicine & Health

01 remedy
[rémədi]

❶ 치료(제)(=cure, treatment) ❷ 해결책
⑤ 해결하다
불면증에 도움이 되는 자연 치료(제)
a natural _____ that helps insomnia

02 therapy
[θérəpi]

치료(법)　　　　　　　　　▶therapist 치료사
물리/방사선 치료 physical/radiation _____

03 first aid

응급 처치　　　　　　　　　▶first aid kit 구급상자
사고 현장에서의 응급 처치가 그의 목숨을 구했다.
The _____ at the scene of the accident saved his life.

04 physician
[fizíʃən]

(내과) 의사(=doctor)　　　　鬼교 physicist 물리학자
담당 의사와 네 건강에 대해 상담해 봐.
Consult with your _____ about your health.

05 surgeon
[sə́:rdʒən]

외과 의사
그 외과 의사가 환자를 수술했다.
The _____ performed an operation on the patient.

06 surgery
[sə́:rdʒəri]

수술(=operation)　　　　▶plastic[cosmetic] surgery 성형 수술
그녀는 다리 수술을 받았다.
She underwent _____ on her leg.

07 checkup
[tʃékʌ̀p]

건강 검진(=medical examination)
정기 건강 검진을 받는 게 중요하다.
It's important to have regular _____s.

08 diagnosis
[dàiəgnóusis]

진단　　　　　　　　　▶diagnose ⑤ 진단하다
정확한 진단은 혈액 샘플을 얻어야 내려질 수 있다.
An exact _____ can be made by obtaining a blood sample.

09 acupuncture
[ǽkjupʌ̀ŋktʃər]

침술[침 치료]
침술은 환자가 통증을 느끼지 못하도록 하는 데 사용될 수 있다.
_____ can be used to keep the patient from feeling pain.

10 acupressure
[ǽkjuprèʃər]

지압 (요법)
지압은 통증을 완화시킨다. _____ relieves pain.

11 crutch
[krʌtʃ]

목발

난 3달 동안 목발을 짚었다.

I was on _____es for three months.

12 pharmacy
[fá:rməsi]

약국(=drugstore), 약학　　　　▶pharmacist 약사(=druggist)

약국은 약이 조제되고 팔리는 가게다.

A _____ is a shop in which medicines are prepared and sold.

13 prescription
[priskrípʃən]

처방(전)　　　　　　　▶prescribe 동 처방하다, 규정하다

처방전 없이도 이 약을 살 수 있나요?

Can I get this medicine without _____?

14 antibiotic
[æ̀ntibaiátik]

항생제

항생제 남용에 대한 우려 concern about the overuse of _____s

15 painkiller
[péinkìlər]

진통제

진통제가 고통을 완화시켜줄 것이다.

The _____ will reduce the pain.

16 pill
[tablet]
[pil] [tǽblit]

알약[정제]

수면제/소화제 sleeping/indigestion _____s

17 dose
[dosage]
[dous] [dóusidʒ]

(약의) 복용량

권장 복용량을 절대 초과하지 마라.

Never exceed the recommended _____.

18 psychiatry
[saikáiətri]

정신 의학[정신과]　　　　▶psychiatric 형 정신 의학의
　　　　　　　　　　　　▶psychiatrist 정신과 의사

정신과 환자/장애/치료 a _____ patient/disorder/treatment

19 psychoanalysis
[sàikouənǽləsis]

정신 분석(학)　　　　　▶psychoanalyst 명 정신 분석가

지그문트 프로이트는 정신 분석의 아버지로 알려져 있다.

Sigmund Freud is known as the father of _____.

20 subconscious
[sʌ̀bkánʃəs]

잠재의식(=unconscious) 형 잠재의식의

잠재의식에 깊이 묻혀 있는 화 anger buried deep in the _____

21 ego
[íːgou]

자아　　　　　　　　　▶egotism[egoism] 이기주의
　　　　　　　　　　　　▶egotist[egoist] 이기주의자
　　　　　　　　　　　　▶superego 초자아

난 내 멍든 자아를 어루만져줄 누군가가 필요해.

I need someone to massage my bruised _____.

의료 · 건강

Part 1

22 narcissism
[ná:rsəsìzm]

자기애(=self-love), 나르시시즘[자기도취증]

그녀는 자기도취증의 강박에 쫓겨 매일 옷을 갈아입는다.

She changes her clothes every day, driven by _____.

23 insanity
[insǽnəti]

정신 이상(=madness ↔ sanity) ▶insane 형 미친[정신 이상의]
(=mad ↔ sane)

그는 정신 이상을 이유로 무죄 판결을 받았다.

He was found not guilty by reason of _____.

24 fitness
[fítnis]

❶ 건강 ❷ 적합성 ▶fit 형 ❶ 건강한 ❷ 알맞은
동 맞다[맞추다]

건강을 증진시키기 위한 운동 프로그램

an exercise program to improve your _____

25 vigor
[vígər]

활기[정력] ▶vigorous 형 활기찬[정력적인]

그는 활기를 되찾아 공부를 시작했다.

He began studying with renewed _____.

26 workout
[wɔ́ːrkàut]

운동[연습] ▶work out 동 운동하다

스트레칭으로 운동을 시작해라.

Start your _____ with some stretching exercises.

27 strain
[strein]

❶ 압박[부담](=stress) ❷ (-s) 가락[선율]

장시간 근무가 그에게 부담을 주어왔다.

The long hours at work have put a _____ on him.

28 obesity
[oubíːsəti]

비만 ▶obese 형 비만인(=fat)

고지방 음식은 비만을 초래할 수 있다.

A diet that is high in fat can lead to _____.

29 sanitation
[sænətéiʃən]

(공중)위생 관리[시설] ▶sanitary 형 위생의[위생적인]
(↔ unsanitary)

질병은 열악한 위생 관리[시설]로 인해 확산될 수 있다.

Disease can spread from poor _____.

30 hygiene
[háidʒiːn]

(개인)위생(=cleanliness)

개인위생/치위생의 중요성 the importance of personal/dental _____

Today's Dessert

The cure for anything is salt water – sweat, tears, or the sea.

삶의 어떠한 상처에 대한 치료제도 소금물이다. 땀, 눈물 혹은 바다.

TEST 06

A 영어는 우리말로, 우리말은 영어로!

1 a first aid kit
2 transplant surgery
3 psychiatric treatment
4 subconscious desires
5 a vigorous workout
6 the stresses and strains

7 약초[한방] 치료　　herbal r_____
8 정기 건강 검진　　regular c_____s
9 정확한 진단　　an exact d_____
10 수면제　　a sleeping p_____
11 열악한 위생 시설　　poor s_____
12 구강 위생　　oral h_____

B 영영사전 뜻풀이에 알맞은 단어 찾기

보기	acupressure　　antibiotic　　narcissism　　psychiatry　　surgeon

1 _____ : a doctor who does operations in a hospital
2 _____ : the study and treatment of mental illnesses
3 _____ : the treatment of pain by a type of massage
4 _____ : excessive self-admiration and self-centeredness
5 _____ : a drug that is used to kill bacteria and cure infections

C 빈칸에 가장 적절한 단어 넣기

보기	crutch　　fitness　　obesity

1 Overeating is the main cause of _____ . 과식은 비만의 주요 원인이다.
2 He can't walk without the aid of _____(e)s. 그는 목발의 도움 없이 걸을 수 없다.
3 I joined a health club to improve my _____ .
나는 건강을 증진시키기 위해서 헬스클럽에 가입했다.

D 알맞은 단어 쌍을 찾아 문장 완성하기

보기	acupuncture – therapy　　dose – painkiller
	pharmacy – prescription　　psychoanalysis – ego

1 I went to the _____ with the _____ . 나는 처방전을 갖고 약국에 갔다.
2 _____ is a form of alternative _____ . 침술은 대체 요법의 한 형태이다.
3 Never exceed the recommended _____ of _____s.
진통제의 권장 복용량을 절대 넘기지 마시오.
4 In Freudian _____ , the self is divided into the id, the _____ , the superego.
프로이트의 정신 분석학에서 자아는 이드, 자아, 초자아로 나뉜다.

ANSWER_____

A 1. 구급상자 2. 이식 수술 3. 정신과 치료 4. 잠재의식적 욕구 5. 활기찬 운동 6. 스트레스와 압박 7. remedy 8. checkup 9. diagnosis
10. pill 11. sanitation 12. hygiene B 1. surgeon 2. psychiatry 3. acupressure 4. narcissism 5. antibiotic C 1. obesity 2. crutch
3. fitness D 1. pharmacy – prescription 2. Acupuncture – therapy 3. dose – painkiller 4. psychoanalysis – ego

의료·건강

Part 1

01 sentiment
[séntəmənt]

❶ 정서(=feeling, emotion)   ▶ sentimental 형 감상적인
❷ 감상(感傷)

반미 정서 anti-U.S. _____

02 sensation
[senséiʃən]

❶ 감각[느낌] ❷ 센세이션[돌풍]   ▶ sensational 형 선정적인[놀라운]
                                  ▶ sensationalism 선정주의

뜨는 것은 쾌감일 수 있다.
Floating can be a pleasant _____.

03 instinct
[ínstiŋkt]

본능   ▶ instinctive 형 본능적인

동물에게는 타고난 생존 본능이 있다.
Animals have a natural _____ for survival.

04 intuition
[ìntjuːíʃən]

직감[직관]   ▶ intuitive 형 직감[직관]적인

나는 위험이 다가오고 있음을 직감으로 알았다.
I knew by _____ that danger was approaching.

05 impulse
[ímpʌls]

충동(=urge)   ▶ impulsive 형 충동적인

충동구매 _____ buying[shopping]

06 contentment
[kənténtmənt]

만족(=happiness ↔ discontent)   ▶ content 형 만족하는 명 내용(물), 함유량

만족이 부보다 낫다.
_____ is better than riches.

07 compassion
[kəmpǽʃən]

동정심[연민](=pity, sympathy)   ▶ compassionate 형 동정적인
                                  ▶ passion 열정

그녀는 아픈 어린이들에게 커다란 동정심을 느꼈다.
She felt great _____ for the sick children.

08 ecstasy
[ékstəsi]

황홀경   ▶ ecstatic 형 황홀한

그녀는 사랑의 황홀경에 빠져 있다.
She is in an _____ of love.

09 zeal
[ziːl]

열의[열성]   ▶ zealous 형 열성적인[열심인]
             ▶ zealot 열광자[광신자]

그들은 결연한 열의로 목표를 추구하고 있다.
They are pursuing their aims with a determined _____.

10 gratitude
[grǽtətjùːd]

감사   ▶ grateful 형 감사하는(↔ ungrateful)

감사의 눈물이 그녀의 눈에 가득 고였다.
Tears of _____ filled her eyes.

11 solitude
[sάlətjùːd]

혼자[즐거운 고독]　　　　▶solitary 혱 ❶ 혼자의, 고독을 즐기는
　　　　　　　　　　　　　　　　❷ 유일한

공부하기 위해서는 즐거운 고독이 필요하다.
You need _____ in order to study.

12 nostalgia
[nɑstǽldʒə]

향수[과거에 대한 그리움]　　　▶nostalgic 혱 과거를 그리워하는
난 학창 시절에 대한 그리움을 느낀다.
I feel _____ for my school days.

13 suspense
[səspéns]

긴장[불안]　　　　　　　▶suspend 동 일시 중지하다, 매달다
나를 계속 긴장하게 하지 마.
Don't keep me in _____.

14 indifference
[indífərəns]

무관심(=apathy)　　　　　▶indifferent 혱 무관심한
물질적 사치품에 대한 무관심　your _____ to material luxuries

15 hatred
[héitrid]

증오[혐오](↔ love)　　　　▶hate 동 몹시 싫어하다[증오하다] 명 증오
싫음은 쉽게 증오로 발전한다.
Dislike easily rises into _____.

16 contempt
[kəntémpt]

경멸[모욕](↔ respect)　　　▶contemptuous 혱 모욕적인
난 부정직한 행동에 대해 경멸을 느낀다.
I feel _____ for dishonest behavior.

17 disgrace
[disgréis]

망신[수치](=dishonor)　　　▶disgraceful 혱 수치스러운
동 망신시키다
그의 행동은 법조계의 수치다.
His actions are a _____ to the legal profession.

18 jealousy
[dʒéləsi]

시기[질투]　　　　　　　유의 envy 부러움
　　　　　　　　　　　　▶jealous 혱 시기[질투]하는
시기는 우정의 적이다.
_____ is an enemy to friendship.

19 heartbreak
[hάːrtbrèik]

상심[비통]　　　　　　　유의 broken heart 상심
　　　　　　　　　　　　▶heartbroken 혱 상심한
　　　　　　　　　　　　▶heartbreaking 혱 가슴 아픈
그는 그녀를 잃는 상심[비통함]을 겪었다.
He suffered the _____ of losing her.

20 melancholy
[mélənkὰli]

우울 혱 우울한
그녀는 깊은 우울 속으로 빠져들었다.
She sank into deep _____.

21 misery
[mízəri]

비참　　　　　　　　　▶miserable 혱 비참한
전쟁은 필연적으로 비참함을 야기한다.
War necessarily causes _____.

22 **panic**
[pǽnik]

극심한 공포[공황]
图 (panicked–panicked) 극심한 공포에 빠지다[빠뜨리다]
아이들은 극심한 공포에 빠져 달아났다.
The children fled in _____.

23 **temper**
[témpər]

❶ (화를 잘 내는) 성질[성깔]
❷ (화난) 기분(=mood)
❸ 마음의 평정

▶lose your temper 화내다
▶bad-tempered 형 화를 잘 내는
▶temperament 기질

조심해. 그는 난폭한 성깔이 있어.
Be careful, he's got a violent _____.

24 **rage**
[reidʒ]

분노[격노](=anger)
图 격노하다

비교 outrage 격분[격노]
图 격분[격노]하게 하다

그는 분노해서 얼굴이 빨개졌다.
His face was red with _____.

25 **fury**
[fjúəri]

분노[격노]
난 분노로 떨었다.
I was shaking with _____.

▶furious 형 격노한, 격렬한

26 **wrath**
[ræθ]

분노[격노]
그는 신의 분노를 두려워했다.
He feared the _____ of God.

27 **agony**
[ǽgəni]

심한 고통(=torment)
누구도 치통의 심한 고통을 오랫동안 참을 수 없다.
Nobody can stand for long the _____ of a toothache.

28 **anguish**
[ǽŋgwiʃ]

심한 고통[비통]
진실을 알지 못하는 심한 고통은 거의 참을 수가 없다.
The _____ of not knowing the truth is almost unbearable.

29 **pang**
[pæŋ]

갑작스러운 고통
질투/죄책감/후회의 갑작스러운 고통 a _____ of jealousy/guilt/regret

30 **woe**
[wou]

❶ 비통 ❷ (-s) 문제[골칫거리]
비통한 이야기 a tale of _____
재정적 문제 financial _____s

▶woeful 형 비통한, 한심한

Today's
Dessert
Patience represses anger, restrains pride, and controls the tongue.
인내는 화를 억제하고 자만심을 자제하고 말을 절제하는 것이다.

TEST 07

A 영어는 우리말로, 우리말은 영어로!

1 a pleasant sensation

2 heart-pounding suspense

3 a pang of jealousy

4 a fiery temper

5 tears of rage

6 a tale of woe

7 반일 정서   anti-Japanese s_____

8 그녀의 우울한 기분   her m_____ mood

9 공황 상태   a state of p_____

10 모성 본능   a maternal i_____

11 여성의 직감   feminine i_____

12 종교적 열성   religious z_____

B 영영사전 뜻풀이에 알맞은 단어 찾기

> 보기   agony   compassion   ecstasy   nostalgia   wrath

1 _____ : extreme anger

2 _____ : a feeling of extreme happiness

3 _____ : sentimental longing for things that are past

4 _____ : extreme physical or mental pain or suffering

5 _____ : a strong feeling of sympathy for the suffering of others

C 표 완성하기

Noun	Meaning	Adjective
1 contentment		
2 gratitude		
3 solitude		
4 misery		
5 fury		

D 빈칸에 가장 적절한 단어 넣기

> 보기   anguish   contempt   disgrace   hatred
>   heartbreak   impulse   indifference

1 She acts on _____. 그녀는 충동적으로 행동한다.

2 He treats her with _____. 그는 그녀를 무관심하게 대한다.

3 His heart was torn with _____. 그의 가슴은 심한 고통으로 찢어졌다.

4 There is no _____ in being poor. 가난한 것은 수치가 아니다.

5 They suffered the _____ of losing a child. 그들은 아이를 잃는 상심[비통함]을 겪었다

6 She looked at him with _____ and _____.
그녀는 증오와 경멸의 시선으로 그를 쳐다봤다.

ANSWER _____

A 1. 쾌감 2. 가슴 뛰는 긴장 3. 질투의 갑작스러운 고통 4. 불같은 성질 5. 분노의 눈물 6. 비통한 이야기 7. sentiment 8. melancholy 9. panic 10. instinct 11. intuition 12. zeal **B** 1. wrath 2. ecstasy 3. nostalgia 4. agony 5. compassion **C** 1. 만족, content 2. 감사, grateful 3. 혼자[즐거운 고독], solitary 4. 비참, miserable 5. 분노[격노], furious **D** 1. impulse 2. indifference 3. anguish 4. disgrace 5. heartbreak 6. hatred, contempt

01 public/private school

공립/사립 학교 ▶ public/private education 공/사교육

나는 공립 학교/사립 학교에 다닌다.

I go to a _____ /_____.

02 kindergarten
[kíndərgà:rtn]

유치원

비교 nursery school[preschool] 유아원(2~5세)

▶ kindergart(e)ner 유치원생

그는 지금 유치원에 다니고, 내년에 초등학교에 들어간다.

He's in _____ now; next year he'll enter elementary school.

03 coeducation
[kòuedʒukéiʃən]

남녀 공학 ▶ coeducational[coed] 형 남녀 공학의

남녀 공학 학교 _____ schools

04 discipline
[dísəplin]

❶ 훈련[훈육] ❷ 규율[자제] ▶ self-discipline 자기 훈련[수양]
❸ 학과 동 훈련[훈육]하다, 징계하다

부모의 훈육 parental _____

학교 규율/군율 school/military _____

05 tuition
[tju:íʃən]

❶ (개인[소그룹]) 수업[교습] ❷ 수업료[등록금](= tuition fees)

그녀는 영어 개인 수업을 받아오고 있다.

She's been getting private _____ in English.

06 tutor
[tjú:tər]

개인[소그룹] 교사 ▶ tutorial 개인[소그룹] 지도
동 개인[소그룹] 지도를 하다

그들은 아들의 영어 공부를 도와줄 개인 교사를 고용했다.

They hired a private _____ to help their son with his English.

07 instructor
[instrʌ́ktər]

강사 ▶ instruction 지도, 지시, (사용) 설명(서)
▶ instruct 동 가르치다, 지시하다

수영/운전 강사 a swimming/driving _____

08 faculty
[fǽkəlti]

❶ (대학의) 전 교원 ❷ 학부 ❸ 능력[기능]

법학부/공학부 the Law/Engineering F_____

시력[시각 기능] the _____ of sight

09 undergraduate
[ʌ̀ndərgrǽdʒuət]

대학 학부생

비교 graduate student 대학원생

▶ graduate 졸업생 동 졸업하다

대부분의 대학 학부생은 학위를 얻는 데 4년이 걸린다.

Most _____s take 4 years to earn a degree.

10 sophomore
[sáfəmɔ̀:r]

(고교/대학) 2학년생

비교 freshman 신입생
junior 마지막 전 학년생
senior 졸업반 학생

이 수업은 2학년생을 위한 것이다.

This class is for _____s.

11 diploma
[diplóumə]

졸업장

고교/대학 졸업장 a high school/college _____

12 degree
[digríː]

❶ 학위
❷ (온도 · 각도의) 도
❸ 정도

▶bachelor's degree 학사 학위
▶master's degree 석사 학위
▶doctorate[Ph.D.] 박사 학위

학사/석사 학위 a bachelor/master's _____

13 certificate
[sərtífikət]

❶ 자격증 ❷ 증명서

비교 qualification (英) 자격증
▶certification 증명[인증](서)
▶certify 통 증명[인증]하다

그녀는 교사 자격증을 취득했다.
She earned her teaching _____.

14 arts [humanities]

인문학

비교 natural science 자연 과학
social science 사회 과학

인문학은 역사, 언어, 철학 등의 교과목이다.
The _____ are subjects, such as history, languages and philosophy.

15 elective
[iléktiv]

선택 과목 형 선거의

비교 required subject 필수 과목

이번 학기 나의 선택 과목 my _____s this semester

16 admission
[ədmíʃən]

❶ 입장[입학] 허가 ❷ 인정[시인]

▶admit 통 ❶ 입장[입학]을 허가하다,
인정[시인]하다

대학 (입학 허가) 지원자들 those applying for _____ to university

17 attendance
[əténdəns]

출석[참석]

▶attend 통 ❶ 출석[참석]하다
❷ 돌보다[시중들다]

선생님은 수업 전에 출석을 체크하신다.
Our teacher checks _____ before class.

18 assignment
[əsáinmənt]

❶ 과제[임무] ❷ 배정

▶assign 통 맡기다[배정하다]

수학/역사 과제 a math/history _____

19 thesis
[θíːsis]

(복수. theses) ❶ 학위 논문 ❷ 논제[명제]

석사/박사 학위 논문 a master's/doctoral _____

20 midterm/ final (exam)

중간/기말고사

우리는 학기마다 중간 · 기말고사를 치른다.
In each term, we have _____ and _____ exams.

21 encyclopedia
[insàikləpíːdiə]

백과사전

백과사전은 특정 주제에 관한 정보를 얻기 위해서 사용될 수 있다.
_____s may be used to obtain information on a particular topic.

22 atlas
[ǽtləs]

지도책

도로 지도책 a road _____

세계 지도책 an _____ of the world

23 dormitory
[dɔ́ːrmətɔ̀ːri]

기숙사(=dorm)

그녀는 대학 구내 기숙사에서 지낸다.

She stays in the campus _____.

24 intellect
[íntəlèkt]

❶ 지성 ❷ 지성인   ▶intellectual 혱 지적인 몡 지식인

그녀의 글은 감정보다 지성에 더 호소한다.

Her writing appeals more to the _____ than the emotion.

25 IQ

아이큐[지능 지수]
(=intelligence quotient)

▶intelligence ❶ 지능 ❷ 첩보 (기관)
▶quotient 지수, (나눗셈의) 몫
▶multiple intelligence 다중 지능

환경적 요인과 유전적 요인이 지능 지수를 결정하는 역할을 한다.

Environmental and genetic factors play a role in determining _____.

26 prodigy
[prádədʒi]

영재[신동]

모차르트는 음악 신동이었다.

Mozart was a musical _____.

27 creativity
[krìːeitívəti]

창의성[창조력]   ▶creativity education 창의성 교육
▶creative 혱 창조적인

창의성 교육은 진행 중인 중요한 주제다.

_____ education is an ongoing critical issue.

28 self-improvement

자기 계발   비교 self development 자기 개발

자기 계발은 훈련이 필요하다.

_____ requires discipline.

29 self-directed learning

자기 주도 학습   ▶self-directed 혱 자기 주도의

무엇이 자기 주도 학습을 효과적이게 하는가?

What makes _____ effective?

30 socialization
[sòuʃəlizéiʃən]

사회화   ▶socialize 동 사회화하다, 사귀다[어울리다]

교육은 가장 중요한 사회화의 동인이다.

Education is the most important agent of _____.

Today's Dessert The main part of intellectual education is not the acquisition of fact but learning how to make facts live.

지적 교육의 주요 부분은 사실의 습득이 아니라 사실이 실생활에서 쓰이도록 하는 법을 배우는 것이다.

TEST 08

A 영어는 우리말로, 우리말은 영어로!

1 free kindergarten education
2 a coed school
3 a bachelor's degree
4 the Arts Faculty
5 the faculty of speech
6 a master's thesis
7 a children's encyclopedia
8 IQ tests
9 creativity education

10 공립 학교   a p _____
11 영어 개인 지도   t _____ in English
12 개인 교사   a private t _____
13 수영 강사   a swimming i _____
14 고교 졸업장   a high school d _____
15 교사 자격증   teaching c _____
16 대학 입학 허가   college a _____
17 중간/기말고사   m _____ / f _____
18 음악 신동   a musical p _____

B 영영사전 뜻풀이에 알맞은 단어 찾기

보기
atlas   discipline   dormitory   elective
socialization   sophomore   undergraduate

1 _____ : a book containing maps
2 _____ : an optional subject of study
3 _____ : a student studying for their first degree
4 _____ : training which produces obedience or self-control
5 _____ : a student in the second year of high school or college
6 _____ : a building at a college or university where students live
7 _____ : the process in which children learn to behave in a way that is accepted by society

C 빈칸에 가장 적절한 단어 넣기

보기
assignment   attendance   intellect
self-directed learning   self-improvement

1 _____ at lectures is compulsory. 강의 출석은 필수적이다.
2 _____ is at the core of success. 자기 계발은 성공의 핵심이다.
3 Schools should nurture a child's _____. 학교는 어린이의 지성을 길러주어야 한다.
4 I stayed late to complete a class _____. 난 수업 과제를 마치기 위해 늦게까지 자지 않았다.
5 The benefits of _____ are widely acknowledged.
자기 주도 학습의 이득이 널리 인정된다.

ANSWER
A 1. 유치원 무상 교육 2. 남녀 공학 학교 3. 학사 학위 4. 인문학부 5. 언어 능력 6. 석사 학위 논문 7. 아동 백과사전 8. 아이큐[지능 지수] 검사 9. 창의성 교육 10. public school 11. tuition 12. tutor 13. instructor 14. diploma 15. certificate 16. admission 17. midterm/final (exam) 18. prodigy   B 1. atlas 2. elective 3. undergraduate 4. discipline 5. sophomore 6. dormitory 7. socialization   C 1. Attendance 2. Self-improvement 3. intellect 4. assignment 5. self-directed learning

01 occupation
[àkjupéiʃən]

❶ 직업(=job, career) ❷ 점령 ▶occupy 통 차지하다, 거주하다,
❸ 거주 점령하다

이름, 주소, 직업 your name, address, and _____

02 vocation
[voukéiʃən]

천직[소명](=calling) ▶vocational 형 직업의

그녀는 교직을 천직으로 여긴다.
She regards the teaching profession as a _____.

03 professionalism
[prəféʃənəlìzm]

전문성 ▶profession 전문직
▶professional 형 전문직[전문가]의
명 전문직 종사자,
프로(↔amateur)

그는 그녀의 전문성을 칭찬했다.
He praised her _____.

04 livelihood
[láivlihùd]

생계(=living)

그는 글을 써서 생계를 꾸려 간다.
He earns his _____ by writing.

05 toil
[tɔil]

노역[고역] 통 힘들게 일하다

평생 동안의 고된 노동으로 그는 늙어 보였다.
A lifetime of hard _____ made him look old.

06 workload
[wə́ːrklòud]

작업[업무/공부]량

학생들은 과중한 공부량에 대해 불평한다.
Students complain about the heavy _____.

07 overtime
[óuvərtàim]

시간 외 근무 (수당)

그들은 일을 끝내기 위해 시간 외 근무를 하고 있다.
They're working _____ to get the job finished.

08 overwork
[óuvərwə̀ːrk]

과로 통 과로하다

과로로 인한 심장 마비 a heart attack brought on by _____

09 workforce
[wə́ːrkfɔ̀ːrs]

전 직원[노동자], 노동력[노동 인구]

숙련된/교육받은 노동력 skilled/educated _____

10 personnel
[pə̀ːrsənél]

❶ 직원들[인원](=staff) 비교 personal 형 개인의
❷ 인사 부서

전 직원들이 회의에 참석해야 한다.
All _____ must attend the meeting.

11 executive
[igzékjutiv]

경영 간부[임원], (the ~) 행정부
⟨형⟩ 경영[행정]의

▶ CEO[Chief Executive Officer] 최고 경영자
▶ execute ⟨동⟩ 실행하다, 처형하다

회사의 경영 간부들 the company's _____ s

12 supervisor
[súːpərvàizər]

감독관

▶ supervision 감독
▶ supervise ⟨동⟩ 감독하다

감독관은 하기 싫어하는 일을 직원들에게 공평하게 배정해야 한다.
A _____ must assign unpopular tasks equally among employees.

13 consultant
[kənsʌ́ltənt]

컨설턴트[상담역/고문]

▶ consultation 상의[상담]
▶ consult ⟨동⟩ 상담[상의]하다,
　　　　　　찾아보다[참고하다]

회사는 상담역[고문]의 조언을 바탕으로 전략을 세웠다.
The company planned its strategy on the basis of the _____ 's
advice.

14 novice
[návis]

초보자(= beginner)

그녀는 기자로서 완전한 초보자다.
She's a complete _____ as a reporter.

15 newbie
[njuːbi]

(컴퓨터[인터넷]) 초보자

이 프로그램은 초보자에게 사용하기 간편하다.
The program is simple to use for _____ s.

16 freelance(r)
[fríːlæ̀ns(ər)]

프리랜서[자유 계약자]

▶ freelance ⟨형⟩ ⟨부⟩ 프리랜서[자유 계약자]의[로]
　　　　　 ⟨동⟩ 프리랜서로 일하다

자유 계약 언론인/작가 a _____ journalist/writer

17 recommendation
[rèkəmendéiʃən]

추천(서), 권고

▶ recommend ⟨동⟩ 추천[권고]하다

그의 이전 고용주가 그에게 추천서를 써주었다.
His former employer wrote him a letter of _____ .

18 promotion
[prəmóuʃən]

❶ 승진 ❷ 홍보[판촉]

▶ promote ⟨동⟩ 촉진[고취]하다, 홍보하다,
　　　　　　승진시키다

승진 전망이 좋은 일자리 a job with good prospects for _____

19 incentive
[inséntiv]

유인책[장려금]

⟨비교⟩ bonus 상여금

생산성 향상을 위한 장려금 an _____ to promote productivity

20 flextime
[flékstàim]

탄력적 근무 시간제
(= flexible working hours)

▶ flexible ⟨형⟩ 융통성 있는[유연한]

그 회사는 탄력적 근무 시간제를 운영한다.
The company runs a system of _____ .

21 retirement
[ritáiərmənt]

퇴직[은퇴]

▶ retiree 퇴직자
▶ retire ⟨동⟩ 퇴직[은퇴]하다

그녀는 작년에 조기 퇴직했다.
She took early _____ last year.

22 pension
[pénʃən]

연금

몇 살 때 연금 수령을 시작할 수 있니?

At what age can you start drawing your _____?

▶pensioner 연금 수령자(=senior citizen)

23 unemployment
[ʌ̀nimplɔ́imənt]

실업[실직]

실업률이 오르고 있다.

The _____ rate is rising.

▶the unemployed 실업자들
▶employment 일자리, 고용

24 capability
[kèipəbíləti]

능력(=ability)

나이는 사람의 능력과 관계가 없다.

Age has nothing to do with a person's _____ies.

▶capable 혱 ~할 수 있는, 유능한

25 competence
[kámpətəns]

능력(↔incompetence)

그는 업무에서 높은 수준의 능력을 보여 주었다.

He demonstrated a high level of _____ in his work.

▶competent 혱 유능한(↔incompetent)

26 craft
[kræft]

❶ 수공예 ❷ 기술[솜씨]
❸ 배·항공기·우주선

전통 수공예 traditional _____s

가구 제작 기술 the _____ of furniture making

▶craftsman 장인(匠人)
▶craftsmanship 솜씨(=workmanship)

27 expertise
[èkspəːrtíːz]

전문 기술[지식]

기술/재정 전문 지식 technical/financial _____

▶expert 전문가

28 proficiency
[prəfíʃənsi]

능숙함[숙달]

그는 영어에서 높은 수준의 숙달에 이르렀다.

He reached a high level of _____ in his English.

▶proficient 혱 능숙한

29 efficiency
[ifíʃənsi]

효율[능률]

공장에서의 능률 향상 improvements in _____ at the factory

▶efficient 효율적인[유능한]

30 morale
[mərǽl]

사기(士氣)

봉급 인상은 직원들 사기를 높여준다.

A raise in salary improves staff _____.

비교 moral 도덕률, 교훈
혱 도덕의

Today's Dessert *Choose a job you love, and you will never have to work a day in your life.*

– Confucius

좋아해서 즐기는 직업을 택하면 평생 하루도 힘들여 일하지 않아도 된다. – 공자

TEST 09

A 영어는 우리말로, 우리말은 영어로!

1 the professionalism of staff
2 skilled workforce
3 a chief executive officer[CEO]
4 a freelance writer
5 a retirement pension
6 production capabilities
7 high morale

8 전문직   professional o_____s
9 생계 수단   a means of l_____
10 시간 외 근무 수당   o_____ pay
11 추천서   a letter of r_____
12 실업률   the u_____ rate
13 미술 공예   arts and c_____s
14 능률 향상   improvements in e_____

B 영영사전 뜻풀이에 알맞은 단어 찾기

보기   competence   expertise   flextime   newbie   toil

1 _____ : a variable work schedule
2 _____ : the ability to do something well
3 _____ : a person who has just started doing something
4 _____ : special skills or knowledge in a particular subject
5 _____ : hard work, especially that which is physically tiring

C 같은 관계 맺어주기

1 staff : personnel = beginner : n_____ [n_____]
2 supervise : supervisor = consult : c_____
3 capable : capability = proficient : p_____

D 빈칸에 가장 적절한 단어 넣기

보기   incentive   overwork   promotion   vocation   workload

1 He impaired his health by _____. 그는 과로로 건강을 해쳤다.
2 He found his true _____ as a writer. 그는 자신의 진정한 천직이 작가라는 걸 발견했다.
3 She's been recommended for _____ by her boss. 그녀는 상사에게서 승진을 추천받았다.
4 The promise of a bonus acted as a(n) _____ to greater efforts.
상여금 지급 약속이 더 열심히 노력하게 하는 유인책으로 작용했다.
5 They have taken on extra staff to cope with the increased _____.
그들은 늘어난 업무량을 감당하기 위해 추가 직원을 채용했다.

ANSWER

A 1. 직원들의 전문성 2. 숙련된 노동력 3. 최고 경영자 4. 자유 계약 작가 5. 퇴직 연금 6. 생산 능력 7. 높은 사기 8. occupation 9. livelihood[living] 10. overtime 11. recommendation 12. unemployment 13. craft 14. efficiency B 1. flextime 2. competence 3. newbie 4. expertise 5. toil C 1. novice[newbie] 2. consultant 3. proficiency D 1. overwork 2. vocation 3. promotion 4. incentive 5. workload

01 carriage
[kǽridʒ]

마차

말이 끄는 마차 a horse-drawn _____

유모차 a baby _____

02 wagon
[wǽgən]

(4륜) 짐마차(=cart)

포장마차 a covered _____

03 path
[pæθ]

(좁은) 길(=track), 진로

자전거 도로 a bicycle _____

태풍의 진로 the _____ of a typhoon

04 lane
[lein]

(좁은) 길, 차선, 항로, 경주로

버스 전용 차선 exclusive bus _____s

05 alley
[ǽli]

골목(길)(=alleyway)   ▶bowling alley 볼링장

뒷골목/막다른 골목 a back/blind _____

06 avenue
[ǽvənjù:]

(Avenue) ~가(街), 가로수길

뉴욕 5번가 the Fifth A_____ of New York

07 pavement
[péivmənt]

포장도로   回교 sidewalk (포장된) 보도[인도]
▶unpaved 형 비포장의

아스팔트 포장도로 an asphalt _____

08 highway
[háiwèi]

고속 도로   ▶information superhighway
(=expressway, freeway)   초고속 정보 통신망

고속 도로 순찰대 the _____ patrol

나는 해안 고속 도로를 따라 운전했다. I drove along the coastal _____.

09 ramp
[ræmp]

경사로, 고속 도로 진입로

휠체어 사용자를 위해 경사로가 출입구에 필요하다.

_____s are needed at exits and entrances for wheelchair users.

10 intersection
[ìntərsékʃən]

교차(점[로])   回교 interchange 입체 교차로
▶intersect 동 교차하다, 가로지르다

다음 교차로에서 우회전하세요.

Turn right at the next _____.

11 milepost [milestone]
[máilpòust] [máilstòun]

❶ 이정표 ❷ (발전의) 중대 사건

철길을 따라 서 있는 낡은 이정표들 the old _____s along the railroad

12 commute
[kəmjúːt]

통근 图 통근하다 ▶commuter 통근자

나의 아침 통근[출근]은 45분 걸린다.

My morning _____ takes 45 minutes.

13 freight
[freit]

화물 (운송)

항공/해상 화물 air/sea _____

14 burden
[bə́ːrdn]

짐, 부담 图 짐[부담]을 지우다 ▶burdensome 图 짐이 되는

당나귀가 무거운 짐을 지고 허우적거렸다.

The donkey struggled under its heavy _____.

15 congestion
[kəndʒéstʃən]

혼잡, 막힘 ▶congested 图 혼잡한, 막힌
참 traffic jam 교통 체증

교통 혼잡 traffic _____

코 막힘 nasal _____

16 honk
[haŋk]

(차의) 경적 소리[빵빵] 참 horn 경적, 뿔, 나팔[호른/트럼펫]
图 경적을 울리다[빵빵거리다]

경적 소리 the _____ of a horn

몇몇 운전자들이 경적을 울렸다. Several drivers _____ed their horns.

17 aviation
[èiviéiʃən]

항공

민간 항공 산업 the civil _____ industry

18 navigation
[nævəgéiʃən]

항해[운항] ▶navigator 항해사[항법사]
▶navigate 图 길을 찾다, 항해하다

과거 항해는 별의 위치에 의존했다.

In the past, _____ depended on the position of the stars.

19 altitude
[æltitʃùːd]

고도

우리 비행기는 고도 15,000미터로 비행하고 있습니다.

We're flying at an _____ of 15,000 meters.

20 vessel
[vésəl]

❶ 배 ❷ (혈)관

화물선/어선 a cargo/fishing _____

21 ferry(boat)
[féri]

나룻배[도선], 연락선

연락선이 서해안에서 침몰했다.

A _____ sank off the west coast.

43

22 liner
[láinər]

대형 여객선

원양 대형 여객선 an ocean _____

23 tanker
[tǽŋkər]

탱커[석유·가스 수송 선박/차량], 유조선(= oil tanker)

유조선이 바다에 수백만 갤런의 기름을 유출시켰다.

The oil _____ spilled millions of gallons of oil into the sea.

24 raft
[ræft]

뗏목, 고무 보트　　　　　　　　▶rafting (스포츠) 래프팅

그는 뗏목을 타고 강을 건넜다.

He crossed the river on a _____.

25 port
[pɔ:rt]

항구(= harbor), 항구 도시　　　▶export 명 동 수출(하다)
　　　　　　　　　　　　　　　▶import 명 동 수입(하다)

어떤 배도 폭풍우 치는 날씨에는 항구를 떠날 수 없다.

No ship can leave _____ in stormy weather.

26 dock
[dɑk]

부두　　　　　　　　　　　비교 wharf 선창
동 (우주선이) 도킹하다　　　　　pier 부두[잔교]

배가 수리를 받기 위해 부두에 있다.

The ship is in _____ for repair.

27 deck
[dek]

갑판　　　　　　　　　　　▶double-decker 2층 버스

거대한 파도가 갑판을 휩쓸고 갔다.

A huge wave swept over the _____.

28 canal
[kənǽl]

운하[수로]

파나마/수에즈 운하 the Panama/Suez C_____

관개 수로 an irrigation _____

29 lighthouse
[láithàus]

등대

등대는 배들을 항구로 인도한다.

A _____ guides ships to a harbor.

30 shipwreck
[ʃíprèk]

난파(선)　　　　　　　　　　▶wreck 잔해, 난파선
동 (be -ed) 난파당하다　　　　　동 망치다, 난파시키다

난파의 생존자들 survivors of the _____

Today's
Dessert

Sail away from the safe harbor. Explore. Dream. Discover. - Mark Twain

안전한 항구에서 떠나 항해하라. 탐험하라. 꿈꾸어라. 발견하라. - 마크 트웨인

TEST 10

A 영어는 우리말로, 우리말은 영어로!

1 a horse-drawn carriage
2 a wagon wheel
3 a garden path
4 an eight-lane highway
5 an electronic navigation system
6 a cruise liner
7 an oil tanker

8 좁은 골목   a narrow a_____
9 화물 열차   a f_____ train
10 교통 혼잡   traffic c_____
11 어선   a fishing v_____
12 군항   a naval p_____
13 파나마 운하   the Panama C_____
14 등대지기   a l_____ keeper

B 영영사전 뜻풀이에 알맞은 단어 찾기

[보기]   altitude   aviation   ferry   intersection   shipwreck

1 _____ : the destruction of a ship in an accident
2 _____ : the operation and production of aircraft
3 _____ : the height of an object or place above the sea
4 _____ : a place where roads, lines etc. cross each other
5 _____ : a boat that transports people or vehicles across water

C 관련된 것끼리 연결하기

1 avenue   •
2 burden   •
3 deck   •
4 pavement   •
5 ramp   •

a. an artificial slope
b. the hard surface of a road
c. a heavy load that you carry
d. the top outside floor of a ship
e. a wide, straight road with trees on both sides

D 빈칸에 가장 적절한 단어 넣기

[보기]   commute   dock   honk   milepost   raft

1 The driver _____(e)d his horn. 운전자가 경적을 울렸다.
2 It takes me too long to _____. 나는 통근하는 데 너무 많은 시간이 걸린다.
3 The ship is unloading at the _____. 배가 부두에서 짐을 내리고 있다.
4 The _____ floated away down the river. 뗏목이 강 아래로 떠내려갔다.
5 The _____ is at the side of road to show distances.
이정표는 거리를 보여 주기 위해서 길가에 있다.

ANSWER_____

A 1. 말이 끄는 마차 2. 짐마차 바퀴 3. 정원의 좁은 길 4. 8차선 고속 도로 5. 전자 항법 장치 6. 대형 유람 여객선 7. 유조선 8. alley 9. freight 10. congestion 11. vessel 12. port 13. Canal 14. lighthouse   B 1. shipwreck 2. aviation 3. altitude 4. intersection 5. ferry   C 1. e 2. c 3. d 4. b 5. a   D 1. honk 2. commute 3. dock 4. raft 5. milepost

Leisure & Entertainment

01 amusement
[əmjúːzmənt]

즐거움[재미], 오락

▶ amusement park 놀이공원[유원지]
▶ amuse 통 즐겁게[재미있게] 하다

어린이 오락 childhood _____ s

02 relaxation
[rìːlækséiʃən]

❶ 휴식[오락] ❷ 완화

▶ relax 통 쉬다(=rest), 안심하다, 긴장을 풀다
▶ relaxed 형 편안한

나는 휴식을 위해 피아노를 친다.
I play the piano for _____ .

03 pastime
[pǽstàim]

취미(=hobby)

정원 가꾸기는 그녀가 좋아하는 취미다.
Gardening is her favorite _____ .

04 amateur
[ǽmətʃùər]

아마추어[비전문가](↔ professional) 형 아마추어의

그 대회는 아마추어와 프로 모두에게 열려 있다.
The contest is open to both _____ s and professionals.

05 maniac
[méiniæk]

미치광이(=madman), 광적 애호가[~광]   ▶ mania 열광

그는 미치광이처럼 운전했다. He drove like a _____ .
축구광 a football _____

06 fanatic
[fənǽtik]

광적 애호가[~광], 광신자

▶ fan 팬[~광]

영화/스포츠광 a film/sports _____
종교적 광신자 a religious _____

07 archery
[áːrtʃəri]

궁도[양궁]

▶ archer 궁수[양궁 선수]

여자 개인 양궁 선수권 대회
the women's individual _____ championships

08 martial art

무술

태권도는 한국의 유명한 무술이다.
Taegwondo is Korea's famous _____ .

09 lottery
[látəri]

복권, 추첨

복권에 당첨된다면 행복해질 거라고 생각하니?
Do you think winning the _____ would make you happy?

10 gambling
[gǽmbliŋ]

도박(=betting)

▶ gamble 통 도박하다(=bet) 명 도박
▶ gambler 도박꾼

복권은 가장 대중적 형태의 도박이다.
The lottery is the most popular form of _____ .

11 tourism
[túərizm]

관광업

▶tour 여행[관광], 순회공연 ⑧ 관광하다
▶tourist 관광객

관광업은 그 나라의 주요 산업이다.
_____ is the country's main industry.

12 backpacking
[bǽkpækiŋ]

배낭여행

▶backpack 배낭 ⑧ 배낭여행을 하다

배낭여행은 젊은이들 사이에 인기가 있다.
_____ is popular among young people.

13 voyage
[vɔ́iidʒ]

긴 항해[우주여행](=journey)

▶voyager 항해자

타이타닉호의 처녀항해 the Titanic's maiden _____

14 cruise
[kruːz]

유람 항해 ⑧ 순항하다

▶cruiser 순양함, 유람용 보트

호화 유람선 a luxury _____ ship

15 expedition
[èkspədíʃən]

탐험[원정](대)

비교 exploration 탐사[답사], 탐구

북극 탐험 an _____ to the North Pole

16 excursion
[ikskɔ́ːrʒən]

소풍[짧은 여행](=trip)

다음 주에 우리는 학교 소풍[수학여행]을 간다.
Next week we're going on a school _____.

17 outing
[áutiŋ]

소풍

바닷가로의 소풍 an _____ to the beach

18 landscape
[lǽndskèip]

풍경(화)

비교 seascape 바다 풍경화

나는 그 풍경의 아름다움에 경탄했다.
I marveled at the beauty of the _____.

19 scenery
[síːnəri]

❶ 경치[풍경] ❷ 무대 장치

▶scene 장면, 현장

여행에서 가장 좋았던 건 멋진 경치였다.
The best part of the trip was the fantastic _____.

20 spectacle
[spéktəkl]

❶ 장관, 구경거리 ❷ (-s) 안경

▶spectator 관객
▶spectacular ⑧ 장관인, 굉장한

지리산의 장관을 본 적이 있니?
Have you seen the grand _____ of Mount Jiri?

21 attraction
[ətrǽkʃən]

❶ 명소[명물] ❷ 끌림[매력]

▶attract ⑧ 끌다[매혹하다]
▶attractive ⑧ 매혹적인

관광[관광객을 끌어들이는] 명소[명물] a tourist _____

22 monument
[mánjumənt]

기념비[탑/상], 유적

비교 memorial 기념비 형 기념의
▶ monumental 형 기념비적인, 엄청난

전몰장병 기념비 a _____ to soldiers killed in the war

23 souvenir
[sù:vəníər]

기념품(=memento)

기념품 가게 a _____ shop

24 accommodation
[əkàmədéiʃən]

(-s) 숙박 시설

▶ accommodate 동 수용하다, 숙박시키다

가격은 항공편과 숙박 시설을 포함한 것이다.
The price includes flights and _____s.

25 jet lag

시차증(제트기 여행 시차로 인한 피로)

여러 시간대를 가로지르는 여행자들은 시차증을 겪는다.
Travelers who cross many time zones suffer from _____.

26 feast
[fi:st]

잔치[연회], 축제(=festival)

결혼 피로연 a wedding _____

27 banquet
[bǽŋkwit]

연회, 성찬

그 도시의 천년을 경축하기 위해 거대한 연회가 계획되었다.
A huge _____ was planned to celebrate the city's millennium.

28 reception
[risépʃən]

환영회[축하연], 환영[반응]

▶ receptionist 접수원

외국 방문객을 위한 공식 환영회
official _____s for the foreign visitors

29 reunion
[ri:jú:njən]

재회 모임[동창회], 재회[재결합]

▶ reunite 동 재회[재결합]하다

고등학교 동창회 a high-school _____

30 hospitality
[hɑspətǽləti]

환대[접대]

비교 hostility 적의[적대 행위]

친절한 환대에 감사드립니다.
Thank you for your kind _____.

Today's Dessert

True relaxation is liberating because it creates no obligations.
진정한 휴식은 아무런 의무도 지우지 않기 때문에 해방시키는 것이다.

TEST 11

A 영어는 우리말로, 우리말은 영어로!

1 an amateur photographer
2 a martial arts expert
3 a Mediterranean cruise
4 an Arctic expedition
5 a school outing
6 a tourist attraction
7 a wedding reception
8 a family reunion

9 놀이공원[유원지]　　an a_____ park
10 축구광　　a football m_____
11 복권 당첨자　　a l_____ winner
12 도박 빚　　a g_____ debts
13 배낭여행　　a b_____ trip
14 시골 풍경　　a rural l_____
15 장관인 경치　　spectacular s_____
16 기념품 가게　　a s_____ shop

B 영영사전 뜻풀이에 알맞은 단어 찾기

보기　accommodation　archery　fanatic　hospitality　voyage

1 _____ : friendly behavior towards visitors
2 _____ : a long journey in a ship or spacecraft
3 _____ : the sport of shooting arrows from a bow
4 _____ : a place for someone to stay, live, or work
5 _____ : a person who is very enthusiastic about something

C 관련된 것끼리 연결하기

1 banquet ·
2 excursion ·
3 monument ·
4 pastime ·

a. a hobby
b. a structure erected as a memorial
c. the short journey made for pleasure
d. a large formal meal for many people

D 빈칸에 가장 적절한 단어 넣기

보기　feast　relaxation　spectacle　tourism

1 The sunrise was a splendid _____. 일출은 멋진 장관이었다.
2 She listens to classical music for _____. 그녀는 휴식을 위해 고전 음악을 듣는다.
3 The film festival is a _____ for moviegoers. 그 영화제는 영화 팬들의 축제다.
4 The island's economy is dependent upon _____. 그 섬의 경제는 관광업에 의존한다.

여가 · 오락
Part 1

ANSWER
A 1. 아마추어 사진작가 2. 무술 전문가 3. 지중해 유람 항해 4. 북극 탐험(대) 5. 학교 소풍 6. 관광 명소[명물] 7. 결혼 축하연 8. 가족 재회 (모임)
9. amusement 10. maniac 11. lottery 12. gambling 13. backpacking 14. landscape 15. scenery 16. souvenir　B 1. hospitality
2. voyage 3. archery 4. accommodation 5. fanatic　C 1. d 2. c 3. b 4. a　D 1. spectacle 2. relaxation 3. feast 4. tourism

01 (a)esthetic
[esθétik]

미학, (-s) (학문 분야) 미학(美學) 형 미(학)의

15초짜리 광고의 미학 the _____ of 15-second advertisements

02 masterpiece
[mǽstərpìːs]

걸작[명작], 대표작
(=masterwork)

▶master 달인[거장], 주인, 석사
통 숙달하다

불후의 명작 an immortal[enduring] _____

03 genre
[ʒáːnrə]

장르[분야]

문학/음악/영화 장르 a literary/musical/film _____

04 avant-garde
[əvàːntgáːrd]

(the ~) 아방가르드[전위 예술가들] 형 아방가르드[전위]의

전위 미술가/작곡가/작가 _____ artists/composers/writers

05 parody
[pǽrədi]

패러디[풍자적 개작]

그 작가는 다른 사람들 작품의 패러디를 쓴다.
The author writes _____ies of other people's works.

06 plot
[plɑt]

❶ (소설·영화·연극의) 줄거리(=storyline)
❷ 음모 통 음모를 꾸미다

단순한/복잡한 줄거리 a(n) simple/intricate _____

07 climax
[kláimæks]

클라이맥스[절정]

오페라는 그녀의 죽음으로 절정에 달한다.
The opera reaches its _____ with her death.

08 narrative
[nǽrətiv]

묘사[기술/서술/이야기] ▶narrate 통 내레이션을 하다, 이야기하다
형 이야기체의

1인칭 시점 묘사[기술/서술/이야기] a first-person _____

**09 myth
[mythology]**
[miθ] [miθálədʒi]

❶ 신화
❷ 잘못된 통념(=fallacy)

비교 legend 전설
▶mythical 형 신화의

고대 그리스 신화 ancient Greek _____s

10 verse
[vəːrs]

운문[시](=poetry), 시의 연[절]

셰익스피어는 대개 운문으로 글을 썼다.
Shakespeare wrote mostly in _____.

11 lyric
[lírik]

❶ 서정시(=lyric poem)   ▶lyricism 서정성
❷ (-s) 노래 가사   형 서정시의

윌리엄 워즈워스는 서정시인이었다.
William Wordsworth was a _____ poet.

12 epic
[épik]

서사시   형 서사시의

호머의 "일리아드"는 유명한 서사시다.
Homer's *Iliad* is a famous _____.

13 prose
[prouz]

산문

나는 시보다 산문을 읽는 것을 더 좋아한다.
I prefer reading _____ to poetry.

14 essay
[ései]

❶ (학생의) 논술   ❷ 수필[시론]

그의 저작에는 시와 수필이 포함되어 있다.
His writings include poetry and _____s.

15 biography/ autobiography
[baiágrəfi] / [ɔ̀:təbaiágrəfi]

전기/자서전

참고 autograph 유명인의 서명[사인]
▶ biographical 형 전기의
▶ autobiographical 형 자서전의

간디의 전기/자서전 Gandhi's _____ / _____

16 oil painting/ watercolor

유화/수채화 (물감)   ▶oil[oil paint] 유화 물감

렘브란트는 17세기 유화의 거장이다.
Rembrandt is the 17-century master of _____.
나는 수채화 물감으로 그리는 걸 더 좋아한다.
I prefer painting with _____s.

예술

Part 1

17 portrait
[pɔ́:rtrit]

초상화   ▶ self-portrait 자화상
▶ portray 동 묘사하다[그리다]

그녀는 자기 초상화를 그리도록 자세를 취했다.
She posed for her _____.

18 mural
[mjúərəl]

벽화

고분 벽화 an ancient tomb _____

19 calligraphy
[kəlígrəfi]

서예

서예에 깃들여 있는 한국인의 예술미 Koreans' artistic beauty in _____

20 ceramic
[səræmik]

(-s) 도예, 도자기   형 도자기의

고려청자 the greenish-blue _____s of the Goryeo Dynasty

21 pottery/ porcelain
[pátəri] / [pɔ́:rsəlin]

도기/자기(=china)

참고 celadon 청자
▶ potter 도공[도예가]

세련된 양식의 도기/자기 a refined style of _____ / _____

22 chorus
[kɔ́:rəs]

후렴(=refrain), 합창단(=choir), 합창(곡)

그들은 교가를 합창했다.

They sang in _____ their school song.

23 chord
[kɔːrd]

화음

비교 cord 끈, (전기) 코드
▶strike[touch] a chord (with)
(~의) 심금을 울리다

화음은 함께 흐르고, 멜로디는 가장자리에 떠 있는 것 같다.

The _____s flow together; a melody seems to be hovering on the edge.

24 tune
[tju:n]

곡조[가락](=melody)
동 조율[조정]하다, (TV·라디오 채널을) 맞추다

나는 기타 곡조에 맞춰 노래를 했다.

I sang a song to the _____ of the guitar.

25 tempo
[témpou]

(음악의) 빠르기, 속도(=pace)

상당히 느린 속도로 연주되는 가락

a tune played at a fairly slow _____

26 playwright
[pléiràit]

극작가(=dramatist)

그녀는 소설가 겸 극작가이다.

She is a novelist and _____.

27 script
[skript]

대본(=screenplay)

비교 scenario 시나리오
▶transcript ❶ (연설·대화를) 문자화한 것
❷ 성적 증명서

두 작가가 대본을 공동 작업했다.

The two writers collaborated on the _____.

28 sequence
[sí:kwəns]

❶ 순서 ❷ 일련의 것들(=series) ❸ (영화의) 일련의 장면

자동차 추격전을 담고 있는 스릴 만점의 일련의 장면

a thrilling _____ that includes a car chase

29 auditorium
[ɔ̀:dətɔ́:riəm]

청중[관객]석, 강당

▶audience 청중[관객], 시청자

청중석이 절반만 찼다.

The _____ was only half full.

30 intermission [interlude]
[ìntərmíʃən] [íntərlù:d]

막간[중간 휴식 시간]

늦게 오신 분은 막간에만 입장이 허용됩니다.

Latecomers will be admitted only during _____.

Today's Dessert

Life is a tragedy when seen in close-up, but a comedy in long-shot.

– Carlie Chapline

인생은 가까이서 보면 비극이지만 멀리서 보면 희극이다. – 찰리 채플린

TEST 12

A 영어는 우리말로, 우리말은 영어로!

1 the plot of the film
2 a third-person narrative
3 an essay test
4 an oil painting
5 an exhibit of ceramics
6 ancient Greek myths

7 음악 장르   a musical g_____
8 전위 예술[미술]   a_____ art
9 자유시   free v_____
10 서정시인   a l_____ poet
11 서사시   an e_____ poem
12 영화 대본   a film s_____

B 영영사전 뜻풀이에 알맞은 단어 찾기

> 보기   auditorium   calligraphy   chord   prose

1 _____ : a large building used for concerts or public meetings
2 _____ : three or more musical notes played at the same time
3 _____ : written language in its usual form, as opposed to poetry
4 _____ : the art of producing beautiful writing using special pens or brushes

C 관련된 것끼리 연결하기

1 aesthetics ·
2 masterpiece ·
3 mural ·
4 pottery ·

a. a great work of art
b. the study of beauty
c. a painting painted on a wall
d. objects made out of baked clay

D 같은 관계 맺어주기

1 portrait : self-portrait = biography : a_____
2 intermission : interlude = dramatist : p_____

E 빈칸에 가장 적절한 단어 넣기

> 보기   chorus   climax   parody   sequence   tempo   tune

1 A _____ is a form of satire. 패러디는 풍자의 한 형태이다.
2 I like _____s with slow _____. 나는 느린 속도의 곡조를 좋아한다.
3 The _____ of events led up to the war. 일련의 사건들이 전쟁을 야기했다.
4 The choir performed the Hallelujah C_____. 합창단은 할렐루야 합창곡을 공연했다.
5 The opera reaches its _____ in the third act. 오페라는 제3막에서 절정에 달한다.

ANSWER

A 1. 영화의 줄거리 2. 3인칭 시점 서술 3. 논술 시험 4. 유화 5. 도자기 전시회 6. 고대 그리스 신화 7. genre 8. avant-garde 9. verse 10. lyric 11. epic 12. script   **B** 1. auditorium 2. chord 3. prose 4. calligraphy   **C** 1. b 2. a 3. c 4. d   **D** 1. autobiography 2. playwright **E** 1. parody 2. tune, tempo 3. sequence 4. Chorus 5. climax

예술

Part 1

01 linguistics
[liŋgwístiks]

언어학

▶ linguistic 혱 언어(학)의
▶ linguist 언어학자

아이의 언어 능력/발달 a child's _____ ability/development

02 lingua franca
[líŋgwəfrǽŋkə]

공용어

영어는 많은 나라에서 공용어다.

English is the _____ in many countries.

03 dialect
[dáiəlèkt]

사투리[방언]

그 지역에서 사용되는 독특한 사투리 the unique _____ used in the area

04 accent
[ǽksènt]

❶ 말씨[사투리] ❷ 강세(=stress) ❸ 강조(=emphasis)

그는 심한 경상도 말씨로 말한다.

He speaks in a strong[heavy] Gyeongsang-do _____.

05 intonation
[ìntənéiʃən]

억양

문장의 의미는 흔히 강세와 억양에 좌우된다.

The meaning of a sentence often depends on stress and _____.

06 slang
[slæŋ]

속어

어디선가 주워들은 속어를 사용하려고 애쓰지 마라.

Don't try to use _____ that you've picked up somewhere.

07 literacy
↔ illiteracy
[lítərəsi] ↔ [ilítərəsi]

읽고 쓰는 능력[활용 능력]
↔ 문맹

▶ literate ↔ illiterate
  혱 읽고 쓸 수 있는 ↔ 문맹의
▶ literary 혱 문학의

컴퓨터 활용 능력 computer _____
문맹률 an _____ rate

08 bilingual
[bailíŋgwəl]

이중 언어 사용자
혱 이중 언어를 사용하는

▶ monolingual/multilingual
  몡 혱 단일/다중 언어 사용자(의)

그녀는 영어와 한국어 이중 언어 사용자이다.

She is _____ in English and Korean.

09 fluency
[flú:ənsi]

유창성[능숙함]

▶ fluent 혱 유창한[능숙한]

영어의 유창성이 이 일에 요구된다.

_____ in English is required for this job.

10 consonant/
vowel
[kánsənənt] / [váuəl]

자음/모음

한글은 14개의 자음과 10개의 모음으로 이루어져 있다.

Hangeul consists of fourteen _____s and ten _____s.

11 **idiom**
[ídiəm]

관용구[숙어]

'under the weather'는 '아픈'을 뜻하는 관용구[숙어]다.

"Under the weather" is an _____ meaning "ill."

12 **usage**
[júːsidʒ]

❶ (언어의) 용법[어법] ❷ 사용(량)

현대 영어 용법에 관한 책 a book on modern English _____

13 **maxim**
[mæksim]

격언[금언]

'아는 것이 힘이다'라는 베이컨의 금언

Bacon's _____ that knowledge is power

14 **quotation**
[kwoutéiʃən]

❶ 인용(문) ❷ 견적　　　　▶quote 통 인용하다 명 인용, 견적

그는 인용들로 자신의 주장을 설명했다.

He illuminated his argument with _____s.

15 **excerpt**
[éksəːrpt]

발췌(= extract)　　　　비교 except 전 접 ~ 제외하고[외에는]

그 연설의 발췌가 신문에 실렸다.

An _____ of the speech appeared in the paper.

16 **anecdote**
[ǽnikdòut]

일화

그는 우리에게 재미있는 일화들을 들려주었다.

He told us interesting _____s.

17 **rhetoric**
[rétərik]

수사(修辭)(법)　　　　▶rhetorical 형 수사적인

수사법은 언어를 사용하는 기술이다.

_____ is the art of using language.

18 **metaphor**
[métəfɔ̀ːr]

은유　　　　비교 simile 직유
▶metaphoric(al) 형 은유의

'너의 미소는 나의 햇빛이다'는 은유다.

"Your smile is my sunshine" is a _____.

19 **analogy**
[ənǽlədʒi]

비유[유추], 유사점

그는 인생을 마라톤에 비유했다.

He drew an _____ between life and a marathon.

20 **irony**
[áiərəni]

반어(법), 얄궂은[뜻밖의] 상황　　　　▶ironic 형 반어적인, 얄궂은[뜻밖의]

인생은 사소한 뜻밖의 상황들로 가득 차 있다.

Life is full of little _____ies.

21 **paradox**
[pǽrədàks]

역설　　　　▶paradoxical 형 역설적인

물을 많이 마시면 목마름을 느끼게 될 수 있다는 건 역설이다.

It's a _____ that drinking a lot of water can make you feel thirsty.

22 satire
[sǽtaiər]

풍자

▶satirical 휑 풍자적인
비교 sarcasm 비꼬는 말

정치 풍자를 하는 코미디언들 comedians that do political _____

23 connotation
[kὰnətéiʃən]

함의[함축적 의미]

비교 denotation 명시적 의미

'전문가'라는 단어는 기술과 탁월함이라는 함축적 의미를 담고 있다.

The word "professional" has _____s of skill and excellence.

24 euphemism
[júːfəmìzm]

완곡어(법)

▶euphemistic 휑 완곡한

'돌아가시다'는 '죽다'의 완곡어이다.

"Pass away" is a _____ for "die."

25 session
[séʃən]

회의[회기], (집단 활동) 기간

브레인스토밍 회의 a brainstorming _____

26 agenda
[ədʒéndə]

❶ 의제 ❷ 해결 과제

오늘 오후 회의의 의제 the _____ for this afternoon's meeting

27 controversy
[kάntrəvəːrsi]

논란

▶controversial 휑 논란거리인

그의 발언은 열띤 논란을 일으켰다.

His remarks provoked heated _____.

28 consensus
[kənsénsəs]

합의[의견 일치]

그들은 그 문제에 대해 합의에 도달했다.

They reached a _____ on the matter.

29 discourse
[dískɔːrs]

담론[담화]

후보들은 진지한 담론에 참여해야 한다.

Candidates should engage in serious _____.

30 forum
[fɔ́ːrəm]

공개 토론의 장, 고대 로마의 광장

텔레비전은 정치적 토론을 위한 중요한 공개 토론의 장이다.

Television is an important _____ for political debate.

Today's Dessert A person who can speak many languages is not more valuable than a person who can listen in one.

여러 언어를 말할 수 있는 사람이 한 가지 언어로 경청할 수 있는 사람보다 더 귀한 것은 아니다.

TEST 13

A 영어는 우리말로, 우리말은 영어로!

1	a lingua franca		**11**	언어 능력	l_____ competence
2	an Irish accent		**12**	지방 사투리	the local d_____
3	bilingual education		**13**	억양 패턴	i_____ patterns
4	English fluency		**14**	속어 표현	a s_____ expression
5	modern English usage		**15**	정보 활용 능력	information l_____
6	a quotation from the Bible		**16**	문맹률	an i_____ rate
7	a humorous anecdote		**17**	자음과 모음	c_____s and v_____s
8	the session of the Assembly		**18**	사회 풍자	social s_____
9	a national consensus		**19**	부정적 함의	a negative c_____
10	serious discourse		**20**	정치적 논란	a political c_____

B 영영사전 뜻풀이에 알맞은 단어 찾기

> 보기   agenda   excerpt   forum   maxim   rhetoric

1 _____ : a well-known phrase or saying

2 _____ : a public meeting for open discussion

3 _____ : a short part taken from a speech, book, film, etc.

4 _____ : a list of the subjects to be discussed at a meeting

5 _____ : the art of using language impressively and persuasively

C 빈칸에 가장 적절한 단어 넣기

> 보기   analogy   euphemism   idiom   irony   metaphor   paradox

1 "The city is a jungle" is a(n) _____. '도시는 정글이다'는 은유다.

2 "More haste, less speed" is a(n) _____. '급할수록 천천히'는 역설이다.

3 "Senior citizen" is a(n) _____ for "old person." '어르신'은 '노인'의 완곡어이다.

4 Life is full of _____(e)s, some funny, some tragic.
인생은 어떤 건 재미있고 어떤 건 비극적인 뜻밖의 상황들로 가득 차 있다.

5 She drew a(n) _____ between childbirth and the creative process.
그녀는 출산을 창조 과정에 비유했다.

6 "To be on top of the world" is a(n) _____ that means to be very happy.
'세상 꼭대기에 있다'는 매우 행복하다는 것을 의미하는 관용구[숙어]다.

ANSWER
A 1. 공용어 2. 아일랜드 말씨 3. 이중 언어 교육 4. 영어 유창성 5. 현대 영어 용법 6. 성경에서의 인용 7. 유머러스한 일화 8. 국회 회기 9. 국민적 합의 10. 진지한 담론 11. linguistic 12. dialect 13. intonation 14. slang 15. literacy 16. illiteracy 17. consonant, vowel 18. satire 19. connotation 20. controversy   B 1. maxim 2. forum 3. excerpt 4. agenda 5. rhetoric   C 1. metaphor 2. paradox 3. euphemism 4. irony(ironies) 5. analogy 6. idiom

언어

Part 1

The Media

대중 매체 관련 명사

01 multimedia
[mʌ̀ltimíːdiə]

멀티미디어[다중 매체]

멀티미디어는 소리, 영상, 그림, 문자 등을 결합한다.

_____ combines sound, video, graphics, and text.

02 newscast
[njúːzkæ̀st]

뉴스 방송

▶ newscaster 뉴스 방송인
▶ broadcast 방송 통 방송하다

저녁 뉴스 방송은 하루 동안의 사건들을 분석 보도한다.

The evening _____ reviews the happenings of the day.

03 channel
[tʃǽnl]

❶ 텔레비전 채널 ❷ 경로
❸ 수로[해협]

비교 canal 운하

케이블/뉴스 채널 a cable/news _____

04 coverage
[kʌ́vəridʒ]

❶ 보도[방송]
❷ (보험의) 보장 (범위)

▶ cover 통 덮다, 취재[보도/방송]하다

선거 운동에 대한 TV 보도 the TV _____ of the election campaign

05 correspondent
[kɔ̀ːrəspándənt]

통신원[특파원](= reporter)

▶ correspondence 서신 (왕래)
▶ correspond 통 소식을 주고받다, 일치하다

정치부 기자/해외 특파원 a political/foreign _____

06 anchor
[ǽŋkər]

❶ 앵커[텔레비전 뉴스 진행자](= anchorperson)
❷ 닻 통 닻을 내리다

그는 9시 뉴스 앵커다.

He is the _____ for the nine o'clock news.

07 journal
[dʒə́ːrnl]

❶ 전문 잡지
❷ 일기(= diary)

▶ journalism 언론
▶ journalist 언론인

과학/의학 전문 잡지 a scientific/medical _____

08 periodical
[pìəriádikəl]

정기 간행물[전문 잡지]

▶ periodic 형 주기적인

기술·과학 정기 간행물 technical and scientific _____s

09 column
[káləm]

❶ (신문·잡지의) 칼럼, 단(段)
❷ 기둥[원주](= pillar)

▶ columnist 특별 기고가

이 신문은 1면이 6단으로 이루어져 있다.

This paper consists of six _____s a page.

10 feature
[fíːtʃər]

❶ 특징 ❷ 특집 (기사/방송) ❸ 이목구비 통 특징으로 하다

지구 온난화에 대한 특집 기사 a _____ on global warming

11 headline
[hédlàin]

(신문 기사의) 표제, (-s) (방송 뉴스의) 주요 뉴스 제목들

신문 기사의 표제는 몇 단어로 기사의 내용을 요약한다.

_____s summarize the content of an article in a few words.

12 deadline
[dédlàin]

마감 (시간/날짜)

마감 시간을 맞추어야 한다는 압박 pressure to meet a _____

13 subscription
[səbskrípʃən]

정기 구독(료)　　　　　　　　　▶subscribe 동 정기 구독[가입]하다

난 영자 신문을 구독하기로 결심했다.

I decided to take out a _____ to an English newspaper.

14 publicity
[pʌblísəti]

❶ 홍보[광고](업)　　　　　　　　▶publicize 동 홍보[광고]하다, 알리다
❷ 매스컴의 관심　　　　　　　　▶publicist 홍보 담당자

신간 서적을 판촉하기 위한 홍보 활동

a _____ campaign to promote the new book

**15 public relations
[PR]**

홍보

홍보 전략/운동 a _____ strategy/campaign

16 sponsor
[spánsər]

광고주, 후원자　동 광고주가 되다, 후원하다

텔레비전 프로그램 광고주 a television program _____

17 copywriter
[kápiràitər]

광고 문안 작성자

광고 문안 작성자는 인상적인 표현을 찾아야 한다.

_____s must look for impressive expressions.

18 classified ad

안내 광고[항목별 광고]　　　　　▶classify 동 분류하다
(=want ad)

일자리를 위한 안내 광고를 확인해 봐라.

Check out the _____s for positions.

19 leaflet
[líːflit]

홍보 전단　　　　　　　　　　비교 flyer 전단

광고 전단 an advertising _____

20 brochure
[brouʃúər]

홍보 소책자(=booklet, pamphlet)

여행안내 소책자 a travel _____

21 bulletin
[búlitən]

❶ 뉴스 단신 ❷ 고시[공고]　　　▶bulletin board 게시판

발표가 게시판에 공고되었다.

An announcement was posted on the _____ board.

22 publication
[pʌ̀bləkéiʃən]

❶ 출판[간행](물) ❷ 발표

▶publish 图 ❶ 출판[간행]하다 ❷ 발표하다
▶publisher 발행인[출판사]

새로운 어휘 책의 출판 the _____ of a new vocabulary book

23 draft
[dræft]

❶ 초안[초고] ❷ 징병
图 ❶ 초안을 작성하다 ❷ 징병하다

그녀의 새 소설의 대략적인 초안 the rough _____ of her new novel

24 manuscript
[mǽnjuskrìpt]

원고

그 저자는 원고를 출판사에 보냈다.
The author sent the _____ to his publisher.

25 format
[fɔ́ːrmæt]

(책·잡지·TV 프로의) 판형[구성/체제]

시각 장애인들을 위한 큰 판형의 책
a large-_____ book for the partially sighted

26 footnote
[fútnòut]

각주

각주를 참조하세요.
Refer to _____s.

27 margin
[máːrdʒin]

❶ 여백 ❷ 차이
❸ 수익 ❹ 가장자리

▶marginal 刨 주변부의, 미미한

누군가가 여백에 메모를 휘갈겨 놓았다.
Someone had scribbled a note in the _____.

28 copyright
[kápiràit]

판권[저작권]

이 책의 저작권은 누가 갖고 있니?
Who owns the _____ of this book?

29 pirate
[páiərət]

❶ 해적 ❷ 저작권 침해자
图 불법 복제하다

▶piracy ❶ 해적질 ❷ 저작권 침해

해적판 서적/시디/소프트웨어 _____ books/CDs/software

30 censorship
[sénsərʃip]

검열

▶censor 검열관 图 검열하다

그 영화는 정부의 검열을 통과하지 못했다.
The film didn't pass government _____.

Today's Dessert

The great lie of the news media: "I am the public."

뉴스 매체의 가장 큰 거짓말: "내가 바로 대중[여론]이다."

TEST
14

A 영어는 우리말로, 우리말은 영어로!

1 interactive multimedia

2 diplomatic channels

3 the press coverage

4 a publicity campaign

5 public relations

6 a classified ad

7 a free leaflet

8 해외 특파원   a foreign c_____

9 의학 전문 잡지   a medical j_____

10 월간 간행물   a monthly p_____

11 과학 출판물   scientific p_____s

12 판권 소유   the ownership of c_____

13 해적판 서적   p_____ books

14 엄격한 검열   strict c_____

B 영영사전 뜻풀이에 알맞은 단어 찾기

| 보기 | brochure   copywriter   format   headline   margin   newscast |

1 _____ : the title of a newspaper report

2 _____ : a news program on radio or television

3 _____ : the empty space at the side of a page

4 _____ : the shape and size of a book, magazine, etc.

5 _____ : someone who writes the words for advertisements

6 _____ : a thin book giving information or advertising something

C 빈칸에 가장 적절한 단어 넣기

| 보기 | deadline   footnote   manuscript   sponsor   subscription   bulletin board |

1 The _____ of the _____ is May 27. 원고 마감은 5월 27일이다.

2 He put the list of players up on the _____. 그는 게시판에 선수 명단을 붙였다.

3 I'll take out a _____ to an English newspaper. 난 영자 신문을 정기 구독할 거야.

4 A _____ is at the bottom of a page in a book. 각주는 책장의 아래쪽에 있다.

5 The company is a major _____ of the Olympics. 그 회사는 올림픽 경기의 주요 후원사다.

D 밑줄 친 단어 뜻 구별하기

1 The ship was at <u>anchor</u>.   the <u>anchor</u> of the evening news

2 thick stone <u>column</u>s   a weekly/science <u>column</u>

3 his handsome <u>feature</u>s   a special <u>feature</u> on education

     a important <u>feature</u> of modern life

4 a <u>draft</u> of the letter   He was <u>drafted</u> into the army.

ANSWER_____

A 1. 쌍방향 멀티미디어 2. 외교 경로 3. 언론 보도 4. 홍보 활동 5. 홍보 6. 안내 광고[항목별 광고] 7. 무료 홍보 전단 8. correspondent 9. journal 10. periodical 11. publication 12. copyright 13. pirate 14. censorship **B** 1. headline 2. newscast 3. margin 4. format 5. copywriter 6. brochure **C** 1. deadline, manuscript 2. bulletin board 3. subscription 4. footnote 5. sponsor **D** 1. 그 배는 닻을 내렸다. / 저녁 뉴스 진행자 2. 두꺼운 돌기둥 / 주간/과학 칼럼 3. 그의 잘생긴 <u>이목구비</u> / <u>교육</u> 관련 특집 / 현대 생활의 중요 <u>특징</u> 4. 편지의 초안 / 그는 군대에 징집되었다.

01 era
[íərə]

(특징적인) 시대(=age, epoch)

세계화 시대 the globalization _____

02 archive
[á:rkaiv]

기록 (보관소)   [혼동] achieve 동 이루다[성취하다]

신문/영화 보관소 the newspaper/film _____

03 throne
[θroun]

왕좌, (the ~) 왕위

누가 그의 뒤를 이어 왕위를 계승할 것인가?

Who will succeed him to the _____?

04 majesty
[mǽdʒəsti]

❶ (Your/His/Her Majesty)   ▶majestic 형 장엄한
(왕 · 여왕의 경칭) 폐하
❷ 장엄함

폐하, 성은이 망극하옵니다. Thank you, your M_____.

05 noble(wo)man
[nóubl(wù)mən]

귀족(=aristocrat)   ▶noble 형 고상한, 귀족의 명 귀족
▶nobility (the ~) 귀족 계급, 고상함

모든 귀족에게 하인이 있었다.

Every _____ had a manservant.

06 knight
[nait]

(중세의) 기사[나이트] 동 나이트 작위를 주다

갑옷 입은 기사들 _____s in armor

07 commoner
[kámənər]

평민   ▶the common man 보통 사람
(=ordinary people)

평민과 결혼한 대가는 왕위의 상실이었다.

The price of marrying the _____ was loss of the crown.

08 slavery
[sléivəri]

노예 (제도)   ▶slave 노예
▶enslave 동 노예로 만들다

노예 제도의 폐지 the abolition of _____

09 feudalism
[fjú:dəlìzm]

봉건 제도   ▶feudal 형 봉건의

봉건 영주/영지 a _____ lord/land

10 imperialism
[impíəriəlìzm]

제국주의   ▶empire 제국
▶imperial 형 제국[황제]의

그녀는 경제 제국주의라는 이유로 미국을 비난했다.

She accused the United States of economic _____.

11 colony
[káləni]

❶ 식민지
❷ 집단[군집]

▶colonial 형 식민지의
▶colonist 식민지 이주자
▶colonization 식민지화

알제리는 이전에 프랑스의 식민지였다.
Algeria was formerly a French _____.

12 arch(a)eology
[à:rkiálədʒi]

고고학

▶arch(a)eologist 고고학자

고고학은 우리를 과거로의 항해로 인도한다.
_____ takes us on a voyage into the past.

13 relic
[rélik]

유물

고고학자들은 고대 문명의 많은 유물들을 발견했다.
The archaeologists found many _____s of an ancient civilization.

14 remains
[riméins]

잔해[유해], 유물[유적]

비교 remain 동 ~인 채로 있다, 남아 있다

폼페이의 고대 유적 the ancient _____ of Pompeii

15 artifact
[á:rtəfæ̀kt]

(도구·장신구·무기 등) 인공 유물

선사 시대의 뼈로 만든 유물들 prehistoric _____s made of bone

16 antique
[æntí:k]

골동품
형 골동품의

▶antiquity 고대 (유물)
▶antiquated 형 구식인

골동품 가게/수집가 an _____ shop/collector

17 treasure
[tréʒər]

보물

▶treasury 재무부, 보고(寶庫)

매장된/침몰된 보물 buried/sunken _____

18 mummy
[mÁmi]

미라

▶mummify 동 미라로 만들다

고대 이집트 미라 an ancient Egyptian _____

19 anthropology
[æ̀nθrəpálədʒi]

인류학

▶anthropologist 인류학자

문화 인류학 cultural _____

20 tribe
[traib]

부족[종족]

▶tribal 형 부족의
▶tribesman 부족[종족] 구성원

원시 유목 부족 a primitive nomadic _____

21 kinship
[kínʃip]

❶ 친족 (관계) ❷ 연대감

각각 다른 민족은 각각 다른 친족 체계를 가진다.
Different ethnic groups have different systems of _____.

22 folklore
[fóuklɔ̀:r]

민간전승[민속]

▶folk 사람들, (-s) 가족, 민속 음악
혱 민속[민간]의

그녀의 책은 민간전승에 바탕을 두고 있다.
Her books are based on _____.

23 heritage
[héritidʒ]

(집단의) 유산

한국의 소중한 문화유산 Korea's valuable cultural _____

24 inheritance
[inhérətəns]

유산[상속]

▶inherit 통 상속받다[물려받다]

그는 일하지 않고 유산에 의존해 산다.
He doesn't work and lives off his _____.

25 legacy
[légəsi]

유산

각 세대는 경험이라는 유산을 다음 세대에 물려준다.
Each generation passes the _____ of its experience on to the next.

26 convention
[kənvénʃən]

❶ 관습(=custom)
❷ 대회(=assembly)
❸ 조약[협정](=treaty)

▶conventional 혱 전통[관습/인습]적인, 재래식의

나는 사회적 관습의 속박으로부터 자유롭고 싶다.
I want to be free from the bondage of social _____s.

27 ritual
[rítʃuəl]

의식[의례](=rite)
혱 의식의, 의례적인

전통적 의식 a traditional _____

28 morality
[mərǽləti]

도덕[윤리](=ethics ↔ immorality)

▶moral 혱 도덕의[도덕적인]
명 (-s) 도덕률, 교훈
▶immoral 혱 부도덕한
▶amoral 혱 도덕관념이 없는

전통적 도덕[윤리] conventional[traditional] _____

29 virtue
[və́:rtʃu:]

선(행)[미덕/장점]

▶virtuous 혱 덕이 있는

겸손의 미덕 the _____ of modesty
유기농의 장점 the _____s of organic farming

30 vice
[vais]

악(행)[악덕/악습],
성·마약 관련 범죄

비교 vice- 접두사 부(副)~
▶vicious 혱 포악한
▶vicious circle[cycle] 악순환

탐욕은 끔찍한 악덕이다.
Greed is a terrible _____.

Today's Dessert If we don't know our own history, we are doomed to live it. – Hannah Arendt
우리가 자신의 역사를 모른다면 그 역사를 살게 되는 악운에 처해진다. – 한나 아렌트

역사·문화 Part 1

TEST 15

A 영어는 우리말로, 우리말은 영어로!

1 a new era of peace
2 knights in armor
3 the abolition of slavery
4 prehistoric artifacts
5 the ties of kinship
6 religious rituals
7 sexual morality

8 제국주의 시대   the age of i_____
9 골동품 가게   an a_____ shop
10 국보   a national t_____
11 이집트 미라   an Egyptian m_____
12 원시 부족들   primitive t_____s
13 문화유산   cultural h_____
14 상속세   an i_____ tax

B 영영사전 뜻풀이에 알맞은 단어 찾기

보기   anthropology   archive   commoner   folklore   relic

1 _____ : a place where historical records are kept
2 _____ : someone who is not a member of the nobility
3 _____ : the study of people, their societies, cultures, etc.
4 _____ : the traditional stories and culture of a group of people
5 _____ : an old object or custom that reminds people of the past

C 빈칸에 가장 적절한 단어 넣기

보기   archeology   colony   legacy   remains   throne   vice   virtue

1 The Greeks have a rich _____ of literature. 그리스인은 풍부한 문학 유산을 가지고 있다.
2 The king's eldest son is the heir to the _____. 왕의 장남이 왕위의 계승자다.
3 The United States was once a _____ of Great Britain. 미국은 한때 영국의 식민지였다.
4 _____ must be punished and _____ rewarded.
   악행은 처벌받고 선행은 보상받아야 한다.
5 _____ is the study of ancient culture through _____.
   고고학은 유물[유적]을 통한 고대 문화에 대한 연구이다.

D 밑줄 친 단어 뜻 구별하기

1 His Majesty the King   the majesty of the Alps
2 social conventions   the UN convention on climate change

역사 · 문화

Part 1

ANSWER
A 1. 평화의 새로운 시대 2. 갑옷 입은 기사들 3. 노예 제도의 폐지 4. 선사 시대 유물들 5. 친족의 유대 6. 종교적 의식 7. 성도덕 8. imperialism
9. antique 10. treasure 11. mummy 12. tribe 13. heritage 14. inheritance   B 1. archive 2. commoner 3. anthropology 4. folklore
5. relic   C 1. legacy 2. throne 3. colony 4. Vice, virtue 5. Archeology, remains   D 1. 국왕 폐하 / 알프스 산맥의 장엄함 2. 사회적 관습 /
유엔 기후 변화 협약

Religion & Philosophy

01 Christian
[krístʃən]

기독교도 형 기독교의

▶ Christianity 기독교
▶ Jesus (Christ) 예수 (그리스도)
비교 Judaism / Jew 유대교 / 유대교도

극소수의 사람들만이 실천적인 기독교도이다.
Very few people are practising _____s.

02 Muslim
[mʌ́zlim]

이슬람교도 형 이슬람교의

▶ Islam 이슬람교
▶ Mohammed[Muhammad] 마호메트

이슬람교도는 이슬람교를 믿는 사람이다.
A _____ is someone who belives in Islam.

03 Buddhist
[bú(:)dist]

불교도 형 불교의

▶ Buddhism 불교
▶ Buddha 부처

불교는 인도에서 기원했다.
_____ had its beginnings in India.

04 Confucian
[kənfjúːʃən]

유교도 형 유교의

▶ Confucianism 유교 비교 Taoism 도교
▶ Confucius 공자

유교는 한국인의 정신을 지배해왔다.
_____ has ruled the Korean minds.

05 monk/nun
[mʌŋk] / [nʌn]

수사/수녀

비교 priest[minister] 성직자
the clergy (집합적) 성직자들

불교 수도승 a Buddhist _____
수녀가 초를 들고 그를 위해 기도했다.
A _____ held a candle while praying for him.

06 shaman
[ʃáːmən]

샤먼[무당]

▶ shamanism 샤머니즘

샤먼은 신령과 이야기하고 병을 고칠 수 있다고 믿어진다.
A _____ is believed to be able to talk to spirits and cure illnesses.

07 hermit
[hə́ːrmit]

(종교적) 은둔자[은자]

은자는 숲속 오두막에서 살고 있다.
The _____ lives in a hut in the forest.

08 pilgrim
[pílgrim]

순례자

▶ the Pilgrim Fathers
1620년 미국에 간 영국 청교도들

많은 순례자들이 예루살렘에 간다. Many _____s go to Jerusalem.

09 cathedral
[kəθíːdrəl]

대성당

커다란 중세 대성당 the large medieval _____

10 monastery
[mánəstèri]

수도원

대부분의 수사들은 수도원에 산다. Most monks live in a _____.

11 shrine
[ʃrain]

성지(聖地)

성지를 방문하는 순례자들 pilgrims visiting a holy _____

비교 temple 사원[절/신전]

---

12 altar
[ɔ́ːltər]

제단

수녀가 제단의 초에 불을 붙였다.
The nun lit the candles on the _____.

비교 alter 동 변하다[바꾸다]

---

13 heaven ↔ hell
[hévən] ↔ [hel]

천국(=paradise) ↔ 지옥

마음은 지옥을 천국으로도, 천국을 지옥으로도 만들 수 있다.
The mind can make a _____ of _____, a _____ of _____.

▶heavenly 형 천국의

---

14 hymn
[him]

찬송가, 찬가

그는 일하면서 찬송가를 부른다.
He sings _____s as he works.

---

15 mercy
[mə́ːrsi]

자비

그는 원수[적]들에게 자비를 베풀었다.
He showed _____ to his enemies.

▶mercy killing 안락사
▶merciful 형 자비로운
▶merciless 형 무자비한

---

16 salvation
[sælvéiʃən]

구원

그들은 세상의 구원을 위해 기도한다.
They pray for the _____ of the world.

---

17 sin
[sin]

(종교·도덕적) 죄(악)

그녀는 죄를 고백하고 용서를 구했다.
She confessed her _____s and asked for forgiveness.

비교 crime (법적) (범)죄
▶sinful 형 죄 많은[죄짓는]

---

18 devil
[dévəl]

(the ~) 악마(=Satan),
마귀(=demon)

천사와 악마는 초자연적인 존재이다.
Angels and _____s are supernatural beings.

비교 evil 악 형 악한, 나쁜

---

19 idol
[áidl]

우상

우상 숭배 the worship of _____s

▶idolize 동 우상화하다[숭배하다]

---

20 superstition
[sùːpərstíʃən]

미신

미신은 박약한 정신이 믿는 종교다.
_____ is the religion of feeble minds.

▶superstitious 형 미신적인

---

21 taboo
[təbúː]

금기[터부] 형 금기시되는

어떤 사람들에게는, 성이 금기시되는 주제다.
For some people, sex is a _____ subject.

비교 tattoo 문신

22 fate
[feit]

운명

비교 Providence 신의 뜻[섭리]
▶the Fates 운명의 세 여신
▶fatal 형 치명적인

아무도 자신의 운명이 어떻게 될지 모른다.
No one knows what their _____ will be.

23 destiny
[déstəni]

운명

▶destined 형 ~할 운명인, ~행(行)의

각자의 운명은 자신의 손에 달려 있다.
Every one's _____ is in his/her own hands.

**24 misfortune
[mischance]**
[misfɔ́ːrtʃən] [mistʃǽns]

불운[불행]

▶fortune ❶ 큰돈[부] ❷ 운(명)
▶unfortunate 형 불운[불행]한(↔fortunate)

불행은 결코 혼자 오는 법이 없다.[설상가상.]
_____s never come single.

25 outlook
[áutlùk]

❶ 관점 ❷ 전망(=prospect)

전 지구적 관점은 복합적 시각과 균형 잡힌 관점을 포함한다.
A global viewpoint includes plural eyes and a balanced _____.

26 perspective
[pərspéktiv]

❶ 관점(=view) ❷ 원근법

우리는 매사를 국제적 관점에서 바라보아야 한다.
We have to look at everything from an international _____.

27 conscience
[kánʃəns]

양심

너는 양심이 시키는 대로 해야 한다.
You have to do what your _____ tells you.

28 idealism
[aidí(ː)əlìzm]

이상주의

▶ideal 형 이상적인 명 이상

젊은 세대의 이상주의 the _____ of the younger generation

29 realism
[rí(ː)əlìzm]

❶ 현실주의
❷ (예술) 사실주의[리얼리즘]

▶real 형 진짜[현실]의

그는 현실주의의 감각[분별력]을 갖고 있다.
He has a sense of _____.

30 materialism
[mətíəriəlìzm]

❶ 물질주의 ❷ 유물론

▶materialistic 형 물질주의의

천박한 물질주의로 가득 찬 세상 a world full of shallow _____

Today's Dessert Any religion or philosophy which is not based on a respect for life is not a true religion or philosophy.

생명에 대한 존중에 바탕을 두지 않는 어떠한 종교나 철학도 참된 종교나 철학이 아니다.

TEST 16

A 영어는 우리말로, 우리말은 영어로!

1 Christian pilgrims

2 Saint Peter's Cathedral

3 salvation from sin

4 the worship of idols

5 a practical outlook on life

6 freedom of conscience

7 독실한 불교도   a devout B _____

8 유교 윤리   C _____ ethics

9 신성한 제단   a sacred a _____

10 찬송가 책   a h _____ book

11 성적 금기   a sexual t _____

12 낙천적 관점   an optimistic o _____

B 영영사전 뜻풀이에 알맞은 단어 찾기

> 보기   hermit   monastery   shaman   shrine

1 _____ : a place where monks live and worship

2 _____ : a person who lives alone, away from society

3 _____ : a person who is believed to be able to talk to spirits

4 _____ : a place that is connected with a holy event or person

C 같은 관계 맺어 주기

1 Christianity : Christian = Islam : M_____

2 god : goddess = monk : n_____

3 misfortune : mischance = fate : d_____

4 angel : devil = heaven : h_____

D 빈칸에 가장 적절한 단어 넣기

> 보기   devil   idealism   materialism   mercy   realism   superstition

1 May God have _____ on your soul. 신께서 네 영혼에 자비를 베푸시길.

2 Talk of the _____, and he will appear. 악마[호랑이]도 제 말 하면 온다.

3 Knowledge is the best remedy for _____. 지식이 미신에 대한 최선의 치료제다.

4 Modern society is full of consumerism and _____.

현대 사회는 소비주의와 물질주의로 가득 차 있다.

5 He tried to achieve a balance between _____ and _____.

그는 이상주의와 현실주의 사이의 균형을 이루려 노력했다.

E 밑줄 친 단어 뜻 구별하기

an international perspective   the artist's use of perspective

ANSWER

A 1. 기독교 순례자들 2. 성 베드로 대성당 3. 죄로부터의 구원 4. 우상 숭배 5. 현실적인 인생관 6. 양심의 자유 7. Buddhist 8. Confucian 9. altar 10. hymn 11. taboo 12. outlook   **B** 1. monastery 2. hermit 3. shaman 4. shrine   **C** 1. Muslim 2. nun 3. destiny 4. hell **D** 1. mercy 2. devil 3. superstition 4. materialism 5. idealism, realism   **E** 국제적 관점 / 화가의 원근법 사용

01 sociology
[sòusiálədʒi]

사회학

▶ sociologist 사회학자
▶ sociological 휑 사회학의
▶ socialization 사회화

사회학은 집단적 측면에서의 인간에 대한 연구다.
_____ is the study of humans in their collective aspect.

02 individualism
[ìndəvídʒuəlìzm]

개인주의

▶ individualist 개인주의자
▶ individualistic 휑 개인주의적인
▶ individuality 개성

자본주의는 경쟁과 개인주의를 장려한다.
Capitalism encourages competition and _____.

03 citizenship
[sítizənʃip]

시민권

▶ citizen 시민

그는 한국과 미국 이중 시민권을 갖고 있다.
He holds dual _____ in Korea and the US.

04 NGO

비정부 기구(non-governmental organization)

그는 비정부 기구 활동에 참여하고 있다.
He is participating in _____ activities.

05 framework
[fréimwèːrk]

뼈대, 체제

▶ frame 틀, 뼈대

사회/정치 체제 a social/political _____

06 infrastructure
[ínfrəstrÀktʃər]

(사회) 기반 시설
(교통·통신·전기·수도 등)

▶ infra- 접두사 아래에
▶ structure 구조(물)

적절한 경제 기반 시설 a suitable economic _____

07 celebrity
[səlébrəti]

❶ 유명인[명사](=star) ❷ 명성

각계각층의 명사들 _____ies from all walks of life

08 prestige
[prestíːʒ]

위신[명망] 휑 명품의

▶ prestigious 휑 명망 있는

그는 우리나라의 국제적 위신을 높였다.
He enhanced our country's international _____.

09 privilege
[prívəlidʒ]

특권[특혜]

▶ privileged ↔ underprivileged
휑 특권을 가진 ↔ 혜택 받지 못한
명 (the ~) 특권층 ↔ 소외 계층

좋은 교육이 부자들의 특권이 되어서는 안 된다.
A good education should not be a _____ of the rich.

10 reputation
[rèpjutéiʃən]

평판[명성]

그 회사는 평판이 좋다/나쁘다.
The company has a good/bad _____.

11 equality ↔ inequality
[ikwáləti] ↔ [ìnikwáləti]

평등 ↔ 불평등

▶equal 형 동일[동등]한 동 같다

평등과 자유의 원칙 the principle of _____ and liberty

12 justice ↔ injustice
[dʒʎstis] ↔ [indʒʎstis]

정의 ↔ 불의

▶just ↔ unjust
형 공정한 ↔ 불공평한[부당한]
▶justify 동 정당화하다

어느 곳의 불의라도 모든 곳의 정의에 대한 위협이 된다.

_____ anywhere is a threat to _____ everywhere.

13 minority
[minɔ́:rəti]

소수 (집단)(↔ majority)

▶minor 형 작은[사소한](↔ major)
명 미성년자, 부전공

민족적/종교적 소수 집단들 ethnic/religious _____ies

14 bias
[báiəs]

편견[편향](=prejudice)
동 편견을 갖게 하다

▶biased 형 편견을 가진[편향된]

학생들은 편견 없이 평가되어야 한다.

Students must be evaluated without _____.

15 stereotype
[stériətàip]

고정 관념

대중 매체에 나타나는 성적 고정 관념 sexual _____ in the media

16 discrimination
[diskrìmənéiʃən]

차별, 구별

▶discriminate 동 차별하다, 구별하다

성/인종 차별 sex/racial _____

17 segregation
[sègrigéiʃən]

분리[차별]

▶segregate 동 분리[차별]하다

인종 분리 제도 the system of racial _____

18 racism
[réisizm]

인종 차별(주의)

비교 sexism 성차별(주의)
▶racist 인종 차별주의자 형 인종 차별의

그들은 인종 차별주의에 맞서 싸우고 있다.

They are fighting _____.

19 violence ↔ non-violence
[váiələns] ↔ [nànváiələns]

폭력 ↔ 비폭력

▶violent 형 폭력적인

여성들에게 가해지는 가정 폭력 domestic _____ against women

20 riot
[ráiət]

폭동[소요]

항의 행진이 폭동으로 급변했다.

The protest march exploded into a _____.

21 turmoil
[tə́:rmɔil]

혼란

정치적/경제적 혼란 political/economic _____

22 overpopulation
[òuvərpàpjuléiʃən]

인구 과잉

인구 과잉을 줄이려는 노력

efforts to reduce _____

▶overpopulated 혱 인구 과잉의

23 density
[dénsəti]

밀도

인구 밀도가 높은 지역

areas of high population _____

▶dense 혱 밀집한, 짙은, 우둔한

24 slum
[slʌm]

도시 빈민가(=ghetto)

도심 빈민가 an inner-city _____

25 anonymity
[ænəníməti]

익명(성)

도시 생활/인터넷의 익명성

the _____ of city life/the Internet

▶anonymous 혱 익명의

26 activism
[ǽktəvìzm]

(사회·정치적) 행동[실천]주의

정치/환경 행동주의

political/environmental _____

▶activist 행동주의자[활동가]

27 feminism
[fémənìzm]

남녀동권주의

그녀는 남녀동권운동에 평생 헌신했다.

She had a lifelong commitment to _____.

▶feminist 남녀동권주의자
혱 남녀동권주의의

28 boycott
[bɔ́ikɑt]

배척[불매/거부] 운동
통 배척[불매/거부] 운동을 하다

그 회사 제품에 대한 불매 운동

a _____ against[on] the company's products

29 petition
[pətíʃən]

진정[탄원/청원](서)
통 진정[탄원/청원]하다

나는 전쟁을 중지시키기 위한 청원서에 서명했다.

I signed a _____ to stop the war.

30 patron
[péitrən]

❶ 후원자(=sponsor)
❷ 고객(=client)

그는 몇몇 자선 단체의 후원자다.

He is a _____ of several charities.

▶patronize 통 ❶ 생색내다
❷ 후원하다

Today's Dessert The sources of our social ills are stupidity, ignorance, greed and love of power.

사회악의 원천은 바로 어리석음과 무지와 탐욕과 권력욕이다.

TEST 17

A 영어는 우리말로, 우리말은 영어로!

1 sociological **research**
2 NGO **activity**
3 competition and **individualism**
4 a social **framework**
5 information **infrastructure**
6 political **bias**
7 racial **segregation**
8 the fight against **racism**
9 political **activism**

10 이중 시민권   dual c_____
11 국제적 위신   international p_____
12 민족적 소수 집단들   ethnic m_____s
13 성차별   sex d_____
14 가정 폭력   domestic v_____
15 교도소 폭동   prison r_____s
16 인구 밀도   population d_____
17 빈민가 지역   a s_____ area
18 급진적 남녀동권주의   radical f_____

B 영영사전 뜻풀이에 알맞은 단어 찾기

보기   celebrity   patron   reputation   stereotype   turmoil

1 _____ : a famous living person
2 _____ : a state of confusion, uncertainty, disorder or anxiety
3 _____ : someone who supports the activities of an organization
4 _____ : the opinion that people have about someone or something
5 _____ : an idea of what a particular type of person or thing is like

C 빈칸에 가장 적절한 단어 넣기

보기   anonymity   boycott   inequality   injustice   petition   privilege

1 We should fight against _____. 우리는 불의에 맞서 싸워야 한다.
2 I signed a(n) _____ to stop the war. 나는 전쟁 종식을 위한 청원서에 서명했다.
3 Witnesses will be guaranteed _____. 증인들은 익명을 보장받게 될 것이다.
4 There are _____(e)s in wealth distribution. 부의 분배에 불평등이 있다.
5 Farmers called for a(n) _____ of imported meat.
농부들은 수입 고기에 대한 불매 운동을 요구했다.
6 A good education should not be a(n) _____ of the rich.
좋은 교육이 부자들의 특권이 되어서는 안 된다.

ANSWER_____

A 1. 사회학 연구 2. 비정부 기구 활동 3. 경쟁과 개인주의 4. 사회 체제 5. 정보 기반 시설 6. 정치적 편향 7. 인종 분리 8. 인종 차별(주의)에 대한 투쟁 9. 정치적 행동주의 10. citizenship 11. prestige 12. minority(minorities) 13. discrimination 14. violence 15. riot 16. density 17. slum 18. feminism   **B** 1. celebrity 2. turmoil 3. patron 4. reputation 5. stereotype   **C** 1. injustice 2. petition 3. anonymity 4. inequality(inequalities) 5. boycott 6. privilege

01 constitution
[kὰnstitjúːʃən]

❶ 헌법 ❷ 체질[건강]

▶constitutional 혱 헌법의

영국에는 성문 헌법이 없다.
Britain has no written _____.

02 legislation
[lèdʒisléiʃən]

법률

▶legislative 혱 입법의
▶legislator 입법자
▶legislature 입법부

아동 보호를 위한 새 법률 new _____ to protect children

03 regulation
[règjəléiʃən]

❶ 규정[법규](=rule)
❷ 규제[조절]

▶regulate 통 규제[조절]하다

교통/안전 법규 traffic/safety _____s

04 offense
[əféns]

❶ 범죄[위반]
❷ 모욕
❸ 공격(진)(↔defense)

▶offend 통 불쾌하게 하다, 범죄를 저지르다
▶offender 범죄자
▶offensive 혱 모욕적인, 공격의

형사 범죄/성범죄 a criminal/sexual _____
중범죄/경범죄 a serious/minor _____

05 violation
[vàiəléiʃən]

위반, 침해

▶violate 통 위반하다, 침해하다

국제법 위반 a _____ of international law

06 delinquency
[dilíŋkwənsi]

(청소년) 비행[범죄]

▶delinquent 비행 청소년 혱 비행의

청소년 비행[범죄]가 급속도로 증가하고 있다.
Juvenile _____ is on the increase at a rapid pace.

07 conspiracy
[kənspírəsi]

음모[공모]

▶conspire 통 음모를 꾸미다[공모하다]

음모론 a _____ theory
살인 음모 _____ to murder

08 murder
[mə́ːrdər]

살인(=homicide)
통 살해하다

비교 assassination 암살
▶murderer 살인자

잔인한 연쇄 살인 a series of brutal _____s

09 robbery
[rábəri]

강도질

▶robber 강도
▶rob 통 강탈하다[털다]

무장 강도 사건들 incidents of armed _____

10 burglar
[bə́ːrglər]

주거 침입 도둑[강도]

▶burglary 주거 침입 도둑[강도]질

지난밤에 우리 집에 도둑이 들었다.
A _____ broke into my house last night.

11 theft
[θeft]

도둑질[절도]   ▶thief 도둑

차량/자전거 절도 car/bicycle _____

12 pickpocket
[píkpàkit]

소매치기   비교 shoplifting 들치기

소매치기가 내 가방을 빼앗아 도망갔다.

A _____ took my bag and ran away. ,

13 assault
[əsɔ́ːlt]

❶ 폭행 ❷ 공격(=attack)   ▶sexual assault 성폭행[강간](=rape)
통 폭행하다, 공격하다

그는 성폭행 혐의로 고소되었다.

He was charged with sexual _____.

14 kidnapping
[kídnæpiŋ]

납치[유괴]   비교 hijack (비행기) 납치
▶kidnap 통 납치[유괴]하다
▶kidnapper 납치[유괴]범

12명 미국 시민의 납치 the _____ of 12 US citizens

15 hostage
[hástidʒ]

인질

기장이 비행기 납치범들에게 인질로 잡혔다.

The captain was taken _____ by the hijackers.

16 arson
[áːrsn]

방화

경찰은 그 화재를 방화 사건으로 간주했다.

Police treated the fire as a case of _____.

17 fraud
[frɔːd]

사기(꾼)

최근의 인터넷 사기 사건 a recent case of _____ on the Internet

18 bribery
[bráibəri]

뇌물 수수   ▶bribe 뇌물 통 뇌물을 주다

그는 뇌물 수수 사건에 연루되었다.

He was involved in a _____ case.

19 jury
[dʒúəri]

배심원단

배심원단이 피고를 유죄라고 평결했다.

The _____ found the accused guilty.

20 defendant
[diféndənt]

피고(=the accused)   비교 plaintiff[accuser] 원고
▶defend 통 방어하다, 변호하다
▶defense 방어, 변호

우리는 피고가 무죄라고 평결한다.

We find the _____ not guilty.

21 prosecutor
[prásikjùːtər]

검사   ▶prosecute 통 기소하다
▶prosecution 기소

검사는 누군가가 유죄라는 것을 입증해야 한다.

A _____ must prove that someone is guilty.

22 attorney
[ətə́ːrni]

변호사[검사](=lawyer)   ▶district attorney 지방 검사

피고 측 변호사 a defense _____

23 alibi
[ǽləbài]

❶ 알리바이[현장 부재 증명] ❷ 변명

완벽한 알리바이 a perfect _____

24 oath
[ouθ]

맹세[서약], 선서

증인들은 선서를 하도록 요구받는다.

Witnesses are required to take an _____.

25 testimony
[téstəmòuni]

증언, 증거   ▶testify 통 증언하다, 증명하다

그의 증언은 그 사건에 결정적인 것이다.

His _____ is crucial to the case.

26 guilt ↔ innocence
[gilt]↔[ínəsəns]

유죄[죄책감] ↔ 무죄[순진함]   ▶guilty ↔ innocent 형 유죄의 ↔ 무죄의

배심원단이 피고의 유죄와 무죄를 결정한다.

The jury determines the defendant's _____ or _____.

27 verdict
[və́ːrdikt]

평결

유죄 평결을 위한 충분한 증거가 없다.

There's not enough evidence for a guilty _____.

28 penalty
[pénəlti]

처벌, 벌금[벌칙]   ▶penalize 통 처벌하다
▶death penalty 사형

휴지 버리지 말 것. 벌금 500달러. No littering. _____ $500.

29 punishment
[pʌ́niʃmənt]

처벌   ▶punish 통 처벌하다
▶capital punishment 사형

법원은 어떤 처벌을 부과할지 결정한다.

The court decides what _____ to impose.

30 confinement
[kənfáinmənt]

감금   ▶confine 통 한정하다, 가두다

그는 독방 감금에 처해졌다.

He was placed in solitary _____.

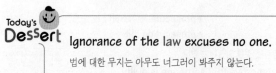

Today's Dessert

Ignorance of the law excuses no one.

법에 대한 무지는 아무도 너그러이 봐주지 않는다.

TEST 18

A 영어는 우리말로, 우리말은 영어로!

1 a written constitution
2 a murder suspect
3 a defense attorney
4 a perfect alibi
5 a guilty verdict
6 capital punishment

7 청소년 범죄   juvenile d_____
8 음모론   a c_____ theory
9 성폭행   sexual a_____
10 방화 사건   a case of a_____
11 보험 사기   insurance f_____
12 독방 감금   solitary c_____

B 영영사전 뜻풀이에 알맞은 단어 찾기

> 보기   legislation   oath   penalty   pickpocket   violation

1 _____ : a law or set of laws
2 _____ : a formal promise to tell the truth in a court
3 _____ : a thief who steals things out of pockets or bags
4 _____ : an action that breaks a law, agreement, principle, etc.
5 _____ : a punishment for breaking a law, rule, or legal agreement

C 표 완성하기

	Crime	Criminal	Verb	Crime	Criminal	Verb
1		thief	steal	3 burglary		break into
2		robber	rob	4 kidnapping		kidnap

D 빈칸에 가장 적절한 단어 넣기

> 보기   bribery   defendant   hostage   jury   prosecutor   testimony

1 The witness is giving false _____. 그 증인은 위증을 하고 있다.
2 The politician was accused of _____. 그 정치인은 뇌물 수수 혐의로 기소되었다.
3 The terrorists have seized 20 _____s. 테러리스트들은 20명의 인질을 붙잡았다.
4 The _____ found the _____ not guilty. 배심원단은 피고가 무죄라고 평결했다.
5 A special _____ was appointed to deal with that case.
특별 검사가 그 사건을 다루기 위해서 임명되었다.

E 밑줄 친 단어 뜻 구별하기

1 traffic regulations   the regulation of public spending
2 a minor offense   I really didn't mean any offense.

ANSWER

A 1. 성문 헌법 2. 살인 용의자 3. 피고 측 변호사 4. 완벽한 알리바이 5. 유죄 평결 6. 사형 7. delinquency 8. conspiracy 9. assault 10. arson 11. fraud 12. confinement   B 1. legislation 2. oath 3. pickpocket 4. violation 5. penalty   C 1. theft 2. robbery 3. burglar 4. kidnapper   D 1. testimony 2. bribery 3. hostage 4. jury, defendant 5. prosecutor   E 1. 교통 법규 / 공공 지출 규제 2. 경범죄 / 난 정말 모욕할 의도가 전혀 없었어.

Agriculture & Industry

01 agriculture
[ǽgrəkʌ̀ltʃər]

농업(=farming), 농학

▶agricultural 형 농업의
▶agriculturalist 농업 전문가

기계화 농업 mechanized _____

02 peasant
[péznt]

영세 농민[소작인]

들에서 힘들게 일하는 농민들 _____s toiling in the fields

03 orchard
[ɔ́ːrtʃərd]

과수원

사과/복숭아 과수원 an apple/a peach _____

04 plantation
[plæntéiʃən]

(열대 지방의) 대규모 재배 농장

커피/목화 재배 농장 a coffee/cotton _____

05 fertilizer
[fə́ːrtəlàizər]

비료

▶fertile 형 비옥한, 생식력 있는
▶fertilize 통 수정시키다, 비옥하게 하다
▶fertility 비옥함, 생식력

천연/인공 비료 natural/artificial _____s
유기/화학 비료 organic/chemical _____s

06 manure
[mənjúər]

(동물 배설물) 거름

비교 compost (썩은 식물) 퇴비

썩은 식물 퇴비와 동물 배설물 거름은 유기 비료이다.
Compost and _____ are organic fertilizers.

07 pesticide
[insecticide]
[péstəsàid] [inséktəsàid]

살충제

비교 herbicide[weedkiller] 제초제
▶pest 해충

살충제를 사용하지 않고 기른 채소
vegetables grown without the use of _____s

08 shovel
[spade]
[ʃʌ́vəl] [speid]

삽

비교 hoe 괭이

그는 삽으로 땅을 파고 있다.
He is digging with a _____.

09 plow
[plau]

쟁기 통 쟁기질하다

비교 rake 갈퀴

황소가 들에서 쟁기를 끌었다.
The ox pulled the _____ through the field.

10 irrigation
[ìrəgéiʃən]

관개

▶irrigate 통 (땅에) 물을 대다

댐은 관개를 위한 물을 공급하는 데 이용된다.
Dams are used to provide water for _____.

11 reservoir
[rézərvwàːr]

저수지
저수지가 가뭄 동안에 말라 버렸다.
The _____ dried up during the drought.

12 barn
[baːrn]

곡식 창고[축사]
곡식 창고가 곡식으로 터질 듯이 차 있다.
The _____ bursts with grain.

13 livestock
[láivstàk]

(집합적) 가축 ▶livestock farming 목축업
그는 가축을 기른다.
He raises _____.

14 shepherd
[ʃépərd]

양치기 비교 cowboy 카우보이
풀을 뜯고 있는 양들을 지키고 있는 양치기들
_____s watching over their grazing sheep

15 ranch
[ræntʃ]

목장 ▶rancher 목장주
소/양 목장 a cattle/sheep _____

16 pasture
[pǽstʃər]

목초지
소들이 목초지에서 풀을 뜯어 먹고 있다.
The cattle are grazing on the _____.

17 hay
[hei]

건초 ▶haystack 큰 건초 더미
해가 나 있는 동안 건초를 만들어라.[기회를 놓치지 마라.]
Make _____ while the sun shines.

18 fishery
[fíʃəri]

어장(=fishing ground), 비교 aquaculture
양어장[양식장](=fish farm) (어류·패류의) 수산 양식[수경 재배]
▶fish farming 물고기 양식업

원양/근해 어장 a deep-sea/an offshore _____

19 mining
[máiniŋ]

광업, 채광 ▶mine 광산 동 채굴하다
▶miner 광부

탄광업/금광업 coal/gold _____

20 petroleum
[pətróuliəm]

석유(=oil)
원유 crude[raw] _____[oil]

21 lumber
[lʌ́mbər]

목재(=timber)
목재 벌목 _____ cutting

22 manufacturing
[mænjufǽktʃəriŋ]

제조(업)

▶manufacture 통 제조하다 명 제조
▶manufacturer 제조업자

제조업 the _____ industry
제조 과정 _____ processes

23 mill
[mil]

❶ 방앗간[제분소] ❷ 분쇄기
❸ 공장

▶watermill 물레방앗간
▶windmill 풍차

제지/철강 공장 a paper/steel _____

24 smokestack
[smóukstæk]

(공장·배의) 높은 굴뚝

[비교] chimney 굴뚝
▶smokestack industry
굴뚝 산업[재래식 산업]

조선과 철강과 같은 굴뚝 산업들
_____ industries such as shipbuilding and steel

25 automation
[ɔ̀ːtəméiʃən]

자동화

▶automate 통 자동화하다
▶automatic 형 자동의

공장/사무 자동화 factory/office _____

26 prefabrication
[prìːfæbrikéiʃən]

조립식 공정

▶fabricate 통 조작하다, 제작하다

조립식 공정은 현대 건축술의 중요한 양상이다.
_____ is an important aspect in modern architecture.

27 warehouse
[wɛ́ərhàus]

창고(=storehouse)

그의 일은 회사의 창고 운영을 관리하는 것이다.
His job is supervising the company's _____ operation.

28 productivity
[pròudʌktívəti]

생산성

▶productive 형 생산적인
▶produce 통 생산하다

생산성을 높이는 방법들 ways of increasing _____

29 competitiveness
[kəmpétətìvnis]

경쟁력, 경쟁심

▶competitive 형 경쟁적인, 경쟁력 있는
▶compete 통 경쟁하다
▶competition 경쟁, 대회[시합]

새로운 기계가 회사의 경쟁력을 강화시켰다.
New machinery has enhanced the company's _____.

30 patent
[pǽtnt]

특허
형 특허의 통 특허를 받다

그는 새 발명품에 대해 특허를 얻었다.
He took out a _____ on his new invention.

Today's Dessert

Make the best quality of goods possible at the lowest cost possible.
– Henry Ford

가능한 한 최고 품질의 제품을 가능한 한 최저 비용으로 만들어라. – 헨리 포드

A 영어는 우리말로, 우리말은 영어로!

1 a peasant farmer

2 a rubber plantation

3 livestock farming

4 crude petroleum

5 the manufacturing industry

6 lumber mill

7 smokestack industries

8 productivity and competitiveness

9 복숭아 과수원　　a peach o_____

10 살충제 사용　　p_____ use

11 갈퀴와 삽　　a rake and s_____

12 관개 수로　　an i_____ canal

13 목우장[소 목장]　　a cattle r_____

14 연안 어장　　a coastal f_____

15 탄광업[채탄]　　coal m_____

16 공장 자동화　　factory a_____

B 영영사전 뜻풀이에 알맞은 단어 찾기

보기　agriculture　plow　reservoir　shepherd　warehouse

1 _____ : the practice or science of farming

2 _____ : a person whose job is to take care of sheep

3 _____ : an artificial lake used for the storage of water

4 _____ : a large building for storing large quantities of goods

5 _____ : a tool used by farmers to turn over the soil before planting crops

C 빈칸에 가장 적절한 단어 넣기

보기　barn　fertilizer　hay　manure　pasture　patent　prefabrication

1 The sheep are grazing on the _____.　양들이 목초지에서 풀을 뜯어 먹고 있다.

2 He applied for a _____ for a new device.　그는 새로운 장치에 대해서 특허를 출원했다.

3 The use of _____ in housing speeds up construction.

주택 건설에서 조립식 공정의 이용은 건축 속도를 빠르게 한다.

4 The cows were feeding on _____ in the _____.

소들이 축사에서 건초를 먹고 있었다.

5 _____ is solid waste from animals used to help plants grow.

거름은 식물이 자라는 걸 돕기 위해 사용되는 동물의 고형 배설물이다.

6 Organic _____s are derived from animal or vegetable matter.

유기 비료는 동물질이나 식물질에서 얻어진다.

ANSWER_____

A 1. 영세 농민[소작인] 2. 고무나무 재배 농장 3. 목축업 4. 원유 5. 제조업 6. 제재소 7. 굴뚝 산업 8. 생산성과 경쟁력 9. orchard 10. pesticide
11. shovel 12. irrigation 13. ranch 14. fishery 15. mining 16. automation　B 1. agriculture 2. shepherd 3. reservoir 4. warehouse
5. plow　C 1. pasture 2. patent 3. prefabrication 4. hay, barn 5. Manure 6. fertilizer

01 economics
[è:kənámiks]

경제학

▶ economy ❶ 경제 ❷ 절약
▶ economic 휑 경제의
▶ economical 휑 경제적인[절약하는]

그는 대학에서 경제학을 공부했다.

He studied _____ at university.

02 supply
↔ demand
[səplái]↔[dimǽnd]

공급 통 공급[제공]하다
↔ 수요, 요구 통 요구하다

수요와 공급의 법칙 the law of s_____ and d_____

03 profit
↔ loss
[práfit]↔[lɔːs]

이익[수익]
↔ 손실[손해]
통 이익을 얻다[주다]

▶ profitable 휑 이익이 되는[유익한]
▶ profitability 수익성

그 회사는 그 거래에서 엄청난 이익/손실을 보았다.

The company made a huge _____ / _____ on the deal.

04 revenue
[révənjùː]

수입[세입]

그 회사의 연간 수입이 10% 늘었다.

The company's annual _____s rose by 10%.

05 expenditure
[ikspénditʃər]

지출[비용/세출], 소비

▶ expend 통 (시간·돈·힘을) 들이다
　[소비하다]

공공 비용/정부 비용/방위비 public/government/military _____

06 corporation
[kɔ̀ːrpəréiʃən]

회사[기업], 법인

▶ corporate 휑 회사[법인]의

무역 회사/다국적 기업 a trading/multinational _____

07 enterprise
[éntərpràiz]

❶ 기업[회사] ❷ 사업
❸ 진취적 기상(=initiative)

▶ enterprising 휑 진취적인

국영 기업/공기업 a state/public _____

08 monopoly
[mənápəli]

독점[전매](권); 독점 기업

▶ monopolize 통 독점하다

정부가 담배 전매권을 갖고 있다.

The government holds a _____ for tobacco.

09 commerce
[kámərs]

상업(=trade)

▶ e-commerce 전자 상거래
▶ commercial 휑 상업의 명 광고 방송
▶ commercialism 상업주의

지역 상업을 촉진시키는 조처들 measures promoting local _____

10 transaction
[trænsǽkʃən]

거래

현금/신용 거래 cash/credit _____s

11 investment
[invéstmənt]

투자 ▶invest 통 투자하다

투자 촉진을 목적으로 하는 세금 감면
tax cuts aimed at stimulating _____

12 retail
[rí:tèil]

소매 통 소매로 팔(리)다 ▶retailer 소매상

소매업/소매가격 a _____ business/price

13 wholesale
[hóulsèil]

도매 형 도매의 ▶wholesaler 도매상

도매가 소매보다 더 싸다.
_____ is cheaper than retail.

14 vendor
[véndər]

노점상 비교 vending machine 자동판매기

노점상들의 외침 the shouts of street _____s

15 merchandise
[mə́:rtʃəndàiz]

상품(=commodity) ▶merchant 상인[무역상]
통 판매하다 ▶merchandiser 상인

선택 가능한 다양한 상품 a wide selection of _____

16 finance
[fáinæns]

재정, 자금 ▶financial 형 재정[금융]의
통 자금을 공급하다

개인/회사 재정 personal/corporate _____

17 budget
[bʌ́dʒit]

예산

회사의 연간 예산 the firm's annual _____

18 currency
[kə́:rənsi]

❶ 통화[화폐] ❷ 통용

외화[외국 화폐] foreign _____

19 property
[prápərti]

❶ 재산, 부동산 ❷ (-ies) 특성 ▶intellectual property 지적 재산

사유 재산 private _____

부동산 가격 _____ prices

20 asset
[ǽset]

자산(↔ liability 부채)

회사의 자산 가치 the value of a company's _____s

자산과 부채 _____s and liabilities

21 bond
[band]

❶ 채권 ❷ 유대 ❸ (-s) 속박 ❹ 접착

그는 약간의 돈을 국채에 투자했다.
He invested some money in government _____s.

경제

Part 1

22 depression
[dipréʃən]

❶ 불경기[불황](= slump) ▶ depress 동 우울하게 하다
❷ 우울(증) ▶ depressed 형 우울[의기소침]한

격심한 경제 불황 a severe economic _____

23 recession
[riséʃən]

경기 후퇴[불경기/불황] 비교 recess 휴식 시간[휴회]
▶ recede 동 물러나다[멀어지다]

많은 사업이 계속되는 불경기 때문에 실패하고 있다.
Many businesses are failing because of the continuing _____.

24 bankruptcy
[bǽŋkrəptsi]

파산 ▶ bankrupt 형 파산한 동 파산시키다
명 파산자

사업이 실패하자 그는 파산했다.
When his business failed he went into _____.

25 consumerism
[kənsú:mərìzm]

❶ 소비 지상주의 ▶ consumer 소비자
❷ 소비자 보호 운동 ▶ consumption 소비

소비 지상주의의 발달 the growth of _____

26 trademark
[tréidmà:rk]

등록 상표(=TM) 비교 brand 상표[브랜드]
▶ trade 무역[거래] 동 무역[거래]하다
▶ trader 상인[무역업자]

등록 상표에 주의하여 모조품을 피하세요.
Look out for our _____, avoid imitations.

27 warranty
[wɔ́(:)rənti]

품질 보증(서)

품질 보증서는 물품에 결함이 없다는 약속이다.
A _____ is a promise that the item has no defects.

28 frugality
[fru:gǽləti]

절약[검소](= thrift) ▶ frugal 형 절약하는(= thrifty)

그녀는 내게 소박함과 절약을 가르쳤다.
She taught me simplicity and _____.

29 extravagance
[ikstrǽvəgəns]

낭비[사치] ▶ extravagant 형 낭비하는[사치스러운]

그들은 낭비를 줄이는 것을 목표로 하고 있다.
They're aimed at reducing _____.

30 luxury
[lʌ́kʃəri]

호화로움[사치], ▶ luxurious 형 호화로운
사치품(↔ necessity 필수품) ▶ luxuriant 형 무성한[풍성한]

컴퓨터는 사치품이 아니라 필수품이다.
The computer is not a _____, but a necessity.

Today's Dessert

There are far more ways to get into debt, than there are to get out of it.
빚에서 벗어나는 길보다 빚지는 길이 훨씬 더 많다.

A 영어는 우리말로, 우리말은 영어로!

1 a multinational corporation

2 a cash transaction

3 an economic depression

4 green consumerism

5 a registered trademark

6 a three-year warranty

7 국가 독점   a state m_____

8 회사 재정   corporate f_____

9 연간 예산   the annual b_____

10 외화   a foreign c_____

11 지적 재산   intellectual p_____

12 최근의 경기 후퇴   the recent r_____

B 영영사전 뜻풀이에 알맞은 단어 찾기

> 보기   asset   commerce   merchandise   vendor

1 _____ : goods that are being sold

2 _____ : the things that a company or a person owns

3 _____ : the activities involved in buying and selling things

4 _____ : a person who sells things, especially on the street

C 같은 관계 맺어 주기

1 invest : investment = bankrupt : b_____

2 luxury : necessity = extravagance : f_____

D 알맞은 단어 쌍을 찾아 문장 완성하기

> 보기   profit – loss   revenue – expenditure
> supply – demand   wholesale – retail

1 He buys _____ and sells _____. 그는 도매로 사서 소매로 판다.

2 The law of _____ and _____ governs the prices of goods.
수요와 공급의 법칙이 상품의 가격을 결정한다.

3 The company's _____(e)s fell 20% due to investment _____(e)s.
그 회사의 수익은 투자 손실로 20% 하락했다.

4 The government does not collect enough _____ to cover its _____.
정부는 지출을 감당할 만큼 충분한 수입[세금]을 거두지 못하고 있다.

E 밑줄 친 단어 뜻 구별하기

1 a commercial <u>enterprise</u>   a spirit of <u>enterprise</u>

2 the <u>bond</u> market   strong family <u>bond</u>s

경제

Part 1

ANSWER_____

A 1. 다국적 기업 2. 현금 거래 3. 경제 불황 4. 녹색[환경 중시] 소비자 운동 5. 등록 상표 6. 3년간의 품질 보증서 7. monopoly 8. finance 9. budget 10. currency 11. property 12. recession **B** 1. merchandise 2. asset 3. commerce 4. vendor **C** 1. bankruptcy 2. frugality **D** 1. wholesale – retail 2. supply – demand 3. profit – loss 4. revenue – expenditure **E** 1. 상업적 기업 / 진취적 기상 2. 채권 시장 / 강한 가족 유대

01 statesman
[stéitsmən]

(존경받는) 정치 지도자

비교 politician 정치가
spokesperson 대변인

존경받는 원로 정치 지도자 a respected elder _____

02 self-reliance
[sélfrilái əns]

자립[독립]
(=independence ↔ dependence)

▶self-reliant 형 자립[독립]적인
(=independent ↔ dependent)
▶rely 동 의존하다, 믿다

경제적 자립 economic _____

03 autonomy
[ɔːtánəmi]

자치(권), 자율(성)

▶autonomous 형 자주적인[자치의]

지방 자치(권) local _____
개인의 자율(성) individual _____

04 federation
[fèdəréiʃən]

연방, 연합[연맹]

▶federal 형 연방의

미합중국은 50개 독립된 주의 연방이다.
The United States is a _____ of 50 individual states.

05 sovereignty
[sávərənti]

주권[통치권]

▶sovereign 군주 형 최고 권력의, 자주의

우리나라 주권의 수호 the defence of our national _____

06 monarchy
[mánərki]

군주제, 군주국
(↔ republic 공화제, 공화국)

▶monarch 군주

입헌 군주제 a constitutional _____

07 aristocracy
[ærəstákrəsi]

(the ~) (집합적) 귀족 (계급)
(=nobility)

▶aristocrat 귀족(=noble(wo)man)
▶aristocratic 형 귀족의(=noble)

귀족 (계급)의 일원 a member of the _____

08 dictatorship
[diktéitərʃip]

독재 (국가)

▶dictator 독재자

군사 독재 (국가) a military _____

09 tyranny
[tírəni]

폭정

▶tyrant 폭군

법[법치]이 끝나는 곳에 폭정이 시작된다.
Where laws end, _____ begins.

10 regime
[rəʒíːm]

정권, 체제

군사/부패한 정권 a military/corrupt _____

11 reign
[rein]

통치 기간 동 통치[지배]하다 비교 rein 고삐, 통제권

세종대왕의 통치 기간 동안 일어난 변화들
changes that took place during the _____ of King Sejong

12 administration
[ædmìnəstréiʃən]

❶ 관리[경영] ❷ 행정부 비교 the executive 행정부
▶administer 동 관리하다, 집행하다
▶administrative 형 관리[행정]의

케네디 행정부 the Kennedy _____
기업 경영(학) business _____

13 ministry
[mínəstri]

(정부의) 부
▶minister ❶ 장관 ❷ 목사
▶prime minister 총리[수상]

외교 통상부 the M_____ of Foreign Affairs and Trade

14 diplomacy
[diplóuməsi]

외교
▶diplomat 외교관
▶diplomatic 형 외교의

국제 외교 international _____

15 doctrine
[dáktrin]

교리, 주의

트루먼주의의 발표 the announcement of the Truman D_____

16 ambassador
[æmbǽsədər]

대사

주미 한국 대사 the Korean A_____ to the United States

17 embassy
[émbəsi]

대사관

워싱턴 디시의 한국 대사관 the Korean E_____ in Washington, D.C.

18 assembly
[əsémbli]

❶ 의회, 집회 ❷ 조립
▶the National Assembly (한국) 국회
비교 Congress 미국 의회
Parliament 영국 의회

법안이 국회에서 통과되었다.
The bill was passed by the National A_____.

19 council
[káunsəl]

지방 의회
비교 counsel 동 상담[조언]하다 명 조언
▶councilman (지방 의회) 의원

지방 의회/시 의회 a local/city _____

20 delegate
[déligət]

대표(=representative)
동 위임하다
▶delegation 대표단

각국 대표들이 회의에 참석했다.
The _____s of each country attended the conference.

21 ballot
[bǽlət]

(무기명) 투표(용지) 비교 ballet 발레

투표는 무기명 투표로 할 것이다.
Voting will be by secret _____.

22 poll
[poul]

❶ 여론 조사(=opinion poll) ❷ (the polls) 투표소
⑧ 여론 조사하다, 득표하다

여론 조사 a public opinion _____

23 referendum
[rèfəréndəm]

국민 투표

그는 국민 투표에서 반대표를 던졌다.
He voted "No" in the _____.

24 capitalism
[kǽpətəlìzm]

자본주의

▶capitalist 자본주의자, 자본가
⑧ 자본주의의
▶capital 자본, 수도, 대문자

현대 산업 자본주의 modern industrial _____

25 socialism
[sóuʃəlìzm]

사회주의

▶socialist 사회주의자 ⑧ 사회주의의

수정 사회주의 revised _____

26 nationalism
[nǽʃənəlìzm]

민족주의, 국수주의

▶nationalist 민족주의자
▶nationality 국적, 민족

세계주의와 민족주의 간의 갈등
the conflict between globalism and _____

27 fascism
[fǽʃizm]

파시즘[독재적 국가 사회주의]

▶fascist 파시스트 ⑧ 파시즘의
비교 totalitarianism 전체주의

그들은 파시즘에 대항했다.
They opposed _____.

28 liberalism
[líbərəlìzm]

자유주의

▶liberal ⑧ 자유주의의 ⑲ 자유주의자
▶liberty 자유

자유 민주주의 _____ democracy

29 conservatism
[kənsə́ːrvətìzm]

보수주의
(↔ progressivism 진보주의)

▶conservative ⑧ 보수적인 ⑲ 보수주의자
(↔ progressive ⑧ 진보적인 ⑲ 진보주의자)

보수적 사회/인생[세계]관 a _____ society/outlook

30 radicalism
[rǽdikəlìzm]

급진주의

▶radical ⑧ 근본적인, 급진적인
⑲ 급진주의자

급진적 좌파 정치가 a _____ left-wing politician

A 영어는 우리말로, 우리말은 영어로!

1 economic self-reliance
2 a military dictatorship
3 a fascist regime
4 international diplomacy
5 the Christian doctrine
6 the National Assembly
7 a public opinion poll
8 liberal democracy

9 지방 자치   local a_____
10 러시아 연방   the Russian F_____
11 국방부   the M_____ of Defence
12 시 의회   a city c_____
13 산업 자본주의   industrial c_____
14 수정 사회주의   revised s_____
15 아랍 민족주의   Arab n_____
16 보수적 견해   c_____ views

B 영영사전 뜻풀이에 알맞은 단어 찾기

> [보기]   referendum   reign   sovereignty   statesman   tyranny

1 _____ : cruel and unfair government
2 _____ : a wise, experienced and respected political leader
3 _____ : a direct vote by the people on an important issue
4 _____ : the period when someone is king, queen, or emperor
5 _____ : the power of a country to control its own government

C 빈칸에 가장 적절한 단어 넣기

> [보기]   ambassador   aristocracy   ballot   delegate   embassy   monarchy

1 We sent two _____(e)s to the meeting.   우리는 회의에 2명의 대표를 보냈다.
2 Dukes and earls were members of the _____.   공작과 백작은 귀족의 일원이었다.
3 The _____ held a reception at the _____.   대사가 대사관에서 환영회를 개최했다.
4 Representatives were elected by secret _____.   대의원들이 무기명 투표로 선출되었다.
5 The French Revolution changed France from a _____ to a republic.
프랑스 혁명은 프랑스를 군주국에서 공화국으로 바꿨다.

D 밑줄 친 단어 뜻 구별하기

1 the Trump <u>administration</u>   business <u>administration</u>
2 a <u>radical</u> difference   <u>radical</u> ideas

ANSWER

A 1. 경제적 자립 2. 군사 독재 (국가) 3. 파시즘 정권 4. 국제 외교 5. 기독교 교리 6. 국회 7. 여론 조사 8. 자유 민주주의 9. autonomy 10. Federation 11. Ministry 12. council 13. capitalism 14. socialism 15. nationalism 16. conservative **B** 1. tyranny 2. statesman 3. referendum 4. reign 5. sovereignty **C** 1. delegate 2. aristocracy 3. ambassador, embassy 4. ballot 5. monarchy **D** 1. 트럼프 행정부 / 기업 경영(학) 2. 근본적 차이 / 급진적인 사상

01 combat
[kámbæt]

전투[싸움] 동 싸우다

쌍방 간의 치열한 전투 fierce _____ between the two sides

02 clash
[klæʃ]

충돌 동 충돌하다   비교 crash 충돌[추락] 동 충돌[추락]하다

의견/문화 충돌 a _____ of opinions/cultures

03 territory
[térətɔ̀:ri]

영토[지역], 영역   ▶ territorial 형 영토의

한국의 영토 Korean _____

점령지 occupied _____

04 frontier
[frʌ̀ntíər]

❶ 미개척지 ❷ 국경(= border, boundary)

우주, 최후의 미개척지 space, the final _____

05 fortress
[fort]
[fɔ́:rtris] [fɔ́:rt]

요새

요새가 공격을 받고 있었다.

The _____ was under attack.

06 foe
[fou]

적(= enemy)

두 나라는 공동의 적에 대항하기 위해 연합했다.

The two countries have united against their common _____.

07 ally
[əlái]

동맹국(↔ enemy),   ▶ alliance 동맹
(the Allies) 연합국   ▶ allied 형 동맹한

그 나라는 동맹국들에게 도움을 요청했다.

The country asked for help from its _____ies.

08 troop
[tru:p]

군대

유엔 평화 유지군 UN peace-keeping _____s

09 corps
[kɔ:r]

군단[부대], 단체[집단]   비교 corpse 시체

의무대 the medical _____

해병대 the Marine C_____

10 warrior
[wɔ́:riər]

(역전의) 용사[전사]

무명용사 unknown _____s

11 veteran
[vétərən]

❶ 참전 용사 ❷ 베테랑[노련한 사람]

2차 세계 대전 참전 용사 a _____ of the Second World War

12 captive
[kǽptiv]

포로(=prisoner)
휑 사로잡힌[포획된]

▶capture 포획 동 포획하다
▶captivate 동 매혹하다

포로 두 명이 달아났다.
Two of the _____ s escaped.

13 civilian
[sivíljən]

민간인

▶civil 휑 시민[민간]의

많은 무고한 민간인들이 전쟁 중에 죽었다.
Many innocent _____ s were killed during the war.

14 aggression
[əgréʃən]

공격(성), 침략

▶aggressive 휑 공격적인

텔레비전의 폭력은 아이들의 공격성을 조장할 수 있다.
Television violence can encourage _____ in children.

15 conquest
[kánkwest]

정복

▶conquer 동 정복하다
▶conqueror 정복자

스페인의 잉카 제국 정복 the Spanish _____ of the Inca Empire

16 revenge
[rivéndʒ]

복수[보복](=vengeance)
동 복수하다(=avenge)

▶revengeful 휑 복수심에 불타는

그들은 보복 공격을 개시했다.
They launched _____ attacks.

17 strategy
[strǽtədʒi]

전략

군사 전략 military _____

18 tactic
[tǽktik]

전술

▶tactical 휑 전술의

이번 폭탄 공격은 테러리스트의 전술 변화를 나타낸다.
These bomb attacks represent a change of _____ s by the terrorists.

19 nuke
[njuːk]

핵무기(=nuclear weapon)

현수막에는 '핵무기 반대!'라고 쓰여 있었다.
"No _____ s!" the banner read.

20 pistol
[pístl]

권총(=gun)

비교 revolver (회전식) 연발 권총
rifle 소총

그는 그녀의 머리에 권총을 겨누었다.
He held a _____ to her head.

21 bullet
[búlit]

총알

▶bullet-proof 휑 방탄의

총알이 그의 가슴을 명중시켰다.
The _____ hit him in the chest.

전쟁 · 평화

Part 1

22 **cannon**
[kǽnən]

대포

▶cannonball 포탄

대포 소리가 주위에 메아리쳤다.
The sound of the _____ echoed around.

23 **artillery**
[ɑːrtíləri]

(대)포, (the ~) 포병(대)

대교 infantry 보병(대)

대포의 굉음은 끔찍했다.
The roar of _____ was awful.

24 **shell**
[ʃel]

❶ (단단한) 껍질 ❷ 포탄

▶seashell 조개껍질[조가비]

포탄을 맞아 집에 불이 났다.
A _____ set fire to a house.

25 **submarine**
[sʌ̀bməríːn]

잠수함
혱 해저의

▶marine 해병 혱 해양의

핵 잠수함 a nuclear _____

26 **spear**
↔ shield
[spiər] ↔ [ʃiːld]

창
↔ 방패 동 보호하다

▶windshield (자동차의) 앞 유리

그는 창을 던졌다. He threw his _____.
인간 방패 a human _____

27 **armor**
[ɑ́ːrmər]

갑옷, (군함 등의) 장갑(裝甲)

▶armored 혱 장갑한

갑옷을 입고 있는 기사 a knight wearing a suit of _____

28 **disarmament**
[disɑ́ːrməmənt]

군비 축소[군축]
(↔ armament 군비 (확충))

▶disarm 동 무장 해제하다

군축 협상 _____ negotiations

29 **ceasefire**
[truce]
[síːsfáiər] [truːs]

휴전[정전]

▶cease 동 중단되다[중단시키다]

휴전 협정 a _____ agreement
휴전을 선언하다/어기다 to call/break a _____

30 **treaty**
[tríːti]

조약

양측이 평화/불가침 조약에 서명했다.
Both sides signed the peace/non-aggression _____.

Today's Dessert

Peace is the happy natural state of man, war his corruption and his disgrace.
평화는 인간의 행복한 자연스러운 상태이며, 전쟁은 타락과 치욕이다.

전쟁 · 평화

Part 1

TEST 22

A 영어는 우리말로, 우리말은 영어로!

1 an ally of the United States
2 the Marine Corps
3 a Vietnam veteran
4 revenge attacks
5 defense strategies
6 bullet-proof glass
7 a non-aggression treaty

8 무장 충돌   an armed c_____
9 한국군   Korean t_____s
10 민간인 사상자들   c_____ casualties
11 무력 정복   military c_____s
12 게릴라 전술   guerrilla t_____s
13 물 대포   a water c_____
14 핵무기 축소   a nuclear d_____

B 영영사전 뜻풀이에 알맞은 단어 찾기

> 보기   artillery   captive   fortress   pistol   warrior

1 _____ : a small gun you can use with one hand
2 _____ : a soldier or fighter who is brave and experienced
3 _____ : large guns, either on wheels or fixed in one place
4 _____ : a person who is kept as a prisoner, especially in a war
5 _____ : a large strong building used for defending an important place

C 관련된 것끼리 연결하기

1 combat   ·
2 foe   ·
3 frontier   ·
4 nuke   ·
5 submarine   ·

a. an enemy
b. a nuclear weapon
c. an underwater ship
d. the border of a country
e. a fight, especially during a war

D 빈칸에 가장 적절한 단어 넣기

> 보기   armor   ceasefire[truce]   shell   spear   territory

1 He hurled his _____. 그는 창을 세게 던졌다.
2 A _____ set fire to a house. 포탄에 맞아 집에 불이 났다.
3 An arrow pierced his _____. 화살이 그의 갑옷을 꿰뚫었다.
4 They agreed to call a(n) _____. 그들은 휴전을 선언하는 데 동의했다.
5 The plane was flying over enemy _____. 비행기가 적지 위를 날고 있었다.

전쟁 · 평화

Part 1

01 zoology/ botany
[zouάlədʒi] [bάtəni]

동물학/식물학

▶zoo 동물원
▶botanic(al) 웹 식물(학)의
참고 biology 생물학

동물학과 식물학은 생명 과학이다.
_____ and _____ are life sciences.

02 organism
[ɔ́ːrgənìzm]

유기체[생물]

▶organ 기관[장기]
▶organic 웹 유기농[유기체]의
▶microorganism[microbe] 미생물

모든 생물은 환경 변화에 적응해야 한다.
All living _____s have to adapt to environmental changes.

03 mammal
[mǽməl]

포유류

고래는 포유류로 분류된다.
Whales are classified as _____s.

04 primate
[práimèit]

영장류

고릴라는 살아 있는 가장 큰 영장류다.
Gorillas are the largest living _____s.

05 reptile
[réptil]

파충류

뱀과 도마뱀과 악어는 파충류다.
Snakes, lizards, and crocodiles are _____s.

06 herbivore/ carnivore
[hə́ːrbəvɔ̀ːr] [kάːrnəvɔ̀ːr]

초식 동물/육식 동물   참고 omnivore 잡식 동물
동물은 초식 동물, 육식 동물, 잡식 동물로 분류될 수 있다.
Animals can be categorized into _____s, _____s and omnivores.

07 predator
[prédətər]

포식자[포식 동물], 약탈자
사자, 늑대 그리고 다른 포식 동물들 lions, wolves and other _____s

08 prey
[prei]

먹잇감 图 (~ (up)on) 잡아먹다
독수리가 먹잇감을 덮쳤다.
An eagle swooped down on its _____.

09 caterpillar
[kǽtərpìlər]

(나비·나방의) 애벌레   참고 larva 유충[애벌레]
애벌레는 나비나 나방으로 변한다.
_____s change into butterflies or moths.

10 herd
[həːrd]

짐승의 떼, 군중   참고 school[shoal] 물고기 떼
pack 사냥 동물의 떼
drove 몰려다니는 동물의 떼

소/코끼리 떼 a _____ of cattle/elephants

11 flock
[flɑk]

새·양 떼, 군중 동 떼 지어 가다

양/까마귀 떼 a _____ of sheep/crows

12 swarm
[swɔːrm]

벌 떼[곤충의 떼], 군중

벌/메뚜기 떼 a _____ of bees/locusts

13 claw
[klɔː]

(새·짐승의) 갈고리 발톱,　　　　비교 paw (발톱 있는 동물의) 발
(게·가재의) 집게발

고양이가 발톱으로 내 다리를 찔렀다.

The cat dug his _____ s into my leg.

14 feather
[féðər]

깃털

같은 깃털을 가진 새들은 함께 모인다.[유유상종.]

Birds of a _____ flock together.

15 plume
[pluːm]

❶ (큰) 깃털 (장식) ❷ (연기·먼지·물·불) 기둥

타조 깃털로 만든 부채 fans made of ostrich _____ s

16 beak
[biːk]

부리(=bill)

새들은 부리를 사용해 먹이를 쪼아 먹는다.

Birds use their _____ s to pick up food.

17 fin
[fin]

지느러미

상어 지느러미 the _____ of a shark

18 aquarium
[əkwɛ́əriəm]

(복수. -s/aquaria) 수족관

나는 수족관에 금붕어를 키우고 있다.

I have a gold fish in my _____.

19 stable
[stéibl]

마구간　　　　　　　　　　▶stabilize 동 안정시키다
형 안정된(↔unstable)　　　　▶stability 안정(성)(↔instability)

그녀는 말을 마구간으로 끌고 갔다.

She led the horse into the _____.

20 hibernation
[hàibərnéiʃən]

겨울잠[동면]　　　　　　　　▶hibernate 동 동면하다

곰은 가을에 동면에 들어간다.

Bears go into _____ in the autumn.

21 veterinarian
[vet]
[vètərənɛ́əriən] [vet]

수의사

농부는 병든 소를 치료하기 위해 수의사를 불렀다.

The farmer called the _____ out to treat a sick cow.

22 stalk
[stɔ:k]

줄기(= stem)
동 ❶ 몰래 뒤쫓다 ❷ 활보하다

비교 trunk 나무줄기
▶ stalking 스토킹

그녀는 튤립의 줄기를 다듬었다.
She trimmed the _____ s of the tulips.

23 twig
[twig]

잔가지

비교 branch 가지
bough 큰 가지

우리는 불을 피우기 위해 마른 잔가지를 모았다.
We collected dry _____ s to start the fire.

24 thorn
[θɔ:rn]

(식물의) 가시

▶ thorny 형 가시가 많은

가시 없는 장미는 없다.
There is no rose without a _____ .

25 petal
[pétl]

꽃잎

비교 pedal 페달 동 페달을 밟다
sepal 꽃받침

꽃잎이 다섯 개인 꽃 a flower with five _____ s

26 pollen
[pálən]

꽃가루[수분]

▶ pollinate 동 수분[가루받이]시키다

꽃가루는 어떤 사람들에게 건초열을 일으킨다.
The _____ causes hay fever in some people.

27 moss
[mɔ:s]

이끼

비교 moth 나방

강 근처의 바위들이 이끼로 덮여 있었다.
The rocks near the river were covered with _____ .

28 fungus
[fʌ́ŋgəs]

(복수. fungi/-es)
(버섯 · 곰팡이 등) 균류

비교 mushroom 버섯
mold 곰팡이

버섯과 곰팡이는 둘 다 균류다.
Mushrooms and mold are both _____ .

29 photosynthesis
[fòutəsínθəsis]

광합성

▶ synthesis 합성, 종합[통합]

식물은 광합성에 이산화탄소를 이용한다.
Plants use carbon dioxide in _____ .

30 hybrid
[háibrid]

❶ (동식물의) 잡종 ❷ 혼성체[혼합물]

밀과 호밀의 잡종 a _____ of wheat and rye
재즈와 록의 혼합 a _____ of jazz and rock

Today's Dessert

Life without love is like a tree without blossoms or fruit. – Kahlil Gibran
사랑이 없는 삶이란 꽃과 열매가 없는 나무와 같다. – 지브란

TEST 23

A 영어는 우리말로, 우리말은 영어로!

1 a living organism

2 the evolution of mammals

3 the claws of a crab

4 corn stalks

5 an allergy to pollen

6 나방 애벌레   a moth c_____

7 갈고리 모양 부리   a hooked b_____

8 물고기 지느러미   a fish's f_____

9 마른 잔가지   dry t_____s

10 장미 꽃잎   rose p_____s

B 영영사전 뜻풀이에 알맞은 단어 찾기

> **보기**   aquarium   hibernation   photosynthesis   plume   veterinarian

1 _____ : a large feather

2 _____ : the state of being asleep for winter

3 _____ : a glass container for fish and other water animals

4 _____ : a person qualified in the medical treatment of animals

5 _____ : the way that green plants make their food using sunlight

C 의미상 더 어울리는 것 고르기

1 (Zoology/Botany) is the scientific study of plants.

2 Lions and tigers are (herbivore/carnivore/omnivore)s.

3 The goat has become the (predator/prey) of a tiger.

4 The dead sheep was covered with (herd/flock/swarm)s of flies.

D 관련된 것끼리 연결하기

1 fungus   •

2 primate   •

3 reptile   •

a. a snake or lizard

b. a mushroom or mold

c. a human, monkey or ape

E 빈칸에 가장 적절한 단어 넣기

> **보기**   hybrid   moss   stable   thorn

1 A rolling stone gathers no _____.   구르는 돌에는 이끼가 끼지 않는다.

2 There is no rose without a _____.   가시 없는 장미는 없다.

3 Lock the _____ after the horse is gone.   소 잃고 외양간 고치기.

4 A mule is a _____ of a male donkey and a female horse.

노새는 수탕나귀와 암말의 잡종이다.

동물·식물   Part 1

ANSWER_____

A 1. 살아 있는 유기체[생물] 2. 포유류의 진화 3. 게 집게발 4. 옥수수 줄기 5. 꽃가루 알레르기 6. caterpillar 7. beak 8. fin 9. twig 10. petal
B 1. plume 2. hibernation 3. aquarium 4. veterinarian 5. photosynthesis   **C** 1. Botany 2. carnivore 3. prey 4. swarm   **D** 1. b 2. c
3. a   **E** 1. moss 2. thorn 3. stable 4. hybrid

01 ecology
[ikάlədʒi]

생태(학)

▶ecological 휑 생태(학)의
▶ecologist 생태학자
▶ecosystem 생태계

식물/동물/인류 생태 plant/animal/human _____

02 contamination
[kəntæmənéiʃən]

오염(=pollution)

▶contaminate 통 오염시키다(=pollute)

방사능/지하수 오염 radioactive/underground water _____

03 global warming

지구 온난화

지구 온난화는 여기에 있고 인간이 야기했으며 이미 위험하다.

_____ is here, human-caused and already dangerous.

04 greenhouse gas

온실가스(온실 효과 유발 가스)

▶greenhouse effect 온실 효과
▶carbon dioxide 이산화탄소(CO_2)
▶methane 메탄(CH_4)

온실가스는 온실 효과의 원인이 된다.

_____es cause the greenhouse effect.

05 fumes
[fju:mz]

(유독) 가스[매연]

▶fume 통 (연기[매연]를) 내뿜다
▶exhaust (gas[fumes]) 배기가스[매연]

자동차 배기가스가 대기를 오염시킨다.

Car exhaust _____ pollute the air.

06 emission
[imíʃən]

배출[방출](물)[배기가스]
▶emit 통 내다[내뿜다]
온실가스 배출을 줄일 조처들

measures which will reduce greenhouse gas _____

07 acid rain

산성비

▶acid (화학) 산 휑 산성의

산성비는 대기 오염의 결과다.

_____ is a result of air pollution.

08 deforestation
[di:fɔ̀ristéiʃən]

삼림 벌채[파괴]
▶deforest 통 삼림을 파괴하다
산림 벌채[파괴]는 홍수와 가뭄을 일으킨다.

_____ causes floods and drought.

09 ozone layer

오존층

▶layer 층
▶CFC[chlorofluorocarbon] 프레온 가스

프레온 가스는 오존층을 감소시킨다.

CFCs deplete the _____.

10 extinction
[ikstíŋkʃən]

멸종

▶extinct 휑 멸종된
▶extinguish 통 불을 끄다, 소멸시키다

멸종 위기에 처한 종 species in danger of _____

11 habitat
[hǽbitæt]

서식지

▶inhabit 통 거주[서식]하다
▶inhabitant 거주자[서식 동물]

축소되는 서식지 shrinking _____ s

12 sanctuary
[sǽŋktʃuèri]

❶ 조수 보호 구역 ❷ 피난처(=refuge)

야생 생물 보호 구역 a wildlife _____

13 detergent
[ditɔ́ːrdʒənt]

세제

세제의 하천 방류가 물고기의 죽음을 초래한다.

The release of _____ s into the river causes the death of fish.

14 sewage
[súːidʒ]

하수

▶sewer 하수관

하수 처리장 a _____ disposal[treatment] plant

15 disposable
[dispóuzəbl]

일회용품 형 일회용의

▶dispose (~ of) 통 처리하다
▶disposal 처리

일회용 종이컵 a _____ paper cup

16 landfill
[lǽndfil]

쓰레기 매립(지)

비교 dump 쓰레기장

쓰레기 매립장에 버려진 유독성 화학 물질

toxic chemicals dumped at _____ sites

17 fallout
[fɔ́ːlàut]

(방사능) 낙진

핵무기 실험으로 생기는 방사능 낙진에 의한 암 사망

cancer deaths caused by _____ from nuclear weapons testing

18 reuse
형[rìːjúːs] 통[rìːjúːz]

재사용 통 재사용하다

▶reusable 형 재사용할 수 있는

많은 가정 쓰레기는 줄일 수 있고, 재사용할 수 있고, 재활용할 수 있다.

A lot of household waste can be reduced, _____ d and recycled.

19 upcycling
[ʌpsáikliŋ]

업사이클링(재활용품을 이용해 더 나은 새 제품을 만드는 과정)

비교 recycling 재활용(품)
▶upcycle 통 업사이클하다

업사이클링은 창조적인 재사용이다. _____ is creative reuse.

20 conservation
[kɑ̀nsərvéiʃən]

(자연) 보호[보존]
(=preservation), 절약

▶conserve 통 보호[보존]하다, 절약하다
▶conservationist 환경 보호 활동가

야생 생물 보호 wildlife _____

에너지 절약 energy _____

21 mound
[maund]

(흙[돌])더미, 작은 언덕

비교 < hill < mountain

작은 흙더미 a small _____ of dirt

서류 더미 a _____ of papers

환경

Part 1

22 ridge
[ridʒ]

산등성이[능선], 용마루

우리는 좁은 산등성이[능선]를 따라 걸었다.

We walked along the narrow mountain _____.

23 meadow
[médou]

풀밭[초원]

초원에서 풀을 뜯고 있는 소 cattle grazing in the _____s

24 wetland
[wétlænd]

습지(대)

습지대의 감소는 생태계의 손상을 가져온다.

The loss of _____s lead to damage of ecosystems.

25 swamp [marsh]
[swɑmp] [mɑːʃ]

늪

늪은 수생 식물에게 비옥한 서식지를 제공한다.

The _____s provide a rich habitat for water plants.

26 brook [creek]
[bruk] [kriːk]

시내[개울]   <stream <river

졸졸 흐르는 시내 a babbling _____

27 strait
[streit]

해협   <channel

베링 해협 the Bering S_____

28 bay
[bei]

만   <gulf

샌프란시스코만 the San Francisco B_____

멕시코만 the G_____ of Mexico

29 glacier
[gléiʃər]

빙하   ▶glacial 형 빙하의

빙하가 녹으면 해수면이 상승한다.

The level of the sea rises as the _____s melt.

30 iceberg
[áisbəːrg]

빙산   ice cap 만년설

빙산의 일각 the tip of the _____

Today's Dessert

There's so much pollution in the air now that if it weren't for our lungs there'd be no place to put it all.

지금 대기 중에는 너무 많은 오염 물질이 있어 만약 우리 폐가 없다면 그 모두를 담을 곳이 없을 것이다.

환경

Part 1

TEST 24

A 영어는 우리말로, 우리말은 영어로!

1 the ecology movement
2 the causes of global warming
3 danger of extinction
4 carbon dioxide emission
5 the depletion of the ozone layer
6 radioactive fallout
7 wildlife conservation

8 농약 오염   pesticide c_____
9 유독 가스   poisonous f_____
10 자연 서식지   a natural h_____
11 조류 보호 구역   a bird s_____
12 합성 세제   a synthetic d_____
13 일회용 면도기   a d_____ razor
14 쓰레기 매립지   a garbage l_____

B 영영사전 뜻풀이에 알맞은 단어 찾기

| 보기 | glacier   meadow   ridge   upcycling |

1 _____ : a field with wild grass and flowers
2 _____ : a long area of high land at the top of a mountain
3 _____ : a large mass of ice that moves slowly down a valley
4 _____ : the reuse of objects or materials to create a product of higher value or quality than the original

C 빈칸에 알맞은 단어 넣어 크기 비교하기

1 m_____ < hill < mountain
2 b_____ [c_____] < stream < river
3 s_____ < channel
4 b_____ < gulf

D 빈칸에 가장 적절한 단어 넣기

| 보기 | acid rain   deforestation   iceberg   reuse   sewage   swamp   wetland |

1 The ship struck a hidden _____. 그 배는 숨겨진 빙산에 부딪쳤다.
2 The _____ is covered with _____. 그 습지대는 늪으로 덮여 있다.
3 Factories dump their _____ into the river. 공장들이 하수를 강에 버린다.
4 _____ causes damage to land and water ecosystems.
   산성비는 땅과 물 생태계에 훼손을 초래한다.
5 _____ is destroying large areas of tropical rain forest.
   산림 벌채[파괴]가 열대 우림의 넓은 지역을 파괴하고 있다.
6 Recycling is good, _____ is better and reducing is best.
   재활용은 좋고, 재사용이 더 좋고, 줄이는 것이 가장 좋다.

ANSWER_____

A 1. 생태 운동 2. 지구 온난화의 원인 3. 멸종 위기 4. 이산화탄소 배출 5. 오존층 감소[파괴] 6. 방사능 낙진 7. 야생 생물 보호 8. contamination
9. fumes 10. habitat 11. sanctuary 12. detergent 13. disposable 14. landfill   B 1. meadow 2. ridge 3. glacier 4. upcycling
C 1. mound 2. brook[creek] 3. strait 4. bay   D 1. iceberg 2. wetland, swamp 3. sewage 4. Acid rain 5. Deforestation 6. reuse

01 meteorology
[mì:tiərálədʒi]

기상학

▶ meteorological 형 기상(학)의
▶ meteorologist 기상학자

기상학은 날씨를 예보하는 데 이용된다.

_____ is used to forecast the weather.

02 precipitation
[prisìpətéiʃən]

강수(량)

▶ precipitate 동 촉발시키다

연간 강수량 annual _____

50% 강수 확률 a 50 percent chance of _____

03 fog/mist
[fɔ(:)g] / [mist]

(짙은) 안개/(엷은) 안개

▶ foggy/misty 형 (짙은)/(엷은) 안개 낀

짙은 안개 thick[heavy] _____

이른 아침 엷은 안개 the early-morning _____

04 frost
[frɔ(:)st]

서리

▶ frosty 형 서리가 내리는
▶ defrost 동 해동하다

농작물의 서리 피해[냉해] _____ damage to crops

05 drizzle
[drízl]

이슬비 동 이슬비가 내리다

가는 이슬비가 오후 내내 내렸다.

Light _____ fell all afternoon.

06 downpour
[dáunpɔ̀:r]

폭우

비교 <torrential rain <flood
▶ pour 동 (퍼)붓다, (액체를) 따르다

폭우로 인한 산사태 the landslide caused by the _____

07 sleet
[sli:t]

진눈깨비

비가 진눈깨비가 되고 난 후 눈이 되었다.

Rain became _____ and then snow.

08 hail
[heil]

우박

▶ hailstone 우박 덩어리
동 ❶ 칭송[환호]하다 ❷ 우박이 떨어지다

골프공만한 우박 _____ the size of golf balls

09 blizzard
[blízərd]

심한 눈보라

비교 snowstorm 눈보라

우리는 심한 눈보라 속에서 꼼짝 못하게 되었다.

We got stuck in a _____.

10 avalanche
[ǽvəlæ̀ntʃ]

눈사태

비교 landslide 산사태

스키를 타던 두 사람이 눈사태로 죽었다.

Two skiers were killed in the _____.

11 gale/gust
[geil] / [gʌst]

강풍/돌풍

비교 **breeze** 산들바람[미풍]
tornado 토네이도[회오리바람]
storm 폭풍(우)

울타리가 강풍에 날려 무너졌다.
The fence was blown down in the _____.

돌풍에 날려 우리 텐트가 뒤집혔다.
A _____ of wind blew our tent over.

12 blast
[blæst]

❶ 돌풍 ❷ 폭발
통 폭파하다, (~ off) 발사되다

▶ **blast-off** (우주선의) 발사

차가운 돌풍이 거리를 휩쓸고 지나갔다.
A _____ of cold air swept through the street.

13 typhoon
[taifúːn]

태풍

비교 **hurricane** 허리케인

태풍이 남부 지역을 강타했다.
The _____ hit the southern parts.

14 thermometer/barometer
[θərmámətər] / [bərámətər]

온도계[체온계]/기압계, 지표[척도]

온도계가 30도를 가리키고 있다.
The _____ registers 30 degrees.

기압계는 대기가 얼마나 무거운지[대기의 압력]를 나타내준다.
A _____ tells how heavy the air is.

15 Celsius/Fahrenheit
[sélsiəs] / [fǽrənhàit]

섭씨(=Centigrade)/화씨

물은 섭씨 0도나 화씨 32도에서 언다.
Water freezes at zero degrees _____ or 32 degrees _____.

16 humidity
[hjuːmídəti]

습도[습기]

▶ **humid** 형 (다)습한

그 방은 상대 습도 50%로 유지된다.
The room is kept at 50% relative _____.

17 moisture
[mɔ́istʃər]

습기[수분]

▶ **moist** 형 촉촉한(=damp)
▶ **moisten** 통 촉촉하게 하다

대기 중에 습기가 많다.
There's a lot of _____ in the air.

18 catastrophe
[kətǽstrəfi]

재앙[재난](=disaster, calamity)

환경/핵/경제 재앙[재난] environmental/nuclear/economic _____

19 hazard
[hǽzərd]

위험 (요소)(=danger)

▶ **hazardous** 형 위험한(=dangerous)

건강/안전에 대한 위험 (요소) a health/safety _____

20 eruption
[irʌ́pʃən]

(화산의) 분출[폭발]

▶ **erupt** 통 (화산이) 분출[폭발]하다

화산 분출[분화] a volcanic _____

21 lava
[láːvə]

용암

비교 **larva** 유충[애벌레]

마그마는 지표면에 도달하면 용암이라고 불린다.
Magma is called _____ when it reaches the earth's surface.

22 ash
[æʃ]

재

▶ashtray 재떨이

재와 용암이 화산에서 분화했다.

_____es and lava erupted from the volcano.

23 tidal wave

해일

▶tide 조수[조류], 흐름
▶tidal 형 조수의

거대한 해일이 섬 마을들을 휩쓸었다.

A vast _____ swept island villages.

24 tsunami
[tsunάːmi]

쓰나미[지진 해일]

▶earthquake 지진

쓰나미는 지진에 의해 일어나는 아주 큰 파도다.

A _____ is a very large wave caused by an earthquake.

25 drought
[draut]

가뭄

강이 가뭄 동안에 말라 버렸다.

The river ran dry during the _____.

26 famine
[fǽmin]

기근

비교 feminine 형 여성의[여성스러운]

아프리카 기근 구호를 위한 호소

an appeal for _____ relief in Africa

27 starvation
[staːrvéiʃən]

기아[아사(餓死)]

▶starve 동 굶주리다[굶어 죽다]

기아로 죽어가는 많은 어린이들 many children dying of _____

28 shortage
[ʃɔ́ːrtidʒ]

부족[결핍](=scarcity)

▶short 형 부족한, 짧은

물/식량/주택 부족

water/food/housing _____

29 refugee
[rèfjudʒíː]

난민

▶refuge 피난(처)

많은 난민들이 피난처를 찾아 국경을 넘었다.

Many _____s crossed the border looking for shelters.

30 survivor
[sərváivər]

생존자

▶survive 동 살아남다, ~보다 오래 살다
▶survival 생존

비행기 추락 사고의 유일한 생존자

the sole _____ of the plane crash

Today's Dessert **The brightest lightning is produced from the darkest storms.**

가장 밝은 번갯불은 가장 어두운 폭풍우에서 만들어진다.

TEST 25

A 영어는 우리말로, 우리말은 영어로!

1 hail the size of golf balls
2 a bomb blast
3 in Celsius or in Fahrenheit
4 a volcanic eruption
5 ashes from volcano
6 the death by starvation
7 survivors of the earthquake

8 연간 강수량   annual p_____
9 된서리   a heavy f_____
10 가는 이슬비   light d_____
11 태풍의 눈   the eye of a t_____
12 화재 위험 (요소)   a fire h_____
13 물 부족   water s_____
14 난민 수용소   a r_____ camp

B 영영사전 뜻풀이에 알맞은 단어 찾기

> 보기   blizzard   downpour   gust   meteorology   sleet

1 _____ : wet, partly melted falling snow
2 _____ : a lot of rain that falls in a short time
3 _____ : a severe snow storm with strong winds
4 _____ : the scientific study of weather conditions
5 _____ : a sudden strong movement of wind, air, rain, etc.

C 빈칸에 가장 적절한 단어 넣기

> 보기   avalanche   barometer   catastrophe   lava   tidal wave

1 _____ poured out of the volcano. 용암이 화산에서 흘러나왔다.
2 He was swept away in an _____. 그는 눈사태에 휩쓸려갔다.
3 The oil spill is an ecological _____. 기름 유출은 생태 재앙이다.
4 The _____ is often caused by an earthquake. 해일은 종종 지진에 의해 일어난다.
5 The skin is a _____ of emotional and physical health.
   피부는 정서적·신체적 건강의 지표다.

D 알맞은 단어 쌍을 찾아 문장 완성하기

> 보기   drought – famine   fog – mist   humidity – moisture

1 _____ is much thicker than _____. 짙은 안개는 옅은 안개보다 훨씬 더 짙다.
2 _____ is a measure of _____ in the atmosphere. 습도는 대기 속 습기의 양이다.
3. The long _____ was followed by months of severe _____.
   오랜 가뭄 후에 몇 달간의 극심한 기근이 이어졌다.

ANSWER_____

A 1. 골프공만 한 우박 2. 폭탄 폭발 3. 섭씨나 화씨로 4. 화산 분출[분화] 5. 화산재 6. 아사 7. 지진의 생존자들 8. precipitation 9. frost 10. drizzle 11. typhoon 12. hazard 13. shortage 14. refugee   **B** 1. sleet 2. downpour 3. blizzard 4. meteorology 5. gust   **C** 1. Lava 2. avalanche 3. catastrophe 4. tidal wave 5. barometer   **D** 1. Fog — mist 2. Humidity — moisture 3. drought — famine

지구 · 우주 관련 명사

The Earth & The Universe

01 geography
[dʒiágrəfi]

지리(학) ▶ geographical 형 지리(학)의

자연/인문 지리학 physical/human _____

02 Arctic/ Antarctic
[áːrktik] / [æntáːrktik]

(the ~) 북극 지방/남극 지방 비교 the North/South Pole 북극/남극
▶ Antarctica 남극 대륙

북극/남극 지방 탐험가/탐험
an _____/_____ explorer/expedition

03 mainland/ island
[méinlæ̀nd] / [áilənd]

본토[대륙]/섬 비교 inland 형 내륙의 부 내륙으로
▶ Isle (섬 이름) 섬
▶ islet 작은 섬

그 연락선은 섬과 본토를 연결한다.
The ferryboat links the _____ to the _____.

04 peninsula
[pənínsjulə]

반도

한반도 the Korean P_____

05 coral reef

산호초 ▶ coral 산호
▶ reef 암초

산호초는 따뜻하고 얕은 바닷물에 길게 줄지어 있는 산호다.
_____ is a long line of coral that lies in warm, shallow sea water.

06 geology
[dʒiálədʒi]

지질(학) ▶ geological 형 지질(학)의
▶ geologist 지질학자

해양 지질학 marine _____

07 crust
[krʌst]

❶ (지구의) 지각(地殼) ❷ 빵 껍질, 딱딱한 층

지질학은 지각에 관한 과학이다.
Geology is the science of the earth's _____.

08 gravel
[grǽvəl]

자갈

자갈길 a _____ path

09 pebble
[pébl]

조약돌[자갈]

그 해변은 하얀 조약돌로 덮여 있었다.
The beach was covered with white _____s.

10 erosion
[iróuʒən]

침식 ▶ erode 동 침식하다

토양/해안 침식을 줄이려는 시도
attempts to reduce soil/coastal _____

11 astronomy
[əstránəmi]

천문학

▶ astronomical 형 천문학의
▶ astronomer 천문학자

항해술은 천문학을 응용한 것이다.
Navigation is an application of _____ .

12 cosmos
[kázməs]

(the ~) (질서 · 조화의) 우주 (=universe)

▶ cosmic 형 우주의

허블 우주 망원경으로 본 우주
_____ from the Hubble Space Telescope

13 chaos
[kéias]

혼돈[무질서]

▶ chaotic 형 혼돈된[무질서한]

그 나라는 정치적 혼돈에 빠졌다.
The country was plunged into political _____ .

14 hemisphere
[hémisfìər]

(지구 · 뇌의) 반구

▶ sphere 구, 영역[분야]

북반구/남반구 the Northern/Southern _____

15 equator
[ikwéitər]

(the ~) 적도

▶ equatorial 형 적도의

적도는 지구를 두 개의 반구로 나눈다.
The _____ divides the globe into two hemispheres.

16 latitude/ longitude
[lǽtətjùːd] / [lándʒətjùːd]

위도/경도

우리의 현재 위치는 북위 37도, 동경 127도다.
Our current position is _____ 37 degrees north, _____ 127 degrees east.

17 orbit
[ɔ́ːrbit]

궤도 통 궤도를 돌다

지구 주위를 도는 달의 궤도 the Moon's _____ around the Earth

18 axis
[ǽksis]

(복수. axes) (지)축

지구는 북극과 남극 사이의 축을 중심으로 돈다.
The Earth rotates on an _____ between the North and South Poles.

19 galaxy
[gǽləksi]

은하계, (the Galaxy) 태양계가 속한 은하계(=the Milky Way)

은하계는 수많은 별들의 거대한 집단이다.
A _____ is a giant family of many millions of stars.

20 constellation
[kànstəléiʃən]

별자리

오리온 별자리의 별 a star in the _____ of Orion

21 sunspot
[sʌ́nspàt]

태양 흑점

태양 흑점은 오존 양을 증가시켜 날씨를 변화시킨다.
_____ s change the weather by increasing the amount of ozone.

22 eclipse
[iklíps]

(해·달의) 식(蝕)

일식/월식/개기식/부분식 a solar/lunar/total/partial _____

23 Mercury/Venus/ Mars/Jupiter
[mə́ːrkjuri] / [víːnəs] / [mɑːrz] / [dʒúːpətər]

수성/금성/화성/목성   비교 Saturn/Uranus/Neptune
토성/천왕성/해왕성

수성, 금성, 지구, 화성, 목성 그리고 토성은 모두 행성이다.

_____, _____, Earth, _____, _____ and Saturn are all planets.

24 comet
[kámit]

혜성

핼리 혜성은 80년마다 한 번씩 돌아온다.

Halley's C_____ comes round once every eighty years.

25 spacecraft
[spéiskræ̀ft]

우주선(= spaceship)

무인/유인 우주선 a unmanned/manned _____

26 probe
[proub]

❶ (space ~) 무인 우주 탐사선 ❷ 조사
동 조사하다

달/화성 무인 탐사선 a lunar/Mars _____

27 blast-off
[blǽstɔ̀ːf]

(우주선의) 발사

▶blast off 동 발사되다
▶blast 돌풍, 폭발 동 폭파하다

(우주선) 발사 10초 전! 10 seconds to _____!

28 aerospace
[ɛ́ərəspèis]

항공 우주 산업

항공 우주 산업 the _____ industry

29 alien
[éiljən]

❶ 외계인 ❷ 체류 외국인
형 외국[외계]의, 낯선

▶alienate 동 소원하게 하다
▶alienation 소외, 이간

다른 행성에 사는 외계인 _____s living on other planets

30 extraterrestrial
[èkstrətəréstriəl]

외계인
형 외계의

▶terrestrial 형 지구의

외계 탐사/생물 _____ exploration/beings

Today's Dessert A human being is a part of a whole, called by us universe, a part limited in time and space. – Albert Einstein

인간은 시·공간적으로 제한받는, '우주'라고 불리는 전체의 일부다. – 아인슈타인

지구·우주 Part 1

TEST 26

A 영어는 우리말로, 우리말은 영어로!

1 mainland China
2 a coral reef
3 a gravel path
4 a pebble beach
5 the Earth's axis
6 Halley's Comet
7 an alien spacecraft
8 a Mars probe

9 북극/남극권   the _____/_____ Circle
10 한반도   The Korean P_____
11 지각(地殼)   the Earth's c_____
12 토양 침식   soil e_____
13 북반구   the northern h_____
14 일식   a solar e_____
15 우주 항공 산업   the a_____ industry
16 외계 생물   e_____ beings

B 영영사전 뜻풀이에 알맞은 단어 찾기

> 보기 chaos   constellation   cosmos   galaxy   sunspot

1 _____ : a small dark area on the sun's surface
2 _____ : one of the large groups of stars in the universe
3 _____ : the universe, considered as a well-ordered system
4 _____ : the state of the universe before there was any order
5 _____ : a group of stars that forms a pattern and has a name

C 표 완성하기

> 보기 astronomy   geography   geology

Subject	the study of ...
1	the universe, stars and planets
2	the earth's rocks, soil and minerals
3	the countries, cities, seas, rivers, mountains, etc. of the world

D 빈칸에 가장 적절한 단어 넣기

> 보기 blast-off   equator   latitude   longitude   orbit

1 Five seconds to _____! 발사 5초 전!
2 Local time is dependent on _____. 지방시(地方時)는 경도에 따라 달라진다.
3 The satellite was launched into _____. 위성이 궤도로 발사되었다.
4 _____ represents the distance north and south of the _____.
   위도는 적도로부터의 남북 거리를 나타낸다.

ANSWER
A 1. 중국 본토 2. 산호초 3. 자갈길 4. 조약돌 해변 5. 지축 6. 핼리 혜성 7. 외계 우주선 8. 화성 무인 탐사선 9. Arctic/Antarctic 10. Peninsula
11. crust 12. erosion 13. hemisphere 14. eclipse 15. aerospace 16. extraterrestrial B 1. sunspot 2. galaxy 3. cosmos 4. chaos
5. constellation C 1. astronomy 2. geology 3. geography D 1. blast-off 2. longitude 3. orbit 4. Latitude, equator

지구 · 우주

Part 1

01 phenomenon
[finámənàn]

(복수. phenomena) 현상
자연/사회 현상 a natural/social _____

▶ phenomenal 혤 놀라운[굉장한]

02 specimen
[spésəmən]

표본[견본](=sample)
혈액 표본 a blood _____

03 hypothesis
[haipáθəsis]

(복수. hypotheses) 가설
(=theory)
추후 연구가 그 가설을 확증할 것이다.
Further research will confirm the _____.

▶ hypothesize 동 가설을 세우다

04 formula
[fɔ́:rmjulə]

(복수. formulas/formulae) (공)식
수학 공식/화학식 a mathematical/chemical _____

▶ formulate 동 고안하다

05 analysis
[ənǽləsis]

분석

그들은 결과를 심층 분석했다.
They carried out an in-depth _____ of the results.

▶ analyze 동 분석하다
▶ analytical 혤 분석적인
▶ analyst 분석가

06 gene
[dʒi:n]

유전자

유전자 조작/치료법 _____ manipulation/therapies

▶ genetic 혤 유전의
▶ genetics 유전학
▶ geneticist 유전학자

07 chromosome
[króuməsòum]

염색체
X/Y/성 염색체 a(n) X/Y/sex _____

08 genome
[dʒí:noum]

게놈(gene+chromosome)
인간 게놈 프로젝트 the Human G_____ Project

09 blueprint
[blú:prìnt]

(세포의) 청사진(=scheme, design)
토마토의 유전적 청사진 the tomato's genetic _____

10 heredity
[hərédəti]

유전
우리는 환경의 영향을 더 받을까 유전의 영향을 더 받을까?
Are we more influenced by environment or _____?

▶ hereditary 혤 유전(성)의

11 mutation
[mjuːtéiʃən]

돌연변이

▶mutate 동 돌연변이하다[돌연변이시키다]

유전적 돌연변이의 결과 the result of genetic _____s

12 physiology
[fiziálədʒi]

생리학, 생리 기능

▶physiological 형 생리적인
▶physiologist 생리학자

생리학은 생물학의 한 분야다.
_____ is a branch of biology.

13 anatomy
[ənǽtəmi]

해부(학), 신체 (구조)

인체 해부학 human _____

14 fossil
[fásəl]

화석

▶fossil fuel 화석 연료
▶fossilize 동 화석화하다

고생물학은 화석을 연구하는 학문이다.
Paleontology is the study of _____s.

15 oxygen/ hydrogen
[ɑ́ksidʒən] / [háidrədʒən]

산소/수소

비교 nitrogen 질소
▶oxide/dioxide 산화물/이산화물

물은 수소와 산소로 이루어진다.
Water consists of _____ and _____.

16 molecule
[máləkjùːl]

분자

▶molecular 형 분자의

질소 분자 a nitrogen _____

17 catalyst
[kǽtəlist]

촉매

비교 enzyme 효소

많은 화학 반응들은 촉매 없이 일어날 수 없다.
Many chemical reactions cannot take place without a _____.

18 physics
[fíziks]

물리학

▶physicist 물리학자
▶physical 형 물질[물리(학)]의, 신체[육체]의

현대 물리학에 끼친 아인슈타인의 영향
the impact of Einstein on modern _____

19 atom
[ǽtəm]

원자

▶atomic 형 원자(력)의

모든 물질은 궁극적으로 원자로 이루어져 있다.
All matter ultimately consists of _____s.

20 nucleus
[njúːkliəs]

(복수. nuclei) (원자 · 세포) 핵

▶nuclear 형 핵의, 원자력의
비교 proton 양성자/neutron 중성자/ electron 전자

원자핵 an atomic _____
세포핵 the _____ of a cell

21 particle
[páːrtikl]

입자, 작은 조각[극소량]

▶elementary particle 소립자

미립자는 육안에는 거의 보이지 않는다.
Minute _____s are hardly visible to the naked eye.

과학

Part 1

22 radiation
[rèidiéiʃən]

방사선[방사능]

▶radioactive 혱 방사성[방사능]의
▶radioactivity 방사능[방사성]
▶radiate 동 방사[방출]하다

핵 발전소에서의 방사능[방사선] 누출
a _____ leak from a nuclear power station

---

23 friction
[fríkʃən]

❶마찰 ❷ 불화[알력]

▶frictionless 혱 마찰이 없는

열은 마찰로 생길 수 있다.
Heat can be produced by _____.

---

24 gravity/ gravitation
[grǽvəti] / [grævətéiʃən]

중력/만유인력

▶gravitational 혱 중력의

중력 the force of _____
뉴턴의 만유인력의 법칙 Newton's law of _____

---

25 optics
[áptiks]

광학

▶optical 혱 광학의
▶optic 혱 눈의

광학은 빛에 관한 학문이다.
_____ is the study of light.

---

26 refraction
[rifrǽkʃən]

굴절

비교 reflection 반사
▶refract 동 굴절하다

곧은 막대기가 물속에 일부 잠겨 있으면 굴절로 인해 구부러져 보인다.
_____ makes a straight stick look bent if it is partly in water.

---

27 ultraviolet rays

자외선
(=ultraviolet light[radiation])

비교 infrared rays[light/radiation] 적외선

자외선은 인간의 건강에 이로운 영향과 해로운 영향 둘 다를 끼친다.
_____ have both beneficial and harmful effects on human health.

---

28 wavelength
[wéivlèŋkθ]

파장

▶wave 파도, 파(동)

장/단파장 long/short _____

---

29 conduction
[kəndʌ́kʃən]

(전기·열의) 전도

▶conductor 지휘자, 전도체

전기의 전도 electrical _____

---

30 vapor
[véipər]

(수)증기

▶water vapor 수증기
▶vaporize 동 기화하다
▶evaporate 동 증발하다

구름은 하늘에 있는 수증기 덩어리이다.
A cloud is a mass of _____ in the sky.

Today's Dessert
Science is simply common sense at its best that is, rigidly accurate in observation, and merciless to fallacy in logic. – Thomas Henry Huxley
과학은 관찰에 엄정하고 논리적 오류에 무자비한 최상의 상식일 뿐이다 . – 토마스 헉슬리

과학 Part 1

TEST 27

A 영어는 우리말로, 우리말은 영어로!

1 a blood specimen

2 a recessive gene

3 fossils of early reptiles

4 oxygen and hydrogen

5 a molecular formula

6 solar ultraviolet rays

7 an infrared wavelength

8 물리적 현상　　a physical p＿＿＿＿＿

9 상세한 분석　　a detailed a＿＿＿＿＿

10 유전 청사진　　a genetic b＿＿＿＿＿

11 원자 입자들　　atomic p＿＿＿＿＿s

12 빛의 굴절　　　the r＿＿＿＿＿ of light

13 열전도　　　　heat c＿＿＿＿＿

14 수증기　　　　water v＿＿＿＿＿

B 영영사전 뜻풀이에 알맞은 단어 찾기

> 보기　catalyst　　genome　　gravity　　nucleus

1 ＿＿＿＿＿ : the central part of an atom or cell

2 ＿＿＿＿＿ : all the genes in one cell of living thing

3 ＿＿＿＿＿ : the force that causes something to fall to the ground

4 ＿＿＿＿＿ : a substance that makes a chemical reaction happen faster

C 표 완성하기

> 보기　anatomy　　optics　　physics　　physiology

Subject	the scientific study of ...
1	light and the way we see
2	the structure of human or animal bodies
3	the way in which the bodies of living things work
4	matter, energy, force and motion, and their interactions

D 빈칸에 가장 적절한 단어 넣기

> 보기　chromosome　　friction　　heredity　　hypothesis　　mutation　　radiation

1 ＿＿＿＿＿ generates heat. 마찰은 열을 발생시킨다.

2 ＿＿＿＿＿ can cause ＿＿＿＿＿. 방사선은 돌연변이를 일으킬 수 있다.

3 ＿＿＿＿＿s replicate before cells divide. 염색체는 세포 분열 전에 자기 복제를 한다.

4 Some diseases are present by ＿＿＿＿＿. 어떤 질병들은 유전에 의해 생긴다.

5 The researcher carried out experiments to test the ＿＿＿＿＿.

연구자는 가설을 검증하기 위해 실험을 실시했다.

과학　Part 1

ANSWER

A 1. 혈액 표본 2. 열성 유전자 3. 초기 파충류의 화석 4. 산소와 수소 5. 분자식 6. 태양 자외선 7. 적외선 파장 8. phenomenon 9. analysis
10. blueprint 11. particle 12. refraction 13. conduction 14. vapor　B 1. nucleus 2. genome 3. gravity 4. catalyst　C 1. optics 2.
anatomy 3. physiology 4. physics　D 1. Friction 2. Radiation, mutation 3. Chromosome 4. heredity 5. hypothesis

01 high technology
첨단 과학 기술(=high tech)
- ▶ high-tech 형 첨단 과학 기술의
- ▶ technologist 과학 기술 전문가
- ▶ technician 기술자[기사]

첨단 과학 기술에 기반을 둔 경제 an economy built on _____

02 innovation
[ìnəvéiʃən]
혁신
- ▶ innovate 동 혁신하다[새것을 도입하다]
- ▶ innovative 형 혁신적인
- ▶ innovator 혁신자

과학 기술의 혁신 속도 the speed of technological _____

03 electronics
[ilèktrániks]
전자 공학, 전자 기기
- 비교 electric(al) 형 전기의
- ▶ electronic 형 전자의
- ▶ electron 전자

전자 산업 the _____ industry
가전제품 consumer _____

04 semiconductor
[sèmikəndΛktər]
반도체
- ▶ conductor ❶ 지휘자 ❷ 전도체
- ▶ conduction (전기·열의) 전도

실리콘은 반도체다. Silicon is a _____.

05 (micro)chip
[(máikrou)tʃip]
(마이크로)칩
실리콘/메모리 칩 a silicon/memory _____

06 circuit
[sə́ːrkit]
❶ 회로 ❷ 순회
전자 회로 an electronic _____
집적 회로 an integrated _____ [IC]

07 electromagnetism
[ilèktroumǽgnətizm]
전자기(電磁氣)
- ▶ electromagnetic 형 전자기의
- ▶ magnet 자석
- ▶ magnetism 자성[자력]

전자(기)파/전자(기)장 an _____ wave/field

08 cellphone
[sélfòun]
휴대폰(=cellular phone, mobile (phone))
- ▶ smart phone 스마트폰
- ▶ cellular 형 세포의
- ▶ mobile 형 이동의

내 휴대폰으로 내게 전화해. Call me on my _____

09 tablet
[tǽblit]
❶ 태블릿 피시
(=tablet computer[PC])
❷ (종이)첩[묶음](=pad 패드), 평판
❸ 알약[정제](=pill)
- ▶ desktop/laptop 탁상용/휴대용 컴퓨터

태블릿 피시는 터치스크린이 있는 휴대용 컴퓨터다.
A _____ is a portable computer with a touch screen.

10 input ↔ output
[ínpùt]↔[áutpùt]
입력[투입] 동 입력[투입]하다
↔ 출력[산출] 동 출력[산출]하다
입력/출력 장치 an _____ / _____ device

11 download ↔ upload
[dáunlòud]↔[ʌ́plòud]

다운로드 툉 다운로드하다 ▶load 짐 툉 싣다
↔ 업로드 툉 업로드하다
나는 인터넷에서 업로드하는 것보다 훨씬 많은 자료를 다운로드한다.
I _____ far more data than I _____ to the Internet from the Internet.

12 update
[ʌ́pdèit]

최신 정보, 업데이트 [반의] upgrade 업그레이드
툉 업데이트하다[갱신하다] 툉 업그레이드하다
[개선하다/승급시키다]

소프트웨어의 업데이트된 버전 an _____d version of the software

13 information superhighway

초고속 정보 통신망[인터넷] ▶(super)highway 고속 도로
(=the Internet)
초고속 정보 통신망[인터넷] 시스템 an _____ system

14 fiber optics

섬유 광학[광섬유] ▶fiber-optic 툉 광섬유의
▶optical fiber 광섬유

광섬유 케이블 _____ cables

15 satellite
[sǽtəlàit]

위성
기상 위성 a weather _____
위성 텔레비전 a _____ TV

16 telecommunications
[téləkəmjùːnikéiʃəns]

(원거리) 통신 ▶communication ❶ 의사소통
❷ (-s) 통신
통신에서의 과학 기술 발달 technological developments in _____

17 teleconference
[tèləkɑ́nfərəns]

원격 (화상) 회의 ▶conference 회의
국제 원격 화상 회의 an international video _____

18 telecommuting
[téləkəmjùːtiŋ]

재택근무(=teleworking) ▶telecommuter[teleworker] 재택근무자
재택근무는 우리의 노동 관행을 완전히 바꿀 것이다.
_____ will transform our working practices.

19 e-commerce
[íkɑ́mərs]

전자 상거래 ▶commerce 상업
(=electronic commerce)
전자 상거래의 폭발적 증가 an explosion of _____

20 GPS

지피에스[전 지구 위치 파악 시스템] ▶position 위치 툉 배치하다
(=global positioning system)
지피에스[전 지구 위치 파악 시스템] 위성 신호 _____ satellite signals

21 AI

인공 지능 ▶artificial 툉 인공[인조]의
(=artificial intelligence) ▶intelligence 지능
인간의 지능을 모방하는 인공 지능
_____ that mimics human intelligence

22 cybernetics
[sàibərnétiks]

사이버네틱스[인공두뇌학]

사이버네틱스[인공두뇌학]는 전자 기계와 인간의 두뇌가 작용하는 방식을 연구한다.
_____ studies the way machines and human brains work.

23 virtual reality

가상 현실

▶virtual 형 ❶ 가상의 ❷ 사실상의
▶reality 현실

가상 현실은 인공적인 3차원 환경이다.
_____ is an artificial, three-dimensional environment.

24 CAD/CAM

캐드/캠[컴퓨터 이용 설계/제조]
(=computer-aided design/
=computer-aided manufacturing)

▶aid 동 돕다
▶manufacturing 제조

캐드/캠은 컴퓨터를 이용해 산업 제품을 설계/제조하는 것이다.
_____/_____ is the use of computers to design/make industrial products.

25 ergonomics
[ə̀:rgənámiks]

인간 공학

▶ergonomic 형 인간 공학의

새로운 인간 공학적 디자인 a new_____ design

26 biotechnology
[bàioʊteknálədʒi]

생명 공학(=biotech)

생명 공학 산업 the _____ industries

27 genetic engineering

유전 공학

▶genetic engineer 유전 공학자
▶genetically engineered[modified]
형 유전자 조작의(=GM)

유전 공학은 생명을 바꾸는 기술이다.
_____ is a technique for changing life.

28 clone
[kloun]

클론[복제 생물]
동 복제하다

▶cloning 클로닝[생물 복제]
▶therapeutic/reproductive cloning
치료/생식 복제

클론[복제 생물]은 부모와 유전적으로 일치한다.
A _____ is genetically identical to its parent.

29 stem cell

줄기세포

▶embryonic stem cell 배아 줄기세포
▶stem 줄기

인간 배아 줄기세포 연구 human embryonic _____ research

30 test-tube baby

시험관 아기

세계 최초의 시험관 아기 the world's first _____

Today's Dessert All new technology is rejected and then accepted.
모든 새로운 과학 기술은 거부되고 나서야 받아들여진다.

A 영어는 우리말로, 우리말은 영어로!

1 high technology industry
2 an electromagnetic wave
3 an input/output device
4 the upload and download speed
5 a weather update
6 fiber-optic technology
7 communications satellite

8 과학 기술 혁신　technological i_____
9 가전제품　consumer e_____
10 휴대폰 사용자들　c_____ users
11 3차원 가상 현실　3 dimensional v_____
12 유전 공학　g_____
13 배아 줄기세포　embryonic s_____s
14 시험관 아기　a t_____

B 영영사전 뜻풀이에 알맞은 단어 찾기

보기　biotechnology　clone　cybernetics　ergonomics　telecommuting

1 _____ : the use of living cells and bacteria in industrial processes
2 _____ : a plant or animal which has the same genes as the original
3 _____ : working at home using a computer connected to your office
4 _____ : the study of how the design of equipment helps people to work better
5 _____ : the study of how information is communicated in human brains and machines

C 약어의 본딧말과 우리말 뜻 밝히기

약어	본딧말	뜻
1 e-commerce		
2 GPS		
3 AI		
4 CAD/CAM		

D 빈칸에 가장 적절한 단어 넣기

보기　circuit　information superhighway　semiconductor　tablet　teleconference

1 The Internet is the _____. 인터넷이 초고속 정보 통신망이다.

2 A(n) _____ is a portable computer with a touch screen.
태블릿 피시는 터치스크린이 있는 휴대용 컴퓨터다.

3 A(n) _____ took place between the executives and headquarters.
원격 화상 회의가 임원들과 본사 간에 열렸다.

4 A microchip is a very small piece of _____ that contains complicated electronic _____s. 마이크로칩은 복잡한 전자 회로들을 포함하는 아주 작은 반도체 조각이다.

ANSWER_____

A 1. 첨단 과학 기술 산업 2. 전자(기)파 3. 입력/출력 장치 4. 업로드와 다운로드 속도 5. 최신 날씨 정보 6. 광섬유 기술 7. 통신 위성 8. innovation 9. electronics 10. cellphone 11. virtual reality 12. genetic engineering 13. stem cell 14. test-tube baby　B 1. biotechnology 2. clone 3. telecommuting 4. ergonomics 5. cybernetics　C 1. electronic commerce 전자 상거래 2. global positioning system 전 지구 위치 파악 시스템 3. artificial intelligence 인공 지능 4. computer-aided design/manufacturing 컴퓨터 이용 설계/제조　D 1. information superhighway 2. tablet 3. teleconference 4. semiconductor, circuit

01 arithmetic
[əríθmətik]

산수 [형] 산수의   [비교] calculation 계산

산수를 공부할 때 더하고 빼고 곱하고 나누는 것을 배운다.

When you study _____ you learn to add, subtract, multiply and divide.

02 algebra
[ǽldʒəbrə]

대수학   ▶ algebraic [형] 대수학의

대수학은 양을 나타내기 위해 문자를 사용한다.

_____ uses letters to represent quantities.

03 geometry
[dʒiámətri]

기하학   [비교] trigonometry 삼각법

르네상스 미술가들은 기하학을 이용해 원근법을 이루었다.

Renaissance artists achieved perspective using _____.

04 statistics
[stətístiks]

통계(학)   ▶ statistic 통계치
     ▶ statistical [형] 통계(상)의
     ▶ statistician 통계학자

통계학은 수학의 한 분야다.

_____ is a branch of mathematics.

05 equation
[ikwéiʒən]

방정식   ▶ equate [동] 동일시하다

방정식 $3x-3=15$에서, x는 6이다.

In the _____ $3x-3=15$, $x=6$.

06 numeral
[njú:mərəl]

숫자(=figure)   ▶ numerous [형] 수많은
     ▶ numerical [형] 수의[수로 나타낸]

아라비아 숫자 Arabic _____ s

07 fraction
[frǽkʃən]

❶ 분수 ❷ 작은 부분[일부]   [비교] friction 마찰, 불화[알력]

1/3과 3/8은 분수다.

1/3 and 3/8 are _____ s.

08 decimal
[désəməl]

소수 [형] 십진법의   [비교] binary [형] 2진법의

0.5와 3.175는 소수다.

0.5 and 3.175 are _____ s.

09 dot
[dɑt]

점 [동] 점점이 흩어져 있다

점들을 연결해 그림을 완성하라.

Join the _____ s up to complete the drawing.

10 dimension
[diménʃən]

❶ 차원 ❷ 크기[치수]   ▶ the fourth dimension 4차원
     ▶ one/two/three-dimensional
     [형] 1/2/3차원의

시간은 4차원이라고 불린다.

The time is called the fourth _____.

11 extent
[ikstént]

정도[범위], 길이[크기]
(=magnitude)

▶ extend 동 뻗(치)다, 연장하다
▶ extension 확장[연장], 내선

난 어느 정도는 그에게 동의한다.

I do agree with him to a certain _____.

12 ratio
[réiʃou]

비(율)

비교 rate 비율, 요금, 속도

학생 대 교사의 비율 the _____ of students to teachers

13 proportion
[prəpɔ́:rʃən]

비(율), 균형

▶ proportional 형 비례하는
▶ portion 부분, 1인분

남녀 비율 the _____ of women to men

14 percentage
[pərséntidʒ]

백분율, (백분율로 나타낸) 비율

비교 percent 퍼센트[%](백분율 단위)

대학을 수료한 여성의 비율은 52퍼센트였다.

The _____ of women completing college was 52 percent.

15 probability
[prùbəbíləti]

확률(=likelihood, chance),
개연성

▶ probable 형 개연성이 있는[~일 것 같은]
▶ probably 부 아마

복권에 당첨될 확률은 매우 낮다.

The _____ of winning the lottery is very low.

16 frequency
[frí:kwənsi]

❶ 빈도 ❷ 주파수

▶ frequent 형 잦은[빈번한]

이 책은 우리에게 어휘 (사용) 빈도를 보여 준다.

This book shows us word _____.

**17 minimum
↔ maximum**
[mínəməm]↔[mǽksəməm]

최소[최저] 형 최소[최저]의
↔ 최대[최고] 형 최대[최고]의

▶ minimize ↔ maximize
동 최소화하다 ↔ 최대화하다
▶ minimal 형 최소의

최소/최대 10명/1주일 a _____/_____ of 10 people/a week

18 multitude
[mʌ́ltətʃùːd]

다수

▶ a multitude of ~ 많은 ~

나는 이전에 그렇게 많은 별들을 본 적이 없었다.

I had never seen such a _____ of stars before.

19 abundance
[əbʌ́ndəns]

풍부함(=wealth)

▶ abundant 형 풍부한
(=plentiful ↔ scarce)

그 섬에는 과일이 풍부하게 자랐다.

Fruit grew in _____ on the island.

20 excess
[ékses]

과도[초과] 형 초과한

▶ excessive 형 지나친[과도한]
▶ exceed 동 초과하다

과도한 열정은 문제를 야기한다.

An _____ of enthusiasm causes problems.

21 surplus
[sɔ́:rplʌs]

❶ 여분[잉여] ❷ 흑자(↔ deficit 적자) 형 여분[잉여]의

식량 여분[잉여] food _____es

무역 흑자/적자 a trade _____/deficit

22 rectangle
[réktæŋgl]

직사각형

비교 square 정사각형
▶rectangular 형 직사각형의
▶triangle 삼각형

직사각형의 네 변 the four sides of a _____

23 polygon
[páligàn]

다각형

▶pentagon/hexagon/octagon
오각형/육각형/팔각형

오각형, 육각형, 팔각형은 모두 다각형이다.
A pentagon, a hexagon and an octagon are all _____s.

24 cube
[kju:b]

❶ 정육면체 ❷ 세제곱

비교 square 제곱
▶cubic 형 세제곱[정육면체]의

정육면체의 6면 the six sides of a _____
2의 세제곱은 8이다. The _____ of 2 is 8.

25 sphere
[sfiər]

❶ 구 ❷ 영역[분야]

비교 circle 원
▶hemisphere (지구·뇌의) 반구

지구는 완전한 구가 아니다.
The Earth is not a perfect _____.

26 spiral
[spáiərəl]

나선(형) 형 나선(형)의 동 나선형으로 움직이다

새들이 천천히 나선형으로 돌았다.
The birds circled in a slow _____.

27 oval
[óuvəl]

계란형[타원형](=ellipse) 형 계란형[타원형]의(=elliptical)

경주로는 타원형이다. The racetrack is an _____.
계란형 얼굴 an _____ face

28 cone
[koun]

원뿔

비교 corn 옥수수
cylinder 원통[원기둥]
▶conic 형 원뿔의

원뿔 모양의 산 a _____-shaped mountain

**29 diameter/
radius**
[daiǽmətər] / [réidiəs]

지름[직경]/반지름[반경]

비교 perimeter 둘레
circumference 원주

원의 반지름은 지름의 반이다.
The _____ of a circle is half the _____.

30 symmetry
[símətri]

대칭, 균형

▶symmetric(al) 형 대칭적인
▶asymmetry 비대칭, 불균형

완벽한 대칭
perfect _____
남녀의 일 사이의 균형
the _____ between men's and women's jobs

Today's
Dessert

Hugs are not measured by quantity; they are measured by quality.

포옹은 양으로 측정되는 게 아니라 질로 측정된다.

A 영어는 우리말로, 우리말은 영어로!

1	Arabic numerals	8	공식 통계	official s_____
2	a tiny dot	9	십진법	the d_____ system
3	the ratio of men to women	10	4차원	the fourth d_____
4	direct proportion	11	확률의 법칙	the laws of p_____
5	the minimum/maximum wage	12	고주파/저주파	a high/low f_____
6	an abundant labor force	13	나선형 은하	a s_____ galaxy
7	perfect symmetry	14	타원형 얼굴	an o_____ face

B 영영사전 뜻풀이에 알맞은 단어 찾기

보기 cube   fraction   multitude   sphere   surplus

1 _____ : an object shaped like a round ball
2 _____ : a division of a number, for example 5/8
3 _____ : a very large number of people or things
4 _____ : an amount which is more than is needed
5 _____ : a solid object with six equal square sides

C 빈칸에 가장 적절한 단어 넣기

보기 diameter   equation   extent   excess   percentage   radius

1 She never eats to _____. 그녀는 절대 과식하지 않는다.
2 In the _____ $2x+1 = 7$, x is 3. 방정식 $2x+1=7$에서, x는 3이다.
3 The figure is expressed as a _____. 그 수치는 백분율로 표시된다.
4 The _____ measures twice the _____. 지름의 길이는 반지름의 2배다.
5 To what _____ was he involved in the affairs? 그는 어느 정도까지 그 일에 연루되었니?

D 주어진 문장 해석하기

1 Mathematics includes arithmetic, algebra, and geometry.

_____

2 A triangle, rectangle, square, and pentagon are all polygons.

_____

수량 · 모양

Part 1

01 sundial/ hourglass
[sándàiəl] / [áuərglæs]

해시계/모래시계

비교 water clock 물시계
pendulum 시계추[진자]

해시계와 모래시계는 과거에 시간을 측정하기 위해 사용되었다.

The _____ and _____ were used to measure time in the past.

02 phase
[feiz]

단계[국면](=period)

비교 pace 속도[보조], 한 걸음

실험 단계 an experimental _____

03 procedure
[prəsí:dʒər]

절차

비교 process 과정[공정]
통 (가공) 처리하다

비자 신청 절차 the _____ for applying for a visa

04 transition
[trænzíʃən]

이행[과도]

▶transitional 형 과도기의

완전한 민주주의로 가는 과도기 the period of _____ to full democracy

05 scope
[skoup]

범위(=range), 여지[기회]

그들은 연구 범위를 확장했다.

They extended the _____ of the study.

06 realm
[relm]

❶ 영역[범위] ❷ 왕국(=kingdom)

예술/과학/교육의 영역 the _____ of art/science/education

07 hub
[hʌb]

중심(=center)

그 지역의 상업 중심지 the commercial _____ of the region

08 core
[kɔːr]

❶ (과일의) 속 ❷ 핵심(=heart)

사과 속 an apple _____

문제의 핵심 the _____ of the problem

09 advent
[ǽdvent]

출현[도래](=appearance)

컴퓨터/인터넷의 출현 the _____ of the computer/the Internet

10 outbreak
[áutbrèik]

(전쟁·사고·질병 등의) 발발[발생] ▶break out
통 (전쟁·사고·질병 등이) 발발[발생]하다

제2차 세계 대전의 발발 the _____ of World War II

식중독의 발생 an _____ of food poisoning

11 prospect
[práspekt]

가망(=possibility), 전망   비교 retrospect 회상[회고]
▶prospective 형 장래의, 유망한

졸업생의 취업 전망이 좋아 보이지 않는다.

Job _____s for graduates don't look good.

12 criterion
[kraitíəriən]

(복수. criteria) 기준[표준]

학업 능력이 입학 허가의 유일한 기준은 아니다.

Academic ability is not the sole _____ for admission.

13 stance
[stæns]

❶ (공개적) 태도[입장] ❷ 자세   비교 stand 동 서 있다 명 태도[입장]

그는 테러리즘에 강경한 태도[입장]를 취했다.

He adopted a tough _____ on terrorism.

공을 치는 자세

the batting _____

14 outage
[áutidʒ]

정전(=blackout)   비교 outrage 격분[격노]
동 격분[격노]하게 하다

정전이 우리를 4시간 동안 어둠 속에 있게 했다.

The power _____ left us in the dark for four hours.

15 mechanism
[mékənìzm]

❶ 기계 장치 ❷ 메커니즘[기제]   ▶mechanic ❶ 정비사 ❷ (-s) 역학

통증은 천연 방어 기제로 작용한다.

Pain acts as a natural defence _____.

16 equilibrium
[ì:kwəlíbriəm]

평형[균형]   ▶equilibrate 동 평형[균형]을 유지하다

신체의 균형 상태에 대한 어떠한 장애도 스트레스를 유발할 수 있다.

Any disturbance to the body's state of _____ can produce stress.

17 pros and cons

이불리[장단점](=advantages and disadvantages)

조기 교육의 장단점   the _____ of early education

18 drawback
[drɔ́:bæk]

결점[문제점](=disadvantage)

유명한 것의 주된 결점 중 하나는 사생활의 결여다.

One of the major _____s of being famous is the lack of privacy.

19 flaw
[flɔ:]

결함[흠](=fault, defect)   ▶flawless 형 흠 없는[완벽한](=perfect)

우리 교육 제도의 많은 결함들 many _____s in our education system

20 shortcoming
[ʃɔ́:rtkʌ̀miŋ]

결점[단점](=defect, weakness)

그는 단점보다 더 많은 장점을 가지고 있다.

He has more strengths than _____s.

21 adversity
[ædvə́:rsəti]

역경   ▶adverse 형 부정적인[불리한]

그녀는 역경 속에서도 항상 쾌활했다.

She was always cheerful in _____.

22 pitfall
[pítfɔ̀:l]

함정[위험] ▶pit 구덩이

온라인 데이트의 숨겨진 함정[위험] the hidden _____ s of online dating

23 brink
[briŋk]

❶ 직전 ❷ 벼랑 끝 ▶on the brink[verge] of ~의 직전에

그 회사는 파산 직전에 있다.
The company is on the _____ of bankruptcy.

24 fragment/ segment
[frǽgmənt] / [ségmənt]

조각[파편]/부분[조각]

깨진 도자기 파편들 _____ s of broken pottery
오렌지 조각들 the _____ s of an orange

25 remnant
[rémnənt]

나머지

어젯밤 식사의 나머지가 아직 식탁에 있다.
The _____ s of last night's meal are still on the table.

26 by-product

부산물

이산화탄소는 연료 연소의 부산물이다.
Carbon dioxide is a _____ of burning fuel.

27 cluster
[klʌ́stər]

무리[송이]
⑧ 무리를 이루다

포도 한 송이 a _____ of grapes
별의 무리[성단(星團)] a _____ of stars

28 concept/ conception
[kάnsept] / [kənsépʃən]

개념/개념[구상] ▶conceive ⑧ 상상하다, 임신하다
▶misconception 오해[잘못된 통념]
(=fallacy)

미의 개념 the _____ of beauty
새로운 장치의 구상 the _____ of a new device

29 scrutiny
[skrú:təni]

정밀 조사

그 문서들은 공개적인 정밀 조사가 이루어져야 한다.
The documents should be available for public _____ .

30 tribute
[tríbju:t]

헌사[헌정]

그 음악회는 그 음악가에 대한 헌정이었다.
The concert was a _____ to the musician.

Today's Dessert He that has never suffered adversity, never knows the full extent of his own life.

역경을 겪은 적이 없는 사람은 자신의 삶 전부를 결코 알지 못한다.

TEST 30

A 영어는 우리말로, 우리말은 영어로!

1 a standard procedure

2 a hub of finance

3 the advent of the Internet

4 the outbreak of war

5 basic concepts

6 a locking mechanism

7 a cluster of stars

8 초기 단계   the initial p_____

9 정전   a power o_____

10 치명적 결함   a fatal f_____

11 유리 파편   glass f_____s

12 식사의 나머지   the r_____s of a meal

13 중립적 태도   a neutral s_____

14 헌정 앨범   a t_____ album

B 관련된 것끼리 연결하기

1 adversity ·

2 core ·

3 criterion ·

4 drawback ·

5 realm ·

a. the central part of a fruit or something

b. a difficult or unlucky situation or event

c. a standard by which something is judged

d. an area of activity, interest, or knowledge

e. a disadvantage of a situation, product, etc.

C 밑줄 친 단어와 비슷한 말 연결하기

1 the scope of the investigation ·

2 the prospect of an improvement ·

3 the main shortcoming of this phone ·

a. defect

b. possibility

c. range

D 빈칸에 가장 적절한 단어 넣기

| 보기 | brink | by-product | equilibrium | pitfall | scrutiny | transition |

1 Supply and demand are in _____. 공급과 수요가 균형을 이루고 있다.

2 Their behavior is under _____ again. 그들의 행동은 다시 정밀 조사를 받고 있다.

3 Many animal species are on the _____ of extinction. 많은 동물 종들이 멸종 직전에 있다.

4 He was well aware of the _____s of running a business.

그는 사업 경영의 함정[위험]을 잘 알고 있었다.

5 One of the _____s of unemployment is an increase in crime.

실업의 부산물들 중 하나는 범죄의 증가이다.

6 Making the _____ from youth to adulthood can be very painful.

청춘기에서 성년기로 이행하는 것은 매우 고통스러울 수 있다.

ANSWER

A 1. 표준 절차 2. 금융의 중심 3. 인터넷의 출현 4. 전쟁의 발발 5. 기본 개념 6. 잠금장치 7. 별의 무리[성단] 8. phase 9. outage 10. flaw 11. fragment 12. remnant 13. stance 14. tribute **B** 1. b 2. a 3. c 4. e 5. d **C** 1. c 2. b 3. a **D** 1. equilibrium 2. scrutiny 3. brink 4. pitfall 5. by-product 6. transition

Putting/Carrying

01 install
[instɔ́:l]

설치하다

▶reinstall 재설치하다
▶installation 명 설치, 장치, 시설
▶installment 명 할부(금)

폐쇄 회로 TV 카메라가 설치되어 있다.
CCTV cameras are _____ed.

02 inject
[indʒékt]

주사[주입]하다

▶injection 명 주사[주입]

그는 인슐린을 주사해야 한다.
He has to _____ himself with insulin.

03 insert
[insə́:rt]

(끼워) 넣다[삽입하다]

▶insertion 명 삽입

구멍에 동전을 넣고 누르시오.
_____ coins into the slot and press.

04 embed
[imbéd]

박다[끼워 넣다]

유리 조각이 그녀의 손에 박혔다.
A piece of glass was _____ded in her hand.

05 enclose
[inklóuz]

❶ 동봉하다 ❷ 둘러싸다

▶enclosure 명 울타리[담]를 친 장소

주문서와 함께 수표를 동봉해 주세요.
Please _____ a check with your order.

06 cram
[kræm]

❶ 밀어[쑤셔] 넣다(=stuff) ❷ 벼락공부하다

8명의 아이들이 차 뒷자리에 밀어 넣어졌다.
Eight children were _____med into the back of the car.

07 choke
[tʃouk]

숨이 막히다[질식하다], 질식시키다

여섯 사람이 가스에 질식해 죽었다.
Six people _____d to death on the fumes.

08 smother
[smʌ́ðər]

❶ 완전히 덮다[불을 덮어 끄다] ❷ 질식사시키다(=suffocate)

난 불길을 덮어 끄기 위해 쿠커 위로 담요를 던졌다.
I threw a blanket over the cooker to _____ the flames.

09 heap
[hi:p]

쌓아 올리다 명 더미(=pile)

그는 불 위에 땔나무를 쌓아 올렸다.
He _____ed logs on the fire.

10 dangle
[dǽŋgl]

매달(리)다(=hang)

그는 절벽에 매달렸다.
He _____d from the cliff.

11 dip
[dip]

❶ 살짝 담그다 ❷ 내려가다
난 물에 손을 살짝 담갔다.
I _____ped my hand in the water.

12 soak
[souk]

❶ 담그다[적시다] ❷ (~ up) 빨아들이다[흡수하다]
요리하기 전에 콩을 물에 담가 두어라.
_____ the beans before cooking.

13 scoop
[sku:p]

❶ 뜨다[퍼내다] ❷ 특종을 보도하다 　명 스쿠프[큰 숟가락], 특종
난 으깬 감자 한 숟가락을 퍼냈다.
I _____ed up a spoonful of mashed potatoes.

14 splash
[splæʃ]

(물을) 튀(기)다[끼얹다/첨벙거리다]
그녀는 얼굴에 찬물을 끼얹었다.
She _____ed cold water on her face.

15 sprinkle
[spríŋkl]

(물·가루를) 뿌리다
생선에 레몬주스를 뿌려라.
_____ the fish with lemon juice.

16 sow
-sowed-sown[sowed]
[sou]

(씨를) 뿌리다
　비교 sew 바느질하다
　saw 톱질하다
3월 말에 씨를 뿌려라.
_____ the seeds in late March.

17 scatter
[skǽtər]

(흩)뿌리다, 흩어지다
꽃들이 떨어져 땅 위에 흩어졌다.
The flowers fell and _____ed on the ground.

18 disperse
[dispə́ːrs]

흩어지다[해산하다]　▶dispersal 명 해산[분산]
경찰은 군중을 해산시키려고 최루탄을 사용했다.
Police used tear gas to _____ the crowd.

19 dispatch
[despatch]
[dispǽtʃ]

발송하다, 파견하다(=send)　명 발송, 파견
물품은 24시간 내에 발송된다.
Goods are _____ed within 24 hours.

20 transport
[trænspɔ́ːrt]

운송[수송]하다 명 운송, 교통　▶transportation 명 운송, 교통
배와 트럭이 기름을 수송하는 데 사용된다.
Ships and trucks are used for _____ing oil.

21 transmit
[trænsmít]

❶ 전송[방송]하다 ❷ 전염시키다　▶transmission 명 전송[방송], 전염
월드컵은 위성으로 생방송될 것이다.
The World Cup will be _____ted live via satellite.

22 transplant
[trænsplǽnt]

이식하다[옮겨 심다]　　　　　　▶plant 심다 圆 식물, 공장[설비]
圆 이식　　　　　　　　　　　▶implant 심다[이식하다]
과학자들은 복제 돼지의 장기를 인간에게 이식하기를 희망한다.
Scientists hope to _____ organs from cloned pigs into humans.

23 shift
[ʃift]

❶ 옮기다　❷ 바꾸다[바뀌다]
圆 ❶ 변화　❷ 교대 근무
그녀는 의자에서 자세를 바꾸었다.
She _____ed her position in the chair.

24 propel
[prəpél]

나아가게 하다[추진하다]　　　　▶propeller 圆 프로펠러
4개의 제트 엔진이 배를 나아가게 한다.
Four jet engines _____ the ship.

25 thrust
-thrust-thrust
[θrʌst]

밀치다[찌르다]
圆 ❶ 찌르기　❷ 요지[취지]
난 손을 호주머니에 찔러 넣었다.
I _____ my hands into my pocket.

26 drag
[dræg]

끌다
의자를 바닥에 끌지 마라.
Don't _____ your chairs along the floor.

27 haul
[hɔːl]

(무거운 것을) 끌어당기다
크레인이 자동차를 개울에서 끌어내기 위해 사용되었다.
A crane was used to _____ the car out of the stream.

28 heave
[hiːv]

❶ (무거운 것을) 들어 올리다　❷ 들썩거리다
그는 어깨 위로 자루를 들어 올렸다.
He _____d the bag onto his shoulder.

29 tug
[tʌg]

(세게) 잡아당기다[끌어당기다]
그는 어머니의 팔을 잡아당겼다.
He _____ged at his mother's arm.

30 jerk
[dʒəːrk]

확 움직이다[당기다]　圆 확 움직임
"무슨 일이야?" 그녀가 고개를 확 들며 물었다.
"What's wrong?" she asked, _____ing her head up.

Today's Dessert

Beware of no man more than of yourself; we carry our worst enemies within us.

너 자신보다 조심해야 할 사람은 아무도 없다. 우리는 자신 속에 최악의 적들을 지니고 있다.

TEST 31

A 밑줄 친 동사에 유의하여 우리말로!

1 to <u>install</u> security cameras

2 to <u>inject</u> yourself with insulin

3 to <u>enclose</u> a check

4 to <u>choke</u> to death

5 to <u>soak</u> the beans

6 to <u>splash</u> cold water

7 to <u>sow</u> the seeds

8 to <u>scatter</u> the onions over the fish

9 to <u>disperse</u> the crowd

10 to <u>transplant</u> organs

11 to <u>thrust</u> the knife

12 to <u>jerk</u> your head up

B 영영사전 뜻풀이에 알맞은 동사 찾기

| 보기 | dip   smother   sprinkle |

1 _____ : to put something briefly into a liquid

2 _____ : to scatter a few bits or drops of something

3 _____ : to cover something completely with something else

C 뒤에 올 가장 적절한 것끼리 연결하기

1 to heap　　·

2 to drag　　·

3 to transport ·

a. the chair

b. passengers

c. food on the plate

D 빈칸에 가장 적절한 동사 넣기

| 보기 | dangle   dispatch   scoop   transmit |

1 The game will be _____(e)d live. 그 경기는 생방송될 것이다.

2 He _____(e)d the sand into a bucket. 그는 모래를 양동이에 퍼 담았다.

3 Goods are normally _____(e)d within 24 hours. 물품은 보통 24시간 내에 발송된다.

4 A light bulb _____(e)d from a wire in the ceiling. 전구가 천장의 전선에 매달려 있었다.

E 의미상 더 어울리는 동사 고르기

1 (Embed / Insert) coins into the slot and press. 구멍에 동전을 넣고 누르시오.

2 The woman gently (heaved / tugged) his arm. 여자가 그의 팔을 부드럽게 잡아당겼다.

01 grip
[grip]

꽉 잡다(=grasp, clasp, clutch) 명 꽉 잡음, 지배, 이해

그녀가 그의 손을 꽉 잡았다.

She _____ped his hand tightly.

02 grab
[græb]

잡아채다[움켜쥐다](=snatch, seize) 명 잡아채기

도둑이 내 가방을 잡아채 달아났다.

The thief _____bed my bag and ran off.

03 pinch
[pintʃ]

꼬집다

그녀가 아기 남동생을 꼬집지 못하게 해.

Stop her _____ing her baby brother.

04 retain
[ritéin]

보유[유지]하다(=keep)

우리는 쌀 수입의 통제권을 보유해야 한다.

We have to _____ control of rice imports.

05 manipulate
[mənípjulèit]

다루다[조작하다], 조종하다 ▶manipulation 명 조작[조종]
▶manipulative 형 조종하는

난 그래픽 이미지를 다룰[조작할] 수 있다.

I can _____ graphic images.

06 imprison
[imprízn]

투옥하다 ▶imprisonment 명 투옥
▶prison 명 감옥[교도소]

정부는 반정부 지도자들을 투옥했다.

The government _____ed opposition leaders.

07 pitch
[pitʃ]

❶ 던지다 ❷ (~ in) 동참하다 ▶pitcher 명 피처[투수], 주전자
명 소리의 높낮이

그는 9회에 두 타자에게 던졌다.

He _____ed to two batters in the ninth inning.

08 fling
-flung-flung
[fliŋ]

내던지다[내동댕이치다]

사람들이 모자를 공중으로 내던졌다.

People _____ their hats into the air.

09 hurl
[həːrl]

내던지다

시위대가 벽돌을 내던지고 있었다.

Demonstrators were _____ing bricks.

10 toss
[tɔ(ː)s]

(가볍게) 던지다 ▶toss and turn 뒤척이다

그 책 좀 던져 줄래?

_____ that book over, will you?

11 flip
[flip]

휙 던지다[뒤집다/넘기다] 명 휙 던지기

난 잡지들을 획획 넘기고 있었다.

I was _____ping magazines.

12 tickle
[tíkl]

간질이다

날 간질이지 마!

Stop _____ing me!

13 stroke
[strouk]

쓰다듬다(=pet) 명 ❶ 뇌졸중 ❷ 치기, (수)영법

좋다면 개를 쓰다듬어도 돼.

_____ the dog if you like.

14 caress
[kərés]

애무하다[어루만지다] 명 애무

그는 부드럽게 그녀의 뺨을 어루만졌다.

Gently he _____ed her cheek.

15 pat
[pæt]

쓰다듬다[토닥거리다]

선생님이 내 머리를 쓰다듬으셨다.

My teacher _____ted me on the head.

16 pound
[paund]

쾅쾅 두드리다(=hammer), 쿵쾅거리다
명 파운드(무게 · 영국 화폐 단위)

누군가가 문을 쾅쾅 두드리고 있었다.

Someone was _____ing at the door.

17 punch
[pʌntʃ]

❶ 주먹으로 치다 ❷ 구멍을 뚫다

그가 나를 주먹으로 쳐서 이빨을 부러뜨렸다.

He _____ed me and knocked my teeth out.

18 thump
[θʌmp]

주먹으로 세게 치다, 쿵쾅거리다 비교 thumb 명 엄지손가락

그녀는 가슴을 주먹으로 세게 쳤다.

She _____ed her chest.

19 slam
[slæm]

쾅 닫(히)다(=bang), 세게 놓다

바람이 문을 쾅 닫히게 했다.

The wind made the door _____ shut.

20 slap
[slæp]

손바닥으로 때리다, 세게 놓다

그녀는 그의 뺨을 때렸다.

She _____ped him across the face.

21 spank
[spæŋk]

(손바닥으로) 엉덩이를 때리다

난 엉덩이를 맞기엔 너무 나이 들었다고 생각해요!

I think I'm too old to be _____ed!

22 thrash
[θræʃ]

❶ (벌로) 때리다 ❷ 심하게 움직이다 ❸ 완패시키다

그는 채찍으로 말을 때렸다.

He _____ed the horse with his whip.

23 smash
[smæʃ]

박살내다[나다], 세게 (부딪)치다

그는 모든 유리창을 박살냈다.

He _____ed all the windows.

24 collide
[kəláid]

충돌하다 ▶collision 몡 충돌

자동차 5대가 안개 속에서 충돌했다.

Five cars _____d in the fog.

25 stab
[stæb]

(칼로) 찌르다(=jab) 비교 sting-stung-stung
(동식물이) 찌르다[쏘다]

그녀는 가슴을 칼로 찔렀다.

She was _____bed in the chest.

26 poke
[pouk]

찌르다, 내밀다(=stick)

그 지팡이를 조심해! 넌 내 눈을 찌를 뻔했어.

Be careful with that stick! You nearly _____d me in the eye.

27 pierce
[piərs]

(꿰)뚫다[관통하다]

그녀는 배꼽을 뚫었다.

She had her belly-button _____d.

28 penetrate
[pénətrèit]

관통하다 ▶penetration 몡 침투[관통]

총알이 그의 뇌를 관통했다.

The bullet _____d his brain.

29 slice
- [slais]

얇게 베다[썰다]
몡 얇은 조각, 부분[몫]

오이를 얇게 썰어라.

Thinly _____ the cucumbers.

30 slash
[slæʃ]

❶ (거칠게) 베다 ❷ 대폭 줄이다 비교 mow (풀을) 깎다[베다]
몡 베기, 사선(/) saw 톱질하다 몡 톱

그녀는 손목을 그어 자살을 기도했다.

She tried to commit suicide by _____ing her wrists.

Today's Dessert

He that grasps too much, holds nothing.

너무 많은 것을 움켜쥐고 있는 사람은 아무것도 제대로 지니지 못한다.

TEST 32

A 밑줄 친 동사에 유의하여 우리말로!

1 to hurl bricks
2 to toss the ball to him
3 to flip over the pages
4 to pat the dog
5 to pound at the door
6 to thrash the child
7 to smash windows
8 to stab him in the chest
9 to have your ears pierced
10 to penetrate his brain
11 to slice cucumbers
12 to slash the tires

B 영영사전 뜻풀이에 알맞은 동사 찾기

보기 | fling   punch[thump]   slap   spank   stroke[caress]

1 _____ : to move your hand gently over something
2 _____ : to throw something somewhere with force
3 _____ : to hit someone with the flat part of your hand
4 _____ : to hit someone very hard with your hand closed
5 _____ : to hit a child on their bottom with your open hand

C 밑줄 친 동사에 유의하여 뜻 구별해 해석하기

1 He gripped my hand firmly.   The thief grabbed my bag and ran off.
2 Stop tickling me!   Stop pinching me!

D 빈칸에 가장 적절한 동사 넣기

보기 | collide   manipulate   poke   retain   slam

1 He _____(e)d the door shut. 그는 문을 쾅 닫았다.
2 Do we _____ control of food imports? 우리는 식량 수입의 통제권을 보유하고 있는가?
3 She _____(e)d him in the ribs with her elbow. 그녀는 팔꿈치로 그의 옆구리를 찔렀다.
4 A car and a truck _____(e)d on the expressway. 승용차와 트럭이 고속도로에서 충돌했다.
5 The mechanical arms are _____(e)d by a computer.
그 기계 팔은 컴퓨터에 의해 조작된다.

ANSWER_____

A 1. 벽돌을 내던지다 2. 그에게 공을 던지다 3. 책장을 휙 넘기다 4. 개를 쓰다듬다 5. 문을 쾅쾅 두드리다 6. 아이를 때리다 7. 유리창을 박살내다 8. 그의 가슴을 칼로 찌르다 9. 귀를 뚫다 10. 그의 뇌를 관통하다 11. 오이를 얇게 썰다 12. 타이어를 베다 B 1. stroke[caress] 2. fling 3. slap 4. punch[thump] 5. spank C 1. 그가 내 손을 꽉 잡았다.(꽉 잡다) / 도둑이 내 가방을 잡아채 달아났다.(잡아채다) 2. 날 간질이지 매!(간질이다) / 날 꼬집지 매!(꼬집다) D 1. slam(slammed) 2. retain 3. poke 4. collide 5. manipulate

01 lean
[liːn]

숙이다[기울다], 기대다 형 군살[기름기]이 없는

그들은 앞으로 몸을 숙이고 있었다.

They were _____ing forward.

02 crook
[krʊk]

구부리다 명 사기꾼 ▶crooked 형 비뚤어진, 부정직한

그녀는 손가락을 구부려 내게 오라고 손짓했다.

She _____ed her finger at me, motioning me to come over.

03 crouch
[kraʊtʃ]

쭈그리고 앉다

그는 그늘에 쭈그리고 앉아 있었다.

He _____ed in the shadows.

04 tilt
[tilt]

기울(이)다(=tip)

그녀는 머리를 한쪽으로 기울였다.

She _____ed her head to the side.

05 roam
[roʊm]

돌아다니다[배회하다](=wander)

난 한 시간 동안 길거리를 배회했다.

I _____ed the streets for an hour.

06 stroll
[stroʊl]

거닐다[산책하다]

우리는 거닐면서 웃고 농담을 주고받았다.

We were _____ing along, laughing and joking.

07 stride
-strode-stridden
[straid]

성큼성큼 걷다[활보하다]

그가 그녀를 향해 성큼성큼 걸어왔다.

He _____ toward her.

08 shuffle
[ʃʌfl]

발을 질질 끌며 걷다

그렇게 발을 질질 끌며 걷지 마!

Don't _____ your feet like that!

09 descend
[disénd]

❶ 내려가다[내려오다](↔rise, ascend) ▶descent 명 하강, 가계
❷ (be -ed from) ~의 자손이다 ▶descendant 명 자손(↔ancestor)

난 계단을 내려오는 그의 발자국 소리를 들었다.

I heard his footsteps _____ing the stairs.

10 bound
[baʊnd]

껑충껑충 달리다
형 ❶ 꼭 ~할 것 같은[해야 하는]
　　❷ ~행의
명 (-s) 한계[한도]

변화 bind-bound-bound 묶다
bounce 튀(기)다, 깡충깡충 뛰다
▶rebound 다시 튀어 나오다

그녀가 계단 아래로 껑충껑충 달려 내려왔다.

She came _____ing down the stairs.

11 hop
[hɑp]

(한 발로) 깡충깡충 뛰다

그녀는 벤치로 한 발로 깡충깡충 뛰어가 신발을 신었다.

She _____ped over to a bench to put on her shoes.

12 dash
[dæʃ]

❶ 급히 달려가다 ❷ 내동댕이치다 명 돌진

사람들이 불구경을 하러 급히 달려 나갔다.

People _____ed out to see the fire.

13 dart
[dɑ:rt]

쏜살같이 움직이다[돌진하다] 명 표창(鏢槍), (-s) 다트 게임

그녀는 앞으로 돌진해 불 속에서 그를 끌어냈다.

She _____ed forward and pulled him away from the fire.

14 sprint
[sprint]

단거리를 전력 질주하다 ▶sprinter 명 단거리 선수
명 단거리 경주

그는 계단을 전력 질주해 올랐다.

He _____ed up the steps.

15 flee
-fled-fled
[fli:]

달아나다[도망치다](=escape)

그의 공격자들은 돌아서서 도망쳤다.

His attackers turned and _____.

16 dodge
[dɑdʒ]

❶ 재빨리 피하다[비키다/움직이다] ▶dodgeball 명 피구
❷ 기피[회피]하다

그는 차들을 재빨리 피하며 뛰어서 길을 건너갔다.

He ran across the road, _____ing the traffic.

17 trace
[treis]

(행방을) 찾아내다[추적하다], 거슬러 올라가다 명 흔적

그들은 실종된 딸의 행방을 찾고 있다.

They are _____ing their missing daughter.

18 trail
[treil]

❶ 뒤쫓다[추적하다](=follow) ❷ (질질) 끌(리)다(=drag)
명 오솔길(=track), 자국[흔적]

경찰이 범인들을 뒤쫓고 있다.

Police have been _____ing the criminals.

19 crawl
[krɔ:l]

기다

아기가 바닥을 기어갔다.

The baby _____ed across the floor.

20 creep
-crept-crept
[kri:p]

살금살금 움직이다, 기다

그녀는 살금살금 그의 뒤로 가서 손으로 그의 눈을 가렸다.

She _____ up behind him and put her hands over his eyes.

21 glide
[glaid]

미끄러지듯 움직이다(=slide), 활공하다

커플들이 댄스 플로어 위를 미끄러지듯 움직이고 있었다.

The couples were _____ing over the dancefloor.

22 skid
[skid]

(차가) 미끄러지다

자동차가 도로에서 미끄러졌다.

The car _____ded off the road.

23 stumble
[stámbl]

❶ 비틀거리다 ❷ 말을 더듬다(=falter)

그는 계단에 걸려 비틀거렸다.

He _____d over the step.

24 tumble
[támbl]

굴러 떨어지다

그녀는 균형을 잃고 굴러 떨어졌다.

She lost her balance and _____d.

25 plunge
[plʌndʒ]

추락[급락]하다, (~ in(to)) 뛰어들다

차가 다리 아래로 추락했다.

The car _____d off a bridge.

26 rotate
[róuteit]

❶ 돌(리)다[회전하다](=turn) ▶rotation 몡 회전, 교대
❷ 교대로 하다

지구는 24시간마다 1회 자전한다.

The Earth _____s on its axis once every 24 hours.

27 revolve
[riválv]

돌(리)다[회전하다] ▶revolution 몡 ❶ 혁명 ❷ 회전
▶revolutionary 혱 혁명적인

바퀴가 돌기 시작했다.

The wheel began to _____.

28 spin
-spun-spun
[spin]

❶ 빙빙 돌(리)다[회전하다] ❷ (실을) 잣다
몡 빙빙 돌기[회전]

비행기의 프로펠러가 회전하고 있었다.

The plane's propellers were _____ning.

29 swirl
[swəːrl]

빙빙 돌(리)다[소용돌이치다] 몡 소용돌이

시냇물이 바위 위에서 소용돌이치고 있다.

The stream is _____ing over the rock.

30 whirl
[hwəːrl]

빙빙[휙휙] 돌(리)다 몡 빙빙[휙휙] 돌기

갈매기들이 항구 상공을 빙빙 돌고 있었다.

The seagulls were _____ing over the harbor.

Today's Dessert

Do not go where the path may lead, go instead where there is no path and leave a trail. - Ralph Waldo Emerson

길이 이끄는 곳으로 가지 말고 대신 길이 없는 곳으로 가 길을 남겨라. - 에머슨

동작

Part 2

TEST 33

A 밑줄 친 동사에 유의하여 우리말로!

1 to <u>lean</u> against the wall

2 to <u>crook</u> your finger

3 to <u>crouch</u> in the shadows

4 to <u>tilt</u> your head

5 to <u>roam</u> the streets

6 to <u>shuffle</u> your feet

7 to <u>dash</u> into the classroom

8 to <u>dart</u> across the road

9 to <u>flee</u> the country

10 to <u>dodge</u> the traffic

11 to <u>trail</u> the criminals

12 to <u>glide</u> over the floor

B 영영사전 뜻풀이에 알맞은 동사 찾기

보기	crawl	hop	spin	sprint	stride

1 _____ : to walk quickly with long steps

2 _____ : to run very fast for a short distance

3 _____ : to turn around and around very quickly

4 _____ : to move by a quick jump or series of jumps

5 _____ : to move along the ground on your hands and knees

C 빈칸에 가장 적절한 동사 넣기

보기	bound	revolve	stroll	swirl

1 The stream is _____ing. 시냇물이 소용돌이치고 있다.

2 The dogs _____(e)d ahead. 개들이 앞으로 껑충껑충 달렸다.

3 The wheel began to _____. 바퀴가 돌기 시작했다.

4 We _____(e)d along the beach. 우리는 해변을 따라 거닐었다.

D 밑줄 친 동사에 유의하여 뜻 구별해 해석하기

He <u>stumbled</u> over the step.   He <u>tumbled</u> down the stairs.

E 빈칸에 가장 적절한 동사 넣기

보기	creep(crept)	plunge	skid	whirl

1 I _____ into my room. 난 내 방 안으로 살금살금 들어갔다.

2 Leaves _____(e)d in the wind. 나뭇잎들이 바람에 빙그르르 돌았다.

3 The car _____(e)d off the road. 자동차가 도로에서 미끄러졌다.

4 The bus _____(e)d into the river. 버스가 강으로 추락했다.

ANSWER
A 1. 벽에 기대다 2. 손가락을 구부리다 3. 그늘에 쭈그리고 앉다 4. 머리를 기울이다 5. 거리를 배회하다 6. 발을 질질 끌며 걷다 7. 교실로 급히 달려 들어가다 8. 도로를 가로질러 돌진하다 9. 그 나라에서 달아나다[도망치다] 10. 차들을 재빨리 피하다 11. 범인을 뒤쫓다 12. 마룻바닥을 미끄러지듯 움직이다 B 1. stride 2. sprint 3. spin 4. hop 5. crawl C 1. swirl 2. bound 3. revolve 4. stroll D 그는 계단에 걸려 비틀거렸다.(비틀거리다) / 그는 계단에서 굴러 떨어졌다.(굴러 떨어지다) E 1. crept 2. whirl 3. skid(skidded) 4. plunge

01 blink
[bliŋk]

❶ 눈을 깜박이다 ❷ 빛이 깜박이다　[비교] wink 한쪽 눈을 깜박이다[윙크하다]
명 깜박임

난 햇빛 속으로 나왔을 때 눈을 깜박였다.

I _____ed as I came out into the sunlight.

02 frown
[fraun]

눈살을 찌푸리다　[비교] grimace 얼굴을 찡그리다
명 찌푸림　　　　　　명 찡그림

그는 그를 보고 웃자 내게 눈살을 찌푸렸다.

He _____ed at me for laughing at him.

03 gaze
[geiz]

응시하다(=stare) 명 응시

난 하늘의 별들을 응시했다.

I _____d at the stars above.

**04 glance/
glimpse**
[glæns] / [glimps]

힐끗 보다 명 힐끗 봄
언뜻 보다 명 언뜻 봄

그는 시계를 힐끗 보았다.

He _____d at his watch.

나는 창문 너머로 그녀를 언뜻 보았다.

I _____d her through the window.

05 glare
[glɛər]

❶ 노려보다 ❷ 눈이 부시게 빛나다 명 노려봄, 눈이 부신 빛

그녀는 화가 나서 그를 노려보았다.

She _____d angrily at him.

**06 peep
[peek]**
[pi:p] [pi:k]

엿보다[훔쳐보다]

그는 창을 통해 그녀의 방을 엿보았다.

He _____ed into her room through the window.

07 overhear
-overheard-overheard
[òuvərhíər]

엿듣다　[비교] oversee-oversaw-overseen
감독하다(=supervise)

난 그들의 대화 일부를 엿들었다.

I _____ part of their conversation.

08 grin
[grin]

활짝 웃다 명 활짝 웃음　[비교] giggle 킥킥 웃다
chuckle 빙긋 웃다

그는 입이 째지게 활짝 웃고 있었다.

He was _____ning from ear to ear.

09 wail
[weil]

울부짖다[통곡하다]　[비교] weep-wept-wept
울다[눈물을 흘리다](=cry)

사람들이 관 주위에 모여 통곡했다.

People gathered around the coffins and _____ed.

10 sob
[sɑb]

흐느껴 울다, 흐느끼며 말하다

"제발 날 떠나지 마." 그가 흐느끼며 말했다.

"Please don't leave me," he _____ bed.

11 exhale
↔ inhale
[ekshéil] ↔ [inhéil]

(숨을) 내쉬다[내뿜다] ↔ 들이쉬다

숨을 깊이 들이쉬고 나서 천천히 내쉬어라.

Take a deep breath, then _____ slowly.

12 gasp
[gæsp]

헉 하고 숨을 쉬다[헐떡이다]   명 헉 하는 숨쉬기[헐떡임]

그는 고통으로 숨을 헐떡였다.

He _____ ed with pain.

13 snore
[snɔːr]

코를 골다   비교 sniff 코를 훌쩍이다,
                              킁킁거리며 냄새를 맡다

코를 곤다면 반듯이 누워 자지 않는 게 좋다.

If you _____, it's better not to sleep on your back.

14 hiccup
[híkʌp]

딸꾹질을 하다   명 딸꾹질

난 계속 웃다가 웃음 때문에 딸꾹질을 했다.

I went on laughing, _____ ing with laughter.

15 burp
[belch]
[bəːrp] [beltʃ]

트림을 하다

갑자기 그녀가 크게 트림을 했다.

Suddenly, she _____ ed loudly.

16 vomit
[vάmit]

토하다(= be sick, throw up)

난 저녁 식사의 대부분을 토했다.

I _____ ed up most of my dinner.

17 suck
[sʌk]

빨다[빨아 먹다]   비교 suckle 젖을 빨다[먹다], 젖을 먹이다

그녀는 빨대로 밀크셰이크의 마지막 한 모금까지 빨아 먹었다.

She _____ ed up the last bit of milkshake with her straw.

18 lick
[lik]

핥다[핥아 먹다]

난 숟가락에서 꿀을 핥아 먹었다.

I _____ ed the honey off the spoon.

19 devour
[diváuər]

❶ 게걸스레 먹다 ❷ 탐독하다

그는 순식간에 샌드위치를 게걸스레 먹어 치웠다.

He _____ ed the sandwiches in seconds.

20 nibble
[níbl]

조금씩[야금야금] 먹다

곤충들이 나뭇잎을 야금야금 먹었다.

Insects _____ d at the tree's leaves.

21 digest
[daidʒést]

소화하다

▶digestion 몡 소화
▶digestive 혱 소화의

대부분의 아기들은 다양한 음식을 쉽게 소화할 수 있다.

Most babies can _____ a wide range of food easily.

22 shiver [quiver]
[ʃívər] [kwívər]

떨다(= shake, tremble)

그는 추위에 떨며 밖에서 기다렸다.

He waited outside, _____ing with cold.

23 wag
[wæg]

(꼬리·손가락·머리를) 흔들다

개는 꼬리를 흔든다.

A dog _____s its tail.

24 flap [flutter]
[flæp] [flʌtər]

퍼덕거리다, 펄럭이다

비교 flatter 아첨하다, 돋보이게 하다

작은 새가 날개를 퍼덕거렸다.

A small bird _____ped its wings.

25 hug
[hʌg]

껴안다[포옹하다] 몡 껴안기[포옹]

우리는 껴안고 웃고 하이 파이브를 했다.

We _____ged, laughed and slapped high-fives.

26 embrace
[imbréis]

껴안다[포옹하다], 받아들이다, 포함하다

그녀는 달려가 어머니를 포옹했다.

She ran to _____ her mother.

27 shrug
[ʃrʌg]

(어깨를) 으쓱하다 몡 (어깨를) 으쓱하기

그는 단지 어깨를 으쓱했을 뿐이다.

He just _____ged his shoulders.

28 sprain
[sprein]

삐다(= twist)

난 계단에서 넘어져 발목을 삐었다.

I fell down the steps and _____ed my ankle.

29 throb
[θrɑb]

욱신[지끈]거리다, 고동치다[울리다] 몡 진동, 욱신거림

그는 머리가 욱신거리고 몸이 아팠다.

His head _____bed, and his body ached.

30 paralyze
[pǽrəlàiz]

마비시키다

▶paralysis 몡 마비

그녀의 다리는 그 충돌로 마비되었다.

Her legs were _____d in the crash.

Today's Dessert

What soap is for the body, tears are for the soul.

비누가 몸을 씻듯이 눈물은 영혼을 씻는다.

TEST 34

A 밑줄 친 동사에 유의하여 우리말로!

1 to overhear the conversation
2 to suck your thumb
3 to lick ice cream
4 to devour sandwiches
5 to digest food
6 to wag its tail
7 to shrug your shoulders
8 to sprain your ankle

B 영영사전 뜻풀이에 알맞은 동사 찾기

| 보기 | blink   glare   paralyze   peep[peek]   sob   wail |

1 _____ : to shut and open your eyes quickly
2 _____ : to cry noisily, breathing in short breaths
3 _____ : to look at something quickly and secretly
4 _____ : to look angrily at someone for a long time
5 _____ : to make a loud, long cry of sadness or pain
6 _____ : to make someone lose the ability to move or feel

C 다음 생리 현상의 우리말 뜻은?

1 hiccup   2 burp[belch]   3 vomit   4 snore

D 빈칸에 가장 적절한 동사 넣기

| 보기 | flap[flutter]   gasp   glance   grin   nibble   throb |

1 He _____(e)d at his watch. 그는 시계를 힐끗 보았다.
2 The bird _____(e)d its wings. 새가 날개를 퍼덕거렸다.
3 He _____(e)d from ear to ear. 그는 입이 째지게 활짝 웃었다.
4 He climbed _____ing for breath. 그는 숨을 헐떡이며 올랐다.
5 He _____(e)d the biscuit cautiously. 그는 조심스럽게 비스킷을 조금씩 먹었다.
6 My feet were _____ing after the long walk. 오래 걸어 내 발이 욱신거렸다.

E 같은 관계 맺어주기

1 stare : gaze = tremble : s_____ [q_____]
2 hurt : ache = hug : e_____
3 descend : ascend = exhale : i_____

ANSWER
A 1. 대화를 엿듣다 2. 엄지손가락을 빨다 3. 아이스크림을 핥아 먹다 4. 샌드위치를 게걸스레 먹다 5. 음식을 소화하다 6. 꼬리를 흔들다 7. 어깨를 으쓱하다 8. 발목을 삐다 B 1. blink 2. sob 3. peep[peek] 4. glare 5. wail 6. paralyze C 1. 딸꾹질을 하다 2. 트림을 하다 3. 토하다 4. 코를 골다 D 1. glance 2. flap[flutter](flapped[fluttered]) 3. grin(grinned) 4. gasp 5. nibble 6. throb(throbbing) E 1. shiver[quiver] 2. embrace 3. inhale

메모

Part 2

01 generate
[dʒénərèit]

만들어 내다[발생시키다]
(= create, produce)
▶ generation 명 ❶ 세대 ❷ 발생
▶ degenerate 악화되다

그 프로그램은 많은 새로운 일자리를 만들어 낼 것이다.
The program would _____ a lot of new jobs.

02 yield
[ji:ld]

❶ 산출[생산]하다(= produce) ❷ (~ to) 굴복하다, 양보하다
명 수확량

저 나무는 열매를 많이 생산한다.
That tree _____s plenty of fruit.

03 reproduce
[rì:prədjú:s]

❶ 생식[번식]하다
❷ 복제[재현]하다
▶ reproduction 명 생식, 복제(품)
▶ reproductive 형 생식[복제]의

연어는 새끼를 번식하기 위해 개울로 되돌아온다.
Salmon return to the stream to _____ offspring.

04 breed
-bred-bred
[bri:d]

❶ 번식하다
❷ 사육[재배]하다, 육종하다
명 품종
▶ breeding 명 번식, 사육[재배], 육종

어떤 나무들은 오염에 견디도록 육종된다.
Some trees are _____ to resist pollution.

05 mate
[meit]

짝짓기[교미]하다 명 짝, 동료

수컷 새는 여러 암컷들과 짝짓기를 한다.
Male birds _____ with several females.

06 cultivate
[kʌ́ltəvèit]

❶ 경작[재배]하다(= grow)
❷ 기르다[함양하다]
▶ cultivation 명 경작[재배], 함양

그 땅은 바위가 너무 많아 경작할 수 없다.
The land is too rocky to _____.

07 consist
[kənsíst]

❶ (~ of) (~로) 이루어져 있다 ❷ (~ in) (~에) 있다[존재하다]

관객은 십 대들로 이루어져 있었다.
The audience _____ed of teenagers.

08 compose
[kəmpóuz]

❶ 구성하다(= make up)
❷ 작곡[작문]하다
▶ be composed of ~로 이루어지다
▶ composition 명 ❶ 구성 ❷ 작품
▶ decompose 분해[부패]하다

물은 수소와 산소로 구성된다.
Water is _____d of hydrogen and oxygen.

09 comprise
[kəmpráiz]

~로 이루어지다[구성되다](= be comprised of), 구성하다

그 집은 2개의 침실과 부엌, 거실로 이루어져 있다.
The house _____s two bedrooms, a kitchen, and a living room.

10 **constitute**
[kánstitʃùːt]

❶ 구성하다 ❷ ~로 여겨지다   ▶constitution 명 ❶ 헌법 ❷ 체질

질소는 지구 대기의 78%를 구성한다.

Nitrogen _____ s 78% of the earth's atmosphere.

11 **compile**
[kəmpáil]

편집하다[엮다]

그들은 새로운 사전을 편집하고 있다.

They are _____ ing a new dictionary.

12 **edit**
[édit]

편집하다[수정하다]   ▶edition 명 (책·신문·잡지의) 판
▶editor 명 편집자
▶editorial 명 사설 형 편집의

신문사는 신문을 인쇄하기 전에 편지들을 편집한다.

The newspaper _____ s letters before printing them.

13 **devise**
[diváiz]

고안[창안]하다   ▶device 명 장치, 방책

한 선생님이 수학을 재미있게 만들 방안으로 그 게임을 고안했다.

A teacher _____ d the game as a way of making math fun.

14 **mold**
[mould]

만들다, 형성하다(=form) 명 ❶ 틀 ❷ 곰팡이

우리의 가치를 형성하는 것은 바로 문화다.

It is culture that _____ s our values.

15 **forge**
[fɔːrdʒ]

❶ 형성[구축]하다 ❷ 위조하다(=counterfeit) ❸ 단조(鍛造)하다

그 사고는 사람들 사이에 긴밀한 유대를 형성했다.

The accident _____ d a close bond among the people.

16 **weave**
-wove-woven
[wiːv]

짜다, 엮다

그들은 전통적인 옷감을 짠다.

They _____ traditional cloth.

17 **synthesize**
[sínθəsàiz]

합성하다, 종합하다   ▶synthetic 형 합성[인조]의
▶synthesizer 명 신시사이저

몸이 자체적으로 합성할 수 없는 많은 비타민이 있다.

There are many vitamins that the body cannot _____ itself.

18 **improvise**
[ímprəvàiz]

즉석에서 하다   ▶improvisation 명 즉흥 연주

재즈 연주자들은 즉흥 연주를 잘한다.

Jazz musicians are good at _____ ing.

19 **duplicate**
통 [djúːplikèit]
명 형 [djúːplikət]

복사[복제]하다(=copy), 되풀이하다 명 사본[복제품] 형 복사[복제]의

많은 사본들이 원본에서 복사될 수 있다.

Many copies can be _____ d from a master copy.

20 **imitate**
[ímitèit]

모방하다, 흉내 내다   ▶imitation 명 모방[흉내], 모조품
▶imitator 명 모방자

자연을 연구해서 모방해라!

Study and _____ nature!

창조

Part 2

21 mimic
-mimicked-mimicked
[mímik]

흉내 내다, 모방하다　명 흉내를 잘 내는 사람

그는 모든 선생님의 억양을 흉내 낼 수 있다.

He can _____ all the teachers' accents.

22 simulate
[símjulèit]

❶ 모의실험을 하다　▶ simulation 명 모의실험
❷ ~인 체하다[시늉하다]　▶ simulator 명 모의실험 장치

우주에서의 상황을 모의실험 하는 기계 장치

a machine that _____s conditions in space

23 disguise
[disgáiz]

변장하다, 숨기다　명 변장

그는 신부로 변장한 채 국경을 넘어 탈출했다.

He escaped across the border, _____d as a priest.

24 adorn
[ədɔ́ːrn]

꾸미다[장식하다](= decorate)　▶ adornment 명 장식(품)

신부의 머리가 흰 꽃으로 장식되었다.

The bride's hair was _____ed with white flowers.

25 illuminate
[ilúːmənèit]

❶ 밝게 비추다[조명하다]　▶ illumination 명 조명
❷ 설명하다

밤에 분수는 아름답게 조명이 된다.

At night the fountain is beautifully _____d.

26 illustrate
[íləstrèit]

❶ 삽화[도해]를 넣다　▶ illustration 명 삽화[도해]
❷ 예를 들어 설명하다　▶ illustrator 명 삽화가

그들은 자신들의 이야기를 쓰고 삽화를 넣게 될 것이다.

They will write and _____ their own stories.

27 scribble
[skríbl]

휘갈겨 쓰다, 낙서하다　비교 graffiti 명 공공장소의 낙서

그는 그녀에게 자신의 전화번호를 휘갈겨 써주었다.

He _____d her his phone number.

28 provoke
[prəvóuk]

❶ 일으키다[유발하다](= cause)　❷ 화나게 하다[도발하다]

그 더러운 전쟁은 빗발치는 저항을 유발했다.

The dirty war _____d storms of protest.

29 spark
[spɑːrk]

❶ 일으키다[유발하다]　❷ 불꽃을 튀기다　명 불꽃

버려진 담배가 산불을 일으킨다.

A discarded cigarette _____s a forest fire.

30 trigger
[trígər]

일으키다[유발하다]　명 방아쇠

암살이 폭동을 일으켰다.

The assassination _____ed off rioting.

Today's Dessert

We have to live in order to create what we are. – Albert Camus

우리는 자신의 정체성을 창조하기 위해 살아야 한다. - 카뮈

TEST 35

A 밑줄 친 동사에 유의하여 우리말로!

1 to generate electricity

2 to yield crops

3 to breed dogs

4 to cultivate potatoes

5 to mold a pot from clay

6 to weave carpets

7 to synthesize sounds

8 to imitate nature

9 to mimic your accents

10 to disguise yourself as a waiter

11 to adorn walls

12 to spark a forest fire

B 영영사전 뜻풀이에 알맞은 단어 찾기

보기 compile   devise   illuminate   improvise   scribble   trigger

1 _____ : to make a light shine on something

2 _____ : to write something quickly and untidily

3 _____ : to make something happen very quickly

4 _____ : to do something without any preparation

5 _____ : to plan or invent a new way of doing something

6 _____ : to make a book using different pieces of information

C 빈칸에 들어가기에 부적절한 하나는?

The audience _____ teenagers. 관객은 십 대들로 이루어져 있다.

① consists of   ② is composed of   ③ comprises

④ is comprised of   ⑤ constitutes

D 빈칸에 가장 적절한 동사 넣기

보기 duplicate   edit   forge   provoke   reproduce   simulate

1 He used a _____(e)d passport. 그는 위조된 여권을 사용했다.

2 The dirty war _____(e)d protests. 그 더러운 전쟁은 저항을 불러일으켰다.

3 The files were _____(e)d illegally. 그 파일은 불법으로 복제되었다.

4 They _____(e)d highlights of the game. 그들은 경기의 주요 장면들을 편집했다.

5 Interviews are _____(e)d in the classroom. 면접이 교실에서 모의실험된다.

6 Most reptiles _____ by laying eggs on land. 대부분의 파충류는 땅에 알을 낳아 번식한다.

ANSWER

A 1. 전기를 발생시키다[발전하다] 2. 농작물을 산출하다 3. 개를 사육[육종]하다 4. 감자를 재배하다 5. 점토로 항아리를 만들다 6. 카펫을 짜다 7. 소리를 합성하다 8. 자연을 모방하다 9. 너의 억양을 흉내 내다 10. 웨이터로 변장하다 11. 벽을 장식하다 12. 산불을 일으키다 B 1. illuminate 2. scribble 3. trigger 4. improvise 5. devise 6. compile C ⑤ D 1. forge 2. provoke 3. duplicate 4. edit 5. simulate 6. reproduce

01 abolish
[əbáliʃ]

폐지하다 ▶abolition 몡 폐지

노예 제도는 미국에서 19세기에 폐지되었다.

Slavery was _____ed in the US in the 19th century.

02 eliminate
[ilímənèit]

제거하다[없애다] ▶elimination 몡 제거

신용 카드가 현금의 필요성을 없앴다.

The credit card _____s the need for cash.

03 erase
[iréis]

지우다[삭제하다] ▶eraser 몡 지우개

난 마음에서 그녀의 이미지를 지울 수가 없다.

I can't _____ her image from my mind.

04 delete
[dilí:t]

지우다[삭제하다] ▶deletion 몡 삭제

난 실수로 파일을 삭제했다.

I have _____d a file by mistake.

05 deplete
[diplí:t]

감소시키다 ▶depletion 몡 감소

석유 비축량이 감소됨에 따라 가격은 계속 오를 것이다.

As oil reserves are _____d, its price will continue to rise.

06 deprive
[dipráiv]

(~ A of B) (A에게서 B를) 빼앗다[박탈하다]

수면을 빼앗기면 몸이 제대로 기능을 발휘할 수 없다.

You can't function properly when you're _____d of sleep.

07 discard
[diská:rd]

버리다

길거리에 쓰레기를 버리지 마라.

Don't _____ your litter in the streets.

08 dispose
[dispóuz]

(~ of) 처리하다 ▶disposal 몡 처리
▶disposable 혱 일회용의 몡 일회용품

전문가들이 핵폐기물을 어디에 어떻게 처리할지 연구하고 있다.

Experts study where and how to _____ of nuclear waste.

09 dispense
[dispéns]

(~ with) ~ 없이 지내다 ▶indispensable 혱 필수 불가결한
(=do without)

우리 격의 없이 지내자.

Let's _____ with the formalities, shall we?

10 expend
[ikspénd]

(시간 · 돈 · 힘을) 들이다[소비하다] ▶expense 몡 비용[경비/지출]
(=spend)

그들은 컴퓨터의 보안을 개선하기 위해 많은 시간과 노력을 들였다.

They _____ed a lot of time and effort to improve computer security.

11 exile
[éɡzail]

망명하게 하다[추방하다] 圆 망명[추방](자)

그 독재자는 자신의 조국에서 추방당했다.

The dictator was _____d from his home country.

12 expel
[ikspél]

쫓아내다[추방하다]

두 소녀가 흡연을 했다는 이유로 학교에서 쫓겨났다.

Two girls were _____led from school for smoking.

13 banish
[bǽniʃ]

쫓아내다[추방하다]　　　　　▶banishment 圆 추방

그는 먼 복도로 쫓겨났다.

He was _____ed to a distant corridor.

14 displace
[displéis]

❶ 쫓아내다 ❷ 대신[대체]하다(=replace)

댐의 건설은 수천 명의 사람들을 내쫓을 것이다.

The building of a dam will _____ thousands of people.

15 dismiss
[dismís]

❶ 무시하다 ❷ 해고하다(=fire, sack) ❸ 떠나게 하다[해산하다]

그는 나의 제안을 비현실적이라고 무시했다.

He _____ed my proposal as unrealistic.

16 withdraw
-withdrew-withdrawn
[wiðdrɔ́ː]

❶ 철수[철회]하다 ❷ 인출하다　　▶withdrawal 圆 철수[철회], 인출

미국은 그 나라에서 군대를 철수했다.

The US has _____ its troops from the country.

17 omit
[oumít]

빠뜨리다[생략하다](=leave out)

어떠한 세부 사항도 빠뜨리지 마세요.

Please don't _____ any details.

18 abbreviate
[əbríːvièit]

줄여[약어로] 쓰다(=shorten)　　▶abbreviation 圆 약어, 축약(형)

'Information technology'는 'IT'로 줄여 쓴다.

"Information technology" is _____d to "IT."

19 extract
[ikstrǽkt]

뽑아내다[추출하다]　　　　　▶extraction 圆 뽑아냄[추출]

기름이 올리브에서 추출된다.

The oil is _____ed from olives.

20 pluck
[plʌk]

잡아 뽑다[따다/뜯다]

그녀는 나무에서 사과 하나를 땄다.

She _____ed an apple off the tree.

21 uproot
[ʌprúːt]

뿌리째 뽑다

나무들이 폭풍에 뿌리째 뽑혔다.

The trees were _____ed in the storm.

22 bleach
[bli:tʃ]

표백[탈색]하다
圐 표백제
그녀는 머리를 금발로 탈색했다.
She _____ed her hair blond.

23 scrub
[skrʌb]

벅벅 문질러 닦다　　　　　　　圓园 rub 문지르다, 닦다
그녀는 바닥을 벅벅 문질러 닦았다.
She _____bed the floor.

24 ruin
[rú:in]

파괴하다[망치다](＝destroy), 파산시키다
圐 폐허[잔해/유적], 파산[파멸]
오랜 파업은 회사를 파산시킬 수도 있다.
A long strike can _____ the company.

25 demolish
[dimáliʃ]

파괴하다
건물 전체가 화재로 파괴되었다.
The entire building was _____ed in the fire.

26 devastate
[dévəstèit]

완전히 파괴[황폐화]하다(＝wreck)
도심이 폭탄으로 완전히 파괴되었다.
The city center was _____d by the bomb.

27 ravage
[rǽvidʒ]

파괴[황폐화]하다
그 지역은 전쟁으로 파괴되었다.
The area has been _____d by war.

28 obliterate
[əblítərèit]

없애다[지우다]
일본은 한국 문화를 없애기 시작했다.
Japan set about _____ing the Korean culture.

29 exterminate
[ikstə́:rmənèit]

몰살시키다
바퀴벌레를 박멸하기란 매우 어렵다.
It is very difficult to _____ cockroaches.

30 extinguish
[ikstíŋgwiʃ]

(불을) 끄다(＝put out)　　　　▶extinguisher 圐 소화기
소방관들이 신고를 받고 불을 끄러 왔다.
Firemen were called to _____ the blaze.

Today's **Dessert**

Reality can *destroy* the dream; why shouldn't the dream *destroy* reality?
현실은 꿈을 파괴할 수 있다. 그렇다면 꿈이 현실을 파괴해서는 왜 안 되겠는가?

TEST 36

A 밑줄 친 동사에 유의하여 우리말로!

1 to <u>eliminate</u> risks

2 to be <u>deprived</u> of your freedom

3 to <u>discard</u> litter

4 to <u>expend</u> energy

5 to <u>omit</u> some details

6 to <u>extract</u> oils from the plants

7 to <u>pluck</u> an apple

8 to <u>uproot</u> weeds

9 to <u>bleach</u> your hair blond

10 to <u>scrub</u> the floor

B 밑줄 친 동사에 유의하여 해석하기

1 I <u>deleted</u> a file by mistake.   Oil reserves were <u>depleted</u>.

2 Experts study where and how to <u>dispose</u> of nuclear waste.

Let's <u>dispense</u> with the formalities, shall we?

C 빈칸에 가장 적절한 동사 넣기

> 보기   abbreviate   abolish   exterminate   extinguish   obliterate

1 This tax should be _____(e)d. 이 세금은 폐지되어야 한다.

2 Firefighters _____(e)d the blaze. 소방관들이 불을 껐다.

3 They used the poison to _____ rats. 그들은 쥐를 박멸하기 위해 독약을 사용했다.

4 "Chief Executive Officer" is _____(e)d as "CEO."

'Chief Executive Officer'는 'CEO'로 줄여 쓴다.

5 The building was completely _____(e)d by the bomb.

그 건물은 폭탄으로 완전히 없어졌다.

제거 · 파괴

Part 2

D 다른 동사들과 의미가 가장 다른 하나는?

1 ① banish   ② displace   ③ expel   ④ exile   ⑤ exhaust

2 ① demolish   ② devastate   ③ erase   ④ ravage   ⑤ ruin

E 밑줄 친 단어 뜻 구별하기

1 I'd like to <u>withdraw</u> $500 from my account.

The US has <u>withdrawn</u> its troops from the country.

2 He was <u>dismissed</u> from the company.

He <u>dismissed</u> my proposal as unrealistic.

ANSWER

A 1. 위험성을 제거하다 2. 자유를 박탈당하다 3. 쓰레기를 버리다 4. 정력을 소비하다 5. 세부 사항을 빠뜨리다 6. 식물에서 기름을 추출하다 7. 사과를 따다 8. 잡초를 뿌리째 뽑다 9. 머리를 금발로 탈색하다 10. 바닥을 벅벅 문질러 닦다   **B** 1. 난 실수로 파일을 삭제했다.(삭제하다) / 석유 비축량이 감소되었다.(감소시키다)   2. 전문가들은 핵폐기물을 어디에 어떻게 처리할지 연구한다.(처리하다) 격의 없이 지내자.(~ 없이 지내다)   **C** 1. abolish 2. extinguish 3. exterminate 4. abbreviate 5. obliterate   **D** 1. ⑤ 2. ③   **E** 1. 제 계좌에서 500달러를 인출하고 싶습니다.(인출하다) / 미국은 그 나라에서 군대를 철수했다.(철수하다) 2. 그는 회사에서 해고당했다.(해고하다) / 그는 나의 제안을 비현실적이라고 무시했다.(무시하다)

01 fuse
[fjuːz]

결합[융합]하다 ▶fusion 몡 결합[융합]

난자와 정자가 하나의 세포로 결합한다.

The egg and sperm _____ together as one cell.

02 integrate
[íntəgrèit]

통합하다(↔ segregate) ▶integration 몡 통합

버스와 지하철 운행이 통합되었다.

Bus and subway services have been _____ d.

03 merge
[məːrdʒ]

합병[통합]하다

그들은 두 회사를 하나로 합병했다.

They _____ d the two companies into one.

04 blend
[blend]

섞(이)다[혼합하다] 몡 혼합물

설탕과 계란, 밀가루를 섞어라.

_____ the sugar, eggs, and flour.

05 mingle
[míŋgl]

섞(이)다[어울리다]

그녀의 흥분은 두려운 감정과 섞여 있다.

Her excitement is _____ d with a feeling of fear.

06 tangle
[tǽŋgl]

엉키다[엉키게 하다]

내 머리카락은 쉽게 엉킨다. My hair _____ s easily.

07 entangle
[intǽŋgl]

걸리게[얽히게] 하다

새가 그물에 걸렸다.

The bird got _____ d in the net.

08 hook
[huk]

❶ 걸다, 낚다 ❷ (~ up) 연결하다
몡 (갈)고리[걸이], 낚싯바늘(=fishhook)

인터넷에 연결되어 있니?

Are you _____ ed up to the Internet?

09 correlate
[kɔ́ːrəlèit]

상호 관련되다[관련시키다] ▶correlation 몡 상관관계
▶relate ❶ 관련되다[관련시키다]
❷ 이야기하다

빈곤은 짧은 수명과 상호 관련된다.

Poverty _____ s with a short life expectancy.

10 incorporate
[inkɔ́ːrpərèit]

포함하다(= include)

어떤 활동을 당신의 생활에 포함하고 싶습니까?

Which activities would you like to _____ in your life?

11 overlap
[òuvərlǽp]

겹치다[중복되다]

나의 음악적 취향은 너의 것과 겹친다.

My musical tastes _____ with yours.

12 assemble
[əsémbl]

❶ 모으다[모이다](=gather)
❷ 조립하다(↔disassemble)

▶assembly 몡 의회, 집회, 조립
▶disassemble 툉 분해[해체]하다

모든 학생이 강당에 모였다.

All the students _____d in the hall.

13 accumulate
[əkjúːmjulèit]

축적하다[축적되다](=build up)　▶accumulation 몡 축적

소수 특권층이 부를 계속 축적하는 것은 부당하다.

It is unjust that a privileged few should continue to _____ wealth.

14 adhere
[ədhíər]

들러붙다, (~ to) 고수하다　▶adhesive 몡 접착제 혱 접착의

이 물고기들 알은 식물 잎에 달라붙는다.

The eggs of these fish _____ to plant leaves.

15 cling
-clung-clung
[kliŋ]

꼭 붙잡다[매달리다], 달라붙다　▶clingy 혱 매달리는, 달라붙는

그는 울부짖으며 어머니에게 매달렸다.

He wailed and _____ to his mother.

16 seal
[siːl]

봉하다, 밀폐하다　몡 ❶ 봉인, 인장 ❷ 바다표범

건물이 밀폐되면 공기가 자유로이 흐르지 못할 수 있다.

As buildings become _____ed, the air may not move freely.

17 sew
-sewed-sewed[sewn]
[sou]

바느질하다[깁다]

비교 saw 톱질하다 몡 톱
sow (씨를) 뿌리다

내 청바지에 헝겊을 대서 좀 기워줄래요?

Can you _____ a patch on my jeans?

18 rip
[rip]

찢(어지)다(=tear), 떼어내다

그녀의 옷이 모두 찢어졌다.

Her clothes were all _____ped.

19 undo
-undid-undone
[ʌndúː]

❶ 풀다(=untie)
❷ 원상태로 돌리다

▶undone 혱 풀린, 끝나지 않은
▶done 혱 다 끝난

난 꾸러미를 조심스럽게 풀었다.

I _____ the package carefully.

20 detach
[ditǽtʃ]

떼다[분리하다](↔attach)

▶detached 혱 무심한[초연한]
▶detachment 몡 무심함[초연], 분리

신청서를 떼어 내 빈 곳을 작성해 주세요.

Please _____ and fill out the application form.

21 isolate
[áisəlèit]

고립시키다(=cut off),
분리[격리]하다

▶isolation 몡 고립, 분리[격리]
▶isolationism 몡 고립[쇄국]주의

그 마을은 홍수로 고립되었다.

The town was _____d by the floods.

22 segregate
[ségrigèit]

분리[차별]하다(↔ integrate)   ▶ segregation 명 분리[차별]

학교는 장애를 가진 아이들을 차별해서는 안 된다.

Schools should not _____ children with disabilities.

23 alienate
[éiljənèit]

소원하게 하다, 소외시키다   ▶ alienation 명 소외
▶ alien 형 낯선, 외국[외계]의
　　　　명 체류 외국인, 외계인

그는 가족으로부터 소외되었다.

He was _____d from his family.

24 exclude
[iksklú:d]

제외[배제]하다(↔ include)   ▶ exclusion 명 제외[배제]
▶ exclusive 형 배타[독점]적인
▶ exclusiveness 명 배타성

판사는 부당하게 얻어진 증거를 배제했다.

The judge _____d evidence which had been unfairly attained.

25 distinguish
[distíŋgwiʃ]

구별[식별]하다   ▶ distinction 명 구별[차이], 차별성
(=tell[know] A from B)

전문가조차 원본[진품]과 가짜를 구별할 수 없다.

Even an expert can't _____ the original from the fake.

26 differentiate
[dìfərénʃièit]

구별하다   ▶ differentiation 명 차별
▶ differential 형 차별의 명 차이

사실과 의견을 구별하는 게 중요하다.

It's important to _____ between fact and opinion.

27 discriminate
[diskrímənèit]

❶ 차별하다 ❷ 구별하다   ▶ discrimination 명 차별, 구별

소수자와 여성을 차별하는 건 불법이다.

It is illegal to _____ against minorities and women.

28 diverge
[divə́:rdʒ]

갈라지다, 다르다   ▶ divergent 형 다른

그 두 종은 수백만 년 전에 갈라졌다.

The two species _____d millions of years ago.

29 classify
[klǽsəfài]

분류하다   ▶ classification 명 분류

법적으로 맥주는 식품으로 분류된다.

In law, beer is _____ied as a food product.

30 categorize
[kǽtəgəràiz]

분류하다   ▶ category 명 범주
▶ categorization 명 범주화

인구는 나이, 성별, 사회 집단에 따라 분류된다.

The population is _____d according to age, sex, and social group.

Today's Dessert

Greed separates us. Dreams and anguish bring us together.

탐욕은 우리를 분열시키고, 꿈과 고통은 우리를 모이게 한다.

TEST 37

A 밑줄 친 동사에 유의하여 우리말로!

1 to fuse jazz and rock
2 to blend eggs and flour
3 to hook up to the Internet
4 to assemble a car
5 to accumulate wealth

6 to cling to your mother
7 to seal the envelope
8 to sew clothes
9 to undo the package
10 to distinguish between right and wrong

B 영영사전 뜻풀이에 알맞은 동사 찾기

보기 adhere entangle exclude isolate overlap

1 _____ : to stick firmly to something
2 _____ : to cover part of the same space
3 _____ : to deliberately not include something
4 _____ : to separate one person or thing from others
5 _____ : to make something become twisted and caught

C 같은 관계 맺어주기

1 tear : rip = classify : c_____
2 distinguish : differentiate = include : i_____
3 integrate : segregate = attach : d_____

D 의미상 더 어울리는 동사 고르기

The two flavors (mingle / tangle) well. 그 두 가지 맛은 잘 섞인다.

E 빈칸에 가장 적절한 동사 넣기

보기 alienate correlate discriminate diverge merge

1 He was _____d from his classmates. 그는 급우들로부터 소외되었다.
2 A high-fat diet _____s with heart disease. 고지방 음식은 심장병과 상호 관련된다.
3 Fact and fiction _____ together in the movie. 그 영화에는 사실과 허구가 함께 섞여 있다.
4 Many species have _____d from a single ancestor.
많은 종이 단일 조상으로부터 갈라졌다.
5 It is illegal to _____ on grounds of race, sex or religion.
인종과 성, 그리고 종교상의 이유로 차별하는 것은 불법이다.

ANSWER
A 1. 재즈와 록을 결합하다 2. 계란과 밀가루를 섞다 3. 인터넷에 연결하다 4. 자동차를 조립하다 5. 부를 축적하다 6. 어머니에게 매달리다 7. 봉투를 봉하다 8. 옷을 바늘질하다[깁다] 9. 꾸러미를 풀다 10. 옳고 그름을 구별하다 B 1. adhere 2. overlap 3. exclude 4. isolate 5. entangle
C 1. categorize 2. incorporate 3. detach D mingle E 1. alienate 2. correlate 3. merge 4. diverge 5. discriminate

153

Change of Possession

01 equip
[ikwíp]

갖추게 하다 ▶equipment 몡 장비[설비]

그 방들은 폐쇄 회로 TV가 갖추어져 있다.

The rooms are _____ped with CCTV.

02 furnish
[fɔ́ːrniʃ]

❶ 가구를 비치하다 ▶furniture 몡 가구
❷ 제공[공급]하다(=provide, supply)

그의 방은 가구가 간단하게 비치되었다.

His room was simply _____ed.

03 impart
[impáːrt]

주다, 전하다(=convey)

난 당장 전해야 할 정보가 있어.

I have information that I can't wait to _____.

04 render
[réndər]

❶ 되게 하다(=make) ❷ 주다[제공하다](=give) ❸ 표현[번역]하다

우리는 어려운 사람들에게 도움을 주어야 한다.

We must _____ assistance to those in need.

05 bestow
[bistóu]

주다[수여하다]

여왕이 그에게 기사 작위를 수여했다.

The Queen _____ed a knighthood on him.

06 endow
[indáu]

❶ (자질을) 주다[부여하다] ▶be endowed with ~을 타고나다
❷ 기금을 기부하다 ▶endowment 몡 기부(금), 자질

극소수의 사람들만이 훌륭한 외모와 두뇌 둘 다를 타고난다.

Few people are _____ed with both good looks and brains.

07 entitle
[intáitl]

❶ 권리[자격]를 주다 ▶title 몡 제목, 권리[자격]
❷ 제목을 붙이다 ▶entitlement 몡 권리[자격] (부여)

종업원들은 건강 보험료를 받을 권리가 있다.

Employees are _____d to receive health insurance.

08 entrust
[intrást]

(~ A with B[B to A])
(A에게 B를) 맡기다[위임하다] ▶trust 신뢰[신용]하다 몡 신뢰[신용]

그녀는 아들의 교육을 그에게 맡겼다.

She _____ed her son's education to him.

09 empower
[impáuər]

권한을 주다 ▶power 몡 힘[권한]

대통령은 사면을 할 권한이 있다.

The President is _____ed to grant a pardon.

10 authorize
[ɔ́ːθəràiz]

권한을 주다[인가하다]
(=sanction)

▶authority 몡 권한[권위], 권위자, 당국
▶authoritative 혱 권위 있는
▶authoritarian 혱 권위주의[독재]적인

이곳은 인가받은 직원들에게만 개방되어 있다.
This is open to _____ d personnel only.

11 allocate
[ǽləkèit]

배정하다

▶allocation 몡 배정

표는 먼저 신청하는 사람들에게 배정될 것이다.
Tickets will be _____ d to those who apply first.

12 assign
[əsáin]

맡기다[배정하다]

▶assignment 몡 과제[임무], 배정

그들은 그 집을 짓는 일을 맡았다.
They was _____ ed the task of building the house.

13 distribute
[distríbjuːt]

배급[분배]하다(=give out)

▶distribution 몡 배급[분배]
▶distributor 몡 배급자

식량이 난민들에게 배급되었다.
Food was _____ d among the refugees.

14 donate
[dóuneit]

기부[기증]하다(=contribute)

▶donation 몡 기부(금)(=contribution)
▶donator[donor] 몡 기부[기증]자

그들은 수익금의 전액을 자선 단체에 기부했다.
They _____ d all profits to charity.

15 dedicate
[dédikèit]

바치다[헌신/헌정하다](=devote)

▶dedicated 혱 헌신적인(=devoted)
▶dedication 몡 헌신(=devotion)

그녀는 어린이 자선 사업에 헌신하고 있다.
She _____ s herself to children's charity work.

16 sacrifice
[sǽkrəfàis]

희생하다, 제물로 바치다   몡 희생, 제물

그는 아이들을 돌보기 위해 유망한 직업을 희생했다.
He _____ d a promising career to look after his kids.

17 submit
[səbmít]

❶ 제출하다(=present)
❷ (~ to) 굴복하다(=give in, yield)

▶submission 몡 제출, 항복[굴복]

신청서는 월요일까지 제출되어야 한다.
The application must be _____ ted by Monday.

18 succumb
[səkám]

(~ to) 굴복[복종]하다

난 유혹에 굴복해 케이크를 먹었다.
I _____ ed to the temptation of cake.

19 surrender
[səréndər]

항복[투항]하다, 넘겨주다

네게 항복하느니 차라리 죽고 싶다.
I would rather die than _____ to you.

20 forfeit
[fɔ́ːrfit]

몰수[박탈]당하다

그는 재산을 몰수당하도록 명령받았다.
He was ordered to _____ his property.

소유·변화

Part 2

21 refund
동[rifʌnd]
명[ríːfʌnd]

환불하다 명 환불

▶refundable 형 환불 가능한
▶non-refundable 형 환불이 안 되는

환불해 주시겠습니까?
Could you _____ my money?

22 restore
[ristɔ́ːr]

회복[복구]하다

▶restoration 명 복구[회복]

정부는 경제를 회복하겠다고 약속한다.
The government promises to _____ the economy.

23 retrieve
[ritríːv]

❶ 되찾다[회수하다]
❷ (정보를) 검색하다

▶retrieval 명 회수

그녀는 귀고리를 되찾으려고 몸을 굽혔다.
She bent down to _____ her earring.

24 inherit
[inhérit]

상속받다[물려받다]

▶inheritance 명 유산, 유전

그녀는 할머니에게서 재산을 상속받았다.
She _____ed a fortune from her grandmother.

25 lease
[liːs]

임대[임차]하다(=rent) 명 임대차 계약

그들은 정부로부터 아파트를 임차하고 있다.
They _____ the apartment from the government.

26 interchange
[ìntərtʃéindʒ]

교환[교체]하다
명 교환, 입체 교차로

비교 exchange 주고받다[교환하다]

두 양념은 서로 쉽게 교체될 수 있다.
The two spices can be easily _____d.

27 barter
[báːrtər]

물물 교환하다 명 물물 교환

그들은 곡물을 소금과 물물 교환했다.
They _____ed their grain for salt.

28 substitute
[sʌ́bstitjùːt]

(~ A for B) (B) 대신 (A를) 사용하다, (~ for) 대신하다
명 대용품, 교체 선수

우리는 건강에 좋은 음식물 대신 비타민 알약을 사용할 수는 없다.
We can't _____ vitamin pills for a healthy diet.

29 utilize
[júːtəlàiz]

이용[활용]하다(=use)

▶utility 명 ❶ (-ies) (전기·수도·가스 등) 공공 서비스
❷ 유용성 ❸ (컴퓨터) 유틸리티

우리는 자원을 최대한 활용해야 한다.
We must _____ our resources best.

30 harness
[háːrnis]

(자연력을) 이용하다 명 마구(馬具), 안전벨트

전기를 생산하기 위해 풍력을 이용할 수 있다.
We can _____ the power of the wind to generate electricity.

Today's Dessert The quickest way to receive love is to give; the best way to keep love is to give it wings.

사랑을 받기 가장 빠른 길은 주는 것이고, 사랑을 유지하기 가장 좋은 길은 그것에 날개를 달아 주는 것이다.

소유·변화 Part 2

TEST 38

A 밑줄 친 동사에 유의하여 우리말로!

1 to <u>furnish</u> a room

2 to <u>impart</u> information

3 to <u>render</u> a service

4 to <u>bestow</u> a title

5 to <u>donate</u> profits

6 to <u>submit</u> an application

7 to <u>succumb</u> to temptation

8 to <u>refund</u> money

9 to <u>restore</u> the economy

10 to <u>inherit</u> a fortune

11 to <u>lease</u> the apartment

12 to <u>harness</u> nuclear fusion

B 영영사전 뜻풀이에 알맞은 동사 찾기

| 보기 | authorize | barter | forfeit | interchange | retrieve | surrender |

1 _____ : to stop fighting and admit defeat

2 _____ : to find something and bring it back

3 _____ : to give official permission for something

4 _____ : to lose something because you have broken a rule

5 _____ : to put each of two things in the place of the other

6 _____ : to exchange for other things rather than for money

C 같은 관계 맺어주기

1 rent : lease = use : <u>u_____</u>

2 devote : dedicate = assign : <u>a_____</u>

3 title : entitle = power : <u>e_____</u>

D 빈칸에 가장 적절한 동사 넣기

| 보기 | distribute | endow | entrust | equip | sacrifice | substitute |

1 _____ dialog for violence. 폭력 대신 대화를 사용해라.

2 The room is _____(e)d with cameras. 그 방은 카메라가 갖추어져 있다.

3 Clothes and blankets have been _____(e)d. 옷과 담요가 배급되었다.

4 He was _____(e)d with her son's education. 그는 그녀의 아들의 교육을 맡았다.

5 Mothers _____ themselves for their children. 어머니는 자식들을 위해 자신을 희생한다.

6 Different people are _____(e)d with different talents.

사람들은 저마다 다른 재능을 타고난다.

ANSWER

A 1. 방에 가구를 비치하다 2. 정보를 <u>전하다</u> 3. 서비스를 제공하다 4. 칭호를 <u>주다</u> 5. 수익금을 <u>기부하다</u> 6. 신청서를 <u>제출하다</u> 7. 유혹에 <u>굴복하다</u> 8. 환불하다 9. 경제를 회복시키다 10. 재산을 <u>상속받다</u> 11. 아파트를 <u>임차하다</u> 12. 핵융합을 <u>이용하다</u> B 1. surrender 2. retrieve 3. authorize 4. forfeit 5. interchange 6. barter C 1. utilize 2. allocate 3. empower D 1. Substitute 2. equip(equipped) 3. distribute 4. entrust 5. sacrifice 6. endow

Helping

01 maintain
[meintéin]

❶ 유지하다(=keep)　　　　▶maintenance 명 유지
❷ 주장하다(=claim)

균형 잡힌 식사를 유지하는 것이 중요하다.
It is important to _____ a balanced diet.

02 sustain
[səstéin]

❶ 유지[지속]시키다　　　　▶sustainable 형 지속 가능한
❷ (피해를) 입다(=suffer)　　▶sustainability 명 지속 가능성

아이들의 관심을 유지하는 것은 어렵다.
It is difficult to _____ children's interest.

03 preserve
[prizə́:rv]

보존[보호]하다　　　　　　▶preservation 명 보존[보호]
　　　　　　　　　　　　▶preservative 명 방부제

우리는 우리의 권리를 보호하기 위해 싸우고 있다.
We are fighting to _____ our rights.

04 conserve
[kənsə́:rv]

보호[보존]하다, 절약하다　　▶conservation 명 자연 보호[보존]

재활용은 자원을 보호하는 데 도움이 된다.
Recycling helps _____ resources.

05 reserve
[rizə́:rv]

❶ 예약하다(=book)　❷ 남겨 두다　▶reservation 명 예약
명 비축(품)

미리 표를 예약해야 하니?
Do you have to _____ tickets in advance?

06 safeguard
[séifgàːrd]

보호하다(=protect)　　　　▶guard 지키다　명 경비[경호]원

산업계는 소비자의 이익을 보호해야 한다.
The industry should _____ the interests of consumers.

07 shield
[ʃiːld]

보호하다[가리다]　명 방패　　▶windshield 명 자동차 앞 유리

오존층은 태양의 자외선으로부터 지구를 보호해 준다.
The ozone layer _____s the earth from the sun's ultraviolet rays.

08 insulate
[ínsəlèit]

❶ 절연[단열/방음]하다　　　▶insulation 명 절연[단열/방음](재)
❷ 격리하다

파이프는 추위에 대비해 단열될 필요가 있다.
Pipes need _____ing against the cold.

09 liberate
[líbərèit]

해방하다　　　　　　　　　▶liberation 명 해방

한국은 1945년 일본으로부터 해방되었다.
Korea was _____d from Japan in 1945.

10 release
[rilíːs]

❶ 풀어 주다[석방하다]　❷ 공개[발표]하다　명 석방, 발표(물)

경찰이 몇몇 남자들을 체포했는데, 그들은 나중에 석방되었다.
Police arrested several men, who were later _____d.

11 rescue
[réskjuː]

구조하다 <small>명</small> 구조

그녀는 불길에서 자신의 아이들을 구조하려다 죽었다.

She died trying to _____ her children from the blaze.

12 rid
-rid-rid
[rid]

(~ A of B) (A에서 B를) 제거하다   ▶get rid of 제거하다[벗어나다]
[(A를 B에서) 벗어나게 하다]

우리는 우리나라에서 핵무기를 제거하기를 원한다.

We want to _____ our country of nuclear weapons.

13 acquit
[əkwít]

무죄 판결[선고]을 하다(↔ convict)

그녀는 살인죄에 대해 무죄를 선고받았다.

She was _____ted of the murder.

14 spare
[spɛər]

❶ 할애하다[내주다] ❷ 피하게 해 주다 ❸ 아끼다
<small>형</small> 여분의 <small>명</small> 여분

미안하지만 시간을 낼 수가 없어.

Sorry, I can't _____ the time.

15 accompany
[əkʌ́mpəni]

❶ 동행[동반]하다 ❷ 반주하다   ▶accompaniment <small>명</small> 반주
   ▶accompanist <small>명</small> 반주자

14세 미만 어린이는 어른과 동행해야 한다.

Children under 14 must be _____ied by an adult.

16 escort
[éskɔːrt]

호위하다

경찰이 그녀를 공항까지 호위했다.

The police _____ed her to the airport.

17 steer
[stiər]

조종하다, 이끌다   ▶steering wheel <small>명</small> 자동차 핸들

우리는 폭풍우 치는 삶의 바다에서 자신의 배를 조종해야 한다.

We must _____ our ship over the stormy ocean of life.

18 usher
[ʌ́ʃər]

안내하다 <small>명</small> 좌석 안내원

그는 그녀를 방으로 안내했다.

He _____ed her into the room.

19 complement
[kámpləmənt]

보완하다 <small>명</small> 보완물   ▶complementary <small>형</small> (상호) 보완적인

그녀와 그는 서로를 잘 보완한다.

She and he _____ each other well.

20 supplement
<small>동</small> [sʌ́pləmènt]
<small>명</small> [sʌ́pləmənt]

보충하다 <small>명</small> 보충(물), 부록   ▶supplemental <small>형</small> 보충의

그들은 부업을 해서 수입을 보충한다.

They _____ their incomes by doing extra jobs.

21 subsidize
[sʌ́bsədàiz]

보조금을 주다   ▶subsidy <small>명</small> 보조금

농업은 정부에 의해 보조금을 받는다.

Farming is _____d by the government.

22 rear
[riər]

기르다(=bring up, raise)
명 뒤(=back) 형 뒤의
곰이 감금 상태로 길러졌다.
The bear has been _____ed in captivity.

23 nurture
[nə́ːrtʃər]

양육[육성]하다 명 양육[육성]
네 속에 있는 잠재력을 육성해라.
_____ potential in yourself.

24 nourish
[nə́ːriʃ]

영양분을 공급하다 ▶nourishment 명 영양분[자양분]
그 크림은 피부에 영양분을 공급하는 비타민 A를 함유하고 있다.
The cream contains vitamin A to _____ the skin.

25 foster
[fɔ́ːstər]

❶ 육성[함양]하다 비교 adopt ❶ 입양하다 ❷ 채택하다
❷ 아이를 맡아 기르다
형 수양[위탁]의
그들은 맡아 기르던 아이를 입양했다.
They adopted a child they had been _____ing.

26 educate
[édʒukèit]

교육하다(=teach, instruct) ▶educated 형 교육받은, 교양 있는
▶education 명 교육
여러분은 마약의 위험에 대해 교육받아야 한다.
You must be _____d about the dangers of drugs.

27 facilitate
[fəsílətèit]

용이하게 하다[촉진하다] ▶facility 명 ❶ 시설 ❷ 재능
컴퓨터가 언어 습득을 용이하게 하기 위해 사용된다.
Computers are used to _____ language learning.

28 promote
[prəmóut]

❶ 촉진[고취]하다 ❷ 홍보하다 ▶promotion 명 승진, 홍보[판촉]
❸ 승진시키다
균형 잡힌 음식이 건강을 증진시킨다.
A balanced diet _____s good health.

29 motivate
[móutəvèit]

동기를 부여하다 ▶motivation 명 동기 부여
▶motive 명 동기
▶motivational 형 동기 부여의
훌륭한 선생님은 학생들에게 동기를 부여해 준다.
A good teacher _____s his/her students.

30 underpin
[ʌ̀ndərpín]

뒷받침하다[지지하다]
여러 이론들이 그의 교수법을 뒷받침한다.
Various theories _____ his teaching method.

Today's Dessert

He has the right to criticize who has the heart to help. – Abraham Lincoln

도와줄 마음이 있는 자만이 비판할 권리가 있다. – 링컨

Helping

TEST 39

A 밑줄 친 동사에 유의하여 우리말로!

1 to <u>sustain</u> life

2 to <u>preserve</u> your rights

3 to <u>conserve</u> resources

4 to <u>reserve</u> tickets

5 to <u>safeguard</u> the environment

6 to <u>insulate</u> a house

7 to <u>release</u> a prisoner

8 to <u>spare</u> the time

9 to <u>steer</u> the ship

10 to <u>supplement</u> your income

11 to <u>nurture</u> potential

12 to <u>nourish</u> the skin

13 to <u>educate</u> the public

14 to <u>promote</u> health

B 영영사전 뜻풀이에 알맞은 단어 찾기

보기 acquit   complement   rescue   subsidize   usher

1 _____ : to pay part of the cost of something

2 _____ : to save someone from a situation of danger

3 _____ : to make a good combination with something else

4 _____ : to help someone to get from one place to another

5 _____ : to decide in a court of law that someone is not guilty

C 빈칸에 가장 적절한 동사 넣기

보기 facilitate   liberate   maintain   motivate   rid   shield

1 Their armies _____(e)d the city. 그들의 군대가 그 도시를 해방시켰다.

2 Will science _____ us of cancers? 과학이 암으로부터 우리를 벗어나게 할 것인가?

3 I _____(e)d my eyes against the glare. 난 섬광을 막으려 내 눈을 가렸다.

4 Structured teaching _____(e)s learning. 조직화된 교육이 학습을 용이하게 하다.

5 He is _____(e)d entirely by self-interest. 그는 완전히 자기 이익에 의해서만 동기가 부여된다.

6 National galleries are _____(e)d at public expense.

국립 미술관은 공공 비용으로 유지된다.

D 밑줄 친 단어 뜻 구별하기

1 The couple <u>adopt</u>ed a child they had been <u>foster</u>ing.

2 She <u>rear</u>s three children alone.

There is a garden at the <u>rear</u> of the house.

3 He <u>accompanied</u> her on the trip.   He <u>accompanied</u> her on the guitar.

ANSWER_____

A 1. 생명을 <u>유지시키다</u> 2. 권리를 <u>보호하다</u> 3. 자원을 <u>보호하다</u> 4. 표를 예약하다 5. 환경을 <u>보호하다</u> 6. 집을 단열하다 7. 죄수를 석방하다 8. 시간을 내다 9. 배를 조종하다 10. 수입을 보충하다 11. 잠재력을 육성하다 12. 피부에 영양분을 공급하다 13. 대중을 교육하다 14. 건강을 증진하다 **B** 1. subsidize 2. rescue 3. complement 4. usher 5. acquit **C** 1. liberate 2. rid 3. shield 4. facilitate 5. motivate 6. maintain **D** 1. 그 커플은 맡아 기르던 아이를 입양했다.(입양하다, 아이를 맡아 기르다) 2. 그녀는 세 아이를 혼자 길렀다.(기르다) / 집 뒤에 정원이 있다.(뒤) 3. 그는 여행에 그녀와 동행했다.(동행하다) / 그는 기타로 그녀의 반주를 했다.(반주하다)

01 ban
[bæn]

금지하다(=prohibit, bar ↔ allow, permit)　명 금지(=prohibition)

그는 1년간 운전이 금지되었다.

He's been _____ned from driving for a year.

02 forbid
-forbade-forbidden
[fərbíd]

금지하다, 막다

그는 출국이 금지되었다.

He was _____ to leave the country.

03 outlaw
[áutlɔ̀ː]

불법화하다　명 범법자[도망자]

싱가포르는 껌을 씹는 걸 불법화하고 있다.

Singapore _____s chewing gum.

04 obstruct
[əbstrʌ́kt]

막다[방해하다]　　　　　　　▶obstruction 명 방해
(=block, bar, prevent)

그는 경찰 공무 집행 방해로 벌금에 처해졌다.

He was fined for _____ing the work of the police.

05 hinder
[híndər]

방해[저해]하다　　　　　　　▶hindrance 명 방해[저해]

그의 직업은 부상으로 방해를 받았다.

His career has been _____ed by injury.

06 disrupt
[dìsrʌ́pt]

방해하다[지장을 주다](=disturb)　▶disruption 명 지장
　　　　　　　　　　　　　　▶disruptive 형 지장을 주는

기후 변화가 농업 경제에 지장을 줄 수도 있다.

Climate change could _____ the agricultural economy.

07 intercept
[ìntərsépt]

가로채다[가로막다]

그의 전화 통화가 가로채여[도청되어] 왔다.

His phone calls had been _____ed.

08 interfere
[ìntərfíər]

간섭[방해]하다　　　　　　　▶interference 명 간섭[방해]

걱정은 아이들의 학업 성취에 방해가 될 수 있다.

Anxiety can _____ with children's performance at school.

09 intrude
[intrúːd]

침범하다, 방해하다　　　　　▶intrusion 명 침범
　　　　　　　　　　　　　　▶intruder 명 침입자

다른 사람들의 사생활을 침범해서는 안 된다.

You shouldn't _____ into the private lives of others.

10 invade
[invéid]

침략하다, 침해하다　　　　　▶invasion 명 침략, 침해
　　　　　　　　　　　　　　▶invader 명 침략자

한국은 여러 차례 침략을 당했다.

Korea has been _____d many times.

11 impair
[impέər]

해치다[손상시키다](= damage)　▶impairment 명 손상, 장애

그 병 때문에 그의 사고력이 손상되었다.

The illness _____ed his ability to think.

12 confine
[kənfáin]

❶ 한정하다(= restrict, limit)　▶confinement 명 감금
❷ 가두다　명 (-s) 한계[경계]　▶confined 형 한정된, 아주 좁은

우리의 논의를 해당 문제에만 한정하자.

Let's _____ our discussion to the matter in question.

13 restrain
[ristréin]

제지[억제]하다　▶restraint 명 제지[억제]

그는 폭력을 사용하지 못하도록 제지되어야 했다.

He had to be _____ed from using violence.

14 suppress
[səprés]

진압하다(= oppress),　▶suppression 명 진압, 억제
억누르다(= repress)

민중 봉기는 무자비하게 진압되었다.

The popular uprising was ruthlessly _____ed.

15 withhold
-withheld-withheld
[wiðhóuld]

주지 않다[보류하다]

당신은 일이 완료될 때까지 요금을 주지 않을 수 있다.

You can _____ the fee until the work is complete.

16 deter
[ditə́:r]

단념시키다[막다](= discourage)

보안 카메라는 사람들이 훔치는 걸 단념하게 하기 위해 설치되었다.

The security camera was installed to _____ people from stealing.

17 threaten
[θrétn]

협박[위협]하다　▶threat 명 협박[위협]

그들은 그가 자신들의 요구대로 하지 않으면 죽이겠다고 협박했다.

They _____ed to kill him unless he did as they asked.

18 menace
[ménis]

위협하다　명 위협, 골칫거리

코끼리가 밀렵꾼들에게 위협받고 있다.

The elephants are _____d by poachers.

19 bully
[búli]

(약자를) 못살게 굴다[위협하다]　명 못살게 구는 자

겁쟁이들은 흔히 약자를 못살게 군다.

Cowards often _____ the weaker.

20 abuse
동 [əbjú:z] 명 [əbjú:s]

❶ 학대하다 ❷ 오용[남용]하다(= misuse)
명 학대, 오용[남용], 욕설

그녀는 어린 시절 성적으로 학대당했다.

She was sexually _____d as a child.

21 exploit
[iksplɔ́it]

❶ 착취하다　▶exploitation 명 착취, 개발
❷ 개발하다, 활용하다

법은 고용주가 종업원들을 착취하지 못하도록 한다.

Laws stop employers from _____ing their employees.

22 persecute
[pə́ːrsikjùːt]

박해하다, 괴롭히다   ▶persecution 몡 박해

청교도들은 박해를 피해 영국을 떠났다.
The Puritans left England to escape being _____d.

23 torture
[tɔ́ːrtʃər]

고문하다
몡 고문

그 정권의 정적들은 고문당했다.
Political opponents of the regime were _____d.

24 distort
[distɔ́ːrt]

왜곡하다[일그러뜨리다]   ▶distortion 몡 왜곡[일그러뜨림]

언론인들이 사실을 왜곡한 죄로 고발되었다.
Journalists were accused of _____ing the facts.

25 contaminate
[kəntǽmənèit]

오염시키다(=pollute)   ▶contamination 몡 오염

식수가 오염되었다.
Drinking water has been _____d.

26 betray
[bitréi]

배신[배반]하다   ▶betrayal 몡 배신[배반]

그녀는 부모님의 신뢰를 배반했다.
She had _____ed her parents' trust.

27 assassinate
[əsǽsənèit]

암살하다   ▶assassination 몡 암살
                             ▶assassinator 몡 암살자

일부 귀빈들은 정치적인 행위로 암살당한다.
Some VIPs are _____d as a political act.

28 execute
[éksikjùːt]

❶ 처형하다   ▶execution 몡 처형, 실행[집행]
❷ 실행[집행]하다   ▶executive 몡 경영 간부[임원],
(=perform, implement)   (the ~) 행정부

수천 명이 정치범으로 처형되었다.
Thousands have been _____d for political crimes.

29 slaughter
[slɔ́ːtər]

도살하다, 대량 학살하다   ▶slaughterhouse 몡 도살장
(=butcher, massacre)

동물들은 도살장에서 도살된다.
The animals are _____ed in slaughterhouses.

30 strangle
[strǽŋgl]

목 졸라 죽이다[교살하다]

희생자는 벨트로 목이 졸려 죽었다.
The victim had been _____d with a belt.

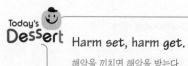

Today's Dessert

Harm set, harm get.
해악을 끼치면 해악을 받는다.

TEST 40

A 밑줄 친 동사에 유의하여 우리말로!

1 to <u>disrupt</u> the meeting
2 to <u>interfere</u> with your work
3 to <u>intrude</u> into the private life
4 to be <u>restrained</u> by police
5 to <u>suppress</u> the uprising
6 to <u>bully</u> the weaker
7 to <u>exploit</u> the poor
8 to <u>betray</u> your trust

B 영영사전 뜻풀이에 알맞은 동사 찾기

> 보기 assassinate   intercept   outlaw   slaughter   strangle   withhold

1 _____ : to murder an important person
2 _____ : to kill someone by pressing their throat
3 _____ : to kill an animal, especially for its meat
4 _____ : to refuse to give someone something
5 _____ : to completely stop something by making it illegal
6 _____ : to stop something before it gets a particular place

C 같은 관계 맺어주기

1 ban : prohibit = block : o_____
2 damage : impair = threaten : m_____
3 pollute : contaminate = restrict : c_____

D 빈칸에 가장 적절한 동사 넣기

> 보기 abuse   deter   forbid   hinder   invade

1 She was _____(e)d as a child. 그녀는 어린 시절 학대당했다.
2 Korea has been _____(e)d many times. 한국은 여러 차례 침략을 당했다.
3 The law _____(e)s racial or sexual discrimination. 법은 인종적·성적 차별을 금지한다.
4 It is not clear whether the death penalty _____(e)s crime.
  사형이 범죄를 단념시키는지는 불분명하다.
5 Parents' wealth may _____ rather than help their children.
  부모의 재산은 자식에게 도움이 되기보다는 방해가 될 수도 있다.

E 의미상 더 어울리는 동사 고르기

1 A young man was (distorted / tortured) to death. 한 젊은이가 고문을 당해 죽었다.
2 He was (executed / persecuted) for murder. 그는 살인죄로 처형되었다.

ANSWER

A 1. 회의를 방해하다 2. 일을 방해하다 3. 사생활을 침범하다 4. 경찰에 의해 제지되다 5. 봉기를 진압하다 6. 약자를 못살게 굴다 7. 가난한 사람들을 착취하다 8. 신뢰를 배반하다 **B** 1. assassinate 2. strangle 3. slaughter 4. withhold 5. outlaw 6. intercept **C** 1. obstruct 2. menace 3. confine **D** 1. abuse 2. invade 3. forbid 4. deter 5. hinder **E** 1. tortured 2. executed

Part 2

막는 · 해치는

01 cooperate
[kouápərèit]

협력[협조]하다

▶ cooperation 명 협력[협조]
▶ cooperative 형 협조적인, 협동의

우리는 다른 나라들과 협력해야 한다.
We should _____ with other countries.

02 collaborate
[kəlǽbərèit]

공동 작업[협력]하다

▶ collaboration 명 공동 작업
▶ collaborative 형 공동의

연구자들은 백신을 개발하기 위해 공동 작업하고 있다.
Researchers are _____ing to develop the vaccine.

03 contend
[kənténd]

❶ 경쟁하다[다투다](= compete) ❷ 주장하다

세 집단이 권력을 다투고 있다.
Three groups are _____ing for power.

04 confront
[kənfrʌ́nt]

닥치다(= face), 맞서다

▶ be confronted[faced] with
~에 직면하다
▶ confrontation 명 대립[대치]

그녀는 돈 문제에 직면했다.
She was _____ed with money problems.

05 cope
[koup]

(~ with) 대처[처리]하다(= manage)

당국은 주택 문제에 대처해야 한다.
The authorities have to _____ with the housing problems.

06 tackle
[tǽkl]

(문제와) 씨름하다[달려들다], 태클하다 명 태클

많은 학교가 약자 괴롭힘 문제와 씨름하고 있다.
Many schools are _____ing the problem of bullying.

07 mediate
[míːdièit]

중재하다

▶ mediation 명 중재
▶ mediator 명 중재자

그가 두 나라 사이의 평화 회담을 중재했다.
He _____d the peace talks between the two countries.

08 negotiate
[nigóuʃièit]

협상[교섭]하다

▶ negotiation 명 협상[교섭]

정부는 테러리스트들과 협상했다.
The government _____d with terrorists.

09 compromise
[kámprəmàiz]

타협하다 명 타협

구성원들이 타협할 때 결정이 내려질 수 있다.
A decision can be reached when the members _____.

10 reconcile
[rékənsàil]

조화시키다, 화해시키다

▶ reconciliation 명 화해, 조화

다른 관점을 조화시키기란 어렵다.
It's difficult to _____ different points of view.

11 regulate
[régjulèit]

규제[조절]하다   ▶regulation 뗑 규정[법규], 규제[조절]
엄격한 규정이 화학 물질의 사용을 규제한다.
Strict rules _____ the use of chemicals.

12 dominate
[dámənèit]

지배하다   ▶domination[dominance] 뗑 지배
                            ▶dominant 톙 지배적인
그 산업은 몇몇 다국적 기업에 의해 지배된다.
The industry is _____d by several multinational companies.

13 domesticate
[dəméstikèit]

길들이다   ▶domesticated 톙 길들여진, 가정적인
                         ▶domestic 톙 국내[가정]의
개는 길들여진 최초의 동물이었다.
Dogs were the first animals to be _____d.

14 tame
[teim]

길들이다 톙 길들여진(↔ wild)
아시아 코끼리는 길들여질 수 있다.
The Asian elephant can be _____d.

15 supervise
[sú:pərvàiz]

감독하다   ▶supervision 뗑 감독
                     ▶supervisor 뗑 감독관
그는 생산 팀을 감독한다.
He _____s a production team.

16 oversee
-oversaw-overseen
[òuvərsí:]

감독하다
그는 그 프로젝트를 감독하도록 임명되었다.
He was appointed to _____ the project.

17 appoint
[əpɔ́int]

임명[지명]하다(= delegate)   ▶appointment 뗑 임명, (만날) 약속
대법원장은 대통령이 임명한다.
The Chief Justice of the Supreme Court shall be _____ed by the President.

18 designate
[dézignèit]

❶ 지명[지정]하다   ▶designation 뗑 지명[지정]
❷ 표시[표기]하다
그는 팀장으로 지명되었다.
He has been _____d as team captain.

19 nominate
[námənèit]

지명[임명]하다   ▶nomination 뗑 지명[임명]
그녀는 최고의 여배우로 지명되었다.
She has been _____d as Best Actress.

20 recruit
[rikrú:t]

모집하다   ▶recruitment 뗑 모집
그들은 자격을 갖춘 직원들을 모집하고 있다.
They're _____ing qualified staff.

21 undertake
-undertook-undertaken
[ʌ̀ndərtéik]

❶ 착수하다   ❷ 약속하다
우리는 간단한 실험에 착수했다.
We _____ simple experiments.

22 comply
[kəmplái]

따르다　　　　　　　　　　▶compliance 명 준수

그는 그녀의 요구에 따랐다.

He ＿＿＿＿＿ied with her request.

23 conform
[kənfɔ́ːrm]

따르다　　　　　　　　　　▶conformity 명 순응

학생들은 교칙에 따르도록 요구된다.

Students are required to ＿＿＿＿＿ to school rules.

24 assimilate
[əsíməlèit]

동화하다, 소화[흡수]하다　　▶assimilation 명 동화, 흡수

이민자들은 그 나라에 동화하려고 노력해야 한다.

Immigrants should try to ＿＿＿＿＿ into the country.

25 violate
[váiəlèit]

위반하다(=break), 침해하다　▶violation 명 위반, 침해

규칙을 위반한 학생들은 벌을 받게 될 것이다.

Students who ＿＿＿＿＿ the rules will be punished.

26 disobey
[dìsəbéi]

불복종하다(↔obey)　　　　▶disobedience 명 불복종
　　　　　　　　　　　　　▶disobedient 형 불복종하는
　　　　　　　　　　　　　▶obey 따르다[순종]하다

그는 명령 불복종으로 처벌받았다.

He was punished for ＿＿＿＿＿ing orders.

27 defy
[difái]

반항[저항]하다　　　　　　▶defiance 명 반항[저항]

몇몇 아이들은 선생님들에게 반항한다.

A few children ＿＿＿＿＿ their teachers.

28 rebel
동[ribél] 명[rébəl]

반항하다　　　　　　　　　▶rebellion 명 반란
명 반역자[반항아]　　　　　▶rebellious 형 반항[반란]의

십 대는 권위에 반항하는 경향이 있다.

Teenagers tend to ＿＿＿＿＿ against authority.

29 disregard
[dìsrigáːrd]

무시하다(=ignore)　　　　▶regard 여기다[간주하다]

그는 나의 조언을 완전히 무시했다.

He totally ＿＿＿＿＿ed my advice.

30 overlook
[òuvərlúk]

❶ 간과하다(=miss, neglect)　❷ 눈감아 주다　❸ 내려다보다(=look over)

넌 중요한 사실 하나를 간과했다.

You have ＿＿＿＿＿ed one key fact.

Today's Dessert

Be kind, for everyone you meet is fighting a harder battle. – Plato

친절해라. 네가 만나는 누구나 힘든 전투에서 싸우고 있는 중이기 때문이다. – 플라톤

TEST 41

A 밑줄 친 동사에 유의하여 우리말로!

1 to <u>cooperate</u> with each other

2 to <u>cope</u> with the problem

3 to <u>negotiate</u> with terrorists

4 to <u>compromise</u> with your enemy

5 to <u>reconcile</u> differences

6 to <u>recruit</u> staff

7 to <u>undertake</u> an experiment

8 to <u>comply</u> with regulations

9 to <u>conform</u> to school rules

10 to <u>assimilate</u> new ideas

B 영영사전 뜻풀이에 알맞은 동사 찾기

> **보기** appoint　dominate　mediate　rebel　violate

1 _____ : to control someone or something

2 _____ : to disobey or do something against a law

3 _____ : to choose someone for a position or a job

4 _____ : to try to end a quarrel between two groups

5 _____ : to fight against or refuse to obey an authority

C 같은 관계 맺어주기

1 domesticate : tame = supervise : o_____

2 face : confront = ignore : d_____

D 빈칸에 가장 적절한 동사 넣기

> **보기** collaborate　contend　defy　nominate　regulate

1 He was _____(e)d as Best Actor. 그는 최고의 배우로 지명되었다.

2 The groups are _____ing for power. 집단들이 권력을 잡으려고 경쟁하고 있다.

3 A few children _____(e)d their teacher. 몇몇 아이들이 선생님에게 반항했다.

4 They _____ to develop the vaccine. 그들은 백신을 개발하기 위해 공동 작업한다.

5 Rules _____ the use of chemicals in food. 규정상 식품에 화학 물질을 사용하는 것을 규제한다.

E 밑줄 친 단어 뜻 구별하기

1 He has been <u>designated</u> as team captain.

　Buildings are <u>designated</u> by red squares on the map.

2 You <u>overlook</u>ed one key fact.　　The room <u>overlook</u>s the ocean.

영 사회적 상호 작용

Part 2

ANSWER

A 1. 서로 협력하다 2. 문제에 대처하다 3. 테러리스트와 협상하다 4. 적과 타협하다 5. 차이를 조화시키다 6. 직원을 모집하다 7. 실험을 착수하다 8. 규정에 따르다 9. 교칙에 따르다 10. 새로운 생각을 흡수하다 **B** 1. dominate 2. violate 3. appoint 4. mediate 5. rebel **C** 1. oversee 2. disregard **D** 1. nominate 2. contend 3. defy(defied) 4. collaborate 5. regulate **E** 1. 그는 팀장으로 지명되었다.(지명하다) / 건물은 지도에서 빨간색 정사각형으로 표시된다.(표시하다) 2. 넌 중요한 사실 하나를 간과했다.(간과하다) / 방에서 바다가 내려다보인다.(내려다보다)

01 convey
[kənvéi]

❶ 전(달)하다(=communicate) ▶conveyor (belt) 몡 컨베이어 벨트
❷ 나르다(=transport)

광고는 마른 게 아름답다는 메시지를 전한다.
Ads _____ the message that thin is beautiful.

02 correspond
[kɔ̀:rəspánd]

❶ 소식을 주고받다 ▶correspondence 몡 서신 (왕래), 관련성
❷ 일치하다[해당하다] ▶correspondent 몡 통신원
  ▶corresponding 혱 상응하는

그녀는 선생님과 소식을 주고받는다.
She _____s with her teacher.

03 converse
[kənvə́:rs]

대화하다 몡혱 반대[역](의) ▶conversation 몡 대화

난 외국인들과 대화하고 싶어.
I want to _____ with foreigners.

04 chatter
[tʃǽtər]

재잘거리다, 지저귀다 ▶chat 잡담하다 몡 잡담
몡 수다 ▶chatty 혱 수다스러운

그녀는 어린애처럼 흥분해서 재잘거렸다.
She _____ed excitedly like a child.

05 gossip
[gásəp]

(남의 사생활에 대해) 잡담하다 몡 (남의 사생활) 잡담

다른 사람들의 사생활에 대해 잡담하기를 피해라.
Avoid _____ing about other people.

06 utter
[ʌ́tər]

말하다, 소리를 내다 ▶utterly 및 완전히
혱 완전한(=absolute)

그는 한마디 말도 하지 않고 고개를 끄덕였다.
He nodded without _____ing a word.

07 pronounce
[prənáuns]

❶ 발음하다 ❷ 선언[선고]하다 ▶pronunciation 몡 발음
  ▶mispronounce 잘못 발음하다

그는 'rice(쌀)'를 'lice(곤충 '이'의 복수)'로 발음했다.
He _____d rice as lice.

08 proclaim
[proukléim]

선언[선포]하다 ▶proclamation 몡 선언[선포]
(=declare, announce)

대통령이 공화국의 독립을 선언했다.
The President _____ed the republic's independence.

09 convict
[kənvíkt]

유죄 판결[선고]을 하다(↔acquit) ▶conviction 몡 ❶ 신념[확신] ❷ 유죄 판결
몡 기결수

그녀는 상점에서 물건을 훔친 죄로 유죄를 선고받았다.
She was _____ed of shoplifting.

10 affirm
[əfə́:rm]

단언하다(=confirm) ▶affirmative 혱 긍정의 몡 긍정

그는 그 소식이 사실이라고 단언했다.
He _____ed that the news was true.

11 assert
[əsə́:rt]

단언[주장]하다(= declare)
▶ assertion 명 단언[주장]
▶ assertive 형 자신감 있는[확신에 찬]

난 한국 음식이 세계 최고라고 단언한다.
I _____ Korean food is the best in the world.

12 narrate
[nǽreit]

내레이션을 하다[해설하다], 이야기하다[서술하다](= relate)
▶ narration 명 해설, 서술
▶ narrator 명 내레이터[해설자]

유명한 배우가 해설하는 다큐멘터리
a documentary _____d by a famous actor

13 depict
[dipíkt]

묘사하다(= describe)
▶ depiction 명 묘사

그 책은 정보화 시대의 삶을 묘사한다.
The book _____s life in the Information Age.

14 portray
[pɔːrtréi]

묘사하다[그리다]
▶ portrait 명 초상화

그 영화는 예수를 인간으로 묘사한다.
The film _____s Jesus as a kind of man.

15 characterize
[kǽriktəràiz]

특징짓다
▶ characterization 명 성격 묘사
▶ characteristic 명 특징 형 특유의

형제애는 배타성이 없는 것으로 특징지어진다.
Brotherly love is _____d by its lack of exclusiveness.

16 clarify
[klǽrəfài]

분명히 하다
▶ clarification 명 설명
▶ clarity 명 명확성

제게 한두 가지만 분명히 해 주시겠습니까?
Could you _____ one or two points for me?

17 specify
[spésəfài]

명시하다
▶ specific 형 특정한, 구체적인
▶ specifically 부 구체적으로, 특별히
▶ specification 명 설명서

필요한 수를 명시해 주세요. Please _____ the number needed.

18 exemplify
[igzémpləfài]

좋은 예가 되다, 예를 들다
▶ example 명 예

동물은 인간의 특성을 보여 주는 좋은 예가 될 수 있다.
Animals can _____ human characteristics.

19 certify
[sə́:rtəfài]

증명[인증]하다
▶ certificate 명 증명서, 자격증
▶ certification 명 인증(서)[자격증]

회계 보고서는 감사에 의해 인증되었다.
The accounts were _____ied by an auditor.

20 testify
[téstəfài]

증언하다, 증명하다
▶ testimony 명 증언, 증거

그녀는 재판에서 증언하기로 동의했다.
She has agreed to _____ at the trial.

21 demonstrate
[démənstrèit]

❶ 입증하다, 시범을 보이다
 (= show, prove, display)
❷ 시위하다(= protest)
▶ demonstration 명 시위, 시범 설명
▶ demonstrative 형 감정을 드러내는

지구가 태양 주위를 돈다는 걸 입증하라.
_____ that the Earth goes round the Sun.

22 manifest
[mǽnəfèst]

드러내다[나타내다]
혱 명백한

고산병은 두통과 피로로 나타난다.
Mountain sickness is _____ed as headache and tiredness.

23 disclose
[disklóuz]

공개하다, 드러내다
(= reveal ↔ conceal)

▶ disclosure 혱 공개

그들은 거래의 세부 내용을 공개하지 않았다.
They didn't _____ details of the transaction.

24 signify
[sígnəfài]

나타내다[의미하다]
(= indicate, signal)

▶ significant 혱 중대한, 의미 있는
▶ significance 혱 중대성, 의미

사자의 이미지는 권력을 나타낸다.
The image of the lion _____ies power.

25 notify
[nóutəfài]

통지[신고]하다(= inform)

▶ notification 혱 통지[신고]

그 결정에 대해 통지를 받았니?
Have you been _____ied of the decision?

26 foretell
-foretold-foretold
[fɔːrtél]

예언하다(= predict, forecast, foresee)

난 미래를 예언할 수 없다.
I cannot _____ the future.

27 prophesy
[práfəsài]

예언하다

▶ prophecy 혱 예언
▶ prophet 혱 예언자

그는 홍수가 땅을 덮을 것이라고 예언했다.
He _____ied that a flood would cover the earth.

28 pledge
[pledʒ]

서약[맹세]하다(= promise, swear)
혱 서약[맹세](= oath)

한국은 난민 지원 사업을 위해 유엔에 100만 달러를 서약했다.
Korea has _____d $1 million to the UN for refugee work.

29 vow
[vau]

맹세[서약]하다 혱 맹세[서약]

난 다시는 담배를 피우지 않겠다고 맹세했다.
I _____ed that I would never smoke again.

30 insure
[inʃúər]

❶ 보장하다[확실히 하다]
(= ensure, make sure)
❷ 보험에 들다

▶ insurance 혱 보험
▶ insurer 혱 보험업자[보험 회사]

우리는 자전거 타는 사람들의 안전을 보장할 수 있는 시설이 필요하다.
We need facilities to _____ the safety of cyclists.

Today's Dessert

Information is giving out. Communication is getting through.

정보는 나누어 주는 것이고, 커뮤니케이션은 서로 통하는 것이다.

TEST 42

A 밑줄 친 동사에 유의하여 우리말로!

1 to <u>convey</u> the message

2 to <u>converse</u> with people

3 to <u>utter</u> a word

4 to <u>proclaim</u> independence

5 to <u>clarify</u> issues

6 to <u>certify</u> the contract

7 to <u>testify</u> at the trial

8 to <u>manifest</u> interest

9 to <u>disclose</u> details

10 to <u>insure</u> the safety

B 영영사전 뜻풀이에 알맞은 동사 찾기

| 보기 | chatter   convict   gossip   pledge   specify |

1 _____ : to state something in an exact and detailed way

2 _____ : to talk quickly in a friendly way without stopping

3 _____ : to decide in a court of law that someone is guilty

4 _____ : to make a formal promise that you will do something

5 _____ : to talk about other people's behavior and private lives

C 같은 관계 맺어주기

1 affirm : assert = foretell : p_____

2 pronounce : declare = depict : p_____

3 narrate : narration = pronounce : p_____

D 빈칸에 가장 적절한 동사 넣기

| 보기 | characterize   demonstrate   notify   signify   vow |

1 We _____(e)d against the war. 우리는 반전 시위를 했다.

2 Bright colours _____ his paintings. 밝은 색은 그의 그림의 특징이다.

3 I _____(e)d that I would never smoke. 난 담배를 피우지 않겠다고 맹세했다.

4 Have you been _____(e)d of the decision? 그 결정에 대해 통지받았니?

5 All those in favor please _____ by saying "Aye."
찬성하는 분은 '네[찬성]'라고 나타내 주세요.

E 밑줄 친 단어 뜻 구별하기

I <u>correspond</u> with her regularly.

Your account of events does not <u>correspond</u> with hers.

소통 1

Part 2

ANSWER

A 1. 메시지를 전하다 2. 사람들과 대화하다 3. 한마디 말하다 4. 독립을 선언하다 5. 문제를 분명히 하다 6. 계약서를 인증하다 7. 재판에서 증언하다 8. 관심을 드러내다 9. 세부 내용을 공개하다 10. 안전을 보장하다 **B** 1. specify 2. chatter 3. convict 4. pledge 5. gossip **C** 1. prophesy 2. portray 3. pronunciation **D** 1. demonstrate 2. characterize 3. vow 4. notify(notified) 5. signify **E** 난 그녀와 정기적으로 소식을 주고받는다.(소식을 주고받다) / 사건에 대한 너의 설명은 그녀의 것과 일치하지 않는다.(일치하다)

01 **assent**
[əsént]

찬성[동의]하다(=agree) 명 찬성[동의](=agreement)

투표자들은 그 제안에 찬성했다.

Voters _____ed to the proposal.

02 **consent**
[kənsént]

허락[동의]하다 명 허락[동의]

그녀의 아버지는 마지못해 결혼을 허락했다.

Her father reluctantly _____ed to the marriage.

03 **concur**
[kənkə́:r]

동의하다

"바로 내 의견이야."라고 그가 동의했다.

"My opinion exactly," he _____red.

04 **accord**
[əkɔ́:rd]

❶ 부여하다 ❷ (~ with) 일치하다 ▶according to ~에 따라[따르면]
명 합의 ▶in accordance with ~에 따라

처벌은 징계 규정과 일치한다.

Punishments _____ with the code of discipline.

05 **acknowledge**
[əknɑ́lidʒ]

❶ 인정하다(=admit, recognize) ❷ 감사를 표하다
❸ 받았음을 알리다

우리는 변화의 필요성을 인정한다.

We _____ the need for change.

06 **concede**
[kənsí:d]

인정하다

난 많은 실수를 했다는 걸 인정했다.

I _____d that I had made a number of errors.

07 **confess**
[kənfés]

자백[고백]하다, 인정하다 ▶confession 명 자백[고백], 인정

그는 21명을 죽였다고 자백했다.

He _____ed that he had killed twenty-one persons.

08 **oppose**
[əpóuz]

반대하다(=be against) ▶opposition 명 반대
▶opponent 명 상대, 반대자

교회는 동성 간의 결혼을 반대한다.

The Church _____s same-sex marriage.

09 **dissent**
[disént]

반대하다[이의를 제기하다] 명 반대(=opposition)

동의(動議)에 이의를 제기하고 싶은 누구든지 지금 손을 들어야 한다.

Anyone wishing to _____ from the motion should now raise their hand.

10 **dispute**
[dispjú:t]

반박하다, 다투다 명 분쟁[논란]

여행이 마음을 넓어지게 한다는 사실을 반박할 사람은 거의 없을 것이다.

Few would _____ that travel broadens the mind.

11 contradict
[kàntrədíkt]

❶ 반박하다 ❷ 모순되다

▶contradiction 몡 모순, 반박
▶contradictory 혱 모순되는

그 연구는 통속적인 미신들을 반박한다.
The research _____ s popular superstitions.

12 grumble
[grʌ́mbl]

투덜거리다(=moan)

농부들은 늘 날씨에 대해 투덜거린다.
Farmers are always _____ ing about the weather.

13 induce
[indʒúːs]

설득[유도]하다(=persuade), 유발하다

아무것도 나를 그에게 투표하도록 설득하지 못할 것이다.
Nothing would _____ me to vote for him.

14 enlist
[inlíst]

❶ 도움을 얻다 ❷ 입대하다

그는 친구들의 도움을 얻었다.
He _____ ed the help of his friends.

15 urge
[əːrdʒ]

촉구하다, 몰아대다
몡 충동(=desire)

▶urgent 혱 긴급한
▶urgency 몡 긴급

우리는 당신들에게 열대 우림을 파괴하는 걸 중단하라고 촉구한다.
We _____ you to stop destroying rain forests.

16 advocate
통 [ǽdvəkèit]
몡 [ǽdvəkət]

지지[옹호]하다 몡 지지[옹호]자

▶advocacy 몡 지지[옹호]

극단주의자들은 공공연히 폭력을 옹호한다.
Extremists openly _____ violence.

17 preach
[priːtʃ]

설교하다

엄마, 설교 좀 그만 하세요. 저도 자신을 돌볼 만큼 컸어요.
Mom, stop _____ ing – I'm old enough to take care of myself.

18 caution
[kɔ́ːʃən]

경고하다[주의를 주다](=warn)
몡 조심[주의/경고]

▶cautious 혱 조심스러운[신중한]
▶precaution 몡 예방책

난 그녀에게 위험을 피하도록 주의를 주었다.
I _____ ed her to avoid dangers.

19 compel
[kəmpél]

강요[강제]하다

▶compelling 혱 강렬한[강력한]
▶compulsion 몡 강요, 강박 충동
▶compulsive 혱 강박적인

법은 고용주가 의료 보험을 제공하도록 강제한다.
The law _____ s employers to provide health insurance.

20 enforce
[infɔ́ːrs]

❶ 집행[시행]하다
❷ 강요[강제]하다

▶force 강요[강제]하다 몡 힘

선생님들은 종종 학생들에게 규율을 강요한다.
Teachers often _____ discipline on their students.

21 oblige
[əbláidʒ]

❶ 강요[강제]하다 ❷ 돕다

▶be obliged to V ~해야 하다
▶obligation 몡 의무

부모들은 자녀를 학교에 보내도록 법으로 강제된다.
Parents are _____ d by law to send their children to school.

소통 2

Part 2

22 exclaim
[ikskléim]

외치다[소리치다](=cry)　　　　▶exclamation 몡 외침

"안 돼!" 그녀가 놀라 소리쳤다.

"No!" she _____ed in shock.

23 chant
[tʃænt]

구호를 외치다[성가를 부르다]
몡 구호[성가]

시위자들은 반정부 구호를 외쳤다.

Protesters _____ed anti-government slogans.

24 mumble
[mʌ́mbl]

중얼거리다(=murmur, mutter)

그는 혼자 중얼거리고 있었다.

He was _____ing to himself.

25 stammer
[stǽmər]

말을 더듬다

그는 화가 날 때마다 말을 좀 더듬는다.

Whenever he is angry, he _____s slightly.

26 brag
[bræg]

자랑하다[뽐내다](=boast)

그는 늘 자신의 돈에 대해 자랑한다.

He's always _____ging about his money.

27 exaggerate
[igzǽdʒərèit]

과장하다　　　　▶exaggeration 몡 과장

그는 어려움을 과장하는 경향이 있다.

He tends to _____ the difficulties.

28 publicize
[pʌ́bləsàiz]

홍보[광고]하다, 알리다　　　　▶publicity 몡 홍보[광고](업), 매스컴의 관심
　　　　▶publicist 몡 홍보 담당자

그 자선 단체의 활동이 대중 매체를 통해 홍보되었다.

The work of the charity has been _____d throughout the media.

29 cite
[sait]

예로 들다, 인용하다　　　　비교 recite 암송하다, 열거하다
　　　　▶citation 몡 인용(문), 표창장

한국은 흔히 떠오르는 정보 기술 강국의 예로 들어진다.

Korea is often _____d as an example of a rising IT power.

30 quote
[kwout]

인용하다　　　　▶quotation 몡 인용(문), 견적
몡 인용, 견적(=estimate)

그는 성경에서 짧은 글 하나를 인용했다.

He _____d a short passage from the Bible.

Today's
Dessert

One of the most important things in communication is to hear what is not being said. – Peter Drucker

커뮤니케이션에서 가장 중요한 것 중 하나는 말해지고 있지 않은 것을 듣는 것이다. – 피터 드러커

A 밑줄 친 동사에 유의하여 우리말로!

1 to <u>consent</u> to the marriage

2 to <u>concur</u> with the view

3 to <u>confess</u> to a crime

4 to <u>dissent</u> from the decision

5 to <u>contradict</u> their claims

6 to <u>enlist</u> your help

7 to <u>advocate</u> peace

8 to <u>preach</u> a sermon

9 to <u>chant</u> slogans

10 to <u>exaggerate</u> the difficulties

11 to <u>publicize</u> the issue

12 to <u>quote</u> a passage

B 영영사전 뜻풀이에 알맞은 동사 찾기

보기 compel   dispute   exclaim   grumble   mumble   stammer

1 _____ : to speak or say very quietly

2 _____ : to force someone to do something

3 _____ : to say something suddenly and loudly

4 _____ : to keep complaining in an unhappy way

5 _____ : to say that something is not correct or true

6 _____ : to speak with a lot of pauses and repeated sounds

C 같은 관계 맺어주기

1 agree : assent = boast : b_____

2 persuade : induce = warn : c_____

D 빈칸에 가장 적절한 동사 넣기

보기 cite   concede   oblige   oppose   urge

1 She _____(e)d him to stay. 그녀는 그에게 머무를 것을 강하게 권유했다.

2 I _____ that I made an error. 난 실수를 했다는 걸 인정한다.

3 Most major papers _____ social reform. 대부분의 주요 신문들은 사회 개혁을 반대한다.

4 I was _____(e)d to comply with his request. 난 그의 요구에 따라야 했다.

5 She _____(e)d three reasons why people get into debt.

그녀는 사람들이 빚지게 되는 세 가지 이유를 예로 들었다.

E 밑줄 친 단어 뜻 구별하기

Please <u>acknowledge</u> receipt of this mail.

We should <u>acknowledge</u> the need for change.

ANSWER_____

A 1. 결혼을 허락하다 2. 그 견해에 동의하다 3.범죄를 자백하다 4. 그 결정에 이의를 제기하다 5. 그들의 주장을 반박하다 6. 너의 도움을 얻다 7. 평화를 지지하다 8. 설교하다 9. 구호를 외치다 10. 어려움을 과장하다 11. 문제를 홍보하다 12. 글귀를 인용하다 B 1. mumble 2. compel 3. exclaim 4. grumble 5. dispute 6. stammer C 1. brag 2. caution D 1. urge 2. concede 3. oppose 4. oblige 5. cite E 이 메일을 받았는지 알려주세요.(받았음을 알리다) / 우리는 변화의 필요성을 인정해야 한다.(인정하다)

01 amuse
[əmjúːz]

즐겁게[재미있게] 하다

▶amusement 몡 즐거움[재미], 오락
▶amused 혱 재미있어[즐거워] 하는
▶amusing 혱 재미있는[즐거운]

그는 아이들을 즐겁게 하려고 우스운 표정을 지었다.
He made funny faces to _____ the children.

02 entertain
[èntərtéin]

❶ 즐겁게[재미있게] 하다
❷ 대접하다

▶entertainment 몡 오락(물), 대접
▶entertaining 혱 재미있는[즐거운]
▶entertainer 몡 연예인

그녀는 춤으로 아이들을 즐겁게 했다.
She _____ed the children with dances.

03 enchant
[intʃǽnt]

매혹하다, 마법을 걸다

▶enchanted 혱 매혹된
▶enchanting 혱 매혹적인

난 그녀가 웃는 모습에 매혹되었다.
I was _____ed by the way she smiled.

04 fascinate
[fǽsənèit]

매혹하다

▶fascination 몡 매혹
▶fascinated 혱 매혹된
▶fascinating 혱 매혹적인

과학은 늘 날 매혹시켜 왔다. Science has always _____d me.

05 captivate
[kǽptəvèit]

매혹하다

▶captivating 혱 매혹적인
▶captive 혱 사로잡힌 몡 포로

그는 그녀의 아름다움에 매혹되었다. He was _____d by her beauty.

06 dazzle
[dǽzl]

❶ 눈부시게 하다
❷ 경탄하게 하다

▶dazzling 혱 눈부신

그녀는 그의 매력에 경탄했다. She was _____d by his charm.

07 tempt
[tempt]

유혹하다[부추기다]

▶temptation 몡 유혹
▶tempting 혱 유혹하는

빨리 재산을 모으는 데 유혹되지 마라.
Don't be _____ed into making a quick fortune.

08 lure
[luər]

유인[유혹]하다 몡 미끼

컴퓨터 게임이 젊은이들을 공부에서 멀어지도록 유혹하고 있다.
Computer games are _____ing youngsters away from their lessons.

09 arouse
[əráuz]

불러일으키다[자극하다],
깨우다(=awaken)

비교 arise 발생하다[일어나다]

그의 행동은 우리의 관심을 불러일으켰다.
His behavior _____d our interest.

10 evoke
[ivóuk]

불러일으키다

그의 외모는 동정심을 불러일으킨다.

His appearance _____s sympathy.

11 inspire
[inspáiər]

고무[격려]하다(=encourage),
영감을 주다

▶inspiration 명 영감
▶inspired 형 영감을 받은[훌륭한]
▶inspiring 형 고무[격려]하는

우리는 팀을 고무시킬 수 있는 지도자가 필요하다.

We need a leader who can _____ the team.

12 stimulate
[stímjulèit]

자극[격려]하다

▶stimulation 명 자극[격려]
▶stimulus(복수 stimuli) 명 자극(제)

격려하는 선생님은 학생들을 성공하도록 자극할 수 있다.

An inspiring teacher can _____ students to succeed.

13 refresh
[rifréʃ]

생기를 되찾게[상쾌하게] 하다

▶refreshed 형 상쾌한
▶refreshing 형 신선한
▶refreshment 명 다과, 음식물, 원기 회복

샤워가 너를 상쾌하게 할 거야. A shower will _____ you.

14 lull
[lʌl]

진정시키다[재우다], (거짓으로) 안심시키다

차의 움직임이 그녀를 잠들게 했다.

The motion of the car _____ed her to sleep.

15 soothe
[su:ð]

진정시키다[달래다]

그녀는 아기를 안고 흔들어 달랬다.

She _____d the baby by rocking it in her arms.

16 sympathize
[símpəθàiz]

(~ with) ❶ 동정하다
❷ 공감하다(=empathize)

▶sympathy 명 동정, 공감
▶sympathetic 형 동정적인, 공감하는

나는 사랑하는 이를 잃은 사람들을 동정한다.

I _____ with those who have lost loved ones.

17 esteem
[istí:m]

존경[존중]하다(=respect, admire)
명 존경[존중]

▶self-esteem 명 자존[자부]심

너 자신보다 다른 사람들을 더 존중하라.

_____ others more than yourselves.

18 adore
[ədɔ́:r]

매우 사랑하다

▶adoration 명 흠모
▶adorable 형 사랑스러운

그녀는 모든 시를 매우 좋아한다. She _____s all poetry.

19 worship
[wə́:rʃip]

예배[숭배]하다 명 예배[숭배]

그들은 모두 같은 신을 숭배한다. They all _____ the same god.

20 idolize
[áidəlàiz]

우상화하다[숭배하다]

▶idol 명 우상

어린 시절 그는 아버지를 우상화했다. As a child, he _____d his father.

21 marvel
[máːrvəl]

경이로워하다[경탄하다]   ▶marvelous 혱 경탄할 만한[멋진]
몡 경이(=wonder, miracle)   (=wonderful)
난 우리에 대한 어머니의 사랑에 경탄한다.
I _____ at my mother's love for us.

22 long
[lɔ(ː)ŋ]

열망[갈망]하다   ▶longing 몡 열망[갈망]
혱 긴 閉 오래
그는 그녀를 다시 만나기를 열망했다.
He _____ed to see her again.

23 yearn
[jəːrn]

갈망[동경]하다   ▶yearning 몡 갈망[동경]
우리는 모두 평화를 갈망한다.
We all _____ for peace.

24 crave
[kreiv]

갈망[열망]하다   ▶craving 몡 갈망[열망]
그녀는 돌봄을 갈망하는 불안정한 어린애다.
She's an insecure child who _____s attention.

25 aspire
[əspáiər]

열망[염원]하다   ▶aspiration 몡 열망[포부](=ambition)
명성을 열망하는 사람들은 그것을 거의 얻지 못한다.
Few people who _____ to fame ever achieve it.

26 detest
[ditést]

몹시 싫어하다[혐오하다]
난 생명에 대한 어떤 형태의 잔인함도 혐오한다.
I _____ any form of cruelty toward life.

27 loathe
[louð]

몹시 싫어하다[혐오하다]
난 정말 쇼핑을 몹시 싫어한다.
I absolutely _____ shopping.

28 deplore
[diplɔ́ːr]

개탄[비난]하다
우리는 무고한 사람들에 대한 폭력의 사용을 개탄한다.
We _____ the use of violence against innocent people.

29 despise
[dispáiz]

경멸하다(=look down (up)on)
난 세습되는 부와 사회 계급을 경멸한다.
I _____ inherited wealth and social class.

30 scorn
[skɔːrn]

경멸하다   ▶scornful 혱 경멸하는
몡 경멸(=contempt, disrespect)
어떤 여성들은 화장품 사용을 경멸한다.
Some women _____ the use of make-up.

Today's Dessert

Love the sinner but hate the sin. – Mahatma Gandhi

죄인은 사랑하되, 죄악은 혐오하라. – 간디

감정 1 Part 2

TEST 44

A 밑줄 친 동사에 유의하여 우리말로!

1 to amuse children
2 to arouse curiosity
3 to evoke sympathy
4 to inspire the team
5 to stimulate interest

6 to soothe the baby
7 to esteem others
8 to worship God
9 to idolize your father
10 to loathe politics

B 영영사전 뜻풀이에 알맞은 동사 찾기

> 보기   adore   deplore   lull   refresh

1 _____ : to cause to feel sleepy, calm or safe
2 _____ : to say or think that something is very bad
3 _____ : to make someone feel less tired or less hot
4 _____ : to love someone very much and feel proud of them

C 빈칸에 가장 적절한 동사 넣기

> 보기   aspire   dazzle   despise   tempt

1 I was _____(e)d to skip class. 난 수업을 빼먹으라는 유혹을 받았다.
2 I _____ inherited wealth and social class. 난 세습되는 부와 계급을 경멸한다.
3 He was _____(e)d by the warmth of her smile. 그는 그녀의 미소의 따뜻함에 경탄했다.
4 Few people who _____ to fame ever achieve it.
   명성을 열망하는 사람들은 그것을 거의 얻지 못한다.

D 다른 동사들과 의미가 가장 다른 하나는?

1 ① captivate   ② charm   ③ enchant   ④ entertain   ⑤ fascinate
2 ① crave   ② desire   ③ marvel   ④ long   ⑤ yearn

E 빈칸에 가장 적절한 동사 넣기

> 보기   detest   lure   scorn   sympathize

1 I _____ any form of violence. 난 어떤 형태의 폭력도 혐오한다.
2 The public _____(e)d with their strike. 대중은 그들의 파업에 공감했다.
3 She _____(e)d his views as old-fashioned. 그녀는 그의 견해를 구식이라고 경멸했다.
4 We are _____(e)d into buying things by advertising.
   우리는 광고에 의해 물건을 사도록 유혹된다.

ANSWER

A 1. 아이들을 즐겁게 하다 2. 호기심을 자극하다 3. 동정심을 불러일으키다 4. 팀을 고무시키다 5. 관심을 자극하다 6. 아기를 달래다 7. 다른 사람들을 존중하다 8. 신을 숭배하다 9. 아버지를 우상화하다 10. 정치를 혐오하다   **B** 1. lull 2. deplore 3. refresh 4. adore   **C** 1. tempt 2. despise 3. dazzle 4. aspire   **D** 1. ④ 2. ③   **E** 1. detest 2. sympathize 3. scorn 4. lure

감정 1

Part 2

01 irritate
[íritèit]

짜증나게 하다(=annoy)
▶ irritation 명 짜증
▶ irritated 형 짜증난
▶ irritating 형 짜증나게 하는

그가 집안일을 돕지 않을 때 날 정말 짜증나게 한다.
It really _____s me when he doesn't help around the house.

02 distress
[distrés]

괴롭히다(=upset) 명 고통, 곤궁, 조난
자신을 괴롭히지 마. Don't _____ yourself.

03 afflict
[əflíkt]

괴롭히다[피해를 입히다]
관절염은 남성보다 여성을 더 괴롭히는 질병이다.
Arthritis is an illness which _____s women more than men.

04 harass
[hərǽs]

괴롭히다[희롱하다]
▶ harassment 명 괴롭힘[희롱]

그녀는 그에게 성희롱을 당했다고 주장했다.
She claimed that she had been sexually _____ed by him.

05 torment
[tɔːrmént]

괴롭히다[학대하다](= torture) 명 심한 고통
그녀는 죄책감으로 괴로워했다.
She was _____ed by feelings of guilt.

06 tease
[tiːz]

놀리다 명 놀림
맘 상해하지 마. 난 단지 놀렸을 뿐인데.
Don't get upset. I was only _____ing.

07 disgust
[disgʌ́st]

역겹게[혐오스럽게] 하다
▶ disgusting 형 역겨운[혐오스러운]
명 역겨움[혐오]

우리는 그 영화의 폭력이 혐오스러웠다.
We were _____ed by violence in the film.

08 discourage
[diskə́ːridʒ]

좌절시키다, 막다[단념시키다]
(↔ encourage)
▶ discouraged 형 좌절한
▶ discouraging 형 좌절시키는
▶ discouragement 명 좌절, 방지

한 번의 실패가 널 좌절시키게 해서는 안 된다.
You should not let one failure _____ you.

09 dismay
[disméi]

실망[낙담]시키다
명 실망[낙담]
▶ dismayed 형 실망[낙담]한

난 그가 거짓말을 했다는 걸 알고 실망했다.
I was _____ed to discover that he'd lied.

10 distract
[distrǽkt]

(주의를) 딴 데로 돌리다
[산만하게 하다](↔ attract)
▶ distraction 명 산만하게 하는 것, 기분 전환
▶ distracted 형 주의가 산만한

내가 공부하고 있는 동안 나를 산만하게 하지 마!
Don't _____ me while I'm studying!

11 perplex
[pərpléks]

당혹하게 하다(=puzzle)

그녀의 증상은 의사들을 당혹하게 했다.

Her symptoms _____ed the doctors.

12 bewilder
[biwíldər]

혼란스럽게[어리둥절하게] 하다
- ▶bewildered 형 어리둥절한
- ▶bewildering 형 어리둥절하게 하는
- ▶bewilderment 명 어리둥절함

나는 그녀의 갑작스러운 기분 변화에 어리둥절했다.

I was _____ed by her sudden change of mood.

13 humiliate
[hju:mílièit]

창피를 주다
- ▶humiliation 명 창피[치욕]
- ▶humiliated 형 창피한
- ▶humiliating 형 치욕적인

그는 그녀가 사람들 있는 데서 그에게 창피를 주려 했다고 비난했다.

He accused her of trying to _____ him in public.

14 overwhelm
[òuvərhwélm]

압도하다
- ▶overwhelmed 형 압도된
- ▶overwhelming 형 압도적인

그는 향수병에 압도되었다.

He was _____ed with a feeling of homesickness.

15 obsess
[əbsés]

집착하게[강박 관념에 사로잡히게] 하다
- ▶obsession 명 집착[강박 관념]
- ▶obsessed[obsessive] 형 집착하는[강박 관념에 사로잡힌]

많은 젊은 여성들이 몸무게에 대한 강박 관념에 사로잡혀 있다.

A lot of young girls are _____ed by their weight.

16 preoccupy
[pri:ákjupài]

마음을 사로잡다
- ▶preoccupation 명 심취[몰두]
- ▶preoccupied 형 몰두하는
- ▶occupy 거주[차지/점령]하다

그녀의 가족 문제들은 계속 그녀의 마음을 사로잡았다.

Her family problems continue to _____ her.

17 beware
[biwɛ́ər]

조심하다

양의 탈을 쓴 늑대를 조심해라.

_____ of a wolf in sheep's clothing.

18 resent
[rizént]

분개하다
- ▶resentment 명 분개
- ▶resentful 형 분개한

그는 장시간 일해야 하는 사실에 분개했다.

He _____ed having to work long hours.

19 inflame
[infléim]

흥분[격분]시키다

그의 논평은 온 나라 사람들을 격분시켰다.

His comments have _____d people all over the country.

20 startle
[stá:rtl]

깜짝 놀라게 하다(=surprise, frighten, alarm, scare)

미안해. 널 놀라게 할 의도는 아니었어.

Sorry, I didn't mean to _____ you.

21 astonish
[əstániʃ]

크게 놀라게 하다
(=amaze, shock)

▶astonishment 명 경악
▶astonished 형 놀란
▶astonishing 형 놀라운

나를 크게 놀라게 하는 것은 그녀에게 두려움이 없는 것이다.
What _____es me is her lack of fear.

22 astound
[əstáund]

크게 놀라게 하다

그는 그녀의 거만함에 크게 놀랐다. He was _____ed by her arrogance.

23 stun
[stʌn]

❶ 크게 놀라게 하다
❷ 기절시키다

▶stunned 형 놀란
▶stunning 형 멋진, 놀라운

그들의 연구 결과는 세계를 크게 놀라게 했다.
The results of their research _____ned the world.

24 horrify
[hɔ́ːrəfài]

공포스럽게 하다

▶horror 명 공포
▶horrifying[horrible, horrific]
  형 공포스러운[끔찍한]

전 국민이 그 살인 행위들에 공포스러워 했다.
The whole country was _____ied by the killings.

25 appall
[əpɔ́ːl]

소름 끼치게[끔찍하게] 하다

▶appalling 형 소름 끼치는[끔찍한]

난 내가 본 것에 소름이 끼쳤다. I was _____ed by what I saw.

26 dread
[dred]

두려워하다 명 두려움

▶dreadful 형 끔찍한(=awful, terrible)

난 기말고사를 치를 걸 두려워하고 있다.
I'm _____ing taking the final exam.

27 exhaust
[igzɔ́ːst]

❶ 탈진시키다
❷ 다 써 버리다[고갈시키다]
명 배기가스

▶exhaustion 명 고갈, 탈진
▶exhausted 형 탈진한(=worn-out)
▶exhausting 형 탈진시키는

정상에 이르렀을 때 우린 탈진했다.
When we reached the summit we were _____ed.

28 grieve
[griːv]

(죽음을) 몹시 슬퍼하다
[슬프게 하다]

▶grief 명 깊은 슬픔
▶grieved 형 몹시 슬퍼하는

그녀는 외아들을 잃어 몹시 슬퍼했다.
She _____d the loss of her only son.

29 mourn
[mɔːrn]

애도하다[애석해하다]

▶mourning 명 애도
▶mournful 형 애절한

그들은 전사한 자식들을 애도했다.
They _____ed for their children, killed in the war.

30 lament
[ləmént]

애통해하다[한탄하다] 명 애도[애가(哀歌)]

국민들은 위대한 지도자의 죽음을 애통해했다.
The nation _____ed the death of its great leader.

Today's Dessert

We are more often frightened than hurt, for our troubles spring more often from fancy than reality.

걱정거리가 현실보다 공상에서 더 자주 생겨나기 때문에, 우리는 실제 다치는 것보다 더 자주 두려워한다.

TEST 45

A 영영사전 뜻풀이에 알맞은 동사 찾기

> 보기   appall   distract   distress   dread   exhaust   lament

1 _____ : to make someone feel very upset

2 _____ : to express sadness and regret about

3 _____ : to make someone feel extremely tired

4 _____ : to fear something that will or might happen

5 _____ : to make someone feel fear, shock, or disgust

6 _____ : to take someone's attention away from something

B 같은 관계 맺어주기

1 alarm : startle = annoy : i_____

2 grieve : mourn = perplex : b_____

3 terror : terrify = horror : h_____

C 빈칸에 가장 적절한 동사 넣기

> 보기   beware   dismay   overwhelm   resent   tease   torment

1 _____ of the dog! 개 조심!

2 I was _____(e)d by mosquitoes. 난 모기들 때문에 괴로웠다.

3 I was _____(e)d at your cynicism. 난 너의 냉소주의에 실망했어.

4 He used to _____ her mercilessly. 그는 그녀를 무자비하게 놀려대곤 했다.

5 She was _____(e)d by feelings of guilt. 그녀는 죄책감에 압도되었다.

6 She _____(e)d him making all the decisions. 그녀는 그가 모든 결정을 하는 데 분개했다.

D 다른 동사들과 의미가 가장 다른 하나는?

① amaze   ② astonish   ③ astound   ④ stun   ⑤ humiliate

E 빈칸에 가장 적절한 동사 넣기

> 보기   afflict   discourage   disgust   harass   inflame   obsess

1 He is _____(e)d with her. 그는 그녀에게 집착하고 있다.

2 His angry speech _____(e)d the people. 그의 성난 연설은 사람들을 격분시켰다.

3 Severe drought has _____(e)d the region. 심한 가뭄이 그 지역에 피해를 입혀 왔다.

4 She has been sexually _____(e)d at work. 그녀는 일터에서 성희롱을 당해 왔다.

5 We were _____(e)d by violence in the film. 우리는 그 영화의 폭력이 혐오스러웠다.

6 You shouldn't let one failure _____ you. 한 번의 실패가 널 좌절시키게 해서는 안 된다.

ANSWER_____

A 1. distress 2. lament 3. exhaust 4. dread 5. appall 6. distract   **B** 1. irritate 2. bewilder 3. horrify   **C** 1. Beware 2. torment 3. dismay 4. tease 5. overwhelm 6. resent   **D** ⑤   **E** 1. obsess 2. inflame 3. afflict 4. harass 5. disgust 6. discourage

감정 2

Part 2

01 revive
[riváiv]

되살리다[소생/회복하다] ▶revive 명 부흥[회복], 재공연[상영]

경제가 회복하기 시작하고 있다.

The economy is beginning to _____.

02 situate
[sítʃuèit]

(~에) 놓다 ▶situation 명 상황, 장소[위치]
▶be situated (~에) 위치하다(=be located)

그 호텔은 해변 가까이에 위치해 있다.

The hotel is _____d near the beach.

03 dwell
-dwelt[dwelled]
-dwelt[dwelled]
[dwel]

살다[거주하다](=live) ▶dwelling 명 주거지[주택]
▶dweller 명 거주자[주민]

그는 숲속에서 살았다.

He _____ in the middle of the forest.

04 reside
[rizáid]

살다[거주하다] ▶residence 명 주거지[주택], 거주
▶resident 명 거주자 형 거주하는
▶residential 형 주거의

많은 한국인이 외국에 산다.

Many Korean people _____ abroad.

05 occupy
[ákjupài]

❶ 거주하다 ❷ 차지하다 ▶occupation 명 직업, 점령, 거주
❸ 점령하다 ▶occupied 형 바쁜, 사용 중인

그는 집세도 안 내고 그 집에 거주한다.

He _____ies the house without paying any rent.

06 inhabit
[inhǽbit]

살다[거주/서식하다] ▶inhabitant 명 거주자[서식 동물]
▶habitat 명 서식지

숲에는 많은 야생 동물들이 서식하고 있다.

The woods are _____ed by many wild animals.

07 populate
[pápjulèit]

살다[거주하다] ▶population 명 인구
▶overpopulation 명 인구 과잉

서울은 세계에서 가장 밀집하여 거주되는[인구 밀도가 높은] 지역 중 하나다.

Seoul is one of the most densely _____d areas in the world.

08 migrate
[máigreit]

이주[이동]하다 ▶migration 명 이주
▶immigrate 이주해 오다
▶emigrate 이주해 가다

새들은 언제 이동해야 하는지 어떻게 알까?

How do birds know when to _____?

09 lodge
[ladʒ]

❶ 숙박하다[숙박시키다] ▶lodging 명 숙소
❷ 박히다 명 오두막 ▶dislodge 제거하다, 몰아내다

그녀는 캐나다에서 현지 가정집에서 숙박했다.

She _____d with a local family in Canada.

10 accommodate
[əkámədèit]

수용하다[숙박시키다] ▶accommodation 명 (-s) 숙박 시설

그 무도장은 700명을 수용할 수 있다.

The ballroom can _____ 700 people.

11 linger
[líŋɡər]

오래 머무르다

그녀의 향기가 오래 머물러 있다.

Her perfume _____s on.

12 lurk
[ləːrk]

숨어 기다리다, 잠복[잠재]하다

누군가가 어둠 속에 숨어 기다리고 있었다.

Someone was _____ing in the shadows.

13 abound
[əbáund]

많이 있다[풍부하다] ▶abundant 형 풍부한
▶abundance 명 풍부함
▶an abundance of 풍부한[많은]

지구가 어떻게 생겨났는지에 대한 이론들이 많이 있다.

Theories _____ about how the earth began.

14 necessitate
[nəsésətèit]

필요로 하다(=need, require) ▶necessity 명 필수품, 필요(성)

돈의 부족은 계획의 변경을 필요로 했다.

Lack of money _____d a change of plan.

15 undergo
-underwent-undergone
[ʌndərɡóu]

겪다[받다](=go through)

그 나라는 커다란 변화를 겪었다.

The country has _____ massive changes.

16 endure
[indʒúər]

견디다[참다]
(=bear, stand, put up with) ▶endurance 명 인내(력)(=patience)

그는 그녀와 떨어져 있는 걸 참을 수 없다.

He can't _____ being apart from her.

17 tolerate
[tálərèit]

용인하다, 견디다[참다] ▶tolerance 명 관용
▶tolerant 형 관대한
▶tolerable 형 참을 수 있는

난 긴 시간을 견딜 수 없었다.

I couldn't _____ the long hours.

18 surmount
[sərmáunt]

극복하다(=overcome) ▶surmountable 형 극복할 수 있는
▶insurmountable 형 극복할 수 없는

여성들은 흔히 경력을 발전시키기 위해 사회적 장벽을 극복해야 한다.

Women often have to _____ social barriers to advance their careers.

19 refrain
[rifréin]

삼가다 명 후렴

이곳에서는 흡연을 삼가 주십시오.

Please _____ from smoking in this area.

20 abstain
[əbstéin]

❶ 삼가다 ❷ (투표에서) 기권하다

여성들은 임신 중에 음주를 삼가야 한다.

Women must _____ from drinking during pregnancy.

21 contain
[kəntéin]

❶ 포함[함유]하다 ❷ 억제하다 ▶container 몡 용기, 컨테이너

그녀는 더 이상 흥분을 억제할 수 없었다.

She couldn't _____ her excitement any longer.

22 strive
-stove-striven
[straiv]

노력[분투]하다(=labor, struggle)

회사는 능률을 더 높이기 위해 노력해야 한다.

The company must _____ for greater efficiency.

23 endeavor
[indévər]

노력하다 몡 노력[시도]

우리는 문제의 원인을 찾아내기 위해 노력하고 있다.

We are _____ing to locate the source of the problem.

24 exert
[igzə́:rt]

❶ (힘을) 행사하다 ▶exertion 몡 노력, 행사
❷ (~ oneself) 노력하다

그는 지칠 줄 모르고 노력해 왔다.

He has _____ed himself tirelessly.

25 pursue
[pərsú:]

❶ 추구하다 ❷ 추적하다 ▶pursuit 몡 추구, 추적

우리는 힘차게 목표를 추구해야 한다.

We must _____ our goals with vigor.

26 venture
[véntʃər]

위험을 무릅쓰고 가다[하다]
몡 모험적 사업

그는 불가능한 것을 위험을 무릅쓰고 하는 걸 즐긴다.

He enjoys _____ing to do something impossible.

27 incline
[inkláin]

(마음이) 기울게 하다[기울다] ▶inclined 혱 ~하고 싶은, 경향이 있는
▶inclination 몡 의향[성향], 경향, 경사도

돈의 부족이 많은 젊은이들을 범죄 쪽으로 기울게 한다.

Lack of money _____s many young people towards crime.

28 accomplish
[əkámpliʃ]

성취하다(=achieve, realize) ▶accomplishment 몡 업적

우리는 하려고 계획했던 모든 것을 성취했다.

We have _____ed all we set out to do.

29 attain
[ətéin]

성취[달성]하다, 이르다[도달하다] ▶attainment 몡 성취[달성], 도달

우리는 목표를 달성할 최선의 방법을 밝혀낼 필요가 있다.

We need to identify the best ways of _____ing our goals.

30 fulfill
[fulfíl]

이행[실현]하다, 충족시키다 ▶fulfillment 몡 이행[실현], 충족
(=carry out, satisfy)

학교는 학생들의 욕구를 충족시켜야 한다.

A school should _____ the needs of its pupils.

Today's
Dessert

He has existed only, not lived, who lacks wisdom in old age.

늙어서도 지혜가 없는 사람은 단지 이 세상에 있었을 뿐 살아 온 것이 아니다.

TEST 46

A 밑줄 친 동사에 유의하여 우리말로!

1 to lodge with a family

2 to accommodate 100 people

3 to undergo a change

4 to refrain from smoking

5 to abstain from alcohol

6 to contain your anger

7 to exert influence

8 to fulfill your dream

B 영영사전 뜻풀이에 알맞은 동사 찾기

> 보기   abound   attain   linger   lurk   migrate

1 _____ : to exist in very large numbers

2 _____ : to succeed in achieving something

3 _____ : to move from one place to another

4 _____ : to wait somewhere quietly and secretly

5 _____ : to continue to exist for longer than is usual

C 같은 관계 맺어주기

1 achieve : accomplish = dwell : r_____

2 revive : revival = pursue : p_____

D 다른 동사들과 의미가 가장 다른 하나는?

① bear　　②endeavor　　③ endure　　④ tolerate　　⑤ put up with

E 빈칸에 가장 적절한 동사 넣기

> 보기   incline   inhabit   necessitate   situate   strive   venture

1 Nothing _____(e)d, nothing gained. 위험을 무릅쓰지 않으면 얻는 것도 없다.

2 We must _____ for greater efficiency. 우리는 능률을 더 높이기 위해 노력해야 한다.

3 The hotel is _____(e)d near the beach. 그 호텔은 해변 가까이에 위치해 있다.

4 His sincerity _____(e)d me to trust him. 그의 진실성이 그를 믿는 쪽으로 나를 기울게 했다.

5 The woods are _____(e)d by wild animals. 숲에는 야생 동물들이 서식하고 있다.

6 Increased traffic _____(e)s widening the road. 증가하는 교통은 도로 확장을 필요로 한다.

F 밑줄 친 단어 뜻 구별하기

Land should be purchased by those who occupy it.

Football occupies most of my leisure time.

ANSWER_____

A 1. 가정집에서 숙박하다 2. 100명을 수용하다 3. 변화를 겪다 4. 흡연을 삼가다 5. 술을 삼가다 6. 화를 억제하다 7. 영향력을 행사하다 8. 꿈을 실현하다 **B** 1. abound 2. attain 3. migrate 4. lurk 5. linger **C** 1. reside 2. pursuit **D** ② **E** 1. venture 2. strive 3. situate 4. incline 5. inhabit 6. necessitate **F** 땅은 거기에 거주하는 사람들에 의해 매입되어야 한다.(거주하다) / 축구는 내 여가 시간의 대부분을 차지한다.(차지하다)

01 emerge
[imə́:rʤ]

나오다, 드러나다
(=appear, come out)

▶ emergence 명 출현
▶ emergency 명 비상(사태)
▶ emerging[emergent] 형 신생의

태양이 구름 뒤에서 나왔다.

The sun _____d from behind the clouds.

02 originate
[ərídʒənèit]

비롯되다, 시작하다

▶ origin 명 기원, 출신
▶ orignal 형 원래의, 독창적인
▶ originality 명 독창성

그 병은 아프리카에서 비롯되었다.

The disease _____d in Africa.

03 derive
[diráiv]

❶ 얻다
❷ 나오다[비롯하다](=be derived)

비교 deprive 빼앗다[박탈하다]

'코리아'라는 이름이 무엇에서 유래했는지 아니?

Do you know what the name "Korea" is _____d from?

04 launch
[lɔ:ntʃ]

❶ 시작[착수]하다(=begin, start) ❷ 진수[발사]하다 ❸ 출시하다

그 단체는 평화 운동을 시작했다.

The organization has _____ed the campaign for peace.

05 embark
[imbá:rk]

❶ (~ (up)on) 시작[착수]하다 ❷ 탑승하다

우리는 새로운 프로젝트에 착수할 것이다.

We're _____ing upon a new project.

06 initiate
[iníʃièit]

❶ 시작[착수]하다 ❷ 가입시키다 ▶ initiative 명 주도권[결단력], 새로운 계획

정부는 경제 개혁 프로그램에 착수했다.

The government has _____d a program of economic reform.

07 commence
[kəméns]

시작하다 ▶ commencement 명 시작[개시]

학년은 3월 초에 시작된다.

The academic year _____s at the beginning of March.

08 persist
[pərsíst]

❶ 끈질기게 계속하다[고집하다]
❷ 지속되다

▶ persistence 명 끈질김[고집], 지속
▶ persistent 형 끈질긴, 지속되는

그녀는 재정 문제에도 불구하고 학업을 끈질기게 계속했다.

She _____ed in studying in spite of financial problems.

09 persevere
[pɜ̀:rsəvíər]

끈질기게 계속하다 ▶ perseverance 명 인내(심)

그녀는 보상 요구를 끈질기게 계속했다.

She _____d in her claim for compensation.

10 erupt
[irʌ́pt]

❶ (화산이) 분출[폭발]하다
❷ 발발하다[터지다](=break out)

▶ eruption 명 분출[폭발], 발발

경찰이 시위 도중 한 학생에게 총을 쏘자 폭력 사태가 터졌다.

Violence _____ed after police shot a student during the demonstration.

11 recur
[rikɔ́ːr]

재발하다, 되풀이되다

병이 재발할 위험이 있다.

There is a danger that the disease may _____.

12 alternate
동 [ɔ́ːltərnèit] 형 [ɔ́ːltərnət]

번갈아 일어나다[하다]
형 번갈아 일어나는

▶ alternately 튀 번갈아
▶ alternative 형 대체[대안]의 명 대안
▶ alternatively 튀 그 대신에

그녀는 웃다 울다를 번갈아 했다.

She _____d between laughing and crying.

13 coincide
[kòuinsáid]

동시에 일어나다, 일치하다

▶ coincidence 명 (우연의) 일치
▶ coincidental 형 우연의 일치인

전시회가 그의 서거 50주년 기념일과 동시에 열린다.

The exhibition _____s with the 50th anniversary of his death.

14 synchronize
[síŋkrənàiz]

동시에 발생하다[시키다], 동기화하다

▶ synchronization 명 동기화

음향은 화면과 동기화되어야[일치되어야] 한다.

The sound has to _____ with the picture.

15 precede
[prisíːd]

앞서다[선행하다](↔ follow)

큰 소리의 폭발이 있고 나서 화재가 뒤따랐다.

The fire was _____d by a loud explosion.

16 ensue
[insúː]

(어떤 일 · 결과가) 뒤따르다

▶ ensuing 형 다음의[뒤이어 일어나는]

내가 그가 한 말에 대해 반대하자 열띤 논쟁이 뒤따랐다.

I objected to what he said and a heated argument _____d.

17 evolve
[iválv]

진화하다

▶ evolution 명 진화
▶ evolutionary 형 진화의

인간이 원숭이에서 진화했다는 걸 믿니?

Do you believe that humans _____d from apes?

18 vanish
[vǽniʃ]

갑자기 사라지다(= disappear)

5명의 소년들이 흔적도 없이 갑자기 사라졌다.

Five boys _____ed without a trace.

19 perish
[périʃ]

(비명에) 죽다, 사라지다

배가 가라앉았을 때 수백 명이 죽었다.

Hundreds _____ed when the ship went down.

20 fade
[feid]

천천히 사라지다, 희미해지다[바래다]

그 밴드의 인기는 최근 몇 해 사이 천천히 사라져 갔다.

The band's popularity has _____d in recent years.

21 recede
[risíːd]

물러나다[멀어지다]

발자국 소리가 저 멀리 멀어져 갔다.

The footsteps were _____ing into the distance.

22 retreat
[ritríːt]

후퇴하다(↔ advance), 물러나다
명 후퇴

그들은 공격을 당해 후퇴해야 했다.
They were attacked and forced to _____.

23 resign
[rizáin]

사임하다(= quit)　　　　　　▶resignation 명 사임

몇몇 검사들이 부패 추문 후에 사임했다.
Several prosecutors _____ed after a corruption scandal.

24 desert
동[dizə́ːrt] 명[dézərt]

버리다[떠나다](= abandon)　비교 dessert 명 후식
명 사막　　　　　　　　　　▶deserted 형 사람이 없는[버려진]

그는 아내와 가족을 버렸다.
He _____ed his wife and family.

25 suspend
[səspénd]

❶ 일시 중지하다, 정학시키다　▶suspension 명 중지, 정직[정학]
❷ 매달다[걸다]

양국 간의 대화가 중지되었다.
Talks between the two countries have been _____ed.

26 halt
[hɔːlt]

멈추다[정지하다] 명 정지　　▶halting 형 더듬거리는[주저하는]

어떻게 범죄의 증가를 멈추게 할 수 있을까?
How can we _____ the increase in crime?

27 adjourn
[ədʒə́ːrn]

휴회[휴정]하다　　　　　　　▶adjournment 명 휴회[휴정]

휴회한 때는 정오 무렵이었다.
It was almost noon when the meeting _____ed.

28 postpone
[poustpóun]

연기하다[미루다](= delay, put off[back])

대기업은 종종 대금 지불을 연기한다.
Big companies often _____ paying their bills.

29 expire
[ikspáiər]

만료되다(= run out)

내 여권이 다음 주에 만료된다.
My passport _____s next week.

30 terminate
[tə́ːrmənèit]

끝나다[종료하다](= end, finish)　▶termination 명 종료, 임신 중절

그들은 나의 계약을 종료시켰다.
They _____d my contract.

Today's Dessert

As long as you continue to work, you can own the dream.
일을 계속하는 한 넌 꿈을 가질 수 있다.

TEST 47

A 밑줄 친 동사에 유의하여 우리말로!

1 to launch the campaign

2 to embark upon a project

3 to initiate legal proceedings

4 to recede into the distance

5 to resign your post

6 to desert your family

7 to be suspended from school

8 to halt traffic

9 to adjourn the meeting

10 to terminate the contract

B 영영사전 뜻풀이에 알맞은 동사 찾기

> 보기   alternate   ensue   originate   recur   synchronize

1 _____ : to happen at the same time and speed

2 _____ : to happen again or happen many times

3 _____ : to start in a particular place or situation

4 _____ : to happen after or as a result of something

5 _____ : to happen or exist one after the other repeatedly

C 같은 관계 맺어주기

1 start : commence = disappear : v_____

2 delay : postpone = persist : p_____

3 come out : emerge = break out : e_____

4 follow : precede = advance : r_____

5 evolve : evolution = coincide : c_____

D 빈칸에 가장 적절한 동사 넣기

> 보기   derive   expire   fade   perish

1 My passport _____s next week. 내 여권은 다음 주에 만료된다.

2 A family of four _____(e)d in the fire. 일가족 4명이 화재로 죽었다.

3 Hopes that they will be found alive are _____ing.

그들이 살아서 발견되리라는 희망이 천천히 사라지고 있다.

4 The word "politics" is _____(e)d from a Greek word meaning "city."

'정치'라는 단어는 '도시'를 의미하는 그리스어 단어에서 나왔다.

ANSWER_____

A 1. 캠페인을 시작하다 2. 프로젝트를 착수하다 3. 법적 절차에 착수하다 4. 저 멀리 멀어지다 5. 사임하다 6. 가족을 버리다 7. 정학당하다 8. 교통을 정지시키다 9. 휴회[정회]하다 10. 계약을 종료시키다   B 1. synchronize 2. recur 3. originate 4. ensue 5. alternate   C 1. vanish 2. persevere 3. erupt 4. retreat 5. coincidence   D 1. expire 2. perish 3. fade(fading) 4. derive

01 emit
[imít]

(빛·소리·액체·기체를) 내다[내뿜다]

▶emission 명 배출(물)[배기가스]

지구는 자연 방사선을 내뿜는다.

The earth _____s natural radiation.

02 discharge
[distʃáːrdʒ]

❶ 방출[배출]하다 ❷ 내보내다 명 방출[배출], 내보냄

하수가 바다로 직접 배출된다.

Sewage is_____ d directly into the sea.

03 glow
[glou]

빛나다(=shine, gleam) 명 부드러운 빛

침대 옆의 램프가 희미하게 빛났다.

The bedside lamp _____ed dimly.

04 glitter
[glítər]

반짝이다(=sparkle) 명 반짝이는 빛

강물이 햇빛에 반짝였다.

The river _____ed in the sunlight.

05 blaze
[bleiz]

활활 타다, 빛나다, 이글거리다(=burn) 명 불길

불이 벽난로에서 활활 타고 있었다.

A fire was _____ing in the fireplace.

06 bang
[bæŋ]

쾅 치다[닫다](=slam) 명 쾅 소리

그는 주먹으로 문을 쾅쾅 쳐 댔다.

He was _____ing on the door with his fist.

07 boom
[buːm]

❶ 우르릉거리다[우렁차게 말하다] ❷ 호황을 맞다[번창하다]
명 붐[호황]

대포 소리가 밤중에 우르릉거렸다.

The cannons _____ed out in the night.

08 zoom
[zuːm]

(붕 소리를 내며) 급히 움직이다(=whizz, zip)

그녀는 차에 뛰어올라 붕 하고 가 버렸다.

She jumped in the car and _____ed off.

09 swish
[swiʃ]

휙[쉭] 움직이다

그들은 줄넘기를 휙 돌리기 시작했다.

They started _____ing a jump rope.

10 snap
[snæp]

❶ 딱 부러지다[소리를 내다]
❷ 스냅 사진을 찍다
❸ (~ at) (동물이) 물려고 하다

▶snap up 덥석 사다

잔가지가 내 발 아래서 딱 부러졌다.

A twig _____ped under my feet.

11 **crack**
[kræk]

갈라지다[금이 가다], 깨(지)다 <u>명</u> 금[틈]

그는 자전거 사고로 쇄골에 금이 갔다.

He _____ed his collarbone in a bike accident.

12 **clatter**
[klǽtər]

달그락[쨍그랑]거리다

쟁반이 미끄러져 쨍그랑 소리를 내며 바닥에 떨어졌다.

The tray slipped and _____ed to the floor.

13 **rattle**
[rǽtl]

덜거덕거리다[딸랑거리다] <u>명</u> 딸랑이

창문이 바람에 덜거덕거렸다.

The window _____d in the wind.

14 **buzz**
[bʌz]

윙윙거리다　　　　　　　▶buzzer <u>명</u> (누르는) 버저

벌들이 꽃들 사이에서 윙윙거렸다.

Bees _____ed among the flowers.

15 **hum**
[hʌm]

콧노래를 흥얼거리다, 윙윙거리다

그는 차를 몰며 혼자 콧노래를 흥얼거렸다.

He _____med to himself as he drove along.

16 **groan**
[groun]

신음하다, 투덜대다(=moan, whine) <u>명</u> 신음

우리 모두는 그의 끔찍한 농담에 신음했다.

We all _____ed at his terrible jokes.

17 **shriek**
[ʃriːk]

날카로운 소리[비명]를 지르다(=scream) <u>명</u> 비명

그들은 비명을 지르며 울면서 끌려갔다.

They were dragged, _____ing and weeping.

18 **howl**
[haul]

(길게) 짖다, 울부짖다

밤의 침묵 속에서 늑대 한 마리가 짖었다.

In the silence of the night, a wolf _____ed.

19 **roar**
[rɔːr]

으르렁거리다(=growl), 고함치다, 크게 웃다 <u>명</u> 으르렁거림, 함성, 폭소

우리는 사자가 으르렁거리는 소리를 들었다.

We heard a lion _____.

20 **toll**
[toul]

천천히 (조)종을 울리다　　　　▶death toll <u>명</u> 사망자 수

<u>명</u> ❶ 통행료 ❷ 사상자 수

멀리서 시간을 알리는 교회 종소리가 울렸다.

In the distance, a church bell _____ed the hour.

21 **stink**
-stank-stunk
[stiŋk]

악취를 풍기다 <u>명</u> 악취

그의 옷은 담배 연기로 악취를 풍긴다.

His clothes _____ of cigarette smoke.

22 perspire
[pərspáiər]

땀을 흘리다(= sweat)　　　　　▶perspiration 명 땀

그녀는 덥고 거북해 땀을 흘리기 시작했다.

She felt hot and awkward and started to _____.

23 bleed
-bled-bled
[bli:d]

피를 흘리다　　　　　▶bleeding 명 출혈
　　　　　　　　　　▶blood 명 피

너 코피가 나네.

Your nose is _____ing.

24 shed
-shed-shed
[ʃed]

❶ 없애다(=get rid of)　　　　　▶bloodshed 명 유혈 사태
❷ 떨어뜨리다[흘리다/비추다]
명 헛간[창고]

나무들은 가을에 잎을 떨어뜨린다.

The trees _____ their leaves in autumn.

25 spit
-spit[spat]-spit[spat]
[spit]

(침을) 뱉다　명 침(=saliva)

많은 사람들이 그의 파렴치한 얼굴에 침을 뱉었다.

Many people _____ in his shameless face.

26 drip
[drip]

똑똑 떨어지다[떨어뜨리다]
명 물방울

그는 팔에 피를 똑똑 떨어뜨리며 들어왔다.

He came in, his arm _____ping blood.

27 leak
[li:k]

새다[새게 하다]　　　　　▶leakage 명 누출[유출]
　　　　　　　　　　　▶leaky 형 새는

기름이 차에서 샜다.

Oil _____ed out of the car.

28 seep
[si:p]

스며 나오다[새다](=ooze, trickle)

살충제가 농지에서 스며 나와 상수도로 흘러 들어가고 있다.

Pesticides are _____ing out of farmland and into the water supply.

29 overflow
[òuvərflóu]

넘쳐흐르다[범람하다]

강물이 둑을 범람했다.

The river had _____ed its banks.

30 sprout
[spraut]

싹트다　명 싹(=shoot)

잡초는 보도의 갈라진 틈새로도 싹튼다.

Weeds _____ even through cracks in the sidewalk.

Today's Dessert　The more you sweat in safety, the less you bleed in danger.

안전할 때 땀을 더 흘리면 위험할 때 피를 덜 흘린다.

TEST **48**

A 영영사전 뜻풀이에 알맞은 동사 찾기

> 보기 blaze   drip   hum   stink   zoom

1 _____ : to let liquid fall in drops
2 _____ : to burn very brightly and strongly
3 _____ : to sing a tune with your lips closed
4 _____ : to move or go somewhere very fast
5 _____ : to have a strong and very unpleasant smell

B 빈칸에 가장 적절한 동사 넣기

> 보기 bang   buzz   crack   howl   rattle   roar   snap

1 Bees were _____ing. 벌들이 윙윙거리고 있었다.
2 We heard a lion _____. 우리는 사자가 으르렁거리는 소리를 들었다.
3 The dogs _____(e)d all night. 개들이 밤새 짖어댔다.
4 The wind had _____(e)d the tree in two. 바람이 나무를 둘로 딱 부러뜨렸다.
5 Concrete _____(e)s in very cold weather. 콘크리트는 아주 추운 날씨에는 갈라진다.
6 He _____(e)d on her door and _____(e)d the handle.
그는 그녀의 문을 쾅쾅 두드리고 손잡이를 덜거덕거렸다.

C 같은 관계 맺어주기

1 shine : glow = sparkle : g_____
2 groan : moan = scream : s_____
3 leak : seep = sweat : p_____

D 빈칸에 가장 적절한 동사 넣기

> 보기 bleed   clatter   overflow   shed   spit[spat]   sprout

1 Your nose is _____ing. 너 코피가 나네.
2 The river had _____ed its banks. 강물이 둑을 범람했다.
3 Weeds _____ even through cracks. 잡초는 갈라진 틈새로도 싹튼다.
4 People _____ in his shameless face. 사람들이 그의 파렴치한 얼굴에 침을 뱉었다.
5 He heard dishes _____ing in the kitchen. 그는 부엌에서 접시들이 달그락거리는 걸 들었다.
6 The factory is _____ing a large number of jobs. 그 공장은 많은 일자리를 없애고 있다.

F 밑줄 친 동사에 유의하여 뜻 구별해 해석하기

1 The cannons <u>boom</u>ed out in the night.   The leisure industry is <u>boom</u>ing.
2 He was <u>discharged</u> from the hospital.
The factory <u>discharge</u>d chemicals into the river.

Part 2 날씨는

01 alter
[ɔ́ːltər]

변하다[바꾸다](= change)   비교 altar 명 제단
▶alteration 명 변화[변경]

그의 얼굴은 많이 변하지 않았다. His face hasn't _____ed much.

02 convert
[kənvə́ːrt]

전환[개조]하다, 개종[전향]하다   ▶conversion 명 전환[개조]
▶convertible 형 전환 가능한

그들은 동물의 배설물을 연료로 전환시킨다.
They _____ animal waste into fuel.

03 transform
[trænsfɔ́ːrm]

변형시키다[완전히 바꾸다]   ▶transformation 명 변형

한국은 주요 산업국으로 완전히 바뀌었다.
Korea has been _____ed into a major industrial nation.

04 adjust
[ədʒʌ́st]

❶ (~ to) 적응하다   ▶adjustment 명 적응, 조정[조절]
❷ 조정[조절]하다

노인들은 아파트 생활에 적응하는 데 곤란을 겪는다.
Old people have trouble _____ing to living in an apartment.

05 modify
[mάdəfài]

❶ 수정[변경]하다(= adapt)   ▶modification 명 수정[변경]
❷ 수식하다   ▶genetically modified[GM]
명 유전자 변형의

우리는 장애인들에게 더 편리하게 하기 위해 디자인을 변경할 수 있다.
We can _____ the design to make it more convenient for the disabled.

06 amend
[əménd]

개정[수정]하다   ▶amendment 명 개정[수정]

그 법은 약자를 보호하기 위해 개정되었다.
The law was _____ed to protect the weak.

07 revise
[riváiz]

수정[개정]하다   ▶revision 명 수정[개정]

새로운 발견이 우리의 생각을 수정하게 했다.
A new discovery made us _____ our ideas.

08 refine
[rifáin]

❶ 개선하다 ❷ 정제하다   ▶refinement 명 개선, 정제
▶refinery 명 정유소[제당 공장]

설탕과 석유는 사용 전에 정제된다.
Sugar and oil are _____d before use.

09 reform
[rifɔ́ːrm]

개혁하다   ▶reformation 명 개혁
명 개혁   ▶reformist 형 개혁적인 명 개혁가

우리는 주택 제도와 복지 규정을 개혁해야 한다.
We should _____ housing system and welfare provision.

10 renew
[rinjúː]

❶ 갱신하다   ▶renewal 명 재개, 갱신
❷ 재개하다(= resume)   ▶renewable 형 재생[갱신] 가능한
(↔ nonrenewable)

난 올해 여권을 갱신할 필요가 있다.
I need to _____ my passport this year.

11 renovate
[rénəvèit]

개조[보수]하다   ▶renovation 몡 개조[보수]

호텔이 개조되고 다시 장식되었다.

The hotel has been _____d and redecorated.

12 innovate
[ínəvèit]

혁신하다[새것을 도입하다]   ▶innovation 몡 혁신
▶innovative 톙 혁신적인
▶innovator 몡 혁신자

그 회사는 새로운 서비스를 도입했다.

The company has _____d new services.

13 reinforce
[rì:infɔ́:rs]

강화[보강]하다(= strengthen)   凾 enforce 집행하다, 강요하다
▶reinforcement 몡 강화[보강]

그 영화는 여성은 예뻐야 한다는 생각을 강화한다.

The film _____s the idea that women should be pretty.

14 enhance
[inhǽns]

향상시키다[높이다](= improve)

인터넷이 교육을 향상시킬 수 있다.

The Internet can _____ our education.

15 intensify
[inténsəfài]

심해지다[강화하다]   ▶intense 톙 극심한[강렬한]
▶intensity 몡 강렬함, 강도[세기]
▶intensive 톙 집중[집약]적인

정부는 범죄와 싸우려는 노력을 강화했다.

The government _____ied efforts to fight crime.

16 magnify
[mǽgnəfài]

확대하다   ▶magnificent 톙 장려한[멋진]
▶magnitude 몡 (큰) 규모, (별의) 광도, (지진의) 진도

그녀의 눈은 두터운 안경으로 확대되었다.

Her eyes were _____ied by her thick glasses.

17 amplify
[ǽmpləfài]

❶ 증폭하다 ❷ 더 자세히 진술[서술]하다

음악이 마이크로 증폭되었다.

The music was _____ied with microphones.

18 diffuse
통[difjú:z] 톙[difjú:s]

확산되다[확산시키다]   ▶diffusion 몡 확산
톙 확산[분산]된

과학 기술은 급속히 확산된다.

Technologies _____ rapidly.

19 dignify
[dígnəfài]

위엄 있어 보이게 하다   ▶dignity 몡 위엄, 존엄성

거대한 그림이 홀의 벽을 위엄 있어 보이게 했다.

A huge picture _____ied the hall wall.

20 enlighten
[inláitn]

이해시키다[깨우치다]   ▶enlightenment 몡 깨달음, (the Enlightenment) 계몽주의

가르침은 학생들에게 단지 지식을 주는 게 아니라 그들을 깨우칠 수 있는 기회이다.

Teaching is an opportunity to _____ students, not just inform them.

21 ventilate
[véntəlèit]

환기하다[통풍시키다]   ▶ventilation 명 환기[통풍]

요리할 때는 부엌을 환기시켜라.

_____ your kitchen when cooking.

22 purify
[pjúərəfài]

정화하다   ▶purification 명 정화
▶purity 명 순수성[깨끗함]

실내 화분 식물들이 공기를 정화하는 데 도움이 된다.

Houseplants help _____ the air.

23 dilute
[dilú:t]

희석하다

약을 물로 희석할 수 있다.

You can _____ the medicine with water.

24 dehydrate
[di:háidreit]

건조[탈수]시키다

우유는 건조되어 가루로 저장된다.

The milk is _____d and stored as powder.

25 evaporate
[ivǽpərèit]

증발하다(액체 → 증기)   ▶vapor 명 (수)증기
▶evaporation 명 증발

햇빛이 나뭇잎의 수분을 증발시킨다.

The sun _____s moisture on the leaves.

26 accelerate
[əksélərèit]

가속화하다   ▶acceleration 명 가속
▶accelerator 명 액셀러레이터
(=gas pedal)

그들은 경제 성장을 가속화하길 원한다.

They want to _____ economic growth.

27 falsify
[fɔ́:lsəfài]

위조[변조/조작]하다   ▶false 형 틀린[가짜의/거짓된]

그 파일은 증거를 조작하기 위해 바뀌었다.

The file was altered to _____ the evidence.

28 degenerate
[didʒénərèit]

악화되다(=worsen ↔ improve)   ▶degeneration 명 악화, 퇴보
형 퇴폐적인[타락한]   ▶degenerative 형 퇴행성의[퇴보적인]

시위가 폭력 사태로 악화되었다.

A demonstration _____d into violence.

29 deteriorate
[ditíəriərèit]

악화되다   ▶deterioration 명 악화

도시 대기의 질이 급속히 악화되고 있다.

Air quality is rapidly _____ing in our cities.

30 dehumanize
[di:hjú:mənàiz]

비인간화하다[인간성을 빼앗다]   ▶dehumanization 명 비인간화

빈곤은 사람들의 인간성을 빼앗는다.

Poverty _____s people.

Today's Dessert

Life improves slowly and worsens fast.

삶은 천천히 개선되고 빠르게 악화된다.

TEST 49

A 밑줄 친 동사에 유의하여 우리말로!

1 to <u>adjust</u> the chair
2 to <u>refine</u> the design
3 to <u>renew</u> your passport
4 to <u>reform</u> education system
5 to <u>enhance</u> the quality of life
6 to <u>purify</u> the water
7 to <u>accelerate</u> growth
8 to <u>ventilate</u> the kitchen
9 to <u>evaporate</u> moisture
10 to <u>falsify</u> a certificate

B 영영사전 뜻풀이에 알맞은 단어 찾기

보기 dehydrate   dignify   enlighten   modify   transform

1 _____ : to explain something to someone
2 _____ : to remove the liquid from a substance
3 _____ : to change something slightly to improve it
4 _____ : to change completely the form of something
5 _____ : to make something seem impressive and important

C 같은 관계 맺어주기

1 change : alter = strengthen : r_____
2 amend : revise = degenerate : d_____

D 빈칸에 가장 적절한 동사 넣기

보기 convert   dehumanize   diffuse   dilute   intensify

1 War _____(e)s people. 전쟁은 사람들의 인간성을 빼앗는다.
2 You can _____ the paint with water. 페인트를 물로 희석할 수 있다.
3 The heat was _____(e)d throughout the room. 열기가 방 전체로 확산되었다.
4 The government _____(e)d efforts to fight crime.
정부는 범죄와 싸우려는 노력을 강화했다.
5 They _____(e)d the spare bedroom into an office.
그들은 여분의 침실을 사무실로 개조했다.

E 의미상 더 어울리는 동사 고르기

1 The company (innovated / renovated) new ideas. 그 회사는 새로운 아이디어를 도입했다.
2 Her eyes were (amplified / magnified) by her thick glasses.
그녀의 눈은 두터운 안경으로 확대되었다.

ANSWER
A 1. 의자를 조정하다 2. 디자인을 개선하다 3. 여권을 갱신하다 4. 교육 제도를 개혁하다 5. 삶의 질을 향상시키다[높이다] 6. 물을 정화하다[정수하다] 7. 성장을 가속화하다 8. 부엌을 환기시키다 9. 수분을 증발시키다 10. 자격증[증명서]을 위조하다 **B** 1. enlighten 2. dehydrate 3. modify 4. transform 5. dignify **C** 1. reinforce 2. deteriorate **D** 1. dehumanize 2. dilute 3. diffuse 4. intensify(intensified) 5. convert **E** 1. innovated 2. magnified

201

Change of States 2

01 flourish
[flə́ːriʃ]

번영[번창/번성]하다(↔ decline)

경제가 호황을 누리고 사업이 번창하고 있다.
The economy is booming and businesses are _____ing.

02 prosper
[prɑ́spər]

번영[번창/번성]하다

▶ prosperity 몡 번영
▶ prosperous 톙 번영하는

우리 모두는 함께 번영해야 한다.
We all should _____ together.

03 thrive
-thrived[throve]
-thrived[thriven]
[θraiv]

번영[번창/번성]하다

많은 식물들이 열대 우림에서 번성한다.
Many plants _____ in tropical rainforests.

04 boost
[buːst]

향상[고양]시키다,
들어[밀어] 올리다

▶ booster 몡 부스터, 강화[촉진]제, 후원자

그 승리는 팀의 자신감을 고양시켰다.
The win _____ed the team's confidence.

05 soar
[sɔːr]

높이 오르다[치솟다]

유가가 치솟았다.
Oil prices have _____ed.

06 inflate
[infléit]

부풀(리)다

▶ inflation 몡 인플레이션[통화 팽창]

그녀의 구명조끼가 부풀지 않았다.
Her life jacket failed to _____.

07 swell
-swelled-swollen
[swel]

붓다[부어오르다]

그녀의 발목이 부어오르기 시작했다.
Her ankle was starting to _____.

08 diminish
[dimíniʃ]

줄(이)다[감소하다](= decrease, reduce, lessen ↔ increase)

인플레이션의 위험이 감소하고 있다.
The threat of inflation is _____ing.

09 dwindle
[dwíndl]

줄어들다

그 도시의 인구가 줄어들고 있다.
The town's population is _____ing away.

10 wane
[wein]

❶ 줄어들다[시들해지다]
❷ (달이) 이지러지다

[비교] wax (달이) 차오르다

스캔들이 그녀의 인기를 시들해지게 했다.
The scandal caused her popularity to _____.

11 shrink
-shrank-shrunk

[ʃriŋk]

줄어들다[줄어들게 하다]　　　▶shrinkage 명 수축[감소]

내 스웨터가 건조기에서 줄어들었다.

My sweater _____ in the dryer.

12 contract
[kəntrǽkt]

❶ 수축[축소]하다(↔ expand)　　▶contraction 명 수축[축소]
❷ 병에 걸리다　❸ 계약하다　　▶contractor 명 계약자
명 계약(서)

금속은 차가워지면 수축한다.

Metal _____s as it cools.

13 compress
[kάmpres]

압축하다　　　　　　　▶compression 명 압축

그 프로그램은 이메일로 보내지는 어떤 데이터든 압축한다.

The program _____es any data sent by email.

14 condense
[kəndéns]

응축[농축/압축]하다

추운 밤 동안에 공기가 응축되어 풀에 이슬이 맺힌다.

During cold nights, air _____s on the grass to form dew.

15 wither
[wíðər]

시들다

들판에 있는 풀들이 시들었다.

Grass _____ed in the fields.

16 rot
[rɑt]

썩다[부패하다](=decay)　　　▶rotten 형 썩은[부패한]

사탕은 이를 썩게 한다.

Candy will _____ your teeth.

17 impoverish
[impάvəriʃ]

가난하게 하다(↔ enrich)　　　▶poverty 명 가난[빈곤]

빚은 많은 가족들을 가난하게 할 수 있을 뿐이다.

Debt can only _____ a lot of families.

18 compound
[kəmpáund]

❶ 악화시키다 ❷ 혼합하다　명 화합물　형 복합의

심한 가뭄이 식량 부족을 악화시켰다.

Severe drought has _____ed food shortages.

19 degrade
[digréid]

❶ 비하하다 ❷ 저하시키다 ❸ 분해하다

그 영화는 여성을 비하한다.

The movie _____s women.

20 collapse
[kəlǽps]

❶ 붕괴하다 ❷ 쓰러지다(=faint)　명 붕괴, 쓰러짐

몇 분 후에 두 번째 건물이 붕괴했다.

Minutes later the second tower _____d.

21 crumble
[krʌ́mbl]

산산이 부서지다, 무너지다

오래된 석조물이 산산이 부서져 나갔다.

The old stonework was _____ing away.

상태 변화 2

Part 2

22 crumple
[krʌ́mpl]

구기다[구겨지다]

그는 그 페이지를 찢어 구겨서 휴지통에 던져 넣었다.

He tore the page out, _____d it, and threw it in the wastepaper basket.

23 shatter
[ʃǽtər]

산산이 부서지다[부수다]

접시가 바닥에 떨어져 산산이 부서졌다.

The plate hit the floor, and _____ed into tiny bits.

24 crush
[krʌʃ]

으스러[쭈그러]뜨리다, 찧다
명 빽빽한 군중

그의 다리가 사고로 으스러졌다.

His leg was _____ed in the accident.

25 mash
[mæʃ]

으깨다

감자를 삶아 으깨어라.

Boil the potatoes and then _____ them up.

26 dissolve
[dizálv]

녹(이)다[용해하다]

두 숟갈의 분말을 따뜻한 물에 녹여라.

_____ two spoons of powder in warm water.

27 thaw
[θɔː]

녹(이)다(=defrost ↔ freeze)
명 해빙(기)

해가 나와 얼음을 녹였다.

The sun came out and _____ed the ice.

28 overturn
[òuvərtə́ːrn]

뒤집히다[전복하다]

그의 차가 전복되어 그는 안에 갇혔다.

His car _____ed, trapping him inside.

29 capsize
[kǽpsaiz]

(배가) 뒤집히다[전복하다]

배가 거친 바다에서 전복되었다.

The ship _____d in rough waters.

30 submerge
[səbmə́ːrdʒ]

물에 잠기다[잠수하다]

잠수함이 잠수했다.

The submarine _____d.

Today's Dessert

To accept good advice is but to increase one's own ability. – *Goethe*

좋은 충고를 받아들이면 자신의 능력이 증가할 뿐이다. – 괴테

Change of States 2

A 밑줄 친 동사에 유의하여 우리말로!

1 to <u>boost</u> your confidence
2 to <u>compress</u> data
3 to <u>compound</u> a problem
4 to <u>crumple</u> the paper

5 to <u>shatter</u> the windows
6 to <u>crush</u> a clove of garlic
7 to <u>mash</u> potatoes
8 to <u>dissolve</u> the sugar

B 영영사전 뜻풀이에 알맞은 단어 찾기

보기	capsize	crumble	dwindle	inflate	soar	submerge

1 _____ : to turn over in the water
2 _____ : to gradually become smaller
3 _____ : to break into very small pieces
4 _____ : to increase quickly to a high level
5 _____ : to increase in size by filling with air
6 _____ : to go under the surface of water or liquid

C 같은 관계 맺어주기

1 decay : rot = flourish : p_____ [=t_____]
2 freeze : thaw = enrich : i_____

D 빈칸에 가장 적절한 동사 넣기

보기	collapse	condense	diminish	shrink(shrank)	swell	wither	wane

1 Grass _____(e)d in the fields. 들판에 있는 풀들이 시들었다.
2 My sweater _____ in the dryer. 내 스웨터가 건조기에서 줄어들었다.
3 Her ankle was starting to _____. 그녀의 발목이 부어오르기 시작했다.
4 The moon waxes and then _____s. 달은 차고 나서 이지러진다[달도 차면 기운다].
5 Steam _____(e)s into water when it cools. 증기는 냉각되면 물로 응축된다.
6 The world's resources are rapidly _____ing. 세계의 자원이 급속히 감소하고 있다.
7 The roof _____(e)d under the weight of snow. 지붕이 눈의 무게로 붕괴했다.

E 밑줄 친 단어 뜻 구별하기

1 Metal <u>contract</u>s as it cools.   Many people <u>contract</u> AIDS.
2 The movie <u>degrade</u>s women.   Plastic goods do not <u>degrade</u>.

ANSWER_____
A 1. 자신감을 고양시키다 2. 데이터를 압축하다 3. 문제를 악화시키다 4. 종이를 구기다 5. 창문을 산산이 부수다 6. 마늘 한 쪽을 찧다 7. 감자를 으깨다 8. 설탕을 녹이다 **B** 1. capsize 2. dwindle 3. crumble 4. soar 5. inflate 6. submerge **C** 1. prosper[thrive] 2. impoverish **D** 1. wither 2. shrank 3. swell 4. wane 5. condense 6. diminish[wane] 7. collapse **E** 1. 금속은 차가워지면 수축한다.(수축하다) / 많은 사람들이 에이즈에 걸린다.(병에 걸리다) 2. 그 영화는 여성을 비하한다.(비하하다) / 플라스틱 제품은 분해되지 않는다.(분해하다)

상태 변화 2

Part 2

01 ponder
[pándər]

숙고하다

그는 계속 그 문제에 대해 숙고했다.

He continued to _____ the problem.

02 deliberate
동[dilíbərèit]
형[dilíbərət]

숙고하다   형 ❶ 의도[계획]적인(=intentional) ❷ 신중한(=careful)

그녀는 그의 말에 대해 숙고했다.

She _____d on his words.

03 contemplate
[kántəmplèit]

고려하다, 숙고하다(=consider)   ▶contemplative 형 명상에 잠기는

그는 자신의 장래를 숙고했다.

He _____d his future.

04 meditate
[médətèit]

❶ 명상하다   画回 mediate 중재하다
❷ (~ on) 숙고하다(=reflect)   ▶meditation 명 명상

그녀는 그날의 일들에 대해 숙고했다.

She _____d on the day's events.

05 suspect
동[səspékt]
명[sáspekt]

의심하다, 혐의를 두다   ▶suspicion 명 혐의[의심]
명 용의자   ▶suspicious 형 의심하는[의심스러운]
                      ▶unsuspecting 형 의심하지 않는

경찰은 그에게 살인 혐의를 두고 있다.

The police _____ him of murder.

06 visualize
[víʒuəlàiz]

마음에 그리다[상상하다]   ▶visualization 명 시각화[상상]
(=picture, imagine)   ▶visual 형 시각의

노인으로서의 네 모습을 마음에 그려 보아라.

Try to _____ yourself as an old man.

07 conceive
[kənsíːv]

❶ 상상하다 ❷ 임신하다   ▶conception 명 개념, 구상
                        ▶inconceivable 형 상상도 할 수 없는

난 누군가가 어떻게 그리 잔인하게 행동할 수 있었는지 상상할 수조차 없다.

I can't _____ how anyone could behave so cruelly.

08 daydream
[déidrì:m]

백일몽을 꾸다[공상에 잠기다]   명 백일몽

무슨 백일몽을 꾸고 있는 거니?

What are you _____ing about?

09 associate
[əsóuʃièit]

연상하다, 연관시키다   명 동료   ▶association 명 협회, 연관[연상]

사람들은 옛날을 좋은 시절로 연상한다.

People _____ the old days with good times.

10 foresee
-foresaw-foreseen
[fɔːrsíː]

예견하다(=predict)   ▶foreseeable 형 예견할 수 있는

그 재해는 예견될 수 없었다.

The disaster could not be _____.

11 recollect
[rèkəlékt]

기억하다(= remember)　　　　　▶recollection 몡 기억

내가 기억하는 건 그녀의 눈동자와 입술뿐이다.

All I _____ is her eyes and lips.

12 comprehend
[kὰmprihénd]

이해하다(= understand)　　　　▶comprehension 몡 이해
　　　　　　　　　　　　　　　▶comprehensible 혱 이해할 수 있는
　　　　　　　　　　　　　　　▶comprehensive 혱 포괄적인

난 무슨 일이 일어났는지 이해하지 못했다.

I didn't _____ what had happened.

13 perceive
[pərsíːv]

감지[인지]하다　　　　　　　　▶perception 몡 지각[인식]
　　　　　　　　　　　　　　　▶perceptual 혱 지각의

난 그의 행동에서 변화를 감지했다. I _____d a change in his behavior.

14 discern
[disə́ːrn]

알아차리다[식별하다]

정치가들은 여론을 알아차리는 데 능하다.

Politicians are good at _____ing public opinion.

15 acquaint
[əkwéint]

알려주다[숙지시키다]　　　　　▶be acquainted (with)
(= familiarize)　　　　　　　　　(~을[와]) 알다[아는 사이다]
　　　　　　　　　　　　　　　▶acquaintance 몡 지인, 면식, 지식

그녀는 학생들에게 그들의 의무를 숙지시켰다.

She _____ed her students with their duties.

16 investigate
[invéstəgèit]

조사[수사]하다(= look into)　　▶investigation 몡 조사[수사]
　　　　　　　　　　　　　　　▶investigator 몡 조사[수사]관

그 연구는 폭력적인 TV 프로그램이 아이들에게 미치는 영향을 조사한다.

The study _____s the impact of violent TV programming on children.

17 inspect
[inspékt]

검사[점검]하다(= examine)　　▶inspection 몡 검사[점검]
　　　　　　　　　　　　　　　▶inspector 몡 검사자

선생님이 돌아다니시면서 우리의 과제를 검사하셨다.

The teacher walked around _____ing our work.

18 inquire
[inkwáiər]

❶ 묻다[문의하다]　　　　　　　▶inquiry 몡 문의, 조사
❷ (~ into) 조사하다

그들은 회사의 금융 거래를 조사했다.

They _____d into the company's financial dealings.

19 browse
[brauz]

❶ 둘러보다[훑어보다]　　　　　▶(web) browser 몡 (웹) 브라우저
❷ 인터넷을 검색하다(= surf)　　　('익스플로러', '크롬' 등)

그는 신문의 구인 광고를 훑어보고 있었다.

He was _____ing the want ads in the newspaper.

20 analyze
[ǽnəlàiz]

분석하다　　　　　　　　　　　▶analysis 몡 분석
　　　　　　　　　　　　　　　▶analyst 몡 분석가
　　　　　　　　　　　　　　　▶analytical 혱 분석적인

그는 환자들의 꿈을 분석했다. He _____d the dreams of his patients.

21 dissect
[disékt]

해부[분석]하다

표본은 주의 깊게 해부되었다.

The specimens were carefully _____ed.

22 decode
[di:kóud]

(암호를) 해독하다(=decipher)   ▶code 몡 암호
                              ▶encode[encrypt] 암호화하다

'게놈 프로젝트'가 유전자 구조의 암호를 해독했다.

The "Genome Project" _____d the password of genetic structures.

23 diagnose
[dáiəgnòus]

진단하다   ▶diagnosis 몡 진단

그녀는 알츠하이머병 진단을 받았다.

She was _____d with Alzheimer's disease.

24 ascertain
[æ̀sərtéin]

확인하다[알아내다]

지방의 양을 확인하려면 라벨을 읽어 보아라.

Read labels to _____ the amount of fats.

25 verify
[vérəfài]

검증하다, 확인하다(=confirm)

너의 이론을 검증할 수 있니?

Are you able to _____ your theory?

26 coordinate
[kouɔ́ːrdənèit]

조직화[조정]하다   ▶coordinator 몡 조정자
                  ▶coordination 몡 조직화[조정]

그가 전체 연구를 조정해 오고 있다.

He has been _____ing the whole research.

27 infer
[infə́ːr]

추론하다   ▶inference 몡 추론

이 통계로부터 많은 것이 추론될 수 있다.

A lot can be _____red from these statistics.

28 equate
[ikwéit]

동일시하다   ▶equation 몡 방정식

대부분의 사람들은 부를 성공과 동일시한다.

Most people _____ wealth with success.

29 formulate
[fɔ́ːrmjulèit]

고안[창안]하다(=devise)   ▶formula(복수 formulas/formulae)
                         몡 (공)식

찰스 다윈은 자연 도태 이론을 창안했다.

Charles Darwin _____d the theory of natural selection.

30 resolve
[rizálv]

❶ 해결하다(=solve)   ▶resolution 몡 결의[결심], 해결
❷ 결심[결의]하다

위기가 협상을 통해 해결되었다.

The crisis was _____d by negotiations.

Today's Dessert

Find out the truth for yourself. Reason it out. That is realization.

스스로 진리를 찾아내라. 이성적으로 진리를 찾아내라. 그것이 깨달음이다.

TEST 51

A 밑줄 친 동사에 유의하여 우리말로!

1 to <u>contemplate</u> studying aboard
2 to <u>foresee</u> the disaster
3 to <u>perceive</u> color
4 to <u>investigate</u> the incident
5 to <u>inspect</u> the goods
6 to <u>inquire</u> into the affairs
7 to <u>analyze</u> dreams
8 to <u>dissect</u> a rat
9 to <u>diagnose</u> diseases
10 to <u>verify</u> a theory
11 to <u>infer</u> from the statistics
12 to <u>formulate</u> a plan

B 영영사전 뜻풀이에 알맞은 동사 찾기

보기 ascertain   associate   coordinate   daydream   discern

1 _____ : to find out something
2 _____ : to think about something pleasant
3 _____ : to make things work effectively as a whole
4 _____ : to connect one thing and another in your mind
5 _____ : to notice something by thinking about it carefully

C 같은 관계 맺어주기

1 understand : comprehend = ponder : d_____
2 remember : recollect = imagine : v_____

D 빈칸에 가장 적절한 동사 넣기

보기 acquaint   browse   conceive   equate   suspect

1 Are you _____(e)d with her? 너는 그녀와 아는 사이니?
2 I cannot _____ he would harm us 난 그가 우리를 해치리라고는 상상할 수조차 없다.
3 The police _____ she killed her child. 경찰은 그녀가 자신의 아이를 죽였을 거라고 의심한다.
4 Most people _____ wealth with success. 사람들 대부분은 부를 성공과 동일시한다.
5 She was _____ing through some magazines. 그녀는 잡지들을 훑어보고 있었다.

E 밑줄 친 동사에 유의하여 뜻 구별해 해석하기

1 He <u>meditated</u> on the meaning of life.   She <u>meditates</u> for an hour every morning.
2 The crisis was <u>resolved</u> by negotiations.   She <u>resolved</u> to stop smoking.

생각 · 연구

Part 2

ANSWER_____
A 1. 유학을 고려하다 2. 재해를 예견하다 3. 색을 인지하다 4. 사건을 수사하다 5. 상품을 검사[점검]하다 6. 사건을 조사하다 7. 꿈을 분석하다 8. 쥐를 해부하다 9. 질병을 진단하다 10. 이론을 검증하다 11. 통계로 추론하다 12. 계획을 고안하다 **B** 1. ascertain 2. daydream 3. coordinate 4. associate 5. discern **C** 1. deliberate 2. visualize **D** 1. acquaint 2. conceive 3. suspect 4. equate 5. browse(browsing) **E** 1. 그는 삶의 의미를 숙고했다.(숙고하다) / 그녀는 매일 아침 1시간 동안 명상을 한다.(명상하다) 2. 위기가 협상을 통해 해결되었다.(해결하다) / 그녀는 담배를 끊기로 결심했다.(결심하다)

01 evaluate
[ivǽljuèit]

평가하다
자신의 일을 평가할 수 있어야 한다.
You should be able to _____ your own work.

▶evaluation 몡 평가

02 assess
[əsés]

평가하다
시험이 학생의 능력을 평가할 수 있는가?
Can examinations _____ a student's ability?

▶assessment 몡 평가

03 appraise
[əpréiz]

평가하다
우리는 어떠한 개발이든 환경 비용을 평가해야 한다.
We should _____ the environmental costs of any development.

▶appraisal 몡 평가

04 estimate
됨[éstəmèit]
몡[éstəmət]

추산[추정]하다(=guess)
몡 추산, 견적(서)

경찰은 군중을 10만 명으로 추산한다.
Police _____ the crowd at 100,000.

▶estimation 몡 판단[평가]
▶overestimate 과대평가하다
▶underestimate 과소평가하다

05 appreciate
[əprí:ʃièit]

❶ 진가를 알아보다
❷ 감사하다

난 훌륭한 예술 작품의 진가를 알아본다. I _____ fine works of art.

▶appreciation 몡 감상(력), 감사
▶appreciative 혱 감탄[감사]하는
▶depreciate 평가 절하하다

06 deem
[di:m]

여기다[간주하다](=consider, regard, judge)
그들은 불법 이민자로 간주되었다.
They were _____ed to be illegal immigrants.

07 attribute
됨[ətríbju:t]
몡[ǽtribju:t]

(~ A to B) (A를 B) 때문이라고 여기다(=ascribe) 몡 속성
한국의 경제 기적은 우리의 부지런함과 창조적 재능 때문이라고 여겨진다.
The Korean economic miracle is _____d to our diligence and creative talents.

08 cherish
[tʃériʃ]

소중히 여기다[아끼다]
난 여전히 그날의 기억을 소중히 여긴다.
I still _____ the memory of that day.

09 compliment
됨[kámpləmènt]
몡[kámpləmənt]

칭찬하다
몡 칭찬[찬사]

선생님은 내 보고서에 대해 칭찬하셨다.
My teacher _____ed me on my report.

비교 complement 보완하다 몡 보완물
▶complimentary 혱 칭찬하는, 무료의

10 flatter
[flǽtər]

아첨하다, 돋보이게 하다
그는 요리 솜씨를 칭찬하며 그녀에게 아첨한다.
He _____s her by praising her cooking.

▶flattery 몡 아첨

11 commemorate
[kəmémərèit]

기념하다(= celebrate)

동상이 100주년을 기념하기 위해 세워졌다.

A statue has been built to _____ the 100th anniversary.

12 compensate
[kámpənsèit]

보상하다 ▶compensation 명 보상(금)

희생자들은 손실에 대해 보상받을 것이다.

Victims will be _____d for their loss.

13 assume
[əsúːm]

❶ 추정[가정]하다 ❷ 맡다 ▶assumption 명 가정
❸ ~인 척하다, 성질을 띠다

네가 안 보여 외출했다고 추정했어.

I didn't see you, so I _____d you'd gone out.

14 presume
[prizúːm]

추정하다 ▶presumably 부 추측건대[아마]

난 우리가 6시까지는 거기에 갈 거라고 추정한다.

I _____ we'll be there by six o'clock.

15 speculate
[spékjulèit]

❶ 추측하다 ❷ 투기하다

내가 무엇을 하게 될지 정확히 추측할 수 없다.

I cannot exactly _____ on what I will do.

16 condemn
[kəndém]

(도덕적으로) 비난[규탄]하다

그 신문은 공정성의 결여로 비난받는다.

The newspaper is _____ed as lacking fairness.

17 denounce
[dináuns]

(공개적으로) 비난하다

우리는 불의와 압제를 비난해야 한다.

We must _____ injustice and oppression.

18 reproach
[ripróutʃ]

책망하다 명 책망

그는 아들의 행동을 책망했다.

He _____ed his son for his behavior.

19 reprove
[riprúːv]

나무라다[꾸짖다]

그녀는 담배를 피운다고 나무람을 들었다.

She was _____d for smoking.

20 scold
[skould]

(아이를) 꾸짖다[야단치다] ▶scolding 명 꾸지람
(= tell off)

그는 지각했다고 그들을 꾸짖었다.

He _____ed them for arriving late.

21 curse
[kəːrs]

욕하다(= swear), 저주하다 명 욕, 저주

그는 술 취하면 늘 욕하기 시작한다.

He always starts _____ing when he gets drunk.

22 mock
[mɑk]

(흉내 내며) 놀리다[조롱하다](=make fun of)　형 가짜[모의]의

그녀는 그가 절뚝거리는 걸 흉내 내며 놀렸다.

She made fun of him by _____ing his limp.

23 sue
[su:]

소송을 제기하다[고소하다]　▶suit[lawsuit] 명 소송

그녀는 의사들을 과실로 고소 중이었다.

She was _____ing doctors for negligence.

24 penalize
[pí:nəlàiz]

처벌하다(=punish)　▶penalty 명 처벌, 벌금[벌칙]

그는 위험한 플레이를 했다고 벌칙을 받았다.

He was _____d for dangerous play.

25 triumph
[tráiəmf]

승리하다
명 승리(감)

▶triumphant 형 의기양양한
▶triumphal 형 개선의

결국 선이 악에 승리할 것이다.

In the end, good shall _____ over evil.

26 prevail
[privéil]

❶ 일반적이다[널리 퍼져 있다]
❷ 승리하다
❸ (~ (up)on) 설득하다

▶prevalent 형 일반적인[널리 퍼져 있는]
▶prevalence 명 유행

정의가 불의에 승리할 것이다.

Justice will _____ over injustice.

27 excel
[iksél]

뛰어나다[탁월하다]

▶excellence 명 뛰어남[탁월함]
▶excellent 형 뛰어난[탁월한]

그녀는 늘 외국어에 뛰어났다.

She has always _____led at foreign languages.

28 exceed
[iksí:d]

초과하다[넘어서다]

▶excess 명 과도 형 초과한
▶excessive 형 과도한
▶exceedingly 부 극도로

노동 시간은 주당 40시간을 초과해서는 안 된다.

Working hours must not _____ 40 hours a week.

29 surpass
[sərpǽs]

능가하다[뛰어넘다]

그는 우리의 모든 예상을 넘어섰다.

He had _____ed all our expectations.

30 transcend
[trænsénd]

초월하다

▶transcendence 명 초월
▶transcendent[transcendental]
　형 초월의[초월적인]

평화에 대한 열망은 정치적 차이를 초월한다.

The desire for peace _____s political differences.

Today's Dessert

Praise a fool, and you make him useful.

바보도 칭찬해 보라. 그러면 쓸모 있게 된다.

Part 2 판단

212

TEST 52

A 밑줄 친 동사에 유의하여 우리말로!

1 to cherish a dream

2 to compensate for the loss

3 to curse your bad luck

4 to mock the idea

5 to surpass your expectations

6 to transcend differences

B 영영사전 뜻풀이에 알맞은 동사 찾기

보기 exceed   excel   presume   scold   triumph

1 _____ : to angrily criticize someone

2 _____ : to do something much better than most people

3 _____ : to be more than a particular number or amount

4 _____ : to gain a victory or success after a difficult struggle

5 _____ : to think that something is true, although you are not certain

C 같은 관계 맺어주기

1 praise : compliment = evaluate : a_____ [a_____]

2 condemn : denounce = celebrate : c_____

3 sue : suit = flatter : f_____

D 빈칸에 가장 적절한 동사 넣기

보기 attribute   deem   estimate   penalize   reproach

1 She _____(e)d him for smoking. 그녀는 그가 담배를 피운다고 책망했다.

2 He was _____(e)d for dangerous play. 그는 위험한 플레이로 벌칙을 받았다.

3 The area has now been _____(e)d safe. 그 지역은 이제 안전한 것으로 여겨진다.

4 The cost of the project is _____(e)d at about 1 million dollars.
그 프로젝트의 비용은 약 백만 달러로 추산된다.

5 His doctor _____s his health problems to a poor diet and a lack of
exercise. 그의 의사는 그의 건강 문제를 빈약한 식사와 운동 부족 때문이라고 여긴다.

E 밑줄 친 단어 뜻 구별하기

1 I appreciate fine works of art.   I appreciate your concern.

2 I assumed you'd gone out.   I assumed an important role.

3 I speculated in stocks.   I cannot speculate on what I will do.

4 Justice will prevail.   I prevailed upon her to admit it.

ANSWER

A 1. 꿈을 소중히 여기다 2. 손해를 보상하다 3. 불운을 저주하다 4. 생각을 조롱하다 5. 예상을 뛰어넘다 6. 차이를 초월하다 B 1. scold 2. excel 3. exceed 4. triumph 5. presume C 1. assess[appraise] 2. commemorate 3. flattery D 1. reproach 2. penalize 3. deem 4. estimate 5. attribute E 1. 난 훌륭한 예술 작품의 진가를 알아본다.(진가를 알아보다) / 당신의 관심에 감사드립니다.(감사하다) 2. 난 네가 외출했다고 추정했어.(추정하다) / 난 중요한 역할을 맡았다.(맡다) 3. 난 주식에 투자했다.(투자하다) / 내가 무엇을 하게 될지 추측할 수 없다.(추측하다) 4. 정의가 승리하리라.(승리하다) / 난 그녀를 설득해 그것을 인정하게 했다.(설득하다)

Part 2

판단

01 prior
[práiər]

❶ (시)전의
❷ 우선하는

▶priority 명 우선 사항, 우선권
▶prioritize 통 우선순위를 매기다

사전 지식/승인/경고 _____ knowledge/approval/warning

그들이 그 재산에 대해 우선권을 가진다.

They have a _____ claim to the property.

02 subsequent
[sʌ́bsikwənt]

그다음의

비교 consequent 결과로 일어나는

사고 그다음에 일어난 사건들

events that happened _____ to the accident

03 simultaneous
[sàiməltéiniəs]

동시의

사용자 20명까지 시스템에 동시에 접근할 수 있다.

Up to twenty users can have _____ access to the system.

04 immemorial
[ìməmɔ́ːriəl]

태곳적[먼 옛날]부터의

▶memorial 기념[추모]의 명 기념비

태고적[먼 옛날]부터의 전통 an _____ tradition

05 initial
[iníʃəl]

처음[초기]의(=first) 명 이름의 첫 글자[머리글자]

산업화의 초기 단계 the _____ stage of industrialization

06 ultimate
[ʌ́ltəmət]

궁극적인[최후의](=final)

네 인생의 궁극적인 목표가 뭐니?

What is your _____ goal in life?

07 timely
[táimli]

적시의[시기적절한]

▶untimely 때 이른[때 아닌]

너의 시기적절한 경고가 우리 목숨을 구했다.

Your _____ warning saved our lives.

08 punctual
[pʌ́ŋktʃuəl]

시간을 지키는

비교 punctuation 명 구두점
puncture 명 구멍[펑크]
▶punctuality 명 시간 엄수

그녀는 늘 약속 시간을 아주 잘 지킨다.

She's always very _____ for appointments.

09 abrupt
[əbrʌ́pt]

❶ 갑작스러운(=sudden, unexpected) ❷ 퉁명스러운

버스가 갑자기 섰다.

The bus came to an _____ halt.

그녀는 내게 몹시 퉁명스러웠다.

She was very _____ with me.

10 prompt
[prɑmpt]

즉각적인[신속한] 통 촉발[유도]하다

즉각적인 조치가 취해져야 한다.

_____ action must be taken.

11 offhand
[ɔ̀(:)fhǽnd]

즉흥적인[즉석의] 🔵 즉석에서[당장]

즉흥적인 발언/대답 an _____ remark/reply

12 momentary
[móuməntèri]

순간적인(=brief) ▶ moment 몡 순간

순간적인 멈춤[휴지]/망설임 a _____ pause/hesitation

순간적인 의식 상실 a _____ loss of consciousness

13 temporary
[témpərèri]

일시적인[임시의](↔ permanent)

일시적인 통증 완화 _____ pain relief

임시직 a _____ job

임시 직원 _____ staff

14 transient [transitory]
[trǽnʃənt] [trǽnsətɔ̀:ri]

일시적인

일시적인 기쁨[즐거움] _____ pleasures[joys]

15 perpetual
[pərpétʃuəl]

끊임없이 계속되는(= permanent)

끊임없이 계속되는 기계들의 소음 the _____ noise of the machines

16 eternal
[itə́:rnl]

영원한(= everlasting) ▶ eternity 몡 영원

우리는 영원한 우정을 맹세했다.

We swore _____ friendship.

17 continuous/ continual
[kəntínjuəs] [kəntínjuəl]

계속되는[끊임없는](= unbroken)/ ▶ continue 통 계속하다
계속되는[(짜증나게) 거듭되는] ▶ continuity 몡 연속성
 ▶ continuation 몡 계속

계속되는 정보의 흐름

a _____ flow of information

18 consecutive
[kənsékjutiv]

연속적인[연이은]

그녀는 9일 연속 결석했다.

She was absent for nine _____ days.

19 successive
[səksésiv]

연속적인[연이은] ▶ succeed 통 ❶ 성공하다 ❷ 뒤를 잇다
 ▶ succession 몡 연속, 계승

팀은 5연승을 했다.

The team has had five _____ victories.

20 sustainable
[səstéinəbl]

지속 가능한(↔ unsustainable) ▶ sustain 통 유지[지속]시키다
 ▶ sustainability 몡 지속 가능성

지속 가능한 경제 성장 _____ economic growth

환경적으로 지속 가능한 사회 an environmentally _____ society

21 durable
[djúərəbl]

오래가는[내구성이 있는] ▶ endure 통 견디다[참다]
(= hard-wearing) ▶ duration 몡 (지속) 기간

기계는 내구성이 있는 재료들로 만들어져야 한다.

The machines have to be made of _____ materials.

시간 · 공간

Part 3

215

22 chronic
[kránik]

만성[고질]의 (=persistent ↔ acute 급성의)

만성 관절염/천식/심장병 _____ arthritis/asthma/heart disease

23 ongoing
[ángòuiŋ]

진행 중인

진행 중인 조사/협상 an _____ investigation/negotiation

24 upcoming
[ápkλmiŋ]

다가오는

다가오는 크리스마스 시즌 the _____ Christmas season

25 annual/ biannual
[ǽnjuəl] / [baiǽnjuəl]

연례[연간]의(=yearly)/연 2회의   비교 biennial 2년마다의[격년의]
                                              quadrennial 4년마다의

연례행사 an _____ event

연 2회 나오는 보고서 a _____ report

26 chronological
[krànəládʒikəl]

시간 순서대로의[연대순의]   ▶ chronology 몡 연대순, 연대표
                                   ▶ chronological age 달력 나이

우리는 문서들을 연대순으로 배열하였다.
We arranged the documents in _____ order.

27 spatial
[spéiʃəl]

공간의   비교 spacious 널찍한
              ▶ space 몡 우주, 공간

아동의 공간 인지 발달
the development of a child's _____ awareness

28 cramped
[krǽmpt]

비좁은

그 부엌은 작고 비좁았다.
The kitchen was small and _____.

29 halfway
[hǽːfwèi]

중간의
뷔 중간에

우리는 중간 지점에서 만났다.
We met at a _____ point.

30 innermost
[ínərmòust]

가장 깊숙한[마음속 깊은]   ▶ inner ↔ outer 안의 ↔ 밖의
(=inmost ↔ outermost)

난 그와 마음속 깊은 생각과 감정을 나눈다.
I share my _____ thoughts and feelings with him.

Today's Dessert

Life just gives you time and space; it's up to you to fill it.

인생은 단지 네게 시간과 공간을 줄 뿐이다. 그걸 채우는 건 네게 달려 있다.

TEST 53

A 영어는 우리말로, 우리말은 영어로!

1 the initial response

2 durable goods

3 an ongoing investigation

4 the upcoming elections

5 in chronological order

6 tests of spatial ability

7 a cramped apartment

8 the halfway stage

9 동시통역　　s_____ interpretation

10 궁극적인 목표　the u_____ goal

11 갑작스러운 변화　an a_____ change

12 신속한 조처　p_____ action

13 즉흥적인 발언　an o_____ remark

14 순간적인 혼란　m_____ confusion

15 임시직　a t_____ job

16 연봉　a_____ salary

B 영영사전 뜻풀이에 알맞은 단어 찾기

| 보기 | perpetual subsequent timely transient |

1 _____ : happening after something else

2 _____ : happening at a suitable moment

3 _____ : continuing only for a short time

4 _____ : continuing all the time without changing or stopping

C 같은 관계 맺어주기

1 prior : priority = eternal : e_____

2 continuous : continual = consecutive : s_____

3 inner : outer = acute : c_____

D 빈칸에 가장 적절한 단어 넣기

| 보기 | immemorial innermost prior punctual sustainable |

1 He's always very _____ for appointments. 그는 늘 약속 시간을 아주 잘 지킨다.

2 I cannot express my _____ feelings to anyone.

난 마음속 깊은 감정을 누구에게도 표현할 수 없다.

3 Markets have been held here since time _____.

시장이 태고적[먼 옛날]부터 여기서 열려왔다

4 You should arrive at least 20 minutes _____ to boarding.

최소한 탑승 20분 전에 도착해야 한다.

5 _____ development is not possible without _____ energy.

지속 가능한 발전은 지속 가능한 에너지 없이는 가능하지 않다.

시간·공간

Part 3

ANSWER

A 1. 초기 반응 2. 내구재 3. 진행 중인 조사 4. 다가오는 선거 5. 시간 순서대로[연대순으로] 6. 공간 능력 테스트 7. 비좁은 아파트 8. 중간 단계 9. simultaneous 10. ultimate 11. abrupt 12. prompt 13. offhand 14. momentary 15. temporary 16. annual　B 1. subsequent 2. timely 3. transient 4. perpetual　C 1. eternity 2. successive 3. chronic　D 1. punctual 2. innermost 3. immemorial 4. prior 5. sustainable

Degree & Power

01 numerous
[njúːmərəs]

(수)많은

▶ numeral 명 숫자

비교 numerical 수의[수로 나타낸]

제가 감사하고 싶은 사람들이 너무 많아 다 언급할 수가 없습니다.
The people I'd like to thank are too _____ to mention.

02 innumerable
[injúːmərəbl]

셀 수 없이 많은[무수한](=countless)

하늘에 무수한 별들이 있다.
There are _____ stars in the sky.

03 multiple
[mʌ́ltəpl]

다수[복수]의

명 배수

▶ multiply 통 곱하다, 증가하다

▶ multitude 명 다수

선다형 시험 _____ choice tests

다의어 words with _____ meanings

04 infinite
[ínfənət]

무한한(↔ finite 한정된)

비교 definite 명확한

무한한 우주 an _____ universe

무한한 가능성 _____ possibilities

05 immense
[iméns]

막대한[엄청난](=enormous)

막대한 부/힘 _____ wealth/power

엄청난 재능/인기 _____ talent/popularity

06 gigantic
[dʒaigǽntik]

거대한

▶ giant 거대한 명 거인

거대한 마천루/기업 a _____ skyscraper/corporation

거대한 파도 _____ waves

07 vast
[væst]

방대한[광대한](=huge)

방대한 양의 정보/지식 _____ quantities of information/knowledge

광대한 열대 우림 지역 _____ areas of rain forest

08 extensive
[iksténsiv]

대규모의[광범위한]

▶ extend 통 연장[확장]하다, 뻗다

▶ extension 명 확장[연장], 내선

광범위한 연구/지식 _____ research/knowledge

09 massive
[mǽsiv]

육중한[거대한/엄청난]

▶ mass 명 덩어리, 대량, 대중, 질량

▶ massiveness 명 육중함

육중한 바위 a _____ rock

거대한 벽 _____ walls

엄청난 노력 a _____ effort

10 substantial
[səbstǽnʃəl]

상당한(=considerable)

상당한 수/양 a _____ number/amount

상당한 변화 a _____ change

11 ample
[ǽmpl]

충분한   ▶ amplify 통 증폭하다

충분한 기회/증거/시간/공간

_____ opportunity/evidence/time/space

12 minute
형 [mainʃúːt] 명 [mínit]

아주 작은[미세한](=tiny) 명 ❶ 분 ❷ (-s) 회의록

미세한 먼지 입자들 _____ particles of dust

13 mighty
[máiti]

강력한[거대한]   ▶ might 명 힘(=strength)

강력한 군대 a _____ army

거대한 미시시피강 the _____ Mississippi

14 formidable
[fɔ́ːrmidəbl]

어마어마한[가공할]

어마어마한 상대/도전 a _____ opponent/challenge

15 potent
[póutnt]

강력한[효력 있는](↔impotent)

강력한 무기 a _____ weapon

효력 있는 약 a _____ medicine

16 intense
[inténs]

극심한[강렬한](=extreme)   ▶ intensify 통 심해지다[강화하다]

                      ▶ intensity 명 강렬함, 강도[세기]

극심한 통증/강렬한 사랑 an _____ pain/love

17 intensive
[inténsiv]

집중[집약]적인   비교 extensive 광대한[광범위한]

1주간의 영어 집중 과정

a one-week _____ course in English

18 drastic
[drǽstik]

과감한[급격한](=radical)

과감한 조치가 취해져야 한다.

_____ measures[action] should be taken.

19 moderate
[mádərət]

❶ 적당한(=reasonable)   ▶ moderation 명 절제[중용]

❷ 온건한(↔extreme)   ▶ in moderation 적당하게

명 온건주의자   (↔to excess 과도하게)

적당한 가격 _____ prices

온건파 당원들 _____ members of the party

20 temperate
[témpərət]

❶ 온화한[온대의] ❷ 차분한

온대/온대 지역 a _____ zone/region

차분한 행동 _____ behavior

21 fragile
[frǽdʒəl]

부서지기 쉬운, 취약한[허약한]   ▶ fragility 명 부서지기 쉬움, 허약

(=delicate ↔strong)

소포에는 '부서지기 쉬움 – 취급 주의'라고 찍혀 있었다.

The parcel was marked F_____ – HANDLE WITH CARE.

22 frail
[freil]

(허)약한[부서지기 쉬운](=weak) ▶**frailty** 명 허약, 약점(=weakness)

그녀는 침대에서 허약한 몸을 일으켰다.

She raised her _____ body in bed.

23 vulnerable
[vʌ́lnərəbl]

상처 받기 쉬운[연약한/취약한] ▶**vulnerability** 명 취약성

폭력 범죄에 취약한 젊은이들

the young who are _____ to violent crime

24 susceptible
[səséptəbl]

민감한[취약한]

나이 든 사람들은 감염증에 더 취약하다.

Older people are more _____ to infections.

25 prone
[proun]

(나쁜 것을) 하기[당하기] 쉬운

아이들은 정크 푸드를 먹기 쉽다.

Kids are _____ to eat junk food.

26 mortal
↔immortal
[mɔ́ːrtl] ↔ [imɔ́ːrtl]

영원히 살지 못하는 ▶**mortality** 명 죽을 운명, 사망자 수
↔ 영원히 사는[불멸/불후의] ▶**immortality** 명 불멸

모든 인간은 영원히 살지 못한다. All human beings are _____.

불멸의 영혼 the _____ soul

불후의 작품/명작 an _____ work/classic

27 fatal
[féitl]

치명적인 ▶**fate** 명 운명
  ▶**fatality** 명 사망자, 치사율

치명적인 질병/사고 a _____ disease/accident

28 destined
[déstind]

❶ ~할 운명인[하기로 되어 있는] ▶**destiny** 명 운명(=fate)
❷ ~행인[가기로 되어 있는] ▶**destination** 명 목적지

우리는 결코 다시 만나지 못할 운명이었다.

We were _____ never to meet again.

29 inevitable
[inévətəbl]

불가피한[필연적인](=unavoidable)

진보와 더불어 변화는 불가피하다.

With progress, change is _____.

30 terminal
[tə́ːrmənl]

(병이) 말기[불치]의 ▶**terminate** 동 종료하다[종료되다]
명 터미널[종점], 단말기 ▶**termination** 명 종료, 임신 중절

말기 암 _____ cancer

말기 환자 a _____ patient

Today's Dessert

He who conquers others is strong; he who conquers himself is mighty.

다른 이들을 정복하는 사람은 강하지만, 자신을 정복하는 사람은 강력하다.

A 영어는 우리말로, 우리말은 영어로!

1 numerous occasions

2 a multiple choice question

3 a massive rock

4 a substantial change

5 ample time

6 a temperate climate

7 a fragile vase

8 frail elderly people

9 accident-prone

10 무한한 잠재력   i_____ potential

11 광범위한 독서   an e_____ reading

12 강력한 군대   a m_____ army

13 어마어마한 상대   a f_____ opponent

14 극심한 통증   an i_____ pain

15 집중 훈련   i_____ training

16 적당한 운동   m_____ exercise

17 치명적 사고   a f_____ accident

18 말기 암   t_____ cancer

B 영영사전 뜻풀이에 알맞은 단어 찾기

> 보기   drastic   gigantic   inevitable   potent   vulnerable

1 _____ : extremely big

2 _____ : powerful and effective

3 _____ : extreme and sudden in action or effect

4 _____ : certain to happen and impossible to avoid

5 _____ : weak and easily hurt physically or emotionally

C 주어진 철자로 시작하는 동의어 쓰기

1 countless = i_____

2 enormous = i_____

3 huge = v_____

4 tiny = m_____

D 빈칸에 가장 적절한 단어 넣기

> 보기   destined   immortal   mortal   susceptible

1 We are all _____ . 우리는 모두 영원히 살지 못한다.

2 We seem _____ never to meet. 우리는 결코 만나지 못할 운명인 것 같다.

3 Do you believe that the soul is _____ ? 넌 영혼이 불멸한다고 믿니?

4 People with high blood pressure are _____ to diabetes.
고혈압이 있는 사람들은 당뇨병에 취약하다.

ANSWER_____
A 1. 수많은 경우들 2. 선다형 문제 3. 육중한 바위 4. 상당한 변화 5. 충분한 시간 6. 온대 기후 7. 깨지기 쉬운 꽃병 8. 허약한 노인들 9. 사고 나기 쉬운 10. infinite 11. extensive 12. mighty 13. formidable 14. intense 15. intensive 16. moderate 17. fatal 18. terminal B 1. gigantic 2. potent 3. drastic 4. inevitable 5. vulnerable C 1. innumerable 2. immense 3. vast 4. minute D 1. mortal 2. destined 3. immortal 4. susceptible

01 **optimistic**
↔ pessimistic
[ɑ̀ptəmístik] ↔ [pèsəmístik]

낙관[낙천]적인 ↔ 비관[염세]적인
▶ optimism/optimist 명 낙관주의/자
▶ pessimism/pessimist 명 비관주의/자

그녀는 결과에 대해 낙관/비관한다.
She is _____ / _____ about the outcome.

02 **extrovert**
↔ introvert
[ékstrəvə̀:rt] ↔ [íntrəvə̀:rt]

외향적인 명 외향적인 사람
↔ 내향[내성]적인
명 내향[내성]적인 사람
▶ extroverted 외향적인
↔ introverted 내향[내성]적인

그녀는 외향적인 데 반해, 그는 내향적이다.
She is an _____, while he is an _____.

03 **sociable**
[sóuʃəbl]

사교적인(=friendly, outgoing
↔ unsociable)
▶ sociability 명 사교성

난 다른 사람들과 함께 있는 걸 좋아하기 때문에 사교적이다.
I am _____ because I love being with other people.

04 **courageous**
[kəréidʒəs]

용감한
(=brave, daring ↔ cowardly)
▶ courage 명 용기(=bravery)

용감한 벗 a _____ companion
용감한 행동/결정 a _____ act/decision

05 **ambitious**
[æmbíʃəs]

야심 찬
▶ ambition 명 야망[야심]

야심 찬 소년[소녀]/젊은이 an _____ boy[girl]/young (wo)men
야심 찬 계획/목표/노력 an _____ plan[project]/goal/effort

06 **industrious**
[indʌ́striəs]

부지런한[근면한](=hard-working)
비교 industrial 산업의
▶ industry 명 ❶ 산업 ❷ 근면

그녀는 유능하고 근면하다.
She is competent and _____.

07 **cowardly**
[káuərdli]

비겁한(↔ brave, courageous)
▶ coward 명 겁쟁이
▶ cowardice 명 겁

무방비한 사람에 대한 비겁한 공격
a _____ attack on a defenseless man

08 **timid**
[tímid]

소심한(=shy ↔ confident)
▶ timidity 명 소심함

난 소심한 아이였다.
I used to be a _____ child.

09 **reserved**
[rizə́:rvd]

❶ 내성적인 ❷ 예약[지정]된
▶ reserve 통 예약하다, 남겨 두다
명 비축(량)

그녀는 수줍음이 많고, 내성적인 소녀다.
She is a shy and _____ girl.
예약[지정]석/지정 주차
_____ seats/parking

10 meek
[miːk]

온순한(=gentle, mild)

그녀는 매우 온순하고 온화해 보인다.

She looks very _____ and mild.

11 courteous
↔ discourteous
[kə́ːrtiəs] ↔ [diskə́ːrtiəs]

예의 바른(=polite, well-mannered)　　▶courtesy 몡 예의
↔ 무례한(=impolite, ill-mannered)

그 직원들은 늘 예의 바르다/무례하다.

The staff are always _____ / _____.

12 considerate
[kənsídərət]

이해심 많은[배려하는]
(↔ inconsiderate)

비교 considerable 상당한
▶consider 통 고려[배려]하다, 여기다
▶consideration 몡 고려[배려]

그는 다른 사람들에 대해 이해심이 많다.

He is _____ of others.

13 earnest
[ə́ːrnist]

성실한[진지한]

성실한 젊은이　an _____ young man

진지한 토론　_____ discussions

14 discreet
[diskríːt]

신중한

비교 discrete 별개의[분리된]

신중한 사람은 소문을 퍼뜨리지 않는다.

A _____ person does not spread rumors.

15 prudent
[prúːdnt]

신중한(↔ imprudent 경솔한)

전문가의 조언을 구하는 게 신중한 것일지도 모른다.

It may be _____ to get some expert advice.

16 altruistic
[æ̀ltruːístik]

이타적인(=selfless ↔ selfish)

그의 동기는 전적으로 이타적이었는가?

Were his motives entirely _____?

17 tolerant
[tálərənt]

관대한(↔ intolerant)

비교 tolerable 참을 수 있는
▶tolerate 통 용인하다, 견디다[참다]
▶tolerance 몡 관용

그녀는 다른 사람들의 결점에 그리 관대하지 못하다.

She's not very _____ of other people's failings.

18 stern
[stəːrn]

엄(격)한(=strict)
몡 선미[고물](↔ bow 이물[뱃머리])

그는 좀처럼 웃지 않는 엄한 사람이다.

He is a _____ man who rarely smiles.

19 stubborn
[stʌ́bərn]

완고한[고집스러운](=obstinate)　▶stubbornness 몡 완고함

완고할수록 넌 더 고립된다.

The more _____ you are, the more isolated you become.

20 arrogant
[ǽrəgənt]

거만한(↔ humble, modest)　▶arrogance 몡 거만

그는 참을 수 없을 정도로 거만했다.

He was unbearably _____.

성격·태도

Part 3

223

21 vain
[vein]

❶ 자만심이 강한(=conceited)
❷ 헛된(=fruitless)

[비교] vein 몡 정맥
▶vanity 몡 자만심
▶in vain 헛되이

그녀는 자만심이 강한 소녀다. She's a _____ girl.

헛된 희망 a _____ hope

22 inquisitive
[inkwízətiv]

호기심이 강한(=curious)

그는 매우 호기심이 강한 아이여서, 늘 "왜요?"라고 묻는다.

He is a very _____ child, always asking "why?"

23 candid
[kǽndid]

솔직한(=frank, honest, truthful)

그는 놀랄 정도로 내게 솔직했다.

He was surprisingly _____ with me.

24 devout
[diváut]

독실한

[비교] devote 동 바치다
▶devotion 몡 헌신[전념]

독실한 불교도/기독교도/이슬람교도

a _____ Buddhist/Christian/Muslim

25 skeptical
[sképtikəl]

회의적인[의심하는](=dubious)

▶skeptic 몡 회의론자
▶skepticism 몡 회의(=doubt)

많은 전문가들은 그의 주장에 회의적이다.

Many experts remain _____ of his claims.

26 cynical
[sínikəl]

냉소적인(↔idealistic)

[비교] ironic 반어적인
satirical 풍자적인
sarcastic 빈정거리는[비꼬는]

인간 본성에 대한 냉소적인 관점 a _____ view of human nature

27 hostile
[hástl]

적대적인(=unfriendly)

▶hostility 몡 적대감[반감]

적대적인 태도 a _____ attitude

적군 _____ forces

28 corrupt
[kərápt]

타락[부패]한(↔fair, honest, just)
동 타락시키다

▶corruption 몡 타락[부패]

부패한 정치인들은 사면되어서는 안 된다.

_____ politicians should not be pardoned.

29 cunning
[kʌ́niŋ]

교활한(=sly) 몡 교활함

교활한 미소/술책 a _____ smile/trick

30 wicked
[wíkid]

사악한(=evil), 심술궂은

사악한 마녀 a _____ witch

심술궂은 유머 감각 a _____ sense of humor

Today's Dessert *Character can be developed not in ease but through experience of trial and suffering.*

인간의 성격은 편안함 속에서가 아니라 시련과 고통의 경험을 통해서만 발전될 수 있다.

TEST 55

A 영어는 우리말로, 우리말은 영어로!

1 a reserved girl/boy
2 an earnest student
3 a prudent choice
4 a stern look
5 an inquisitive child
6 cynical view of life

7 거만한 태도   an a_____ attitude
8 솔직한 고백   a c_____ confession
9 독실한 불교도 a d_____ Buddhist
10 부패한 정권   a c_____ regime
11 교활한 술책   a c_____ trick
12 사악한 행위   a w_____ deed

B 가장 적절한 내용의 문장이 되도록 연결하기

1 A sociable person ·
2 An ambitious person ·
3 An industrious person ·
4 A considerate person ·
5 A discreet person ·

a. works hard.
b. enjoys being with other people.
c. has a strong desire to be successful.
d. is careful about what he/she says or does.
e. thinks of other people's wishes and feelings.

C 주어진 철자로 시작하는 반의어 쓰기

1 optimistic ↔ p_____
2 extrovert ↔ i_____
3 courageous ↔ c_____

4 confident ↔ t_____
5 courteous ↔ d_____
6 selfish ↔ a_____

D 빈칸에 가장 적절한 단어 넣기

| 보기 | hostile | meek | skeptical | stubborn | tolerant | vain |

1 He is as _____ as a mule. 그는 노새처럼 완고하다.
2 She looks very _____ and mild. 그녀는 매우 온순하고 온화해 보인다.
3 Men can be as _____ as women. 남성은 여성만큼 자만심이 강할 수 있다.
4 The rich are _____ to the reform. 부자들은 개혁에 적대적이다.
5 I'm _____ about what I read in the press. 난 신문에서 읽는 것에 대해 의심한다.
6 We need to be _____ of different points of view.
우리는 다른 관점에 대해 관대할 필요가 있다.

성격 · 태도

Part 3

ANSWER_____
A 1. 내성적인 소녀/소년 2. 성실한 학생 3. 신중한 선택 4. 엄한 표정 5. 호기심 강한 아이 6. 냉소적인 인생관 7. arrogant 8. candid 9. devout
10. corrupt 11. cunning 12. wicked B 1. b 2. c 3. a 4. e 5. d C 1. pessimistic 2. introvert 3. cowardly 4. timid 5. discourteous 6.
altruistic D 1. stubborn 2. meek 3. vain 4. hostile 5. skeptical 6. tolerant

01 slim
[slim]

❶ 날씬한(=slender), 얇은 ❷ 아주 적은
동 (~ down) 날씬하게 하다
그녀는 아름다운 날씬한 몸매를 가지고 있다.
She's got a lovely _____ figure.

02 plump
[plʌmp]

통통한[포동포동한]
그 아이는 볼이 통통하고 발그레하다.
The child has _____ rosy cheeks.

03 stout
[staut]

❶ 뚱뚱한 ❷ 튼튼한
그는 나이가 들면서 뚱뚱해졌다.
He became _____ as he grew older.

04 lame
[leim]

❶ 다리를 저는 ❷ 어설픈   ▶lame duck 명 레임덕
(임기 말 권력 누수 현상)
다리를 저는 개/말 a _____ dog/horse
어설픈 변명/사과 a _____ excuse/apology

05 dynamic
↔static
[dainǽmik]↔[stǽtik]

(역)동적인 명 역학, 동력
↔ 정적인[정체된] 명 잡음, 정전기
한국은 역동적인 나라다.
Korea is a _____ country.
집값이 장기간 정체되어 있다.
House prices have been _____ for a long period.

06 brisk
[brisk]

❶ 활발한[빠른](=energetic) ❷ (날씨가) 상쾌한
활발한 걸음/거래/시장 a _____ walk[pace]/trade/market
상쾌한 가을 날씨 _____ fall weather
상쾌한 바람 a _____ wind

07 intriguing
[intrí:giŋ]

아주 흥미로운   ▶intrigue 동 ❶ 호기심을 불러일으키다
❷ 모의하다 명 모의[음모]
이들 발견은 아주 흥미로운 의문들을 제기한다.
These discoveries raise _____ questions.

08 keen
[ki:n]

❶ 열심인[열망하는] ❷ 예민한[예리한]
예민한 후각/청각 a _____ sense of smell/hearing

09 blunt
[blʌnt]

무딘[뭉툭한]
그는 둔기로 머리를 맞았다.
He was hit over the head with a _____ instrument.

10 spontaneous
[spɑntéiniəs]

자연스러운[즉흥적인]   ▶spontaneity 몡 자연스러움[즉흥성]

자연스러운[즉흥적인] 환호/반응 a _____ cheer/reaction

11 reluctant
[rilʌ́ktənt]

내키지 않는[마지못해 하는]   ▶reluctance 몡 내키지 않음
(↔ eager, keen, willing)

그는 그 일에 착수하는 것이 내키지 않았다.

He was _____ to undertake the job.

12 inert
[inə́ːrt]

움직이지 않는[활동력이 없는]   ▶inertia 몡 타성, 관성

그는 움직이지 않은 채 침대에 누워 있었다.

He lay, _____, in his bed.

13 monotonous
[mənɑ́tənəs]

단조로운(=repetitive)

단조로운 일/목소리 a _____ job/voice

14 arduous
[ɑ́ːrdʒuəs]

몹시 힘든[고된]

고된 일/훈련/공부/여정 an _____ job/training/study/journey

15 flexible
[fléksəbl]

융통성 있는, 유연한   ▶flexibility 몡 융통성[유연성]
(↔ inflexible, rigid)

생각을 더 융통성 있게 해라. Be more _____ in your thinking.

유연한 나뭇가지 _____ branches

유연한 몸/소재 a _____ body/material

16 elastic
[ilǽstik]

탄력[신축성] 있는   ▶elasticity 몡 탄력[탄성]
몡 고무 밴드(=rubber band)

신축성 있는 섬유/소재 _____ fibers/material

17 versatile
[və́ːrsətl]

다재다능한, 다용도[다목적]의

다재다능한 배우 a _____ actor

다용도 도구 a _____ tool

18 eloquent
[éləkwənt]

웅변적인[유창한](=expressive)   ▶eloquence 몡 웅변

지지를 위한 웅변적인 호소 an _____ appeal for support

19 transparent
[trænspέərənt]

투명한(=clear)   ▶transparency 몡 투명성

투명한 플라스틱 용기 a _____ plastic container

20 superficial
[sùːpərfíʃəl]

피상[표면]적인(=shallow)

그 주제에 대한 피상적인 지식 a _____ knowledge of the subject

21 fluffy
[flʌ́fi]

솜털 같은[가볍고 부드러운]   비교 downy 솜털로 덮인

가볍고 부드러운 수건/스웨터/담요 a _____ towel/sweater/blanket

솜털 같은 흰 구름 _____ white clouds

Part 3

특장

22 cozy
[kóuzi]

아늑한[편안한]　　　　　　　▶coziness 명 아늑함

그 방은 따뜻하고 아늑했다.

The room was warm and _____.

23 tidy
[táidi]

정돈된[깔끔한](=neat ↔ untidy, messy)

그녀의 방은 늘 말쑥하고 정돈되어 있다.

Her room is always neat and _____.

24 shabby
[ʃǽbi]

낡은, 초라한

낡은 옷/가구/빌딩 _____ clothes/furniture/buildings

25 sticky
[stíki]

끈적거리는　　　　　　　▶stick 동 붙(이)다, 찌르다 명 막대기

그의 손가락은 잼으로 끈적거렸다.

His fingers were _____ with jam.

26 foul
[faul]

역겨운[더러운](=disgusting)

동 반칙하다 명 반칙

역겨운 냄새 a _____ smell

더러운 공기 _____ air

27 vulgar
[vʌ́lgər]

❶ 상스러운[야비한] ❷ 조잡[조야]한(=tasteless)

상스러운 언어 _____ language

조야한 무늬의 셔츠 a _____ patterned shirt

28 coarse
[kɔːrs]

❶ 거친[굵은](=rough) ❷ 상스러운[야비한]

거친 천 a _____ cloth

상스러운 농담 _____ jokes

29 crude
[kruːd]

❶ 대략의 ❷ 조잡한 ❸ 상스러운 ❹ 천연 그대로의

조잡한 목제 다리 a _____ wooden bridge

상스러운 발언 a _____ remark

30 obscene
[əbsíːn]

음란한[외설의]

음란한 제스처/전화 an _____ gesture/phone call

특성 Part 3

Today's Dessert　In order to create there must be a dynamic force, and what force is more potent than love?

창조하기 위해서는 역동적인 힘이 있어야 하는데, 무슨 힘이 사랑보다 더 강력할 수 있겠는가?

TEST 56

A 영어는 우리말로, 우리말은 영어로!

1 a dynamic personality
2 an intriguing possibility
3 spontaneous applause
4 an arduous task
5 a superficial examination
6 a shabby coat
7 sticky fingers
8 vulgar language

9 날씬한 몸매   a s_____ figure
10 다리를 저는 개   a l_____ dog
11 정체된 인구   a s_____ population
12 무딘 칼   a b_____ knife
13 탄력 붕대   an e_____ bandage
14 정돈된 책상   a t_____ desk
15 거친 손   c_____ hands
16 음란 전화   an o_____ phone call

B 영영사전 뜻풀이에 알맞은 단어 찾기

| 보기 | cozy   foul   monotonous   plump |

1 _____ : dirty and smelling bad
2 _____ : small, comfortable, and warm
3 _____ : slightly fat in a fairly pleasant way
4 _____ : boring because of always being the same

C 관련된 것끼리 연결하기

1 brisk   •   a. fairly fat and heavy
2 fluffy   •   b. able to be seen through
3 stout   •   c. quick, energetic and active
4 transparent   •   d. very light and soft to touch

D 빈칸에 가장 적절한 단어 넣기

| 보기 | eloquent   flexible   inert   reluctant   versatile |

1 He lay, _____, in his bed. 그는 움직이지 않은 채 침대에 누워 있었다.
2 My schedule is quite _____. 내 일정은 꽤 융통성이 있다.
3 Eyes are more _____ than lips. 눈은 입보다 더 웅변적이다.
4 Eggs are an extremely _____ food. 계란은 아주 다용도로 쓰이는 식품이다.
5 She was _____ to admit she was wrong. 그녀는 마지못해 자신이 틀렸다고 인정했다.

E 밑줄 친 단어 뜻 구별하기

1 keen students   a keen sense of smell
2 crude oil   a crude remark   a crude estimate

ANSWER

A 1. 역동적인 성격 2. 아주 흥미로운 가능성 3. 자연스러운[즉흥적인] 박수갈채 4. 고된 일 5. 피상적인 조사 6. 낡은 외투 7. 끈적거리는 손가락 8. 상스러운 언어 9. slim 10. lame 11. static 12. blunt 13. elastic 14. tidy 15. coarse 16. obscene B 1. foul 2. cozy 3. plump 4. monotonous C 1. c 2. d 3. a 4. b D 1. inert 2. flexible 3. eloquent 4. versatile 5. reluctant E 1. 열심인 학생들 / 예민한 후각 2. 원유[천연 그대로의 석유] / 상스러운 발언 / 대략적인 추산

01 objective
↔subjective
[əbdʒéktiv]↔[səbdʒéktiv]

객관적인 명 목표
↔주관적인

객관적 사실 an _____ fact
주관적 판단 a _____ judgment

▶objectivity ↔ subjectivity
　명 객관성 ↔ 주관성

02 rational
[ræʃənl]

이성적인[합리적인]
(↔ irrational)
인간은 이성적인 동물이다.
Man is a _____ animal.

▶rationality 명 합리성
▶rationalization 명 합리화

03 sensible
[sénsəbl]

분별 있는[합리적인]

분별 있는 사람 a _____ person
합리적인 가격/생각/선택 a _____ price/idea/choice

비교 sensitive 세심한, 예민한[민감한]
▶sensibility 명 감성[감수성]

04 empirical
[impírikəl]

실증적인

실증적 자료/증거/지식/연구
_____ data/evidence/knowledge/research

05 consistent
[kənsístənt]

일관된(↔ inconsistent)
우리는 규칙을 적용하는 데 일관되어야 한다.
We must be _____ in applying the rules.

▶consistency 명 일관성

06 coherent
[kouhíərənt]

조리 있는(↔ incoherent)

그 사건에 대한 조리 있는 설명 a _____ account of the incident

▶coherence 명 조리[통일성]
▶cohesion 명 결속

07 absurd
[əbsə́ːrd]

터무니없는[부조리한](= ridiculous)
그건 터무니없는 생각인 것 같다.
It seems an _____ idea.

08 compatible
[kəmpǽtəbl]

양립할 수 있는, 호환되는
(↔ incompatible)
그의 견해는 그녀의 것과 양립할 수 없다.
His view isn't _____ with her own.

▶compatibility 명 양립 가능성, 호환성

09 feasible
[fíːzəbl]

실행[실현] 가능한(= practicable)
기술적으로 가장 실현 가능한 대안
the most technically _____ alternative

10 plausible
[plɔ́ːzəbl]

그럴듯한
그의 이야기는 그럴듯하게 들렸다.
His story sounded _____.

11 apt
[æpt]

❶ ~하는 경향이 있는[~하기 쉬운] ❷ 적절한

음식은 여름에 빨리 부패하기 쉽다.

Foods are _____ to go bad quickly in summer.

12 liable
[láiəbl]

❶ ~할 것 같은(= likely), ~하기 쉬운(= prone)
❷ 법적 책임이 있는

우리는 피곤하면 실수하기 쉽다.

We're _____ to make a mistake when we're tired.

13 reliable
[riláiəbl]

믿을 수 있는
(= dependable ↔ unreliable)

믿을 수 있는 소식통에서 나온 정보

the information from a _____ source

비교 reliant 의존하는
▶ rely 동 의존하다, 믿다

14 handy
[hǽndi]

유용한(= useful)

유용한 도구/장치/요리책 a _____ tool/gadget/cookbook

15 functional
[fʌ́ŋkʃənl]

기능(성)의[실용적인]

기능성 의복/가구 _____ clothing/furniture

▶ function 명 기능 동 기능하다
▶ functionalism 명 기능주의
▶ dysfunctional 기능 장애의

16 utilitarian
[ju:tìlətέəriən]

❶ 실용적인 ❷ 공리주의의   ▶ utilitarianism 명 공리주의

실용적인 가구/물건/건물 _____ furniture/objects/buildings

17 hands-on
[hǽndzán]

직접 해 보는[실천하는]

그것은 직접 해 보는 경험을 얻는 기회였다.

It was a chance to get some _____ experience.

18 authentic
[ɔːθéntik]

진짜의(= genuine, real ↔ fake)   ▶ authenticity 명 진짜임

피카소의 진짜 작품[진품] an _____ work by Picasso

19 sheer
[ʃiər]

❶ 순전한(= pure), 엄청난 ❷ 몹시 가파른 ❸ 아주 얇은

순전한 행운/기쁨 _____ luck/joy

엄청난 양의 일 the _____ amount of work

몹시 가파른 절벽 _____ cliffs

아주 얇은 스타킹 _____ stockings

20 thorough
[θə́:rou]

철저한

철저한 조사 a _____ investigation

비교 through 전 부 (관)통하여
▶ thoroughness 명 철저

21 intact
[intǽkt]

손상되지 않은[온전한]

폭격에도 불구하고 그 집은 아직 손상되지 않았다.

Despite the bombing, the house was still _____.

22 partial
[pá:rʃəl]

❶ 부분적인 ▶partiality 몡 편애[편파]
❷ 편파적인[불공평한](=biased ↔ impartial)

부분적인 성공 a _____ success

편파적인 심판 a _____ referee

23 apparent
[əpǽrənt]

❶ 분명한(=clear, obvious) ❷ 외관상[겉보기]의

그는 분명한 이유도 없이 갑자기 떠났다.

He left suddenly, for no _____ reason.

24 evident
[évədənt]

분명한[명백한] ▶self-evident 자명한
▶evidence 몡 증거

그가 진실을 말하지 않고 있다는 것은 분명했다.

It was _____ that he was not telling the truth.

25 explicit
[iksplísit]

분명한[명확한], 노골적인(↔ implicit 암묵적인)

명확한 지시 _____ instructions

노골적인 가사의 노래 a song with _____ lyrics

26 vivid
[vívid]

생생한[선명한]

생생한 기억/묘사 a _____ memory/description

27 vague
[veig]

모호한[막연한/희미한] ▶vagueness 몡 모호함

모호한 대답/막연한 생각/희미한 기억

a _____ answer/idea/memory

28 ambiguous
[æmbígjuəs]

애매모호한 ▶ambiguity 몡 애매모호함
(↔ clear, obvious, unambiguous)

내 질문에 대한 그의 애매모호한 대답

his _____ reply to my question

29 subtle
[sʌ́tl]

미묘한(↔ obvious)

미묘한 차이 a _____ difference

30 fuzzy
[fʌ́zi]

❶ 불분명한[애매한] ▶fuzzy theory 몡 퍼지 이론
❷ 솜털로 덮인

불분명한 이미지/생각 _____ images/ideas

솜털 스웨터/담요 a _____ sweater/blanket

Today's Dessert

Men have no right to what is not reasonable.

인간은 합리적이지 않은 것에 대해서는 어떠한 권리도 없다.

TEST 57

A 영어는 우리말로, 우리말은 영어로!

1 a subjective judgement

2 rational behavior

3 consistent improvement

4 hands-on experience

5 thorough preparation

6 an ambiguous question

7 fuzzy ideas

8 합리적인 조언　s＿＿＿＿＿ advice

9 조리 있는 설명　a c＿＿＿＿＿ account

10 실현 가능한 해결책　a f＿＿＿＿ solution

11 그럴듯한 설명　a p＿＿＿＿＿ explanation

12 유용한 도구　a h＿＿＿＿＿ tool

13 기능성 의복　f＿＿＿＿＿clothing

14 생생한 기억　v＿＿＿＿＿ memories

B 영영사전 뜻풀이에 알맞은 단어 찾기

| 보기 | explicit | intact | subtle | utilitarian |

1 ＿＿＿＿＿ : not broken, damaged, or spoiled

2 ＿＿＿＿＿ : expressed in a way that is very clear and direct

3 ＿＿＿＿＿ : not loud, bright, noticeable or obvious in any way

4 ＿＿＿＿＿ : designed to be useful and practical rather than attractive

C 주어진 철자로 시작하는 동의어 쓰기

1 ridiculous = a＿＿＿＿＿

2 dependable = r＿＿＿＿＿

3 genuine = a＿＿＿＿＿

4 obvious = a＿＿＿＿＿

D 빈칸에 가장 적절한 단어 넣기

| 보기 | apt | compatible | empirical | evident | vague |

1 He gave only a ＿＿＿＿＿ answer. 그는 모호한 대답만 해주었을 뿐이다.

2 Old people are ＿＿＿＿＿ to be forgetful. 노인들은 잘 잊어버리는 경향이 있다.

3 It was ＿＿＿＿＿ that he had studied hard. 그가 열심히 공부했다는 것은 분명했다.

4 The printer is not ＿＿＿＿＿ with my computer. 그 프린터는 내 컴퓨터와 호환되지 않는다.

5 They collected plenty of ＿＿＿＿＿ data from their experiments.

그들은 실험에서 많은 실증적 자료를 모았다.

E 밑줄 친 단어 뜻 구별하기

1 the main objective　　　an objective assessment

2 sheer slopes　　　sheer coincidence

3 a partial success　　　a partial referee

ANSWER

A 1. 주관적 판단 2. 이성적[합리적] 행동 3. 일관된 개선 4. 직접 해 보는 경험 5. 철저한 준비 6. 애매모호한 질문 7. 불분명한 생각 8. sensible 9. coherent 10. feasible 11. plausible 12. handy 13. functional 14. vivid　B 1. intact 2. explicit 3. subtle 4. utilitarian　C 1. absurd 2. reliable 3. authentic 4. apparent　D 1. vague 2. apt 3. evident 4. compatible 5. empirical　E 1. 주목표 / 객관적 평가 2. 몹시 가파른 비탈 / 순전한 우연의 일치 3. 부분적인 성공 / 편파적인 심판

Excellence & Importance

01 superb
[su:pə́:rb]

최고[최상]의(= excellent)

최고의 공연 a _____ performance

02 supreme
[səprí:m]

최고의 ▶ **supremacy** 명 패권[우위]

최고 사령관 the _____ commander

최고 권위 _____ authority

03 foremost
[fɔ́:rmòust]

최고의[앞선](= leading, top) ▶ **first and foremost** 무엇보다 먼저

세계 최고의 소프라노 가수

the world's _____ soprano

04 prime
[praim]

주요한(= main), 최상의

주요 용의자 a _____ suspect

최상의 위치 a _____ location

05 dominant
↔ recessive
[dámənənt] ↔ [risésiv]

(유전적) 우성의, 지배적인 ▶ **dominate** 동 지배하다
↔ 열성의

열성/우성 유전자 a _____/_____ gene

06 fundamental
[fʌndəméntl]

근본[기본]적인(= basic)

근본적인 변화/차이 a _____ change/difference

기본 원칙 a _____ principle

기본적 인권 _____ human rights

07 underlying
[ʌ́ndərlàiiŋ]

❶ 근본적인[근원적인] ▶ **underlie** 동 기저를 이루다
❷ 밑에 있는

그 사고의 근본적인 원인 the _____ cause of the accident

08 requisite
[rékwəzit]

필요한(= required, necessary) ▶ **prerequisite** 명 전제 조건
명 필수품[요소]

필요한 자격 the _____ qualifications

09 indispensable
[ìndispénsəbl]

필수 불가결한(= essential) ▶ **dispense** 동 (~ with) ~ 없이 지내다

비옥한 토양은 농사에 필수 불가결하다.

Fertile soil is _____ for farming.

10 imperative
[impérətiv]

필수적인[긴요한](= vital) 명 필수 과제

문제가 심각해지기 전에 지금 행동하는 것이 긴요하다.

It's _____ to act now before the problem gets serious.

11 compulsory
[kəmpʌ́lsəri]

의무적인[강제적인]

비교 **compulsive** 강박적인
▶**compel** 동 강요[강제]하다

의무 교육/학교 교육 _____ education/schooling

12 obligatory
[əblígətɔ̀:ri]

의무적인(↔ optional)

▶**oblige** 동 강요[강제]하다
▶**obligation** 명 의무

군 복무는 모든 남성에게 의무적이다.
Military service is _____ for all men.

13 mandatory
[mǽndətɔ̀:ri]

의무적인

차 안에서 안전벨트를 착용하는 것은 의무적이다.
It's _____ to wear seat belts in cars.

14 prominent
[prɑ́mənənt]

중요한[저명한](=well-known), 두드러진

중요한[저명한] 과학자 a _____ scientist

15 eminent
[émənənt]

저명한

저명한 역사학자 an _____ historian

16 renowned
[rináund]

유명한(=famous)

▶**renown** 명 명성

세계적으로 유명한 그 분야 전문가 a world _____ expert in the field

17 obscure
[əbskjúər]

잘 알려지지 않은[무명의](=unknown), 난해한[불분명한]
동 가리다

무명의 시인 an _____ poet
난해한 시/강의 an _____ poem/lecture

18 peripheral
[pərífərəl]

중요하지 않은, 주변[말초]의

지엽적인 문제/역할 a _____ issue/role
주변 장치들 _____ devices
말초신경 _____ nerves

19 trivial
[tríviəl]

하찮은[사소한](=insignificant)

사소한 문제에 귀중한 시간을 낭비하지 마라.
Don't waste your precious time on _____ matters.

20 splendid
[spléndid]

화려한[훌륭한/멋진]

일출은 멋진 광경이었다.
The sunrise was a _____ spectacle.

21 magnificent
[mæɡnífəsnt]

장려한[멋진](=grand)

▶**magnificence** 명 장려함[멋짐]

산 정상에서의 장려한 경치 _____ views from the summit

22 marvelous
[mάːrvələs]

놀라운[멋진](=wonderful)

▶marvel 동 경이로워하다[경탄하다]
명 경이

네 기억력은 정말 놀랍구나!
Your memory is really _____!

23 fabulous
[fǽbjuləs]

❶ 훌륭한[멋진] ❷ 엄청난[굉장한]

훌륭한[멋진] 공연 a _____ performance
굉장한 아름다움 _____ beauty

24 gorgeous
[gɔ́ːrdʒəs]

아름다운[매력적인/멋진](=beautiful, lovely)

너 참 아름답게 보이는구나!
You look _____!

25 elegant
[éligənt]

우아한[고상한](=stylish)

▶elegance 명 우아[고상]함

우아한 여성/정장 an _____ woman/suit

26 exquisite
[ikskwízit]

우아한[정교한]

우아한 보석 an _____ piece of jewelry

27 clumsy
[klʌ́mzi]

서투른[어색한]
(=awkward ↔ sensitive, elegant)

▶clumsiness 명 서투름[어색함]

그는 그녀에게 키스하려는 서투른 시도를 했다.
He made a _____ attempt to kiss her.

28 invaluable
[invǽljuəbl]

매우 귀중한

비교 valueless 가치 없는
▶valuable 값비싼[귀중한]
명 (-s) 귀중품

네 조언은 우리에게 매우 귀중했어.
Your advice has been _____ to us.

29 worthy
[wə́ːrði]

가치 있는, 훌륭한,
(~ of) ~할[받을] 가치가 있는
(=deserve)

▶worth ~의 가치가 있는 명 가치
▶worthwhile 가치 있는
▶unworthy 가치가 없는

주목/언급할 가치가 있는 책
a book _____ of attention[notice]/mention

30 state-of-the-art
[stéitəvðiάːrt]

최신식[최첨단]의

최첨단 과학 기술 _____ technology

TEST 58

A 영어는 우리말로, 우리말은 영어로!

1 a superb meal
2 the supreme commander
3 a dominant/recessive gene
4 the fundamental change
5 an underlying cause
6 a gorgeous view
7 a worthy winner

8 중요한 역할　　a p_____ role
9 저명한 과학자　an e_____ scientist
10 지엽적인 역할　a p_____ role
11 사소한 문제　　a t_____ problem
12 훌륭한 공연　　a f_____ performance
13 우아한 여성　　an e_____ woman
14 최첨단 컴퓨터　a s_____ computer

B 영영사전 뜻풀이에 알맞은 단어 찾기

> 보기　clumsy　　exquisite　　invaluable　　requisite

1 _____ : extremely useful
2 _____ : needed for a particular purpose
3 _____ : extremely beautiful and very delicately made
4 _____ : moving or doing things in a very awkward way

C 주어진 철자로 시작하는 동의어 쓰기

1 compulsory = o_____ = m_____
2 splendid = m_____ = m_____

D 빈칸에 가장 적절한 단어 넣기

> 보기　foremost　imperative　indispensable　obscure　prime　renowned

1 The details of his life remain _____.　그의 세부적인 삶은 잘 알려지지 않은 채로 남아 있다.
2 He's one of the world _____ scholars.　그는 세계 최고의 학자 중 하나다.
3 It's _____ that you should rest for a week.　넌 1주일 동안 휴식하는 게 필수적이다.
4 Smoking is the _____ cause of lung cancer.　담배는 폐암의 주요한 원인이다.
5 The region is _____ for its outstanding natural beauty.
그 지역은 빼어난 자연미로 유명하다.
6 The Internet has become a(n) _____ part of our lives.
인터넷은 우리 삶의 필수 불가결한 부분이 되었다.

ANSWER_____

A 1. 최고의 식사　2. 최고 사령관　3. 우성/열성 유전자　4. 근본적인 변화　5. 근본적인 원인　6. 아름다운 경치　7. 훌륭한 우승자　8. prominent　9. eminent　10. peripheral　11. trivial　12. fabulous　13. elegant　14. state-of-the-art　B 1. invaluable　2. requisite　3. exquisite　4. clumsy C 1. obligatory, mandatory　2. magnificent, marvelous　D 1. obscure　2. foremost　3. imperative　4. prime　5. renowned　6. indispensable

아수성 · 중요성

Part 3

유사성 • 차이 관련 형용사

01 ordinary
↔ **extraordinary**
[ɔ́:rdənèri] ↔ [ikstrɔ́:rdənèri]

보통의[평범한] ↔ 보통이 아닌[비범한]
보통 사람들 _____ people
비범한 재능 an _____ talent

02 normal
↔ **abnormal**
[nɔ́:rməl] ↔ [æbnɔ́:rməl]

정상[보통]의 ↔ 비정상의 ▶normality ↔ abnormality 명 정상 ↔ 이상
정상/비정상 수준의 콜레스테롤
a(n) _____ / _____ level of cholesterol

03 abstract
↔ **concrete**
[ǽbstrækt] ↔ [kánkri:t]

추상적인 ↔ 구체적인 ▶abstraction 명 관념, 추출
추상적 생각/개념 an _____ idea/concept
구체적 증거 _____ evidence

04 commonplace
[kámənplèis]

평범한[흔한] 명 평범한[흔한] 것
외국 휴가 여행이 흔해졌다.
Foreign vacations have become _____.

05 equivalent
[ikwívələnt]

같은[동등한](=equal) 명 상당하는 것[등가물]
1마일은 약 1.6킬로미터와 같다.
A mile is _____ to about 1.6 kilometers.

06 homogeneous
[hòumədʒí:niəs]

동질의 ▶homogeneity 명 동질성
(=uniform ↔ heterogeneous 이질의)
동질 집단/인구/이웃 a _____ group/population/neighborhood

07 unanimous
[ju:nǽnəməs]

만장일치의 비교 majority vote[decision] 명 다수결
▶unanimity 명 만장일치
만장일치의 투표/결정 a _____ vote/decision

08 sole
[soul]

하나뿐인[유일한](=only) 명 발바닥[구두창]
사고의 유일한 생존자 the _____ survivor of the accident

09 varied
[vέərid]

다양한(=various) 비교 variable 가변적인 명 변수
▶vary 통 다르다, 달라지다
다양한 의견/관심 _____ opinions/interests
다양한 음식/삶 a _____ diet/life

10 diverse
[divə́:rs]

다양한[상이한] ▶diversity 명 다양성(=variety)
▶diversify 통 다양화하다
팝 음악과 고고학 같은 다양한[상이한] 주제들
subjects as _____ as pop music and archaeology

11 distinct
[distíŋkt]

❶ 구별되는[별개의]
❷ 뚜렷한[분명한]

▶distinction 몡 구별[차이], 차별성
▶distinguish 통 구별[식별]하다

그 단어는 두 가지 구별되는 의미를 가진다.
The word has two _____ meanings.

분명히 가스 냄새가 났다.
There was a _____ smell of gas.

12 distinctive
[distíŋktiv]

독특한[특이한]

그녀는 독특한 목소리를 가졌다.
She's got a _____ voice.

13 discrete
[diskrí:t]

별개의[분리된](=separate)   비교 discreet 신중한

변화는 일련의 별개의 단계들을 거쳐 일어난다.
The change happens in a series of _____ steps.

14 remarkable
[rimá:rkəbl]

주목할 만한(=outstanding)   ▶remark 몡 의견[발언]
                              통 (의견을) 말하다

주목할 만한 업적 a _____ accomplishment

15 striking
[stráikiŋ]

두드러진[눈에 띄는](=marked)

부와 빈곤의 두드러진 대조
a _____ contrast between wealth and poverty

16 ingenious
[indʒí:njəs]

기발한[독창적인]   비교 ingenuous 순진한

독창적인 생각/방법 an _____ idea/method

17 inherent
[inhíərənt]

고유한[내재하는]

모든 사업은 자체의 고유한 위험이 있다.
Every business has its own _____ risks.

18 intrinsic
[intrínsik]

고유한[본질적인]   비교 extrinsic 외적인[외부의]

교육의 고유한[본질적인] 가치 the _____ value of education

19 innate
[inéit]

타고난[선천적인](=natural)

어린이는 언어를 배울 수 있는 선천적 능력이 있다.
Children have an _____ ability to learn language.

20 peculiar
[pikjú:ljər]

❶ 이상한(=odd, strange)
❷ 특유의[독특한](=unique)

▶peculiarity 몡 특이함

이상한 맛/느낌/표정 a _____ taste/feeling/expression
한국 특유의 관습 a custom _____ to Korea
독특한 스타일 a _____ style

21 weird
[wiərd]

기이한   ▶weirdo 몡 기인[괴짜]

기이한 생각/꿈/소녀 a _____ idea/dream/girl

22 bizarre
[bizáːr]

기이한   비교 **bazaar** 명 바자회

기이한 이야기/복장 a _____ story/outfit

기이한 행동 _____ behavior

23 freak
[friːk]

기이한 명 ~광(=fanatic), 기인[괴짜]

기이한 사고/폭풍 a _____ accident/storm

컴퓨터/영화광 a computer/movie _____

24 exotic
[igzátik]

이국적인, 외래의

이국적인 장소 an _____ place

외래 식물 an _____ plant

25 morbid
[móːrbid]

병적인

죽음에 대한 병적인 매혹 a _____ fascination with death

26 approximate
형 [əpráksəmət]
동 [əpráksəmèit]

대략의(=rough ↔ exact)   ▶**approximately** 부 대략
동 비슷하다[가깝다]

이 방의 대략적인 크기가 얼마니?

What's the _____ size of this room?

27 straightforward
[strèitfóːrwərd]

❶ 간단한(=simple ↔ complicated)
❷ 솔직한(=frank)

간단한 문제/과정/프로그램

a _____ matter/process/program

그는 우리에게 매우 솔직했다.

He was very _____ with us.

28 elaborate
형 [ilǽbərət]
동 [ilǽbərèit]

정교한
동 더 자세히 설명하다

정교한 디자인/무늬/계획/준비

_____ designs/patterns/plans/preparations

29 intricate
[íntrikət]

복잡한   ▶**intricacy** 명 복잡함

복잡한 구성의 소설 a novel with an _____ plot

30 sophisticated
[səfístəkèitid]

❶ 세련된(=refined)   ▶**sophistication** 명 정교화, 세련
❷ 정교한(=advanced)

세련된 남성/여성 a _____ man/woman

세련된 스타일/취향 _____ styles/tastes

정교한 소프트웨어/의술 _____ software/medical techniques

유사성 · 차이   Part 3

Today's Dessert

Two people can look at the exact same thing and see something totally different.

두 사람은 정확히 같은 것을 쳐다보면서도 완전히 다른 것을 볼 수 있다.

TEST 59

A 영어는 우리말로, 우리말은 영어로!

1 an extraordinary woman
2 varied opinions
3 diverse political views
4 an ingenious idea
5 intrinsic beauty
6 an innate ability
7 a weird dream
8 the approximate number
9 a sophisticated conversation

10 비정상적 행동   a_____ behavior
11 추상화   a_____ paintings
12 구체적 증거   c_____ evidence
13 동질 집단   a h_____ group
14 만장일치의 결정   a u_____ decision
15 주목할 만한 진보   r_____ progress
16 두드러진 대조   a s_____ contrast
17 이국적인 장소   an e_____ place
18 복잡한 패턴[무늬]   i_____ patterns

B 영영사전 뜻풀이에 알맞은 단어 찾기

| 보기 | bizarre   elaborate   morbid   straightforward |

1 _____ : very unusual or strange
2 _____ : very detailed and complicated
3 _____ : simple and easy to understand
4 _____ : too interested in unpleasant subjects, especially death

C 빈칸에 가장 적절한 단어 넣기

| 보기 | commonplace   discrete   equivalent   inherent   peculiar |

1 Foreign vacations have became _____. 외국 휴가 여행이 흔해졌다.
2 Dance is a(n) _____ part of our culture. 춤은 우리 문화의 고유한 부분이다.
3 A mile is _____ to about 1.6 kilometers. 1마일은 약 1.6킬로미터와 같다.
4 There was a(n) _____ smell in the kitchen. 부엌에서 이상한 냄새가 났다.
5 The insect passes through several _____ stages. 곤충은 몇 개의 분리된 단계를 거친다.

D 밑줄 친 단어 뜻 구별하기

1 a freak accident   a computer freak
2 the sole survivor of the accident   a cut on the sole of his foot
3 two distinct meanings   a distinct smell of gas   a distinctive sound

ANSWER

A 1. 비범한 여성 2. 다양한 의견들 3. 다양한[상이한] 정치적 견해 4. 독창적인 생각 5. 고유한[본질적인] 아름다움 6. 선천적 능력 7. 기이한 꿈 8. 대략적인 수 9. 세련된 대화 10. abnormal 11. abstract 12. concrete 13. homogeneous 14. unanimous 15. remarkable 16. striking 17. exotic 18. intricate   B 1. bizarre 2. elaborate 3. straightforward 4. morbid   C 1. commonplace 2. inherent 3. equivalent 4. peculiar 5. discrete   D 1. 기이한 사고 / 컴퓨터광 2. 사고의 유일한 생존자 / 그의 발바닥의 베인 상처 3. 두 가지의 구별되는 의미들 / 뚜렷한 가스 냄새 / 독특한 소리

01 masculine ↔ feminine
[mǽskjulin] ↔ [fémənin]

남성의[남성다운] ↔ 여성의[여성스러운]

▶ male ↔ female
형 명 남성[수컷](의) ↔ 여성[암컷](의)

남성다운/여성스러운 외모/목소리

a _____/_____ appearance/voice

02 maternal ↔ paternal
[mətə́ːrnl] ↔ [pətə́ːrnl]

어머니의 ↔ 아버지의

비교 parental 부모의

모성애/모성 본능 _____ love/instinct

부성애/아버지의 권위 _____ love/authority

03 marital
[mǽrətl]

결혼의

비교 martial 군사[전쟁]의

(미혼/기혼/이혼의) 결혼 상태[여부] _____ status

04 eligible
[élidʒəbl]

자격이 있는

19세 이상의 사람들만 투표할 자격이 있다.

Only people over 19 are _____ to vote.

05 monetary
[mánətèri]

통화[화폐]의

정부의 통화 정책 the government's _____ policy

06 preliminary
[prilímənèri]

예비의 명 예비, 예선

예비회담 _____ talks

예선 _____ rounds

07 eco-friendly
[iːkoufréndli]

환경친화[친환경]적인(= environment(ally)-friendly)

환경친화[친환경] 제품/포장/사업/기업

an _____ product/packaging/business/corporation

08 renewable
[rinjúːəbl]

재생[갱신] 가능한

▶ renew 동 갱신하다, 재개하다
▶ renewal 명 재개, 갱신

풍력과 태양열 발전 같은 재생 가능한 에너지원

_____ sources of energy such as wind and solar power

09 medi(a)eval
[mìːdíːvəl]

중세의

중세사/중세 유럽 _____ history/Europe

10 divine
[diváin]

신의[신성한]

실수하는 것은 인간의 일이고, 용서하는 것은 신의 일이다.

To err is human, to forgive _____.

11 **sacred**
[séikrid]

신성한, 종교의

신성한 맹세 a _____ vow

종교 의식 a _____ ceremony

12 **secular**
[sékjulər]

세속의[비종교의](↔ religious)

세속[비종교] 음악/교육 _____ music/education

13 **verbal**
↔ **nonverbal**
[vɔ́:rbəl] ↔ [nὰnvɔ́:rbəl]

언어[구두]의 ↔ 말을 쓰지 않는[비언어적]

구술 능력 _____ skills

비언어적 의사소통 _____ communication

14 **attentive**
[əténtiv]

주의[귀]를 기울이는(↔ inattentive)

귀를 기울이는 청중 an _____ audience

15 **wholesome**
[hóulsəm]

❶ 건강에 좋은(= healthy)
❷ 건전한

균형이 잘 잡힌 건강에 좋은 식사 well-balanced _____ meals

16 **stale**
[steil]

신선하지 않은(↔ fresh), 진부한

신선하지 않은 빵 _____ bread

진부한 표현 _____ expressions

17 **toxic**
[táksik]

유독한[독성의](= poisonous)　비교 toxin 명 독소

유독성 화학 물질 _____ chemicals

맹독성 살충제 a highly _____ pesticide

18 **contagious**
[kəntéidʒəs]

(접촉) 전염성의(= infectious)

그 감염증은 전염성이 매우 강하다.

The infection is highly _____.

19 **mobile**
[móubəl]

이동의(↔ immobile)　▶ **mobility** 명 이동[유동]성
　　　　　　　　　▶ **mobilize** 동 동원하다

이동식 장비 _____ equipment

이동 상점/도서관 a _____ store/library

20 **ubiquitous**
[juːbíkwətəs]

어디에나 있는[유비쿼터스]

커피숍은 요즘 어디에나 있다.

Coffee shops are _____ these days.

유비쿼터스 컴퓨팅/네트워크

_____ computing/networks

21 **aerial**
[έəriəl]

항공의, 공중의

항공 사진 an _____ photograph

공중 폭격 an _____ bombing

22 hollow
[hάlou]

속이 빈, 우묵한, 공허한(=empty)

속이 빈 나무 a _____ tree

우묵한 눈 _____ eyes

23 vacant
[véikənt]

비어 있는, 멍한   ▶vacancy 몡 빈자리, 빈방

단 하나의 빈 좌석 a single _____ seat

멍한 표정 a _____ look

24 dazed
[deizd]

멍한(=confused)   ▶daze 몡 멍한 상태

그녀는 멍한 표정을 지었다.

She wore a _____ expression.

25 somber
[sάmbər]

침울한(=serious, solemn), 어둠침침한

침울한 얼굴/기분 a _____ face/mood

26 stricken
[stríkən]

고통받는[시달리는]

빈곤에 시달리는 가정들/지역들 poverty-_____ families/areas

27 stranded
[strǽndid]

오도 가도 못하게 된(=stuck)

승객들은 철도 파업으로 오도 가도 못하게 되었다.

Passengers were left _____ because of the rail strike.

28 wretched
[rétʃid]

불쌍한[비참한](=miserable), 지독한

그들의 비참한 생활 상태 their _____ living conditions

29 adverse
[ædvə́ːrs]

부정적인[불리한](↔favorable)   ▶adversity 몡 역경

부정적인 비판 _____ criticism

불리한 상황/조건 _____ circumstances/conditions

30 reverse/
inverse
[rivə́ːrs] / [invə́ːrs]

반대[역]의 몡 반대[역] /   ▶reverse 동 뒤바꾸다[뒤집다]
반비례의 몡 반대[역]

반대 방향으로 in the r_____ direction

역순으로 in r_____ order

반비례 i_____ proportion

반비례 관계 an i_____ relationship

Today's Dessert

Our five senses are incomplete without the sixth – a sense of humor.

우리의 다섯 가지 감각[오감]은 여섯 번째인 '유머 감각'이 없으면 불완전한 것이다.

TEST 60

A 영어는 우리말로, 우리말은 영어로!

1 the International Monetary Fund
2 an attentive audience
3 stale cake
4 a mobile home
5 the wretched girl
6 adverse weather conditions
7 an inverse relationship

8 결혼의 행복   m _____ bliss
9 예비회담   p _____ talks
10 중세 건축   m _____ architecture
11 신의 섭리   d _____ providence
12 유독 가스   t _____ fumes
13 항공 사진   an a _____ photograph
14 멍한 표정   a d _____ expression

B 영영사전 뜻풀이에 알맞은 단어 찾기

| 보기 | eco-friendly   somber   ubiquitous   vacant |

1 _____ : sad and serious
2 _____ : seeming to be everywhere
3 _____ : not filled, used, or lived in
4 _____ : designed not to harm the environment

C 주어진 철자로 시작하는 반의어 쓰기

1 masculine ↔ f _____
2 maternal ↔ p _____
3 sacred ↔ s _____
4 verbal ↔ n _____

D 빈칸에 가장 적절한 단어 넣기

| 보기 | contagious   eligible   renewable   stranded   stricken |

1 The patient is still highly _____. 그 환자는 아직 매우 전염성이 높다.
2 We should help famine-_____ countries. 우리는 기근으로 고통받는 나라를 도와야 한다.
3 The strike left tourists _____ at the airport.
파업 때문에 관광객들은 공항에서 오도 가도 못하게 되었다.
4 When are you _____ to vote in your country? 당신 나라에서는 언제 투표할 자격이 있나요?
5 Wind, solar, and biomass are emerging _____ sources of energy.
풍력, 태양열, 바이오매스가 신흥 재생 가능 에너지원이다.

E 밑줄 친 단어 뜻 구별하기

1 wholesome food   wholesome fun
2 a hollow tree   hollow eyes   hollow promises

ANSWER

A 1. 국제 통화 기금 2. 귀를 기울이는 청중 3. 신선하지 않은 케이크 4. 이동식 주택 5. 불쌍한 소녀 6. 불리한 기상 조건 7. 반비례 관계 8. marital
9. preliminary 10. medi(a)eval 11. divine 12. toxic 13. aerial 14. dazed   B 1. somber 2. ubiquitous 3. vacant 4. eco-friendly   C 1.
feminine 2. paternal 3. secular 4. nonverbal   D 1. contagious 2. stricken 3. stranded 4. eligible 5. renewable   E 1. 건강에 좋은 식
품[건강식] / 건전한 놀이 2. 속이 빈 나무 / 우묵한 눈 / 공허한 약속들

어원(Word Origin), 어떻게 할 것인가?

비슷한 형태의 단어들을 어원 중심으로 암기하려 들면 헷갈려서 오히려 역효과가 날 수 있습니다.

영어 단어는 고대 영어 · 라틴어 · 그리스어 · (고대) 프랑스어 등 여러 근원에서 나온 것으로, 〈접두사Prefix + 어근Root + 접미사Suffix〉로 구성됩니다.

e.g. dehumanize : de(반대非)+human(인간)
　　　　　　　　접두사　　　　어근

+ize(~화하다)＝비인간화하다
(동사)접미사

War dehumanizes people.

현대 영단어에 접두사Prefix와 접미사Suffix는 살아남았지만, 어근Root은 일부를 제외하고 거의 다 변형되었습니다.

따라서 기본 단어들을 충분히 습득한 다음에, 어려운 단어들로 확장해 나가기 위한 방편으로 어원의 꽃인 접두사Prefix와 영문법 기초인 품사를 만드는 접미사Suffix에 집중해서 학습하는 것이 효과적입니다.

수 | 능 | 필 | 수

접두사
Prefix 40

어근
Root 30

접미사
Suffix 20

권장 학습법

과학적 · 경제적 · 효과적으로 제시된 수능필수 어원(접두사+어근+접미
사)을 초고속으로 완전정복해 보세요!

접두사 Prefix 40

01 PRE- 미리, 앞에

prerequisite	전제 조건	A degree is an essential prerequisite for employment. 학위가 취업을 위한 필수 전제 조건이다.
presuppose	상정하다[전제로 하다]	The idea of heaven presupposes the existence of God. 천국의 개념은 신의 존재를 상정한다.
preliminary	예비의	the preliminary rounds of the contest 그 경연의 예선전

precaution 예방책   **pre**view 시사회   **pre**dict 예측하다

preheat 예열하다   **pre**historic 선사 시대의   **pre**mature 너무 이른

02 FORE- 미리, 앞에

foresee	예견하다	It is impossible to foresee how life will work out. 삶이 어떻게 풀릴지 예견하는 것은 불가능하다.
foregoing	앞서 말한	the foregoing discussion 앞서 말한 논의
foremost	최고의[앞선]	the world's foremost authority on the subject 그 주제에 대한 세계 최고 권위자

forearm 팔뚝   **fore**father 선조   **fore**finger 집게손가락

forehead 이마   **fore**cast 예보하다   **fore**tell 예언하다

03 PRO- 앞으로

proclaim	선언[선포]하다	The president proclaimed a state of emergency. 대통령이 비상사태를 선포했다.
provoke	유발[도발]하다	The announcement provoked a storm of protest. 그 발표는 거센 항의를 유발했다.
proficient	능숙한	She's proficient in several languages. 그녀는 몇 개 언어에 능숙하다.
prominent	중요한[두드러진]	He played a prominent part in the game. 그는 그 경기에서 중요한 역할을 했다.

progress 진보[진전]   **pro**secution 기소   **pro**test 항의

prophesy 예언하다   **pro**mpt 즉각적인[신속한]

04 ANTE[I]- 전에
POST- 후에

antecedent	선행 사건[선조]	antecedent events 선행 사건들

antique 골동품   **anti**quity 고대 (유물)   **ante** meridiem[a.m.] 오전

anticipate 예상하다   **anti**quated 구식인   **post**modernism 포스트모더니즘

postscript[PS] 추신   **post**-war 전후의

05 RE-   다시, 뒤로

reconstruct	재건[재구성]하다	After the earthquake, many houses were reconstructed. 지진 후에 많은 집들이 재건되었다.
restrain	제지[억제]하다	He managed to restrain his anger. 그는 간신히 화를 참았다.
retrieve	회수[검색]하다	to retrieve information from the database 데이터베이스에서 정보를 검색하다

rearrange 재배열하다   **re**consider 재고하다   **re**gress 퇴보[퇴행]하다
renovate 개조[보수]하다   **re**pay 갚다   **re**produce 복제[번식]하다

06 UN-   반대, 아닌

undo	풀다[원상태로 돌리다]	to undo a button/knot/zip 단추를 끄르다/매듭을 풀다/지퍼를 열다
unavoidable	불가피한	unavoidable delays 불가피한 지연
unbiased	편견 없는	an unbiased judge 편파적이지 않은 심판[판사]

unlock (자물쇠를) 열다   **un**plug 플러그를 뽑다   **un**aware 알지 못하는
uncertain 불확실한   **un**fair[**un**equal] 불공평한   **un**willing 꺼리는

07 IN/IM- IL/IR-   반대, 아닌

invalid	무효의	The treaty was declared invalid. 그 조약은 무효라고 선언되었다.
impartial	공정한	an impartial inquiry/observer 공정한 조사/관찰자
irrelevant	무관한	Many people consider politics irrelevant to their lives. 많은 사람들은 정치가 자기 삶과 무관하다고 생각한다.

injustice 불의   **in**competent 무능한   **im**mature 미숙한
imperfect 불완전한   **il**literate 문맹의   **ir**rational 비이성적인

08 DIS-   반대, 아닌, 떨어져

disgrace	망신[수치]	His behavior has brought disgrace on his country. 그의 행동은 자신의 나라에 수치를 안겨 주었다.
disapprove	반대하다	She wants to be an actress, but her parents disapprove. 그녀는 배우가 되고 싶지만 부모님이 반대하신다.
discriminate	차별[구별]하다	practices that discriminate against women and in favor of men 여성에게 불리하고 남성에게 유리하게 차별하는 관행들

disbelief 불신   **dis**honesty 부정직함   **dis**card 버리다
disconnect 끊다   **dis**obey 불복종하다   **dis**solve 녹(이)다

09 DE- 반대, 아래로

decode	(암호를) 해독하다	The software decodes the information. 그 소프트웨어가 정보를 해독했다.
decompose	분해[부패]하다	a decomposed body 부패된 시체
dehydrate	탈수[건조]하다	Exercising in this heat will dehydrate you. 이런 더위에 운동하는 건 너를 탈수 상태가 되게 할 것이다.

decentralize 분권화하다   **de**frost 해동하다   **de**humanize 비인간화하다
degrade 비하하다   **de**preciate 평가 절하하다   **de**spise 경멸하다

10 NON- A(N)- 아닌, 없는

nonprofit	비영리의	an independent nonprofit organization 비영리 독립 단체
apathy ·	무관심	widespread public apathy 팽배한 대중의 무관심
anonymity	익명(성)	He agreed to give an interview on condition of anonymity. 그는 익명을 조건으로 인터뷰에 응했다.

nonviolence 비폭력   **non**sense 말도 안 되는 것   **non**existent 존재하지 않는
nongovernmental 비정부의   **non**verbal 비언어적인   **a**moral 도덕관념이 없는

11 ANTI- 반대, 맞서

antibiotic	항생제	effective antibiotic treatment 효과적인 항생제 치료
anticancer	항암의	anticancer drugs 항암제
antisocial	반사회적인	antisocial behavior 반사회적 행동

antiseptic 소독제   **anti**-American 반미의   **anti**government 반정부의
antinuclear 반핵의   **anti**virus 항바이러스의   **anti**war 반전의

12 CONTRA[O]- COUNTER- 반대, 맞서

controversy	논란	The President resigned amid considerable controversy. 대통령은 상당한 논란 속에 사임했다.
contradict	반박하다	He contradicted the rumor. 그는 그 소문을 반박했다.
counterfeit	위조의	counterfeit money 위조지폐

contrary 반대의   **counter**attack 반격   **counter**part 상대 쪽
counteract 대응하다   **counter**balance 균형을 맞추다   **counter**productive 역효과인

13 OB- 맞서, 향하여
WITH- 맞서/뒤로

oblige	강제하다 [의무를 지우다]	Employers are legally obliged to pay the minimum wage. 고용주는 법적으로 최저 임금을 지불할 의무가 있다.
obsess	생각을 사로잡다	He is obsessed by the war. 그는 전쟁 생각에 사로잡혔다.
withstand	견뎌 내다	They withstood cold and hunger. 그들은 추위와 굶주림을 견뎌 냈다.

obstacle 장애(물)　　**ob**literate 없애다[지우다]　　**ob**struct 방해하다
offend 불쾌하게 하다　　**with**draw 철수[인출]하다　　**with**hold 주지 않다

14 MIS- 나쁜, 잘못된

mischief	못된 짓[장난]	Those children are always getting into mischief. 저 아이들은 항상 못된 짓을 꾸민다.
mislead	오도하다	Politicians have misled the public. 정치가들이 대중을 오도했다.
misuse	남용[오용]하다	individuals who misuse power for their own ends 자기 자신의 목적을 위해 권력을 남용하는 개인들

misconception 오해　　**mis**deed 비행[악행]　　**mis**inform 잘못된 정보를 주다
misinterpret 잘못 해석하다　　**mis**judge 오판하다　　**mis**treat 학대하다

15 BENE- 좋은
MAL- 나쁜

beneficial	유익한[이로운]	A good diet is beneficial to health. 좋은 음식은 건강에 이롭다.
benevolent	자애로운	a benevolent smile/attitude 자애로운 미소/태도
malnutrition	영양실조	refugees suffering from malnutrition 영양실조에 시달리는 난민들

benefactor 후원자　　**bene**ficiary 수혜자　　**bene**fit 이익[혜택]
beneficent 선을 행하는[도움이 되는]　　**mal**formed 기형인　　**mal**icious 악의적인

16 AD-/AC- 향하여

adore	매우 사랑하다 [흠모하다]	It's obvious that she adores him. 그녀가 그를 흠모하는 게 분명하다.
adorn	장식하다	The walls were adorned with paintings. 벽들은 그림들로 장식되어 있었다.
advocate	지지[옹호]하다	The group does not advocate the use of violence. 그 단체는 폭력 사용을 지지하지 않는다.

adhere 달라붙다　　**ad**journ 휴회하다　　**ad**minister 관리하다
accord 부여[일치]하다　　**ac**cumulate 축적하다　　**ac**knowledge 인정하다

17 IN-/IM- 안에, 안으로

innovate 혁신하다 We must constantly innovate to ensure success.
우리는 성공을 보장하려면 끊임없이 혁신해야 한다.

intrude 침범하다 The government shouldn't intrude into citizens' private
lives. 정부는 시민들의 사생활을 침범해서는 안 된다.

impoverish 가난하게 하다 The dictator enriched himself but impoverished his
people. 그 독재자는 자신은 부유하게 했지만 국민들은 가난하게 했다.

inflate 부풀(리)다   **in**habit 거주[서식]하다   **in**sert 삽입하다
insulate 절연[단열]하다   **im**migrate 이주해 오다   **im**plant 심다[이식하다]

18 E(X)- 밖으로, 떨어져

exclude 제외[배제]하다 Until 1920, women were excluded from the right to vote
in the U.S. 1920년까지 미국에서 여성은 선거권에서 배제되었다.

exploit 착취[개발]하다 They were accused of exploiting migrant workers.
그들은 이주 노동자들을 착취한 혐의로 기소되었다.

evaporate 증발하다 Heat until all the water evaporates.
수분이 모두 증발할 때까지 가열해라.

exhale 내쉬다   **ex**ile 추방하다   **ex**pire 만료되다
extinguish 불을 끄다   **e**rosion 침식   **e**voke 불러일으키다

19 OUT-
EXTRA- 밖에, 밖으로

outcome 결과 We are confident of a successful outcome.
우리는 성공적인 결과를 확신한다.

outstanding 뛰어난[현저한] an outstanding player/achievement/success
뛰어난 선수/성과/성공

extravagant 낭비하는 She's got very extravagant tastes.
그녀는 낭비벽이 심하다.

outbreak 발발[발병]   **out**skirts 변두리(교외)   **out**put 출력[산출]
outdate 구식이 되게 하다   **out**law 불법화하다   **out**going 외향적인
extraordinary 보통이 아닌[비범한]   **extra**terrestrial 외계인   **ext**rovert 외향적인 사람

20 OVER- 너무, 위로

overtake 앞지르다[추월하다] Obesity may overtake smoking as the leading cause of
deaths. 비만이 주요 사망 원인으로 흡연을 앞지르게 될지도 모른다.

overthrow 타도하다 The President was overthrown by a people's revolution.
그 대통령은 시민 혁명으로 타도당했다.

overturn 뒤집(히)다 The car skidded and overturned.
그 차가 미끄러지면서 뒤집혔다.

overdo 너무 하다   **over**eat 과식하다   **over**estimate 과대평가하다
overlap 겹치다   **over**load 과적하다   **over**crowded 초만원[과밀]의

21 SUPER- SUR-
초-[너머], 위에

superficial	피상[표면]적인	superficial differences/similarities 피상적인 차이점들/유사점들
surpass	뛰어넘다	He hopes to surpass the world record. 그는 세계 기록을 뛰어넘기를 바란다.
surrender	항복하다[넘겨주다]	The terrorists surrendered to police. 테러리스트들이 경찰에 투항했다.

superego 초자아   **super**power 초강대국   **super**stition 미신

superhuman 초인적인   **super**natural 초자연적인   **sur**plus 여분[잉여]

22 UP- DOWN-
위로
아래로

uproot	뿌리째 뽑다	to uproot evil practices 악폐를 근절하다
downpour	폭우	a sudden downpour of rain 갑작스러운 폭우

upbringing 양육[교육]   **up**rising 봉기   **up**load 업로드하다

upcoming 다가오는   **up**hill 오르막의[언덕 위로]   **up**right 똑바른

downfall 몰락   **down**turn 감소[하락/하강]   **down**load 다운로드하다

downplay 경시하다   **down**hill 내리막의[언덕 아래로]

23 UNDER-
아래에

undergo	겪다	Children undergo a transformation when they become teenagers. 아이들은 십 대가 되면 변화를 겪는다.
underlie	기저를 이루다	These ideas underlie much of his work. 이러한 생각들이 많은 그의 작품의 기저를 이루고 있다.
undertake	착수하다	to undertake a task/project 과제/프로젝트에 착수하다

undergraduate 대학 학부생   **under**wear 속옷   **under**estimate 과소평가하다

undermine 약화시키다   **under**lying 근본적인   **under**privileged 혜택을 못 받는

24 SUB-
아래에

subsidize	보조금을 주다	The projects are subsidized by the government. 그 프로젝트는 정부 보조금을 받는다.
subjective	주관적인	a subjective point of view 주관적인 관점
subsequent	그다음의	subsequent events/generations 그다음 사건들/세대들

submarine 잠수함   **sub**title 자막[부제]   **sub**urb 교외

submerge 물에 잠기다   **sub**conscious 잠재의식의   **sub**tropical 아열대의

25 INTER- 사이에, 서로

intervene 개입하다 to intervene in the crisis 위기 사태에 개입하다

interdependent 상호 의존적인 interdependent economies/organizations/relationships
상호 의존적인 경제/기관들/관계

interracial 다른 인종 간의 interracial marriage 타인종 간의 결혼

interchange 교환   **inter**mission 중간 휴식 시간   **inter**section 교차(로)
intercept 가로채다   **inter**relate 서로 관련되다   **inter**mediate 중간의

26 CO-
CON/COM- 함께
COL/COR-

compromise 타협 The two sides finally reached a compromise.
양측은 마침내 타협에 이르렀다.

coincide 동시에 일어나다 The population increase coincided with industrial growth.
인구 증가와 산업 성장이 동시에 일어났다.

consistent 일관된 The data show consistent results.
그 데이터는 일관된 결과를 보여 준다.

coexist 공존하다   **con**dense 응축[농축]하다   **com**patible 양립 가능한[호환되는]
collaborate 공동 작업하다   **col**lide 충돌하다   **cor**respond 일치[해당]하다

27 SYN-/SYM- 함께

synchronize 동시에 발생하다
[동기화하다] The sound track did not synchronize with the action.
사운드 트랙이 동작과 동기화되지 않았다.

synthesize 합성[종합]하다 Scientists synthesize new drugs.
과학자들이 신약을 합성한다.

sympathize 동정[공감]하다 I find it very hard to sympathize with them.
나는 그들을 동정하기가 몹시 힘들다.

synonym 동의어   **syn**opsis 개요   **sym**bolize 상징하다
symphony 교향곡   **sym**metrical 대칭적인   **syl**lable 음절

28 TRANS- 건너, 통하여

transcend 초월하다 Love transcends time and space.
사랑은 시공을 초월한다.

transplant 이식하다 Doctors transplanted one of his kidneys into his sister.
의사들이 그의 신장 하나를 그의 누이에게 이식했다.

transparent 투명한 transparent glass 투명한 유리

transaction 거래   **trans**formation 탈바꿈[변신]   **trans**it 운송[교통]
transition 이행[과도]   **trans**mit 전송하다   **trans**ient 일시적인

29 DIA- 통하여

dialect	사투리[방언]	They speak a southern dialect. 그들은 남부 지방 사투리로 말한다.
diagnose	진단하다	He was diagnosed as a diabetic. 그는 당뇨병이라는 진단을 받았다.

diabetes 당뇨병   **dia**gnosis 진단   **dia**gonal 대각선[사선]

diagram 도표   **dia**meter 지름[직경]   **dia**rrhea 설사

diaper 기저귀

30 PER- 통하여

perplex	당혹하게 하다	They were perplexed by his response. 그들은 그의 반응에 당혹했다.
persevere	끈질기게 계속하다	You have to persevere with difficult tasks. 힘든 일은 끈질기게 계속해야 한다.
persist	끈질기게 계속하다	She persisted in her search for the truth. 그녀는 끈질기게 진실 찾기를 계속했다.

perfume 향수[향기]   **per**spective 관점   **per**spire 땀을 흘리다

pervade 널리 퍼지다   **per**manent 영구[영속]적인   **per**petual 끊임없이 계속되는

31 PARA- 옆에

parasite	기생 생물[기생충]	Many diseases are caused by parasites. 많은 질병이 기생충에 의해 발병된다.
paralysis	마비	paralysis of both legs 양 다리 마비
paraphrase	바꾸어 말하다	Try to paraphrase the question. 그 질문을 바꾸어 말해 보아라.

paradigm 모델[패러다임]   **para**dox 역설   **para**graph 문단[단락]

parameter 한도[파라미터]   **par**ody 패러디   **para**llel 평행한

32 AB(S)- 떨어져

abuse	남용[학대]	He was arrested on charges of corruption and abuse of power. 그는 부패 및 권력 남용 혐의로 체포되었다.
abortion	낙태	to support/oppose abortion 낙태를 찬성하다/반대하다
abstract	추출하다[끌어내다]	She abstracted the main points from the argument. 그녀는 그 주장에서 요점을 끌어냈다.

absence 결석[결여]   **ab**sorption 흡수   **ab**breviate 약어로 쓰다

abstain 삼가다   **ab**normal 비정상적인   **ab**surd 터무니없는

33 SE- 떨어져

secrecy	비밀 (유지)	the need for absolute secrecy 절대적인 비밀 유지의 필요성
segregate	분리[차별]하다	a culture in which women are segregated from men 여성이 남성으로부터 차별받는 문화
separable	분리될 수 있는	Physical health is not easily separable from mental health. 신체 건강은 정신 건강과 쉽게 분리될 수 없다.

seclusion 호젓함   **se**curity 보안   **se**duction 유혹
selection 선정[선발]   **se**paration 분리   **se**verity 심각성

34 UNI- 하나

uniformity	동일[획일]성	There is a uniformity of opinion among the students. 학생들 사이에 의견의 동일성이 있다[모두가 같은 의견이다].
unilateral	일방[단독]의	a unilateral decision 일방적인[단독] 결정
unanimous	만장일치의	The decision was not unanimous. 그 결정은 만장일치가 아니었다.

unicorn 유니콘[일각수]   **uni**fication 통일[통합]   **uni**son 일치, 제창
universality 보편성   **uni**cellular 단세포의   **uni**sex 남녀 공용의

35 MONO- 하나
BI- 둘

monopoly	독점(권)	Electricity, gas and water have been considered to be monopolies. 전기, 가스, 수도는 독점 서비스로 여겨져 왔다.
bilateral	쌍방의	bilateral relations/agreements/trade 쌍방 관계/합의/무역
bilingual	두 개 언어를 쓰는	Their kids are bilingual. 그들의 아이들은 두 개 언어를 쓴다.

monogamy 일부일처제   **mono**log(ue) 독백   **bi**ped 두 발 동물
biannual 연 2회의   **bi**ennial 격년의   **bi**nary 2진법의

36 SEMI-/HEMI- 반
AMBI- 둘 다

semiconductor	반도체	semiconductor production technology 반도체 생산 기술
hemisphere	(지구 · 뇌) 반구	the left/right cerebral hemisphere 좌/우 대뇌 반구
ambivalent	반대 감정이 병존하는 [애증이 엇갈리는]	She has an ambivalent attitude towards him. 그녀는 그에 대해 애증이 엇갈리는 태도를 보인다.

semicircle 반원(형)   **semi**final 준결승   **semi**annual 반년마다의
semi-skilled 반숙련된   **ambi**dextrous 양손잡이의   **ambi**guous 모호한

37 MULTI-   많은, 여러

multiply	곱하다 [크게 증가하다]	Cigarette smoking multiplies the risk of cancer. 흡연은 암의 위험을 크게 증대시킨다.
multicultural	다문화의	multicultural families 다문화 가정들
multilateral	다자간의	multilateral negotiations 다자간 협상

multitasking 다중 작업 **multi**tude 다수 **multi**lingual 여러 언어를 쓰는

multinational 다국적의 **multi**ple 다수[복수]의 **multi**purpose 다목적의

38 MICRO-   아주 작은

microbe	미생물	Some microbes can cause diseases. 일부 미생물들은 질병을 일으킬 수 있다.
microwave	전자레인지	Reheat the soup in the microwave. 수프를 전자레인지에 다시 데워라.
microscopic	미세한[현미경으로 봐야만 보이는]	a microscopic creature/particle 현미경으로 봐야만 보이는 생물/입자

microorganism 미생물 **micro**biology 미생물학 **micro**chip 마이크로칩

microeconomics 미시 경제학 **micro**phone 마이크 **micro**scope 현미경

39 AUTO-   스스로

autocracy	독재 정치	the difference between democracy and autocracy· 민주주의와 독재의 차이
autonomy	자치권[자율성]	The teacher encourages individual autonomy. 그 선생님은 개인의 자율성을 장려한다.
automate	자동화하다	The entire manufacturing process has been automated. 전 제조 공정이 자동화되었다.

autobiography 자서전 **auto**graph 유명인 서명 **auto**mation 자동화

automobile 자동차 **auto**pilot 자동 조종 장치 **auto**nomous 자주적인

40 BE-   되게 하다

betray	배신[배반]하다	They betrayed their country for personal gain. 그들은 개인적 이익을 위해 조국을 배신했다.
beware	조심하다	You should beware of making hasty decisions. 성급한 결정을 하지 않도록 조심해야 한다.
bewilder	어리둥절하게 하다	He was bewildered by her reaction. 그는 그녀의 반응에 어리둥절했다.

behave 행동하다 **be**hold 보다 **be**little 비하하다

besiege 포위하다 **be**stow 주다[수여하다] **be**loved 대단히 사랑받는

어근

01 CED[CEED/CESS]　　가다(go)

con**cede**	인정하다	to _____ your error 잘못을 인정하다
pre**cede**	앞서다[선행하다]	a type of cloud that _____s rain 비에 앞서 오는 종류의 구름
re**cede**	물러나다[멀어지다]	The footsteps was _____ing. 발소리가 멀어져 갔다.
ex**ceed**	초과하다[넘어서다]	to _____ your expectations 예상을 넘어서다
pro**ceed**	진행하다, 나아가다	to _____ with the case 소송을 진행하다
pro**cess**	과정, 가공[처리]하다	the learning _____ 학습 과정
pro**cess**ion	행렬[행진]	a torchlight _____ 횃불 행진
pro**ced**ure	절차	legal _____s 법적 절차

02 VENT[VENE]　　오다(come)

ad**vent**	출현[도래]	the _____ of the Internet 인터넷의 출현
pre**vent**	막다[방지하다]	to _____ accidents 사고를 방지하다
inter**vene**	개입하다	to _____ in disputes 분쟁에 개입하다

03 CEIVE　　잡다(hold)

con**ceive**	상상하다	to _____ a plot 구성[음모]을 상상하다
de**ceive**	속이다	to _____ the public 대중을 속이다
per**ceive**	감지[인지]하다	to _____ a change 변화를 감지하다

빈칸에 알맞은 단어 넣기

보기
concede
precede
recede
exceed
proceed

01 (1) Work is _____ing slowly. 작업은 천천히 진행되고 있다.

　　(2) I _____ that there may be difficulties. 나는 어려움이 있을지도 모른다는 것을 인정한다.

　　(3) Your achievements have _____ed expectations. 너의 성과는 예상을 넘어섰다.

　　(4) Dinner will be _____d by a short speech from the chairman.
　　　만찬은 회장의 짧은 연설 뒤에 이어질 것이다.

보기
prevent
intervene

02 (1) The accident could have been _____ed. 그 사고는 방지되었을 수도 있었다.

　　(2) We need the courts to _____ in this dispute.
　　　우리는 법정이 이 분쟁에 개입할 것을 필요로 한다.

보기
conceive
deceive
perceive

03 (1) I _____d that she had been crying. 나는 그녀가 울고 있었다는 걸 감지했다.

　　(2) His parents punished him for trying to _____ them.
　　　그의 부모는 그들을 속이려 한다고 그를 벌주었다.

ANSWER

01. (1) proceed (2) concede (3) exceed (4) precede　　02. (1) prevent (2) intervene　　03. (1) perceive (2) deceive

04 **CIP** 잡다(hold)

anti**cip**ate 예상[기대]하다(= expect) to _____ developments 발전을 기대하다
parti**cip**ate 참가[참여]하다 to _____ in the discussions 논의에 참여하다

05 **SUME** 잡다(hold)

as**sume**
❶ 추정[가정]하다 to _____ the worst 최악을 가정하다
❷ 맡다 to _____ responsibility 책임을 맡다
❸ ~인 척하다 to _____ an air of indifference 무관심한 척하다
❹ 성질을 띠다 to _____ importance 중요성을 띠다

pre**sume** 추정하다 to be _____d innocent 무죄로 추정되다
re**sume** 다시 시작하다[재개하다] to _____ work/training 일/훈련을 재개하다

06 **TAIN** 가지다(have)

con**tain**
❶ 포함[함유]하다 to _____ alcohol 알코올을 포함하다
❷ 억제하다 to _____ your excitement 흥분을 억제하다

main**tain**
❶ 유지하다 to _____ high standards 높은 수준을 유지하다
❷ 주장하다 to _____ your innocence 결백을 주장하다

ob**tain** 얻다[획득하다] to _____ permission 허가를 얻다

re**tain** 보유[유지]하다 to _____ control of food imports
식량 수입의 통제권을 보유하다

sus**tain**
❶ 유지[지속]시키다 to _____ economic growth 경제 성장을 지속시키다
❷ (피해를) 입다

빈칸에 알맞은 단어 넣기

| 보기 |

anticipate
participate

04 (1) We don't _____ any major problems.
우리는 무슨 큰 문제가 있을 것으로 예상하지 않는다.

(2) Everyone in the class is expected to _____ in the discussions.
반의 모두가 논의에 참여할 것으로 기대된다.

assume
presume
resume

05 (1) She hopes to _____ work after the baby is born.
그녀는 아기가 태어난 후 일을 다시 시작하기를 바란다.

(2) It is _____d that stress is caused by too much work.
스트레스는 과로로 유발된다고 추정된다.

contain
maintain
obtain
sustain

06 (1) Try to _____ a healthy weight. 건강한 체중을 유지하려고 노력해라.

(2) The information is difficult to _____. 그 정보는 얻기 어렵다.

(3) Hope _____s us during difficult times.
희망은 힘든 시기 동안 우리를 살아가게 해 준다[유지시켜 준다].

(4) Soya milk _____s low fat and high protein. 두유는 저지방과 고단백질을 함유한다.

ANSWER

04. (1) anticipate (2) participate 05. (1) resume (2) assume[presume] 06. (1) maintain[sustain] (2) obtain (3) sustain (4) contain

07 TRIBUTE　　　　주다(give)

at**tribute** (~ to)	~ 때문이라고 여기다	to _____ your success to luck 성공을 행운 때문이라고 여기다
con**tribute**	기부하다, 기여하다	to _____ to charity 자선 단체에 기부하다
dis**tribute**	분배[배급]하다	to _____ food 식량을 배급하다

08 DIC　　　　말하다(say)

ad**dic**t	중독자	a(n) alcohol/drug _____ 알코올/마약 중독자
contra**dic**t	❶ 반박하다 ❷ 모순되다	to _____ your claims 주장을 반박하다
pre**dic**t	예측하다	to _____ earthquakes 지진을 예측하다
de**dic**ate	바치다	to _____ yourself to charity work 자선 사업에 헌신하다

09 SCRIB　　　　쓰다(write)

a**scrib**e	(탓)으로 돌리다	to _____ your failure to bad luck 실패를 불운 탓으로 돌리다
de**scrib**e	묘사[기술]하다	to _____ your friend 친구를 묘사하다
pre**scrib**e	❶ 처방하다 ❷ 규정하다	to _____ the drug 약을 처방하다
sub**scrib**e	정기 구독[가입]하다	to _____ to a magazine 잡지를 정기 구독하다
tran**scrib**e	베껴 쓰다[받아쓰다]	to _____ the statements 진술을 받아쓰다

빈칸에 알맞은 단어 넣기

| 보기 |

attribute
contribute
distribute

07 (1) The volunteers _____ their own time to the project.
자원봉사자들은 그 프로젝트에 자신의 시간을 바친다.

(2) She _____s her success to hard work and a little luck.
그녀는 자신의 성공을 근면과 약간의 행운 때문이라고 여긴다.

(3) The organization _____d food to the earthquake victims.
그 단체는 지진 피해자들에게 식량을 배급했다.

contradict
predict
dedicate

08 (1) No one can _____ the future. 아무도 미래를 예측할 수 없다.

(2) He _____(e)d the charges of his critics. 그는 비판하는 사람들의 비난을 반박했다.

(3) She _____(e)d herself to helping the poor. 그녀는 가난한 사람들을 돕는 데 자신을 바쳤다.

ascribe
describe
prescribe
subscribe
transcribe

09 (1) This drug should not be _____d to children.
이 약은 아이들에게 처방되어서는 안 된다.

(2) I _____ to several newspapers and magazines.
나는 몇 개의 신문과 잡지를 정기 구독하고 있다.

(3) The report _____s the rise in asthma to the increase in pollution.
그 보고서는 천식의 증가를 오염의 증가 탓으로 돌린다.

ANSWER

07. (1) contribute　(2) attribute　(3) distribute　　**08.** (1) predict　(2) contradict　(3) dedicate　　**09.** (1) prescribe　(2) subscribe　(3) ascribe

10 FORM　　　　만들다

conform	따르다	to _____ to customs 관습에 따르다
perform	❶ 공연하다 ❷ 수행하다	to _____ tasks 일을 수행하다
reform	개혁하다	to _____ the unfair system 불공정한 제도를 개혁하다
transform	변형시키다 [완전히 바꾸다]	to _____ your life 인생을 완전히 바꾸다

11 DUC　　　　(이)끌다(draw, lead)

induce	설득하다, 유발하다	a stress-_____d allergy 스트레스로 유발된 알레르기
reduce	줄이다[축소하다]	"_____ Speed Now." "속도를 줄이시오."(표지판)
reproduce	❶ 생식[번식]하다 ❷ 복제[재현]하다	cells _____ing themselves 자기 복제하는 세포

12 TRACT　　　　끌다(draw)

abstract	추상적인 (↔ concrete)	_____ ideas/concepts 추상적 생각/개념
attract	끌다[매혹하다]	to _____ attention 주의를 끌다
distract	(주의를) 딴 데로 돌리다	to _____ attention 주의를 딴 데로 돌리다
extract	뽑아내다[추출하다]	to have your tooth _____ed 이를 뽑다
subtract	빼다(= deduct ↔ add)	to _____ 30 from 45 45에서 30을 빼다

빈칸에 알맞은 단어 넣기

보기
conform
perform
reform
transform

10 (1) The law needs to be _____ed. 그 법은 개혁될 필요가 있다.

　　(2) He refused to _____ to the local customs. 그는 지역 관습을 따르는 것을 거부했다.

　　(3) The Internet has _____ed many retail businesses.
　　　　인터넷이 많은 소매업을 완전히 바꾸어 놓았다.

induce
reduce
reproduce

11 (1) Nothing would _____ me to take the job.
　　　　아무것도 내가 그 일을 맡도록 설득하지 못할 것이다.

　　(2) The helmet law should _____ injuries in motorcycle accidents.
　　　　헬멧 법은 오토바이 사고에서 부상을 줄일 것이다.

　　(3) It is illegal to _____ books without permission from the publisher.
　　　　출판사의 허락 없이 책을 복제하는 것은 불법이다.

attract
distract
extract
subtract

12 (1) Try not to _____ the other students. 다른 학생들을 산만하게 하지 않도록 해라.

　　(2) We can _____ essential oils from plants. 우리는 식물에서 정유를 추출할 수 있다.

　　(3) What _____ed me most to the job was the chance to travel.
　　　　나를 그 일로 가장 끌었던 것은 여행의 기회였다.

ANSWER

10. (1) reform (2) conform (3) transform　**11.** (1) induce (2) reduce (3) reproduce　**12.** (1) distract (2) extract (3) attract

13 PEL   밀다, 몰다 (push, drive)

com**pel**	강요[강제]하다	to be _____led to resign 사임을 강요당하다
ex**pel**	쫓아내다[추방하다]	to be _____led for spying 스파이 행위로 추방되다
pro**pel**	나아가게 하다[추진하다]	a boat _____led by a motor 모터로 추진되는 보트

14 FER   나르다, 보내다 (carry, send)

in**fer**	추론[추리]하다	to _____ the meaning 의미를 추론하다
trans**fer**	❶ 옮기다, 전학[전근]하다	to _____ to another school 다른 학교로 전학하다
	❷ 갈아타다	to _____ from the bus to the subway 버스에서 지하철로 갈아타다

15 MIT   보내다 (send)

ad**mit**	❶ 인정하다 ❷ 허락하다	to _____ to your mistakes 실수를 인정하다
com**mit**	❶ 저지르다 ❷ 약속하다 ❸ 헌신하다	to _____ murder/suicide 살인/자살하다
e**mit**	내다[내뿜다]	to _____ infra-red rays 적외선을 방출하다
o**mit**	빠뜨리다[생략하다]	to _____ details 세부 사항을 생략하다
per**mit**	허락[허가]하다	Smoking is not _____ted. 흡연은 허락되지 않는다.
sub**mit**	❶ 제출하다 ❷ (~ to) 굴복하다	to _____ your application 신청서를 제출하다
trans**mit**	전송하다	to _____ the information 정보를 전송하다
dis**miss**	❶ 무시하다 ❷ 해고하다	to _____ the proposal 제안을 무시하다 to be unfairly _____ed 부당하게 해고되다

빈칸에 알맞은 단어 넣기

보기

compel
expel
propel

13 (1) He was _____led from school for bad behavior. 그는 비행으로 학교에서 쫓겨났다.

    (2) The law can _____ fathers to make regular payments for their children.
법은 아버지가 자녀들에게 정기적으로 돈을 지불하도록 강제할 수 있다.

infer
transfer

14 (1) She _____red from another school last year. 그녀는 작년에 다른 학교에서 전학 왔다.

    (2) Much of the meaning must be _____red from the context.
의미의 많은 부분은 문맥에서 추론되어야 한다.

admit
commit
emit
omit
permit
submit
transmit
dismiss

15 (1) They _____ted your name from the list. 그들이 당신의 이름을 명단에서 빠뜨렸다.

    (2) Don't be afraid to _____ to your mistakes. 실수를 인정하기를 두려워하지 마라.

    (3) No government can _____ its public opinion. 어떤 정부도 여론을 무시할 수 없다.

    (4) Completed projects must be _____ted by 25 April.
완성된 프로젝트가 4월 25일까지 제출되어야 한다.

ANSWER

13. (1) expel (2) compel   14. (1) transfer (2) infer   15. (1) omit (2) admit (3) dismiss (4) submit

16 JECT　　　　　　　　　　던지다(throw)

inject	주사[주입]하다	to _____ insulin 인슐린을 주사하다
project	❶ 계획 (사업) ❷ 예측[계획]하다 ❸ 영사[투사]하다	the _____ed housing development 계획된 주택 개발
reject	거부[거절]하다	to _____ the proposal 제안을 거부하다

17 POSE　　　　　　　　　　놓다(put)

compose	❶ 구성하다 ❷ 작곡하다	to _____ a song 노래를 작곡하다
dispose (~ of)	처리하다	to _____ of waste 쓰레기를 처리하다
expose	노출시키다, 폭로하다	to be _____d to light 빛에 노출되다
impose	부과하다, 강요하다	to _____ taxes 세금을 부과하다
oppose	반대하다	to _____ the death penalty 사형을 반대하다

18 PRESS　　　　　　　　　　누르다

compress	압축하다, 요약하다	_____ed air 압축 공기
oppress	억압하다	to _____ minorities 소수자를 억압하다
repress	억누르다	to _____ the urge 충동을 억제하다
suppress	진압하다, 억누르다	to _____ the uprising 봉기를 진압하다

빈칸에 알맞은 단어 넣기

보기
inject project reject
compose dispose expose impose oppose
compress oppress repress suppress

16 (1) She _____ed his offer of help. 그녀는 그의 지원 제의를 거절했다.

(2) Chemicals are _____ed into the fruit to reduce decay.
화학 약품이 부패를 줄이기 위해 과일에 주입된다.

17 (1) It is difficult to _____ of nuclear waste. 핵폐기물을 처리하는 것은 어렵다.

(2) The government _____s heavy taxes on cigarettes.
정부는 담배에 무거운 세금을 부과한다.

(3) The workers were _____d to dangerous chemicals.
작업자들은 위험한 화학 물질에 노출되었다.

(4) The legal system is _____d of people, and people make mistakes.
법 제도는 사람들로 구성되는데, 사람들은 실수를 한다.

(5) There was a campaign to _____ the building of a nuclear reactor.
원자로 건설을 반대하는 캠페인이 있었다.

18 (1) Political dissent was brutally _____ed. 정치적 반대가 잔인하게 탄압되었다.

(2) An MP3 is a _____ed digital music file. MP3는 압축된 디지털 음악 파일이다.

ANSWER

16. (1) reject (2) inject　　17. (1) dispose (2) impose (3) expose (4) compose (5) oppose　　18. (1) suppress[oppress/repress] (2) compress

19 QUIRE — 찾다(look for)

ac**quire**	얻다[획득/습득]하다	to _____ the skills	기술을 습득하다
in**quire**	문의하다	to _____ about train times	열차 시간에 대해 문의하다
re**quire**	필요로 하다[요구하다]	to _____ surgery	수술을 필요로 하다

20 SPIRE — 숨 쉬다(breathe)

a**spire**	열망하다	to _____ to a teaching career	교직을 열망하다
in**spire**	고무하다[영감을 주다]	Music _____s me. 음악은 내게 영감을 준다.	
per**spire**	땀을 흘리다(=sweat)	your _____ing face	땀 흘리는 얼굴
re**spire**	호흡하다	to _____ with difficulty	어렵게 호흡하다

21 SENT — 느끼다(feel)

as**sent**	찬성[동의]하다	to _____ to the suggestion	제안에 찬성하다
con**sent**	허락[동의]하다	to _____ to the plan	계획에 동의하다
dis**sent**	반대하다	to _____ from the decision	결정에 반대하다
re**sent**	분개하다	to _____ the criticism	비난에 분개하다

빈칸에 알맞은 단어 넣기

보기
acquire
inquire
require

19 (1) The wearing of seat belts is _____d by law. 좌석 벨트 착용은 법으로 요구된다.

(2) I'm calling to _____ about your advertisement.
광고에 대해 문의하려고 전화합니다.

(3) The college _____d a reputation for very high standards.
그 대학은 아주 높은 수준으로 명성을 얻었다.

aspire
inspire
perspire
respire

20 (1) Fish use their gills to _____. 물고기는 호흡하기 위해 아가미를 사용한다.

(2) She _____d to a scientific career. 그녀는 과학 관련 직업을 열망했다.

(3) He has _____d us to live better lives. 그는 우리가 더 나은 삶을 살도록 고무했다.

assent
consent
dissent
resent

21 (1) Several scientists _____ed from the decision.
몇몇 과학자들이 그 결정에 반대했다.

(2) She bitterly _____s being treated like a child.
그녀는 아이 취급당하는 것에 몹시 분개한다.

(3) He reluctantly _____ed to his daughter's marriage.
그는 딸의 결혼을 마지못해 허락했다.

ANSWER

19. (1) require (2) inquire (3) acquire　**20.** (1) respire (2) aspire (3) inspire　**21.** (1) dissent (2) resent (3) consent

22 **SIST** 서다(stand)

as**sist**	돕다(=help)	to _____ the police 경찰을 돕다
per**sist**	끈질기게 계속하다 [고집하다]	to _____ with your studies 공부를 끈질기게 계속하다
re**sist**	저항하다, 참다[견디다]	to _____ change 변화에 저항하다

23 **STITU** 세우다(stand)

| con**stitu**te | ❶ ~로 여겨지다
❷ 구성하다 | to _____ a criminal offence 형사상 범죄로 여겨지다 |
| in**stitu**te | ❶ 기관[연구소]
❷ 도입[시작]하다 | research _____ s 연구소
to _____ measures 조치를 도입하다 |

24 **SPECT** 보다(see)

in**spect**	검사[점검]하다	to _____ the scene 현장을 점검하다
pro**spect**	가망, 전망	_____ s for growth 성장 전망
retro**spect**	회상[회고]	in _____ 회상해 보면[돌이켜 보면]
per**spect**ive	❶ 관점(=view) ❷ 원근법	from a global _____ 세계적 관점에서 the use of _____ 원근법의 사용

빈칸에 알맞은 단어 넣기

보기

assist
persist
resist

22 (1) We'll do all we can to _____ you.
우리는 당신을 돕기 위해 우리가 할 수 있는 모든 일을 할 것입니다.

(2) The rich _____ paying their fair share of taxes.
부자들은 자신들의 합당한 몫의 세금을 내는 것에 저항한다.

(3) She _____ed in her refusal to admit responsibility.
그녀는 책임을 인정하기를 고집스럽게 거부했다.

constitute
institute

23 (1) The new management intends to _____ a number of changes.
새 경영진은 많은 변화를 도입할 작정이다.

(2) The increase in racial tension _____s a threat to our society.
인종 간 긴장의 증가는 우리 사회에 위협으로 여겨진다.

inspect
prospect
retrospect
perspective

24 (1) The goods are _____(e)d for defects before being packaged.
상품은 포장되기 전에 결함이 검사[점검]된다.

(2) In _____, I made the right decision. 돌이켜 보면, 나는 올바른 결정을 했다.

(3) There is no immediate _____ of peace. 즉시 평화가 올 가망은 없다.

(4) He helped us see the problem from a new _____.
그는 우리가 그 문제를 새로운 관점에서 보도록 도왔다.

ANSWER

22. (1) assist (2) resist (3) persist　**23.** (1) institute (2) constitute　**24.** (1) inspect (2) retrospect (3) prospect (4) perspective

25 VIS　　　　　　　　보다(see)

de**vis**e	고안[창안]하다	to _____ a method 방법을 고안하다
impro**vis**e	즉석에서 하다	an _____d speech 즉흥 연설
re**vis**e	수정[개정]하다	to _____ plans 계획을 수정하다
super**vis**e	감독[관리]하다	to _____ exams 시험을 감독하다

26 RUPT　　　　　　　　깨뜨리다(break)

ab**rupt**	❶ 갑작스러운 ❷ 퉁명스러운	an _____ change of plan 갑작스러운 계획 변경
cor**rupt**	타락[부패]한, 타락시키다	a _____ regime 부패한 정권
dis**rupt**	방해하다[지장을 주다]	to _____ the meeting 회의를 방해하다
e**rupt**	(화산이) 분출하다	The volcano _____ed. 화산이 분출했다.
inter**rupt**	방해하다, 중단하다	Stop _____ing me! 내 말을 가로막지 마!

27 TEND　　　　　　　　뻗치다(stretch)

con**tend**	❶ 경쟁하다[다투다] ❷ 주장하다	to _____ for power 권력을 다투다
in**tend**	의도[작정]하다	to _____ to study harder 더 열심히 공부할 작정이다
pre**tend**	~인 척하다	to _____ not to notice 알아차리지 못한 척하다

빈칸에 알맞은 단어 넣기

보기
devise
improvise
revise
supervise

25 (1) We have to _____ our plans because of the delays.
우리는 지연 때문에 계획을 수정해야 한다.

(2) He had to _____ his speech when he forgot his notes.
그는 메모를 잊어버려서 즉흥 연설을 해야 했다.

(3) They have _____d a new method for converting sunlight into electricity.
그들은 햇빛을 전기로 바꾸는 새로운 방법을 고안했다.

disrupt
erupt
interrupt

26 (1) The barking dogs _____ed my sleep. 짖는 개들이 나의 수면을 방해했다.

(2) The game was _____ed several times by rain.
그 경기는 비 때문에 여러 차례 중단되었다.

(3) An immense volume of rocks and lava was _____ed.
엄청난 양의 암석과 용암이 분출되었다.

contend
intend
pretend

27 (1) I didn't _____ to hurt you. 나는 당신의 감정을 상하게 하려는 의도는 아니었어요.

(2) We _____ed (that) nothing had happened. 우리는 아무 일도 일어나지 않은 척했다.

(3) She _____s the new law will only benefit the wealthy.
그녀는 새로운 법이 부자들에게 이익이 될 뿐이라고 주장한다.

ANSWER

25. (1) revise (2) improvise (3) devise　**26.** (1) disrupt[interrupt] (2) interrupt[disrupt] (3) erupt　**27.** (1) intend (2) pretend (3) contend

28 VOLV　　　　돌다, 말다(turn, roll)

evolv**e**　　진화하다　　to _____ from a single ancestor
단일 조상으로부터 진화하다

involv**e**　　❶ 포함[수반]하다　　to _____ the risk 위험을 포함하다
❷ 관련[참여]시키다　　to be _____d in the project 프로젝트에 참여하다

revolv**e**　　돌다[회전하다]　　The Earth _____s on its axis.
지구는 축을 중심으로 회전한다.

29 VERT[VERS]　　　　돌다(turn)

convert　　전환하다, 개종하다　　a sofa that _____s into a bed 침대로 전환되는 소파

invert　　뒤집다[거꾸로 하다]　　the _____ed pyramid 역 피라미드

converse　　대화하다　　to _____ with her 그녀와 대화하다

reverse　　뒤바꾸다[뒤집다]　　to _____ a decision 결정을 뒤집다

30 FIN　　　　끝, 경계(end, boundary)

confine　　제한[한정]하다, 감금하다　　to _____ your discussion to the matter
논의를 그 문제에 한정하다

define　　정의하다　　to _____ freedom 자유를 정의하다

refine　　개선하다, 정제하다　　to _____ the designs 디자인을 개선하다

빈칸에 알맞은 단어 넣기

ㅣ보기ㅣ

evolve
involve
revolve

28 (1) Any investment _____s an element of risk. 어떤 투자든 위험 요소를 포함한다.

(2) Bacteria are _____ing resistance to antibiotics.
박테리아는 항생제에 대한 내성을 진화시키고 있다.

(3) The restaurant slowly _____s, giving excellent views.
그 식당은 천천히 회전하면서, 멋진 경치를 제공한다.

convert
invert
converse
reverse

29 (1) The Supreme Court _____d the decision. 대법원이 그 판결을 뒤집었다.

(2) _____ the cake onto a rack and let it cool. 케이크를 받침대 위에 뒤집어서 식혀라.

(3) We _____ed our oil boiler to gas to save money.
우리는 돈을 절약하기 위해 기름보일러를 가스로 전환했다.

confine
define
refine

30 (1) Please _____ your comments to 200 words.
당신의 논평을 200자까지로 한정해 주십시오.

(2) The term "mental illness" is difficult to _____.
'정신 질환'이라는 용어는 정의하기가 어렵다.

(3) We've _____d the system since it was first launched.
우리는 그 시스템이 처음 출시된 이래 계속 그것을 개선해 왔다.

ANSWER

28. (1) involve (2) evolve (3) revolve　　**29.** (1) reverse (2) Invert[Reverse] (3) convert　　**30.** (1) confine (2) define (3) refine

접 미 사 Suffix 20

명사 접미사 | Noun Suffixes

01	**-ant**	applicant 지원자	descendant 자손[후손]	immigrant 이민자
		inhabitant 거주자[서식 동물]	participant 참가자	pollutant 오염 물질
	-ent	correspondent 통신원[특파원]	opponent 상대[반대자]	component 요소[부품]

02	**-ee/er/or**	employee 고용인	explorer 탐험가	supervisor 감독관
	-ian	humanitarian 인도주의자	vegetarian 채식주의자	veterinarian 수의사
	-ist/ism	optimist 낙관[낙천]주의자	specialist 전문가	racism 인종 차별(주의)

03	**-al**	approval 승인[인정]	denial 부인[부정]	disposal 처리
		refusal 거절[거부]	removal 제거	withdrawal 철수[인출]
	-age	coverage 보도[방송]	heritage (집단의) 유산	leakage 누출[유출]

04	**-ance**	acceptance 받아들임[수락/수용]	assistance 도움[지원]	defiance 반항[저항]
		endurance 인내력	maintenance 유지	resemblance 닮음[유사점]
		tolerance 관용	ignorance 무지[무식]	significance 중대성[의미]

05	**-ence**	coexistence 공존	disobedience 불복종	preference 선호
		adolescence 청소년기	competence 능력	negligence 부주의[태만/과실]
	-(en)cy	efficiency 효율[능률]	fluency 유창성[능숙함]	accuracy 정확(성)

06	**-ation**	democratization 민주화	industrialization 산업[공업]화	memorization 암기
		realization 깨달음[실현]	conservation 자연 보호[보존]	globalization 세계화
	-ion	addiction 중독	completion 완료[완성]	exclusion 제외[배제]

07	**-(i)ty**	causality 인과 관계	continuity 연속성	diversity 다양성
		originality 독창성	prosperity 번영	sensibility 감성[감수성]
		simplicity 단순성	penalty 처벌[벌금]	specialty 전문[전공]

08	**-dom/tude**	boredom 지루함[권태]	gratitude 고마움[감사]	magnitude (큰) 규모(震度/光度)
	-hood/ship	brotherhood 형제애[인류애]	citizenship 시민권[시민 의식]	ownership 소유(권)
	-ment/ness	agreement 동의[합의/협정]	encouragement 격려	quickness 빠름[기민함]

동사 접미사 | Verb Suffixes

09	**-ate**	**activate** 작동[활성화]하다 **formulate** 고안하다 **necessitate** 필요로 하다	**assimilate** 동화[소화/흡수]하다 **initiate** 시작[착수]하다 **negotiate** 협상[교섭]하다	**differentiate** 구별하다 **integrate** 통합하다 **vaccinate** 예방 접종을 하다
10	**-ify**	**beautify** 아름답게 하다 **intensify** 심해지다[강화하다] **signify** 나타내다[의미하다]	**clarify** 분명히 하다 **justify** 정당화하다 **simplify** 단순화하다	**exemplify** 좋은 예가 되다 **purify** 정화하다 **specify** 명시하다
11	**-ize**	**characterize** 특징짓다 **harmonize** 조화를 이루다 **standardize** 표준화하다	**generalize** 일반화하다 **idolize** 우상화하다 **sympathize** 동정[공감]하다	**globalize** 세계화하다 **stabilize** 안정시키다 **visualize** 상상하다
12	**-en**	**flatten** 평평[납작]해지다[하게 하다] **moisten** 촉촉해지다[하게 하다]	**heighten** 높이다 **thicken** 걸쭉해지다[짙게 하다]	**lessen** 줄(이)다 **worsen** 악화시키다
	en-	**enlarge** 확대하다	**enslave** 노예로 만들다	**entitle** 권리[자격]를 주다

형용사 접미사 | Adjective Suffixes

13	**-able** **-ible**	**admirable** 존경[감탄]할 만한 **audible** 들리는 **eligible** 자격이 있는	**practicable** 실행 가능한 **accessible** 접근[이용] 가능한 **irresistible** 저항할 수 없는	**sustainable** 지속 가능한 **convertible** 전환 가능한 **negligible** 무시해도 될 정도의
14	**-al**	**accidental** 우연한 **exceptional** 예외적인[특출한] **intentional** 의도[고의]적인	**confidential** 비밀[기밀]의 **immemorial** 태곳적부터의 **minimal** 최소의	**empirical** 실증적인 **influential** 영향력 있는 **sentimental** 감상[感傷]적인
15	**-ant** **-ent**	**abundant** 풍부한 **dependent** 의존[의지]하는 **persistent** 끈질긴[지속되는]	**dominant** 지배적인[우성의] **emergent** 신생의 **prevalent** 일반적인[널리 퍼져 있는]	**resistant** 저항하는[잘 견디는] **insistent** 주장[고집]하는 **proficient** 능숙한
16	**-ary**	**complementary** 보완적인 **legendary** 전설적인	**complimentary** 칭찬하는[무료의] **monetary** 통화[화폐]의	**customary** 관례인 **voluntary** 자발적인
	-y	**fatty** 지방이 많은	**filthy** 아주 더러운	**moody** 침울한[기분 변화가 심한]
17	**-ic**	**democratic** 민주주의의 **periodic** 주기적인	**energetic** 정력적인 **sarcastic** 빈정거리는[비꼬는]	**enthusiastic** 열렬한[열광적인] **synthetic** 합성[인조]의
	-ical	**analytical** 분석적인	**ecological** 생태계[학]의	**psychological** 심리의
18	**-ive**	**affirmative** 긍정의 **defensive** 방어[수비]의 **productive** 생산적인	**conservative** 보수적인 **interactive** 상호 작용[대화형]의 **progressive** 진보적인	**constructive** 건설적인 **persuasive** 설득력 있는 **responsive** 즉각 반응[호응]하는
19	**-ous**	**capricious** 변덕스러운 **miraculous** 기적적인 **prestigious** 명망 있는	**courteous** 예의 바른 **mischievous** 짓궂은 **simultaneous** 동시의	**harmonious** 조화로운 **nutritious** 영양분이 풍부한 **spontaneous** 자연스러운[즉흥적인]
20	**-ful**	**eventful** 다사다난한 **meaningful** 의미 있는	**forgetful** 잘 잊어버리는 **shameful** 수치스러운[부끄러운]	**healthful** 건강에 좋은 **wasteful** 낭비하는
	-less	**boundless** 무한한	**penniless** 무일푼인	**speechless** 할 말을 잃은[말문이 막힌]

더 이상 헷갈림 (Confusion) 금지

수 | 능 | 적 | 중

다의어 30

흔히 쓰이는 여러 뜻들을 가지는 기본 단어로,
시험에 자주 나오는 대표적 다의어·30 엄선.

혼동어 120

철자·발음은 비슷한데 의미나 용법이 서로 다른 단어들로,
헷갈리기 쉬워 수능을 비롯한 여러 시험에
단골로 등장하는 대표적 혼동어 120 엄선.
동사 중심 | 형용사 중심 | 명사 중심 | 품사 혼합

권장 학습법

1. 다의어/혼동어의 뜻과 모양(철자)을 비교하며 익힐 것!

2. 오른쪽 예구 빈칸을 채우며 머리에 새길 것!

3. 바로 아래 Quiz를 풀며 확실한 되새김질!

다의어

30

01 account

❶ 계좌, (-s) 회계   a bank/savings _____ 은행/예금 계좌
❷ 설명, (~ for) 설명하다(=explain)   to give an _____ of the incident 그 사건을 설명해 주다
❸ (~ for) 차지하다   to _____ for 12% of the total 전체의 12%를 차지하다

▶ on account of = because of
▶ take account of [take ~ into account] 고려하다

02 address

❶ 주소(를 쓰다)   What's your _____? 주소가 어떻게 되니?
❷ 연설(하다), 직접 말하다   to deliver an _____ 연설을 하다
❸ 다루다   to _____ a(n) problem[issue] 문제를 다루다
❹ (~ as) ~라고 부르다   to be _____ed as "sir" '선생님'이라고 불리다

03 apply

❶ 지원[신청]하다   to _____ to a university 대학에 지원하다
     to _____ for a passport 여권을 신청하다
❷ 적용하다   to _____ new technology to farming 신기술을 농업에 적용하다
❸ (~ yourself (to)) (~에) 전념하다   to _____ yourself to studying 공부에 전념하다

밑줄 친 단어의 뜻은?

01 (1) What's your <u>account</u> number please?
     (2) How do you <u>account for</u> their success?
     (3) The Chinese market <u>accounts for</u> 50% of the company's revenue.

02 (1) I'll give you my email <u>address</u> and phone number.
     (2) The new President delivered his inaugural <u>address</u>.
     (3) Our products <u>address</u> the needs of real users.
     (4) The president should be <u>address</u>ed as "Mr. President."

03 (1) I <u>applied</u> to four universities and was accepted by all of them.
     (2) They <u>applied</u> a new technique to solve an old problem.
     (3) You would pass your exams if you <u>applied</u> yourself.

ANSWER

01. (1) 계좌 번호가 어떻게 되세요? (2) 그들의 성공을 어떻게 설명하겠어요? (3) 중국 시장이 그 회사 수익의 50%를 차지한다.   02. (1) 제 이메일 주소와 전화번호를 알려드릴게요. (2) 새 대통령이 취임 연설을 했다. (3) 우리 제품은 실제 사용자의 필요를 다룬다. (4) 대통령은 '미스터 프레지던트'라고 불려야 한다.   03. (1) 나는 4개의 대학에 지원해서 모든 곳에서 받아들여졌다. (2) 그들은 오래된 문제를 해결하기 위해 새로운 기법을 적용했다. (3) 네가 전념하면 시험에 합격할 텐데.

04 **bear**-bore-borne

❶ 참다[견디다](=endure)   to _____ the pain 고통을 참다

❷ 떠맡다   to _____ the responsibility/costs 책임/비용을 떠맡다

❸ 지탱하다[견디다](=hold)   to _____ your weight 몸무게를 지탱하다

❹ 지니다[가지다](=keep, have)   to _____ in mind 마음에 지니다

❺ 곰

05 **beat**-beat-beaten

❶ 이기다(=defeat), 능가하다   We _____ them at soccer.

우리는 축구에서 그들을 이겼다.

❷ 두드리다[때리다]   to _____ a drum 드럼을 치다

❸ 고동치다, 고동[박동]   Your heart is _____ing.

너의 심장이 뛰고 있다.

❹ 박자[비트](=rhythm)   the _____ of the music 음악의 박자

06 **bow**

❶ 절(하다), 고개를 숙이다   to _____ low to the audience 청중[관객]에게 절하다

❷ 구부러지다   The pines _____ed in the wind. 소나무가 바람에 구부러졌다.

❸ 뱃머리[이물]   from _____ to stern 뱃머리에서 선미까지

❹ (쏘는/현악기의) 활(로 켜다)   a _____ and arrow 활과 화살

❺ 나비매듭   a _____ tie 나비넥타이

밑줄 친 단어의 뜻은?

04 (1) She can't bear being laughed at.

(2) Developed countries have to bear the responsibility for environmental problems.

(3) It is too thin to bear your weight.

(4) He bears no resentment towards them.

05 (1) We beat them 7 to 4.

(2) Someone is beating at the door.

(3) Your heart beats 70 times a minute.

06 (1) She bowed her head in shame.

(2) His back was bowed under the weight of his pack.

(3) The deck was cleaned from bow to stern.

ANSWER

04. (1) 그녀는 놀림을 받는 것을 참지 못한다. (2) 선진국은 환경 문제에 대한 책임을 떠맡아야 한다. (3) 그것은 너무 얇아 네 체중을 견디지 못한다. (4) 그는 그들에게 분한 마음을 갖고 있지 않다.   05. (1) 우리는 그들을 7 대 4로 이겼다. (2) 누군가가 문을 두드리고 있다. (3) 심장은 1분에 70번 뛴다.   06. (1) 그녀는 수치심에 고개를 숙였다. (2) 그의 등은 짐의 무게로 구부러졌다. (3) 갑판이 뱃머리에서 선미까지 청소되었다.

07 **capital**

❶ 수도   Cairo is the _____ of Egypt.
카이로는 이집트의 수도다.

❷ 자본(의)   foreign _____ 외국 자본

❸ 대문자(의)   to write in _____s[_____ letters] 대문자로 쓰다

❹ 사형의   _____ offence[crime] 사형 죄

08 **charge**

❶ 요금, 청구하다   gas/admission _____s 가스 요금/입장료

❷ 책임   to take _____ of the company 회사의 책임을 맡다

❸ 기소/비난(하다), 혐의   a(n) murder/assault _____ 살인/폭행 혐의

❹ 돌격(하다)   to _____ at the enemy 적에게 돌격하다

❺ 충전하다   to _____ the battery 배터리를 충전하다

09 **command**

❶ 명령[지휘](하다)(=order)   troops under his _____ 그의 지휘하의 부대

❷ 받다   to _____ respect/support 존경/지지를 받다

❸ 내려다보이다   to _____ a fine view 멋진 경치가 내려다보이다

❹ 구사력   a good _____ of English 훌륭한 영어 구사력

밑줄 친 단어의 뜻은?

07 (1) The government is eager to attract foreign capital.

(2) Homicide that occurs during the kidnapping is a capital crime.

08 (1) We won't charge you for delivery.

(2) She asked to speak to the person in charge.

(3) He was charged with murder.

(4) They charged at the enemy.

(5) The shaver can be charged up.

09 (1) He commanded his men to retreat.

(2) She commands the respect of her students.

(3) The hotel commands a fine view of the sea.

(4) Applicants are expected to have a good command of English.

ANSWER_____

07. (1) 정부는 외국 자본을 유치하는 데 열심이다. (2) 납치 중에 발생하는 살인은 사형 죄이다.   08. (1) 우리는 배달료를 청구하지 않습니다. (2) 그녀는 책임자에게 말하겠다고 요구했다. (3) 그는 살인죄로 기소되었다. (4) 그들은 적에게 돌격했다. (5) 그 면도기는 충전될 수 있다.   09. (1) 그는 부하들에게 후퇴하라고 명령했다. (2) 그녀는 학생들의 존경을 받는다. (3) 그 호텔은 아름다운 바다 전망이 내려다보인다. (4) 지원자들은 훌륭한 영어 구사력을 갖출 것이 요구된다.

10 company

❶ 회사(=business, firm)	an insurance _____	보험 회사
❷ 함께 있음[동반, 교제]	I enjoy his _____.	
	난 그와 함께 있는 게 즐겁다.	
❸ 손님들, 친구들	to have _____	손님들이 와 있다
❹ (공연) 단체	a theater/dance _____	극단/무용단

11 contract

❶ 계약(하다)	to enter into[make] a _____	계약을 맺다
❷ 수축[축소]하다(↔ expand)	Metal _____s as it cools.	
	금속은 차가워지면서 수축한다.	
❸ 병에 걸리다	to _____ AIDS	에이즈에 걸리다

12 correspond

❶ 일치하다	Your account and hers do not _____.
	당신의 설명과 그녀의 것이 일치하지 않는다.
❷ 해당하다	The broad lines on the map _____ to roads.
	지도 위의 굵은 선은 도로에 해당한다.
❸ 소식을 주고받다	I _____ with her regularly.
	난 정기적으로 그녀와 소식을 주고받는다.

밑줄 친 단어의 뜻은?

10 (1) Company profits were 5% higher than last year.

    (2) We enjoy each other's company.

    (3) People judge you by the company you keep.

    (4) He joined a theater company.

11 (1) They are contracted to work 35 hours a week.

    (2) The heart muscles contract to expel the blood.

    (3) Two-thirds of the adult population there has contracted AIDS.

12 (1) Your account of events does not correspond with hers.

    (2) In some countries, the role of prime minister corresponds to that of president.

    (3) We haven't corresponded in years.

ANSWER

10. (1) 회사 수익이 작년보다 5% 높았다. (2) 우리는 서로 함께 있는 게 즐겁다. (3) 사람들은 네가 사귀는 친구들을 보고 너를 판단한다. (4) 그는 극단에 가입했다.   11. (1) 그들은 주당 35시간 일하도록 계약되어 있다. (2) 심근은 혈액을 내보내기 위해 수축한다. (3) 그곳 성인 인구의 2/3가 에이즈에 걸려 있다.   12. (1) 사건들에 대한 당신의 설명은 그녀의 것과 일치하지 않는다. (2) 일부 국가에서는 수상의 역할이 대통령의 그것에 해당한다. (3) 우리는 몇 년 동안 소식을 주고받지 않았다.

13 count

❶ 세다[계산하다]　　　　　　　　　to _____ from 1 to 10　1부터 10까지 세다

❷ 여기다[간주하다]　　　　　　　　to _____ yourself lucky　자신을 운이 좋다고 여기다

❸ 중요하다(=matter)　　　　　　　Every vote _____s.　모든 (투)표가 중요하다.

　　　　　　　　　　　　　　　　　Don't _____ on anyone.　아무도 믿지 마.

❹ (~ (up)on) 믿다[기대하다]

14 cover

❶ 가리다[덮다], 덮개[뚜껑/표지]　　to _____ your face with your hands　손으로 얼굴을 가리다

❷ 다루다[포함하다]　　　　　　　　to _____ all aspects　모든 측면을 다루다

❸ (거리를) 가다　　　　　　　　　to _____ 10 miles　10마일을 가다

❹ 취재[보도]하다　　　　　　　　　to _____ the war　전쟁을 취재[보도]하다

❺ 돈을 대다　　　　　　　　　　　to _____ your expenses　비용을 대다

❻ (보험으로) 보장하다　　　　　　　to _____ your damage　손해를 보장하다

15 decline

❶ 감소[하락](하다)　　　　　　　　economic _____　경기 하락

　　　　　　　　　　　　　　　　　Car sales have _____d.

　　　　　　　　　　　　　　　　　자동차 판매량이 감소했다.

❷ 거절[사양]하다　　　　　　　　　to _____ an offer/invitation　제의/초대를 거절하다

밑줄 친 단어의 뜻은?

13 (1) She is counting calories.

　　(2) I count you as my best friend.

　　(3) Every point in this game counts.

　　(4) I'm counting on you to help me.

14 (1) He laughed to cover his nervousness.

　　(2) The survey covers all aspects of the business.

　　(3) By sunset we had covered thirty miles.

　　(4) The KBS will cover all the major games.

　　(5) Your parents will have to cover your tuition fees.

15 (1) The number of tourists to the resort declined by 5% last year.

　　(2) I offered to give them a lift but they declined.

ANSWER

13. (1) 그녀는 칼로리를 계산하고 있다. (2) 난 널 가장 친한 친구로 여긴다. (3) 이 경기에서는 모든 점수가 중요하다. (4) 난 네가 날 도와주리라 믿고 있어.
14. (1) 그는 초조함을 가리기 위해 웃었다. (2) 그 조사는 그 사업의 모든 측면을 다룬다. (3) 해 질 무렵까지 우리는 30마일을 갔었다. (4) KBS는 모든 주요
경기를 보도[방송]할 것이다. (5) 너의 부모님이 네 학비를 대셔야 할 것이다. 15. (1) 작년에 그 휴양지의 관광객 수가 5% 감소했다. (2) 내가 그들에게 태
워주겠다고 제의했지만 그들은 사양했다.

16 engagement

❶ 약혼	to break off your _____ 파혼하다
❷ 약속	a prior _____ 선약
❸ 교전	an _____ with the enemy 적과의 교전
❹ 관여[참여]	_____ with the problems 그 문제들에 대한 관여

17 fair

❶ 타당한	a _____ wage/price 타당한 임금/가격
❷ 공정한[공평한](=just↔unfair)	a _____ distribution of wealth 부의 공정한 분배
❸ 금발의, 흰 피부의	_____ hair 금발
❹ (날씨가) 맑은(=fine)	a _____ day 맑은 날
❺ 꽤 큰[많은]	a _____ size/amount 꽤 큰 크기/꽤 많은 양
❻ 박람회	a book/job _____ 도서/취업 박람회

18 figure

❶ 수치, 숫자, 계산하다	sales _____s 판매 수치
❷ 인물	a leading _____ 주도적인 인물
❸ 모습, 몸매	to have a good _____ 멋진 몸매를 가지다
❹ 도표, 도형	_____ 3 도표 3
❺ (~ out) 이해하다[알아내다]	to _____ it out 그것을 이해하다

밑줄 친 단어의 뜻은?

16 (1) Their engagement was announced in the paper.

(2) I had to refuse because of a prior engagement.

(3) The general tried to avoid an engagement with the enemy.

(4) Many students pass without any real engagement in learning.

17 (1) What do you think is the fairest solution?

(2) We demand a fairer distribution of wealth.

(3) She has long fair hair.

(4) A fair number of people came along.

18 (1) The figure has risen to 1 million.

(2) He is a leading figure in the music industry.

(3) She's always had a good figure.

(4) I can't figure out how to do this.

ANSWER

16. (1) 그들의 약혼이 신문에 발표되었다. (2) 나는 선약 때문에 거절해야 했다. (3) 그 장군은 적과의 교전을 피하려고 했다. (4) 많은 학생들이 학습에 진정으로 참여하지 않고 그냥 지나친다. 17. (1) 가장 타당한 해결책이 무엇이라고 생각하니? (2) 우리는 더 공정한 부의 분배를 요구한다. (3) 그녀는 긴 금발을 하고 있다. (4) 꽤 많은 수의 사람들이 왔다. 18. (1) 수치가 100만으로 올랐다. (2) 그는 음악 산업에서 주도적인 인물이다. (3) 그녀는 언제나 몸매가 멋지다. (4) 나는 이것을 어떻게 하는지 이해할 수 없다.

19 issue

❶ 쟁점, 문제 — a sensitive/controversial _____ 민감한/논란이 많은 쟁점

❷ (잡지 · 신문의) 호[판] — the latest _____ of *Time* '타임지' 최근호

❸ 발표하다 — to _____ a statement 성명을 발표하다

❹ 발급[발행](하다) — to _____ a passport/stamps 여권을 발급하다/우표를 발행하다

20 mark

❶ 자국(을 남기다) — to leave dirty _____ s 더러운 자국을 남기다

❷ 표시(하다) — to make _____ s with a pencil 연필로 표시하다

❸ 기념하다 — to _____ your birthday 생일을 기념하다

❹ 특징짓다 — a life _____ ed by suffering 고통으로 특징지어진 삶

21 match

❶ 성냥 — to strike a _____ 성냥을 켜다

❷ 어울리다, 어울리는 것 — The outfit _____ es.
그 옷은 어울린다.

❸ 일치하다, 대등하다 — The copy _____ es the original.
복사본은 원본과 일치한다.

❹ 맞수[호적수](=rival) — to meet your _____ 맞수를 만나다

❺ 경기(=game) — a football/tennis _____ 축구/테니스 경기

밑줄 친 단어의 뜻은?

19 (1) Money is not an issue.

(2) He issued a statement denying the charges.

(3) New members will be issued with a temporary identity card.

20 (1) A large scar marked his cheek.

(2) Prices are marked on the goods.

(3) Your birthday will be marked with a party.

(4) His songs are marked by profound lyrics.

21 (1) Does this shirt match these pants?

(2) His actions do not match his words.

(3) I was no match for him at tennis.

ANSWER

19. (1) 돈이 문제가 아니다. (2) 그는 혐의를 부인하는 성명을 발표했다. (3) 신입 회원들에게는 임시 신분증이 발급될 것이다. **20.** (1) 큰 흉터 자국이 그의 뺨에 남아 있었다. (2) 가격은 상품에 표시되어 있다. (3) 네 생일은 파티로 기념될 거야. (4) 그의 노래들은 심오한 가사가 특징이다. **21.** (1) 이 셔츠가 이 바지와 어울리니? (2) 그의 행동은 말과 일치하지 않는다. (3) 나는 테니스에서 그의 맞수가 못 되었다.

22 observe

❶ 관찰하다(=watch)   to _____ the world 세상을 관찰하다
❷ 준수하다(=obey)   to _____ the rules 규칙을 준수하다
❸ 말하다[논평하다]   "You look great," she _____d.
                                     "너 멋져 보여."라고 그녀가 말했다.

23 operate

❶ 작동하다   to _____ the machine 기계를 작동하다
❷ 운영하다[되다]   to _____ an emergency hospital 응급 병원을 운영하다
❸ 수술하다   to _____ on your eyes 눈을 수술하다
❹ 작전을 벌이다   soldiers _____ing overseas 해외에서 작전을 벌이는 군인들

24 raise

❶ (들어) 올리다   to _____ your hand/prices 손을 들다/가격을 올리다
❷ 모으다   to _____ money for charity 자선기금을 모으다
❸ 제기하다, 일으키다   to _____ the question 문제를 제기하다
                           to _____ doubts/fears 의심/공포를 일으키다
❹ 기르다   to be born and _____d 태어나 길러지다
                           to _____ cattle/corn 소/옥수수를 기르다
❺ 임금 인상   to ask for a _____ 임금 인상을 요구하다

밑줄 친 단어의 뜻은?

22 (1) The role of scientists is to <u>observe</u> and describe the world.

    (2) You must <u>observe</u> the rules.

    (3) She <u>observed</u> that we need a reliable leader.

23 (1) Most domestic freezers <u>operate</u> at below -18 .

    (2) A new late-night service is <u>operating</u>.

    (3) The doctor <u>operated</u> on her eyes.

24 (1) She <u>raised</u> a hand in greeting.

    (2) They are <u>raising</u> funds to help needy youngsters.

    (3) The book <u>raises</u> many important questions.

    (4) I was born and <u>raised</u> a city child.

ANSWER

22. (1) 과학자의 역할은 세상을 관찰하고 설명하는 것이다. (2) 너(희)는 규칙을 준수해야 한다. (3) 그녀가 우리는 믿을 수 있는 지도자가 필요하다고 말했다.
23. (1) 대부분의 가정용 냉동고는 영하 18도로 작동된다. (2) 새로운 심야 서비스가 운영되고 있다. (3) 의사가 그녀의 눈을 수술했다. 24. (1) 그녀가 인사로 손을 들어 올렸다. (2) 그들은 어려운 청소년들을 돕기 위해 기금을 모으고 있다. (3) 그 책은 많은 중요한 문제들을 제기한다. (4) 나는 도시 아이로 태어나 길러졌다.

25 refer (~ to)

❶ 언급하다[부르다]   to _____ to the matter 그 문제를 언급하다

❷ 찾아보다   to _____ to a dictionary 사전을 찾아보다

❸ 가리키다[관련되다]   The asterisk _____s to a footnote.
           별표는 각주를 가리킨다.

❹ 보내다   to _____ them to a specialist 그들을 전문가[전문의]에게 보내다

26 spell

❶ 철자를 쓰다[말하다]   to _____ your surname 성의 철자를 쓰다

❷ 초래하다   to _____ disaster 재앙을 초래하다

❸ (~ out) 자세히 설명하다 to _____ it out 그것을 자세히 설명하다

❹ 주술[주문], 매력   to cast a _____ 주술을 걸다

❺ (짧은) 기간   a cold/wet _____ 잠깐 동안의 추위/궂은 날씨

27 suit

❶ 정장, ~복   a smart _____ and tie 단정한 정장과 넥타이

❷ 맞다[적합하다]   to _____ your needs 필요에 맞다

❸ 어울리다   Red _____s you.
           빨간색이 네게 어울린다.

❹ 소송(=lawsuit)   a civil/divorce _____ 민사/이혼 소송

밑줄 친 단어의 뜻은?

25 (1) We agreed never to <u>refer to</u> the matter again.

  (2) You may <u>refer to</u> your notes if you want.

  (3) The figures <u>refer to</u> our sales.

  (4) My doctor <u>refer</u>red me <u>to</u> a specialist.

26 (1) How do you <u>spell</u> your surname?

  (2) Their carelessness <u>spelled</u> disaster for all of us.

  (3) The contract <u>spelled</u> out the terms of his employment.

27 (1) He's wearing a black <u>suit</u>.

  (2) Choose a book to <u>suit</u> your particular needs.

  (3) That coat really <u>suits</u> you.

  (4) She has filed <u>suit</u> against him.

ANSWER

25. (1) 우리는 그 문제를 다시는 <u>언급하지</u> 않기로 합의했다. (2) 원하면 노트를 <u>찾아봐도</u> 된다. (3) 그 수치들은 우리의 판매량을 <u>가리킨다</u>. (4) 내 주치의가 나를 전문의에게 <u>보냈다</u>. 26. (1) 당신의 성은 철자를 어떻게 <u>씁니까</u>? (2) 그들의 부주의가 우리 모두에게 재앙을 <u>초래했다</u>. (3) 계약서가 그의 고용 조건을 <u>자세히 설명했다</u>. 27. (1) 그는 검은 <u>정장</u>을 입고 있다. (2) 당신의 특정한 필요에 <u>맞는</u> 책을 선택하라. (3) 그 코트는 너에게 정말 <u>어울린다</u>. (4) 그녀는 그를 상대로 <u>소송</u>을 제기했다.

28 subject

❶ 주제, 주어	a _____ of conversation 대화의 주제
❷ 과목	my favorite _____ 내가 가장 좋아하는 과목
❸ 실험 대상[피험자]	the _____s of the experiment 실험 대상
❹ ~될 수 있는	to be _____ to delay 지연될 수 있다
❺ 달려 있는, 따라야 하는	to be _____ to a law 법을 따라야 하다
❻ 강요하다	to _____ him to questioning 그에게 심문을 강요하다
❼ 지배하에 두다[복속시키다]	to _____ other countries 다른 나라들을 복속시키다

29 term

❶ 용어	a legal/technical _____ 법률/기술 용어
❷ 기간, 기한	your _____ in office 임기
	in the long/short _____ 장기/단기적으로
❸ (-s) 조건	the _____s of the contract 계약 조건

▶in terms of [in ~ terms] ~ 면에서[~에 관하여]

30 yield

❶ 산출[생산]하다	to _____ good results 좋은 결과를 산출하다
❷ (~ to) 굴복[항복]하다	to _____ to temptation 유혹에 굴복하다
❸ (~ to) 양보하다	to _____ to pedestrians 보행자에게 양보하다

밑줄 친 단어의 뜻은?

28 (1) The morality of capital punishment is a subject for debate.

(2) The subjects of this experiment are men aged 18-20.

(3) Flights are subject to delay because of the fog.

(4) The plan is subject to your approval.

(5) The prisoners were subjected to torture.

(6) The Roman Empire subjected most of Europe to its rule.

29 (1) "Multimedia" is the term for any technique combining sounds and images.

(2) In the long term, alcohol causes high blood pressure.

(3) They negotiated the terms of the agreement.

30 (1) The research has yielded useful information.

(2) He reluctantly yielded to their demands.

(3) You must yield to pedestrians in the crosswalk.

ANSWER

28. (1) 사형의 도덕성이 논쟁의 주제이다. (2) 이 실험의 피험자들은 18세부터 20세까지의 남성이다. (3) 항공기는 안개 때문에 지연될 수 있다. (4) 그 계획은 당신의 승인에 달려 있다. (5) 죄수들은 고문을 강요받았다. (6) 로마 제국은 대부분의 유럽을 자기 지배하에 두었다. **29.** (1) '멀티미디어'는 소리와 이미지를 결합하는 기법에 대한 용어이다. (2) 장기적으로 알코올은 고혈압을 초래한다. (3) 그들은 합의[계약] 조건을 협상했다. **30.** (1) 그 연구 조사는 유용한 정보를 생산했다. (2) 그는 마지못해 그들의 요구에 굴복했다. (3) 횡단보도에서는 보행자에게 양보해야 한다.

혼 동 어

120 명사 | Noun

01 chord : code : cord

chord	❶ 화음 ❷ 심금	to strike[touch] a _____ 심금을 울리다
code	❶ 법규[규정]	the civil/criminal _____ 민법/형법
	❷ 암호, 코드[부호]	messages written in _____ 암호로 쓰인 메시지
		a bar/zip _____ 바코드/우편 번호
cord	끈[줄], (전기) 코드[선]	the phone _____ 전화선[전화기 코드]

02 pear : peer : pier

pear	(먹는) 배	a _____ tree 배나무
peer	또래	_____ pressure 또래로부터 받는 압력
	图 응시하다	to _____ into the dark 어둠 속을 응시하다
pier	부두[잔교]	a yacht tied up at a _____ 부두[잔교]에 매인 요트

03 sauce : saucer : source : resource

sauce	소스	tomato/cheese _____ 토마토/치즈 소스
saucer	받침 접시	a cup and _____ 컵과 받침 접시
source	원천, 근원	a _____ of information 정보원
resource	(-s) 자원	natural _____s 천연자원

빈칸에 알맞은 단어 넣기

보기: chord code cord

01 (1) The school has a dress _____. 그 학교는 복장 규정이 있다.

(2) She wore an ID card on a _____ around her neck.
그녀는 목에 줄로 신분증을 걸고 있었다.

(3) A _____ is three or more musical notes played together.
화음은 함께 연주되는 세 개 이상의 음이다.

보기: pear peer pier

02 (1) He is respected by his _____s. 그는 또래에게 존경을 받는다.

(2) The ferry leaves from _____ 3. 페리[연락선]는 제3 부두에서 출발한다.

(3) _____s are one of the most versatile fruits with delicious taste.
배는 맛있는 최고의 다용도 과일 중 하나다.

보기: sauce saucer source resource

03 (1) He refused to reveal his _____s of information.
그는 자신의 정보원을 밝히기를 거부했다.

(2) I tried several _____s before I found one I liked.
나는 여러 소스를 먹어본 후에 내가 좋아하는 것을 찾아냈다.

(3) We must make the most efficient use of the available _____s.
우리는 이용 가능한 자원을 최대한 효율적으로 활용해야 한다.

ANSWER

01. (1) code (2) cord (3) chord 02. (1) peer (2) pier (3) Pear 03. (1) source (2) sauce (3) resource

04 altitude : aptitude : attitude

altitude	고도	at an _____ of 40,000 feet	4만 피트의 고도로
aptitude	소질[적성]	a natural _____ for the work	그 일에 대한 천부적 소질
attitude	태도	a positive/negative _____	긍정적/부정적 태도

05 arm : arms

arm	팔 图 무장시키다	_____ in _____	서로 팔짱을 끼고
arms	무기(=weapons)	an _____ race	군비 (확장) 경쟁

06 ballet : ballot

ballet	발레	a _____ dancer	발레 무용수
ballot	(무기명) 투표(용지)	by secret _____	비밀 무기명 투표로

07 biography : autobiography : autograph

biography	전기	Gandhi's _____	간디의 전기
autobiography	자서전	his _____	그의 자서전
autograph	유명인의 서명[사인]	to sign _____s	사인을 하다

빈칸에 알맞은 단어 넣기

보기
altitude
aptitude
attitude

04 (1) We are flying at an _____ of 7,000 meters. 우리는 7,000미터의 고도로 날고 있다.

(2) He shows a natural _____ for the subject. 그는 그 과목에 천부적인 소질을 보인다.

(3) I have a positive _____ about the changes.
나는 변화에 대해 긍정적인 태도를 갖고 있다.

arm
arms

05 (1) We walked along _____ in _____. 우리는 서로 팔짱을 끼고 걸어갔다.

(2) The government is selling _____ to other countries.
그 정부는 다른 나라들에게 무기를 팔고 있다.

ballet
ballot

06 (1) She wants to be a _____ dancer. 그녀는 발레리나가 되고 싶어 한다.

(2) The chairperson is chosen by secret _____. 의장은 비밀 무기명 투표로 선출된다.

biography
autobiography
autograph

07 (1) Could I have your _____? 사인 좀 해 주시겠어요?

(2) I read her _____ last year. 나는 작년에 그녀의 자서전을 읽었다.

(3) He wrote a _____ of Admiral Yi Sun-shin. 그는 이순신 장군의 전기를 썼다.

ANSWER

04. (1) altitude (2) aptitude (3) attitude　**05.** (1) arm, arm (2) arms　**06.** (1) ballet (2) ballot　**07.** (1) autograph (2) autobiography (3) biography

08 cloth : clothes : clothing

cloth	옷감[천]	cotton/woollen/silk _____	면/모/명주 옷감
clothes	옷[의복] ·복수 취급	to put on/take off _____	옷을 입다/벗다
clothing	(특정 종류의) 옷[의복]	food, _____ and shelter	의식주
	·셀 수 없는 명사	a few item[article]s of _____	몇 점의 의복

09 complement : compliment

complement	보완물	Wine is a _____ to grilled dishes.	
	통 보완하다	포도주는 석쇠로 구운 요리의 보완물이다.	
compliment	칭찬[찬사]	to pay him a _____	그를 칭찬하다
	통 칭찬하다		

10 corps : corpse

corps	군단[부대], 단체[집단]	the Signal C_____	통신대
corpse	시체	a decaying _____	부패하고 있는 시체

11 emergence : emergency

emergence	출현[발생], 탈출	the _____ of new technologies	새로운 과학 기술의 출현
emergency	비상(사태)	to declare a state of _____	비상사태를 선포하다

빈칸에 알맞은 단어 넣기

보기
cloth
clothes
clothing

08 (1) Wipe the surface with a damp _____. 표면을 젖은 천으로 닦아라.

(2) Why don't you take those wet _____ off? 그 젖은 옷을 벗지 않을래?

(3) Food, _____, and shelter are things that every person needs.
의식주는 모든 사람이 필요한 것이다.

complement
compliment

09 (1) My teacher gave me a _____. 선생님이 나를 칭찬해 주셨다.

(2) The scarf is a perfect _____ to her outfit.
그 스카프는 그녀의 옷을 완벽히 보완해 주는 것이다.

corps
corpse

10 (1) They are a _____ of trained and experienced doctors.
그들은 훈련받고 경험 있는 의사들 집단이다.

(2) The _____ was found by children playing in the woods.
시체가 숲속에서 놀던 아이들에 의해 발견되었다.

emergence
emergency

11 (1) The government has declared a state of _____. 정부는 비상사태를 선포했다.

(2) The _____ of the Internet has changed the world.
인터넷의 출현이 세상을 변화시켰다.

ANSWER

08. (1) cloth (2) clothes (3) clothing　　**09.** (1) compliment (2) complement　　**10.** (1) corps (2) corpse　　**11.** (1) emergency (2) emergence

12 gem : germ

gem	보석(=jewel)	precious _____s 값비싼 보석
germ	❶ 세균[병균]	Disinfectant kills _____s.
	❷ 싹[배아]	살균제가 병균을 죽인다.

13 geography : geology : geometry

geography	지리(학)	physical/human _____ 자연/인문 지리학
geology	지질(학)	the _____ of Jeju Island 제주도의 지질
geometry	기하학	the laws of _____ 기하학 법칙들

14 hardship : hardness

hardship	어려움[곤란]	economic _____ 경제적 어려움
hardness	단단함	the _____ of glass 유리의 단단함

15 hospitality : hostility

hospitality	환대[접대]	Thank you for your _____.
		당신의 환대에 감사합니다.
hostility	적의[적대 행위]	_____ towards foreigners 외국인에 대한 적의[적대 행위]

빈칸에 알맞은 단어 넣기

보기

gem
germ

12 (1) He came up with a _____ of an idea. 그가 보석 같은 아이디어[참 좋은 생각]를 내놓았다.

(2) Dirty hands can be a breeding ground for _____s.
더러운 손은 세균들의 온상일 수가 있다.

geography
geology
geometry

13 (1) I don't know the _____ of the area. 나는 그 지역의 지리를 모른다.

(2) _____ is the study of the rocks, soil, etc. 지질학은 암석, 토양 등에 관한 학문이다.

(3) _____ is the study of the angles and shapes. 기하학은 각과 도형에 관한 학문이다.

hardship
hardness

14 (1) Many people are suffering economic _____.
많은 사람들이 경제적 어려움을 겪고 있다.

(2) The wood's _____ makes it suitable for carving.
나무는 그 단단함 때문에 조각에 적합하다.

hospitality
hostility

15 (1) Thanks for your _____ over the past few days.
지난 며칠 동안의 당신의 환대에 감사해요.

(2) They showed open _____ to their new neighbors.
그들은 새로운 이웃들에게 노골적인 적의를 보였다.

ANSWER

12. (1) gem (2) germ   13. (1) geography (2) Geology (3) Geometry   14. (1) hardship (2) hardness   15. (1) hospitality (2) hostility

16 conscience : consciousness

conscience	양심	freedom of _____ 양심의 자유
▶conscientious	웹 양심적인[성실한]	a _____ student 양심적인[성실한] 학생
consciousness	의식	political _____ 정치의식
▶conscious	웹 의식하는[의식적인]	a _____ effort/decision 의식적인 노력/결정

17 likelihood : livelihood

likelihood	가능성(=probability)	little/lower/high _____ 적은/낮은/높은 가능성
livelihood	생계	a means of _____ 생계 수단

18 manner : manners

manner	방식, 태도	in the normal _____ 정상적인 방식으로 a friendly/relaxed _____ 친절한/편한 태도
manners	예의	to have good/bad _____ 예의가 바르다/바르지 못하다

19 mass : mess : moss : moth

mass	덩어리, 대중, 질량	the _____ media 대중 매체
mess	엉망 통 (~ up) 망치다	What a _____! 정말 엉망이구나!
moss	이끼	_____-covered walls 이끼로 덮인 벽
moth	나방	a _____ caterpillar 나방 애벌레

빈칸에 알맞은 단어 넣기

보기

conscience
consciousness

16 (1) She lost _____ briefly. 그녀는 잠시 의식을 잃었다.

(2) You should decide what to do according to your own _____.
너는 너 자신의 양심에 따라 무엇을 할지 결정해야 한다.

likelihood
livelihood

17 (1) It's difficult to earn a _____ as an artist. 예술가로 생계를 꾸려 나가기란 어렵다.

(2) A poor diet increases the _____ of serious health problems.
빈약한 식사는 심각한 건강 문제의 가능성을 증가시킨다.

manner
manners

18 (1) He has excellent _____. 그는 정말 예의가 바르다.

(2) She answered in a businesslike _____. 그녀는 사무적인 태도로 대답했다.

mass
mess
moss
moth

19 (1) The rocks near the river are covered with _____. 강가 바위들은 이끼로 덮여 있다.

(2) They are drawn to money like a _____ to a flame.
그들은 불꽃에 뛰어드는 나방처럼 돈에 끌렸다.

(3) The national emergency management system was a _____.
국가 위기[비상] 관리 체계가 엉망이었다.

ANSWER

16. (1) consciousness (2) conscience   17. (1) livelihood (2) likelihood   18. (1) manners (2) manner   19. (1) moss (2) moth (3) mess

20 pace : phase : phrase

pace	속도, 한 걸음	the _____ of change in our lives 삶에서의 변화의 속도
phase	단계[국면]	an experimental _____ 실험 단계
phrase	어구	the _____ "survival of the fittest" '적자생존'이라는 어구

21 physician : physicist

physician	(내과) 의사(=doctor)	a family _____ 가정의[주치의]
physicist	물리학자	a theoretical _____ 이론 물리학자

22 rein : reign

rein	고삐, 통제권	to pull on the _____s 고삐를 당기다
reign	통치 기간 동 통치[지배]하다	the _____ of King Sejong 세종대왕의 통치 기간

23 state : statue : status

state	❶ 상태 ❷ 국가, 주	your mental/physical _____ 정신/신체 상태
statue	조각상	a bronze _____ 청동 조각상
status	지위[신분]	a high social _____ 높은 사회적 지위

빈칸에 알맞은 단어 넣기

보기
pace
phase
phrase

20 (1) We can learn at our own _____. 우리는 우리 자신의 속도로 배울 수 있다.

(2) It's just a _____ you're going through. 그건 단지 네가 거치고 있는 한 단계일 뿐이다.

(3) He uses the _____ "you know" so often.
그는 "있잖아[알잖아]"란 어구를 너무 자주 사용한다.

physician
physicist

21 (1) Consult with your _____. 담당 의사와 상담해 봐.

(2) He's known to be an outstanding nuclear _____.
그는 뛰어난 핵물리학자로 알려져 있다.

rein
reign

22 (1) We need to keep a _____ on our spending.
우리는 지출의 고삐를 조일[지출을 억제할] 필요가 있다.

(2) He was a popular ruler throughout his _____.
그는 통치 기간 내내 인기 있는 통치자였다.

state
statue
status

23 (1) The country is drifting into a _____ of chaos.
그 나라는 혼돈 상태로 빠져들고 있다.

(2) We seek to improve the social _____ of disabled people.
우리는 장애인들의 사회적 지위를 향상시키려고 한다.

ANSWER

20. (1) pace (2) phase (3) phrase   **21.** (1) physician (2) physicist   **22.** (1) rein (2) reign   **23.** (1) state (2) status

24 success : succession

success	성공	Confidence is the key to _____. 자신감이 성공의 비결이다.
succession	❶ 연속	a _____ of events 연속적인[일련의] 사건 four times in _____ 연속해서 4번
	❷ 계승	_____ to the throne 왕위 계승

25 sympathy : empathy : apathy

sympathy	동정(심)[연민], 공감	to feel/express _____ 동정을 느끼다/표하다
empathy	공감 (능력)[감정이입]	to feel/have _____ 공감하다/공감 능력이 있다
apathy	무관심[무심/냉담]	widespread _____ 만연한 무관심

26 tone : tune

| tone | 어조[말투], 음조, 색조 | a friendly/angry _____ 친절한/화난 어조
the guitar's clean _____ 기타의 맑은 음조 |
| tune | 곡조[가락](=melody)
통 조율[조정]하다 | an old familiar _____ 오래된 친숙한 곡조
to _____ the piano 피아노를 조율하다 |

27 vacation : vocation

| vacation | 방학[휴가] | your summer _____ 여름휴가 |
| vocation | 천직[소명](=calling) | your true _____ in life 삶에서의 진정한 천직[소명] |

빈칸에 알맞은 단어 넣기

보기

success
succession

sympathy
empathy
apathy

tone
tune

vacation
vocation

24 (1) Failure is but a stepping stone to _____. 실패는 성공의 디딤돌이다.

(2) After graduation he had a _____ of temporary jobs.
졸업 후에 그는 연속적인[일련의] 임시직들을 가졌다.

25 (1) She doesn't have any _____ with the poor.
그녀는 가난한 사람들과의 어떠한 공감 능력도 없다.

(2) We feel a deep _____ for the families of the victims.
우리는 희생자 가족들에게 깊은 동정심을 느낀다.

(3) People shows surprising _____ toward social problems.
사람들은 사회 문제에 대해 놀라운 무관심을 보인다.

26 (1) He was humming a familiar _____. 그는 귀에 익은 곡조를 흥얼거리고 있었다.

(2) Don't speak to me in that _____ of voice. 그런 말투로 내게 말하지 마.

27 (1) We had a restful _____ at the beach. 우리는 해변에서 편안한 휴가를 보냈다.

(2) Nursing is not just a job—it's a _____.
간호직은 단지 하나의 직업이 아니라 천직이다.

ANSWER

24. (1) success (2) succession   25. (1) empathy[sympathy] (2) sympathy (3) apathy   26. (1) tune (2) tone   27. (1) vacation (2) vocation

28 adapt : adopt

adapt	❶ 적응하다(=adjust)	to _____ to the new environment 새로운 환경에 적응하다
	❷ 조정하다(=modify)	
	❸ 개작[각색]하다	to be _____ed for TV 텔레비전전용으로 각색되다
adopt	❶ 입양하다	to _____ children 아이들을 입양하다
	❷ 채택하다	to _____ the new policy 새로운 정책을 채택하다

29 arise : arouse: rouse

arise (-arose-arisen)	발생하다, 일어나다	A crisis has _____. 위기가 발생했다.
arouse	불러일으키다, 깨우다	to _____ your interest/curiosity 너의 관심/호기심을 불러일으키다
rouse	깨우다, 불러일으키다	to be _____d from sleep 잠에서 깨다

30 deprive : derive

deprive (~ of)	빼앗다[박탈하다]	to be _____d of your basic rights 기본권을 박탈당하다
derive	❶ 얻다	to _____ pleasure from studying 공부에서 즐거움을 얻다
	❷ 나오다[비롯하다]	to be _____d from Latin 라틴어에서 나오다

빈칸에 알맞은 단어 넣기

보기

adapt
adopt

28 (1) He was _____ed as an infant. 그는 유아 때 입양되었다.

(2) She has _____ed to the new school easily. 그녀는 새 학교에 쉽게 적응했다.

(3) The party is expected to _____ the new policy.
그 당은 새로운 정책을 채택할 것으로 예상된다.

arise
arouse
rouse

29 (1) The phone _____d me from my sleep. 전화가 나를 잠에서 깨웠다.

(2) Her irresponsible comments _____d public anger.
그녀의 무책임한 발언은 대중의 분노를 불러일으켰다.

(3) Emotional or mental problems can _____ from a physical cause.
정서적 또는 정신적 문제가 신체적 요인으로 발생할 수도 있다.

deprive
derive

30 (1) Many English words are _____d from French. 많은 영어 단어가 프랑스어에서 나왔다.

(2) I _____ great satisfaction from our friendship.
나는 우리의 우정에서 큰 만족을 얻는다.

(3) They were imprisoned and _____d of their basic rights.
그들은 투옥되어 기본권을 박탈당했다.

ANSWER

28. (1) adopt (2) adapt (3) adopt   29. (1) rouse[arouse] (2) arouse[rouse] (3) arise   30. (1) derive (2) derive (3) deprive

31 exchange : replace : substitute

exchange (A for B)	(A를 B로) 교환하다	to _____ a black jacket for a blue one 검은 재킷을 파란 것으로 교환하다
replace (A with B)	(A를 B로) 대신[교체]하다	to _____ a worn tire with a new one 헌 타이어를 새것으로 교체하다
substitute (A for B / B with A)	(B) 대신 (A를) 사용하다	to _____ dialog for violence 폭력 대신 대화를 사용하다

32 expand : expend : extend

expand	확대[확장/팽창]하다 (↔ contract)	Water _____s as it freezes. 물은 얼면 팽창한다.
expend	들이다[소비하다] (= spend)	to _____ energy/time 에너지/시간을 들이다
extend	연장[확장]하다, 뻗다	to _____ a deadline 마감을 연장하다

33 force : enforce : reinforce

force	강요하다	to be _____d to resign 사임을 강요당하다
enforce	❶ 집행하다 ❷ 강요하다	to _____ a law 법을 집행하다
reinforce	강화[보강]하다	to _____ stereotypes 고정 관념을 강화하다

Q ⎯보기⎯ **빈칸에 알맞은 단어 넣기**

보기: exchange / replace / substitute

31 (1) These coupons can be _____d for food. 이 쿠폰들은 음식으로 교환될 수 있다.

(2) You can _____ pasta for the rice in this recipe.
이 조리법에서 쌀 대신 파스타를 사용할 수 있다.

(3) It is not a good idea to _____ meals with snacks.
식사를 간식으로 대신하는 것은 좋은 생각이 아니다.

보기: expand / expend / extend

32 (1) She _____ed her visit by two days. 그녀는 방문을 이틀 연장했다.

(2) The vocabulary _____s through reading. 어휘는 독서를 통해 확장된다.

(3) You _____ so much effort for so little return.
너는 너무 적은 수익을 위해 너무 많은 노력을 들인다.

보기: force / enforce / reinforce

33 (1) It's the job of the police to _____ the law. 법을 집행하는 것은 경찰의 일이다.

(2) They _____d us to work long hours without pay.
그들은 우리에게 무보수로 장시간 일하도록 강요했다.

(3) The political confusion _____s the country's economic decline.
정치적 혼란은 나라의 경제적 쇠퇴를 강화한다.

ANSWER

31. (1) exchange (2) substitute (3) replace[substitute]　**32.** (1) extend (2) expand (3) expend　**33.** (1) enforce (2) force (3) reinforce

34 lie : lay

lie	❶ (-lay-lain) 눕다, 있다	to _____ down on the grass 풀밭에 눕다
	❷ (-lied-lied) 거짓말하다	to _____ about your age 나이에 대해 거짓말하다
lay (-laid-laid)	놓다[눕히다], (알을) 낳다	to _____ your hand on his shoulder 그의 어깨 위에 손을 얹다

35 migrate : emigrate : immigrate

migrate	이주[이동]하다	Swallows _____ south in winter. 제비는 겨울에 남쪽으로 이동한다.
emigrate	이주해[이민] 가다	to _____ to Australia 호주로 이민 가다
immigrate	이주해[이민] 오다	to _____ to Korea from China 중국에서 한국으로 이민 오다

36 praise : appraise : apprise

praise	칭찬하다	to be _____d by your teacher 선생님께 칭찬받다
appraise	평가하다(=evaluate)	to _____ the environmental costs 환경 비용을 평가하다
apprise	알리다(=inform)	to _____ me of the situation 내게 상황을 알리다

빈칸에 알맞은 단어 넣기

보기
lie
lay

34 (1) _____ on your back. 똑바로[등을 대고] 누워라.

(2) The camera cannot _____. 카메라는 거짓말하지 못한다.

(3) She _____ the baby down on the bed. 그녀는 아기를 침대에 눕혔다.

migrate
emigrate
immigrate

35 (1) My uncle _____d to Canada. 우리 삼촌은 캐나다로 이민 가셨다.

(2) They _____d to Korea from China. 그들은 중국에서 한국으로 이민 왔다.

(3) Many people _____d from rural to urban areas in search of work.
많은 사람들이 일자리를 찾아 농촌에서 도시로 이주했다.

praise
appraise
apprise

36 (1) She _____d my cooking. 그녀는 나의 요리를 칭찬했다.

(2) He coolly _____d the situation. 그는 상황을 냉정히 평가했다.

(3) Please _____ me of any change in the situation.
내게 상황의 어떤 변화라도 좀 알려 주세요.

ANSWER

34. (1) Lie (2) lie (3) laid **35.** (1) emigrate[migrate] (2) immigrate[migrate] (3) migrate **36.** (1) praise (2) appraise (3) apprise

37 defer : deter

| defer | 미루다[연기하다]
(=postpone) | to _____ your decision 결정을 연기하다 |
| deter | 단념시키다[막다] | Can the death penalty _____ crime?
사형이 범죄를 막을 수 있을까? |

38 delete : deplete

| delete | 삭제하다 | to _____ a file 파일을 삭제하다 |
| deplete | 감소시키다 | to _____ the ozone layer 오존층을 감소시키다 |

39 doubt : suspect

| doubt | (사실이 아닐 거라고)
의심하다 | I _____ the story.
난 그 이야기를 의심한다. |
| suspect | (사실일 거라고)
의심하다 | The doctors _____ pneumonia.
의사들은 폐렴을 의심한다. |

40 fall : fell

| fall
(-fell-fallen) | 떨어지다,
넘어[쓰러]지다 | The leaves are starting to _____.
나뭇잎들이 떨어지기 시작하고 있다. |
| fell | (베어) 넘어[쓰러]뜨리다 | The trees were _____ed.
나무들이 베여 넘어졌다. |

빈칸에 알맞은 단어 넣기

보기
defer
deter

37 (1) Please let me _____ the payment. 지불을 좀 연기하게 해 주십시오.

(2) The heavy fines should _____ people from smoking in public places.
무거운 벌금이 사람들이 공공장소에서 흡연하는 걸 막을 것이다.

delete
deplete

38 (1) Your name has been _____d from the list. 당신 이름은 명단에서 삭제되었어요.

(2) If we continue to _____ the earth's natural resources, we will cause serious damage to the environment.
우리가 지구의 천연자원을 계속 감소시킨다면 환경에 심각한 피해를 초래할 것이다.

doubt
suspect

39 (1) I _____ you are lying to me. 나는 네가 내게 거짓말하고 있다고 의심한다.

(2) I never _____ed you would succeed. 나는 네가 성공하리라는 걸 결코 의심하지 않았다.

fall
fell

40 (1) The tree was about to _____. 나무가 막 쓰러지려고 했다.

(2) Thousands of trees are being _____ed at this moment.
이 순간에도 수많은 나무들이 베여 넘어지고 있다.

ANSWER

37. (1) defer (2) deter   38. (1) delete (2) deplete   39. (1) suspect (2) doubt   40. (1) fall (2) fell

41 find : found

find (-found-found)	찾(아내)다[발견하다]	to _____ the keys 열쇠를 찾다
found	설립하다(=establish)	to _____ a company 회사를 설립하다

42 innovate : renovate

innovate	혁신하다 [새것을 도입하다]	to _____ new ideas/products 새로운 생각/제품을 도입하다
renovate	개조[수리]하다	to _____ the historic hotel 역사적으로 중요한 호텔을 개조하다

43 rise : raise

rise (-rose-risen)	오르다	Smoke is _____ing into the air. 연기가 공중으로 피어오르고 있다.
raise	올리다	to _____ a hand 손을 올리다

44 steal : rob

steal (물건 from 사람) (-stole-stolen)	(사람에게서 물건을) 훔치다	to _____ money from you 네게서 돈을 훔치다
rob (사람 of 물건)	(사람에게서 물건을) 강탈하다[털다]	to _____ the bank of $1 million 은행에서 백만 달러를 털다

빈칸에 알맞은 단어 넣기

보기
find
found

41 (1) Can you _____ my bag for me? 내 가방 좀 찾아 주겠니?

(2) The university was _____ed in 1957. 그 대학은 1957년에 설립되었다.

innovate
renovate

42 (1) The old factory has been _____d as a gallery.
오래된 공장이 미술관으로 개조되었다.

(2) The company _____d a new operating system.
그 회사는 새로운 운영 체제를 도입했다.

rise
raise

43 (1) Who _____s house prices? 누가 집값을 올리는가?

(2) House prices are _____ing sharply. 집값이 급격하게 오르고 있다.

steal
rob

44 (1) They _____bed her of her life savings. 그들은 그녀에게서 평생 모은 돈을 강탈했다.

(2) He has been _____ing money from us for years.
그는 수년 동안 우리에게서 돈을 훔치고 있다.

ANSWER

41. (1) find (2) found   42. (1) renovate (2) innovate   43. (1) raise (2) rise(rising)   44. (1) rob (2) steal

45 alive : live : lively

alive	(서술적) 살아 있는	They're lucky to be _____. 그들은 다행히 살아 있다.
live	(명사 앞) ❶ 살아 있는(=living) ❷ 생방송[실황]의	_____ animals 살아 있는 동물 _____ coverage of the World Cup 월드컵 생중계
lively	활기찬[활발한]	_____ debate 활발한 토론

46 alone : lone : lonely

alone	(서술적) ❶ 혼자 ❷ 외로운	He was _____ there. 그는 거기에 혼자 있었다. I feel _____. 난 외로움을 느낀다.
lone	(명사 앞) 혼자의 (=solitary)	a _____ traveler 혼자 여행하는 사람
lonely	외로운[쓸쓸한] (=lonesome)	a _____ life/old man 외로운 삶/노인

47 complementary : complimentary

complementary 상호 보완적인	_____ colors 보색 a _____ relation 상호 보완적 관계
complimentary ❶ 무료의 ❷ 칭찬하는	_____ tickets 무료 티켓 a _____ remark 칭찬하는 말

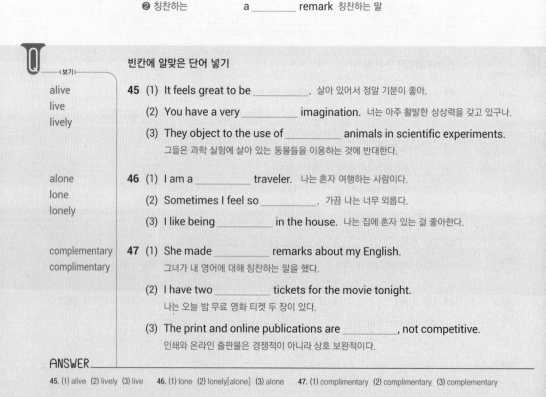

빈칸에 알맞은 단어 넣기

┤보기├

alive
live
lively

45 (1) It feels great to be _____. 살아 있어서 정말 기분이 좋아.

(2) You have a very _____ imagination. 너는 아주 활발한 상상력을 갖고 있구나.

(3) They object to the use of _____ animals in scientific experiments.
그들은 과학 실험에 살아 있는 동물들을 이용하는 것에 반대한다.

alone
lone
lonely

46 (1) I am a _____ traveler. 나는 혼자 여행하는 사람이다.

(2) Sometimes I feel so _____. 가끔 나는 너무 외롭다.

(3) I like being _____ in the house. 나는 집에 혼자 있는 걸 좋아한다.

complementary
complimentary

47 (1) She made _____ remarks about my English.
그녀가 내 영어에 대해 칭찬하는 말을 했다.

(2) I have two _____ tickets for the movie tonight.
나는 오늘 밤 무료 영화 티켓 두 장이 있다.

(3) The print and online publications are _____, not competitive.
인쇄와 온라인 출판물은 경쟁적이 아니라 상호 보완적이다.

ANSWER

45. (1) alive (2) lively (3) live   46. (1) lone (2) lonely[alone] (3) alone   47. (1) complimentary (2) complimentary (3) complementary

48 confident : confidential

confident	❶ 자신 있는	a _____ voice/manner	자신 있는 목소리/태도
	❷ 확신하는	to be _____ of success	성공을 확신하다
confidential	비밀[기밀]의	a _____ report	기밀 보고서

49 credible : incredible : credulous : incredulous

credible	믿을 수 있는	a _____ explanation	믿을 수 있는 설명
incredible	믿을 수 없는, 엄청난	an _____ story	믿을 수 없는 이야기
credulous	쉽게 믿는[속는]	_____ investors	쉽게 믿는[속는] 투자가들
incredulous	믿지 않는	an _____ look	믿지 않는 표정

50 finite : infinite : definite

finite	한정된	the earth's _____ resources	지구의 한정된 자원
infinite	무한한	an _____ universe	무한한 우주
definite	명확한	a _____ answer	명확한 대답

빈칸에 알맞은 단어 넣기

보기		
confident confidential	**48**	(1) I'm _____ you will succeed. 나는 네가 성공하리라 확신한다.
		(2) These documents are completely _____. 이 서류들은 완전히 기밀이다.
		(3) I am _____ about my ability to do the job. 나는 그 일을 할 수 있는 내 능력에 자신 있다.
credible incredible credulous incredulous	**49**	(1) I'm _____ at the news. 나는 그 뉴스를 믿지 않는다.
		(2) The story is hardly _____. 그 이야기는 거의 믿을 수 없다.
		(3) Few people are _____ enough to believe such nonsense. 그런 말도 안 되는 걸 믿을 만큼 쉽게 속는 사람들은 거의 없다.
finite infinite definite	**50**	(1) I need a _____ answer by tomorrow. 나는 내일까지 명확한 답이 필요하다.
		(2) The earth's natural resources are _____. 지구의 천연자원은 한정되어 있다.
		(3) She has _____ patience when she's dealing with children. 그녀는 아이들을 다룰 때는 무한한 인내심이 있다.

ANSWER

48. (1) confident (2) confidential (3) confident　　49. (1) incredulous (2) credible (3) credulous　　50. (1) definite (2) finite (3) infinite

51 imaginable : imaginary : imaginative

imaginable	상상할 수 있는	every _____ treatment 상상할 수 있는 모든 치료법
imaginary	상상[가상]의	_____ fears 가상의 공포
imaginative	상상력이 풍부한 [창의적인]	an _____ child/idea 상상력이 풍부한 아이/창의적인 생각

52 intellectual : intelligent : intelligible

intellectual	지적인	_____ ability/development 지적 능력/발달
intelligent	총명한, 지능이 있는	_____ students 총명한 학생들
intelligible	쉽게 이해될 수 있는	an _____ plan 쉽게 이해될 수 있는 계획

53 intense : intensive : extensive

intense	극심한[강렬한]	an _____ pain/desire 극심한 고통/강렬한 욕구
intensive	집중[집약]적인	an _____ course in English 영어 집중 과정
extensive	대규모의[광범위한]	_____ knowledge 광범위한 지식

빈칸에 알맞은 단어 넣기

보기

imaginable
imaginary
imaginative

51 (1) We made _____ use of colors in this book.
우리는 이 책에서 색들을 창의적으로 활용했다.

(2) A lonely child sometimes creates an _____ friend to play with.
외로운 아이는 때때로 함께 놀 가상의 친구를 만들어 낸다.

(3) Smart phones allow us to do things that were hardly _____ only a few years ago. 스마트폰은 우리가 몇 년 전만 해도 거의 상상할 수 없던 것들을 하게 한다.

intellectual
intelligent
intelligible

52 (1) She's a hard worker but she's not very _____.
그녀는 열심히 일하는 사람이지만 그리 총명하지는 않다.

(2) His lecture was readily _____ to all the students.
그의 강의는 모든 학생들에게 쉽게 이해될 수 있었다.

(3) I like detective stories and romances–nothing too _____.
나는 추리 소설과 로맨스를 좋아한다 – 너무 지적이지 않은.

intense
intensive
extensive

53 (1) The typhoon caused _____ damage. 그 태풍은 대규모의 피해를 가져왔다.

(2) The President is under _____ pressure to resign.
대통령은 극심한 사임 압력을 받고 있다.

(3) After six months' _____ training, he could fly the aircraft.
6개월의 집중 훈련 후에 그는 항공기를 조종할 수 있었다.

ANSWER

51. (1) imaginative (2) imaginary (3) imaginable   **52.** (1) intelligent (2) intelligible (3) intellectual   **53.** (1) extensive (2) intense (3) intensive

54 liable : reliable : reliant

liable	❶ ~할 것 같은 [하기 쉬운]	to be _____ to make mistakes 실수를 하기 쉽다
	❷ 법적 책임이 있는	to be _____ for any damage 어떤 손상에 대해서도 법적 책임이 있다
reliable	믿을 수 있는	a _____ source 믿을 수 있는 소식통
reliant	의존하는	to be _____ on the Internet 인터넷에 의존하다

55 literal : literary : literate

literal	문자 그대로의	a _____ meaning/interpretation 문자 그대로의 의미/해석
literary	문학의	a _____ work/critic 문학 작품/평론가
literate	읽고 쓸 수 있는 (↔ illiterate)	Half of the children are _____. 그 아이들의 절반이 읽고 쓸 수 있다.

56 respectable : respectful : respective

respectable	존경할 만한[훌륭한]	hard-working, _____ people 근면하고 존경할 만한 사람들
respectful	존중하는[경의를 표하는]	to be _____ of one another 서로 존중하다
respective	각자[각각]의	the _____ roles of men and women 남성과 여성 각자의 역할

빈칸에 알맞은 단어 넣기

─ 보기 ─
liable
reliable
reliant

54 (1) You will be _____ for any damage caused.
당신은 야기되는 모든 손상에 대해 법적 책임을 지게 됩니다.

(2) We are looking for someone who is _____ and hard-working.
우리는 믿을 수 있고 근면한 사람을 찾고 있다.

(3) Most college students remain _____ on their parents' support.
대부분의 대학생은 부모의 지원에 계속 의존한다.

literal
literary
literate

55 (1) Do his books have any _____ merit? 그의 책들은 문학적 가치가 있는가?

(2) She is _____ in both English and French.
그녀는 영어와 프랑스어 둘 다 읽고 쓸 수 있다.

(3) The _____ meaning of "television" is "seeing from a distance."
'텔레비전'의 문자 그대로의 의미는 '멀리서 보기'이다.

respectable
respectful
respective

56 (1) He continues to lead a _____ life. 그는 계속 존경할 만한 삶을 산다.

(2) We chatted about our _____ childhoods.
우리는 우리 각자의 어린 시절에 대해 이야기를 나누었다.

(3) You should be more _____ of other people's points of view.
너는 다른 사람들의 관점을 더 존중해야 한다.

ANSWER

54. (1) liable (2) reliable (3) reliant　**55.** (1) literary (2) literate (3) literal　**56.** (1) respectable (2) respective (3) respectful

57 sensational : sensible : sensitive : sensory

sensational	선정적인[놀라운]	_____ newspaper stories 선정적인 신문 기사
sensible	분별 있는[합리적인]	a _____ person/solution 합리적인 사람/해법
sensitive	❶ 세심히 배려하는	a _____ man 세심히 배려해 주는[예민한] 남자
	❷ 예민[민감]한	_____ skin 민감한 피부
sensory	감각의	_____ stimuli 감각 자극

58 tolerable : intolerable : tolerant

tolerable	참을 수 있는	a _____ level/degree 참을 수 있는 수준/정도
intolerable	참을 수 없는	an _____ burden/situation 참을 수 없는 부담/상황
tolerant	관대한(↔intolerant)	a _____ attitude/society 관대한 태도/사회

59 valuable : invaluable : valueless

valuable	값비싼[귀중한]	a _____ painting 값비싼 그림
invaluable	매우 귀중한	_____ help/information 매우 귀중한 도움/정보
valueless	가치 없는[무가치한] (=worthless)	_____ currency 가치 없는 통화

Q 보기 **빈칸에 알맞은 단어 넣기**

sensational
sensible
sensitive
sensory

57 (1) My teacher gave me some _____ advice. 선생님이 내게 합리적인 조언을 좀 해 주셨다.

(2) Some children are overly _____ to certain _____ stimuli.
어떤 아이들은 어떤 감각 자극에 너무 민감하다.

(3) The _____ newspapers gave a lot of coverage to the scandal.
선정적인 신문들이 그 스캔들에 대한 많은 보도를 했다.

tolerable
intolerable
tolerant

58 (1) This kind of behavior is not _____. 이러한 종류의 행동은 참을 수 없다.

(2) This situation is totally _____ to us. 이 상황은 우리에게 완전히 참을 수 없다.

(3) He has a _____ attitude towards other religions.
그는 다른 종교들에 대해 관대한 태도를 갖고 있다.

valuable
invaluable
valueless

59 (1) No one's life is _____. 누구의 삶도 무가치하지 않다.

(2) Your help has been _____ to me. 너의 도움이 내게 매우 귀중했어.

(3) The volunteers provide a very _____ service to the community.
자원봉사자들은 지역 사회에 아주 귀중한 봉사를 제공한다.

ANSWER
57. (1) sensible (2) sensitive, sensory (3) sensational **58.** (1) tolerable (2) intolerable (3) tolerant **59.** (1) valueless (2) invaluable (3) valuable

60 anonymous : unanimous

anonymous	익명의	an _____ donor[benefactor] 익명의 기부자
unanimous	만장일치의	by a _____ vote 만장일치의 표결로

61 comparable : comparative

comparable	비슷한[비교할 만한]	to be _____ in size 크기가 비슷하다
comparative	상대적인[비교적] (=relative)	_____ freedom/wealth 상대적 자유/부

62 competent : competitive

competent	유능한	a _____ mechanic 유능한 수리공
competitive	❶ 경쟁적인	a _____ game/market 경쟁적인 게임/시장
	❷ 경쟁력 있는	at _____ prices 경쟁력 있는 가격으로

63 comprehensible : comprehensive

comprehensible	이해할 수 있는	to be _____ to the average reader 일반 독자들이 이해할 수 있다
comprehensive	포괄[종합]적인	a _____ report/study 포괄[종합]적인 보고/연구

빈칸에 알맞은 단어 넣기

보기

anonymous
unanimous

60 (1) We reached a _____ decision on the proposal.
우리는 그 제안에 대해 만장일치의 결정에 이르렀다.

(2) The bomb threat was made by an _____ caller.
익명으로 전화한 사람에 의해 폭파 위협이 있었다.

comparable
comparative

61 (1) She is living in _____ comfort. 그녀는 비교적 안락하게 살고 있다.

(2) Our school's test scores are _____ to the national average.
우리 학교의 시험 성적은 전국 평균과 비슷하다.

competent
competitive

62 (1) He's very _____ in his work. 그는 자기 일에 아주 유능하다.

(2) The new technology gives them a _____ advantage.
신기술이 그들에게 경쟁 우위를 가져다준다.

comprehensible
comprehensive

63 (1) They speak in barely _____ slang. 그들은 거의 이해할 수 없는 은어로 말한다.

(2) We offer a _____ range of services. 우리는 포괄적인 범위의 서비스를 제공한다.

ANSWER

60. (1) unanimous (2) anonymous　**61.** (1) comparative (2) comparable　**62.** (1) competent (2) competitive　**63.** (1) comprehensible (2) comprehensive

64 compulsive : compulsory

| compulsive | 강박적인 | _____ overeating/spending 강박적인 과식/소비 |
| compulsory | 의무적인[강제적인] | _____ education 의무 교육 |

65 considerable : considerate

| considerable | 상당한 | a _____ amount of money 상당한 금액의 돈 |
| considerate | 이해심 많은[배려하는] | to be _____ of others 다른 사람들을 배려하다 |

66 discreet : discrete

| discreet | 신중한 | a _____ person 신중한 사람 |
| discrete | 별개의[분리된] | your own _____ identity 자신의 별개의 정체성 |

67 economic : economical

| economic | 경제의 | _____ growth 경제 성장 |
| economical | 경제적인[절약하는] | A small car is more _____. 소형차가 더욱 경제적이다. |

Q 빈칸에 알맞은 단어 넣기

보기
compulsive
compulsory

64 (1) She has a _____ eating disorder. 그녀는 강박적인 식이 장애가 있다.

(2) School uniform is _____ in many schools. 교복은 많은 학교에서 의무적이다.

considerable
considerate

65 (1) I've saved a _____ amount of money. 나는 상당한 금액의 돈을 모았다.

(2) She is one of the most _____ people I know.
그녀는 내가 아는 가장 이해심 많은 사람들 중 한 명이다.

discreet
discrete

66 (1) He's very _____ about his personal life. 그는 사생활에 대해서 아주 신중하다.

(2) The change happens in a series of _____ steps.
변화는 일련의 별개의 단계로 일어난다.

economic
economical

67 (1) The country's _____ growth is incredible. 그 나라의 경제 성장은 믿을 수 없다.

(2) We offer quality products at _____ prices.
우리는 양질의 제품을 경제적인 가격으로 제공한다.

ANSWER

64. (1) compulsive (2) compulsory   65. (1) considerable (2) considerate   66. (1) discreet (2) discrete   67. (1) economic (2) economical

68 effective : efficient

| effective | ❶ 효과적인 (원하는 결과를 얻는) ❷ 시행되는 | a highly _____ treatment 매우 효과적인 치료 |
| efficient | ❶ 효율[능률]적인 (낭비하지 않는) ❷ 유능한 | the _____ use of energy 에너지의 효율적인 이용 |

69 fluent : affluent

| fluent | 유창한 | to be _____ in English 영어가 유창하다 |
| affluent | 부유한(=wealthy) | an _____ society/country 부유한 사회/나라 |

70 historic : historical

| historic | 역사적으로 중요한 | _____ buildings/occasions 역사적으로 중요한 건물/사건 |
| historical | 역사(상)의 | _____ figures/context/novels 역사상 실존 인물/역사적 맥락[배경]/역사 소설 |

71 industrial : industrious

| industrial | 산업의 | _____ production/development 산업 생산/발전 |
| industrious | 근면한 | an _____ worker 근면한 일꾼 |

빈칸에 알맞은 단어 넣기

보기
effective
efficient

68 (1) He is an _____ worker. 그는 유능한 일꾼이다.

(2) The drug is an _____ treatment. 그 약은 효과적인 치료제다.

fluent
affluent

69 (1) She speaks _____ English and a little China.
그녀는 영어를 유창하게 말하고 중국어를 조금 한다.

(2) Obesity has become a big issue in _____ societies.
비만은 부유한 사회의 큰 문제가 되었다.

historic
historical

70 (1) The film is based on _____ facts. 그 영화는 역사적 사실에 근거를 두고 있다.

(2) They returned safely from their _____ flight into space.
그들은 역사적인[역사적으로 중요한] 우주 비행에서 무사히 귀환했다.

industrial
industrious

71 (1) Koreans are _____ people. 한국인은 근면한 민족이다.

(2) _____ production has risen by 0.5% since January.
산업 생산이 1월 이후로 0.5% 증가했다.

ANSWER

68. (1) efficient (2) effective　**69.** (1) fluent (2) affluent　**70.** (1) historical (2) historic　**71.** (1) industrious (2) industrial

72 ingenious : ingenuous

ingenious	기발한[독창적인]	an _____ method 기발한 방법
ingenuous	순진한	You're too _____.
		넌 너무 순진해.

73 jealous : zealous

| jealous | 시기[질투]하는 | a _____ wife/husband 질투하는 아내/남편 |
| zealous | 열성적인[열심인] | _____ supporters 열성적인 지지자들 |

74 loyal : royal

| loyal | 충실한[충성스러운] | a _____ supporter of the team 팀의 충성스러운 지지자 |
| royal | 왕의 | the _____ family/palace 왕실/왕궁 |

75 marital : martial

| marital | 결혼(생활)의 | _____ status (미혼/기혼/이혼의) 결혼 상태[여부] |
| martial | 군사[전쟁]의 | _____ arts 무술 _____ law 계엄령 |

빈칸에 알맞은 단어 넣기

─┤보기├─

ingenious
ingenuous

72 (1) You're being deliberately _____. 너는 일부러 순진한 척하고 있어.

(2) He is _____ at finding ways to work more quickly.
그는 더 빨리 일하는 법을 찾아내는 데 기발하다.

jealous
zealous

73 (1) His success made some of his friends _____.
그의 성공은 일부 그의 친구들이 시기하게 했다.

(2) She was one of the President's most _____ supporters.
그녀는 대통령의 아주 열성적인 지지자들 중 한 사람이었다.

loyal
royal

74 (1) He comes from _____ blood. 그는 왕족 출신이다.

(2) The team has many _____ fans. 그 팀은 많은 충성스러운 팬이 있다.

marital
martial

75 (1) He is a _____ arts expert. 그는 무술의 달인이다

(2) They've enjoyed many years of _____ bliss.
그들은 여러 해 동안 결혼 생활의 행복을 누려 왔다.

ANSWER

72. (1) ingenuous (2) ingenious　　73. (1) jealous (2) zealous　　74. (1) royal (2) loyal　　75. (1) martial (2) marital

76 momentary : momentous

| momentary | 순간적인 | a _____ silence 순간적인 침묵 |
| momentous | 중대한 | a _____ decision 중대한 결정 |

77 regretful : regrettable

| regretful | 유감스러워하는 [후회하는] | a _____ look 후회하는 표정 |
| regrettable | 유감스러운 (=unfortunate) | a _____ error 유감스러운 실수 |

78 social : sociable

| social | 사회의 | _____ justice 사회 정의 |
| sociable | 사교적인(=friendly) | a pleasant, _____ couple 상냥하고 사교적인 커플 |

79 spatial : spacious

| spatial | 공간의 | _____ awareness 공간 인식 (능력) |
| spacious | 널찍한(=roomy) | a _____ room 널찍한 방 |

빈칸에 알맞은 단어 넣기

보기
momentary
momentous

76 (1) Today is a _____ day in my life. 오늘은 내 삶의 중대한 날이다.

(2) He experienced a _____ loss of consciousness.
그는 순간적인 의식 상실을 경험했다.

regretful
regrettable

77 (1) It was a _____ mistake. 그것은 유감스러운 실수였다.

(2) He is _____ about not coming with us.
그는 우리와 함께 오지 않은 걸 유감스러워한다[후회한다].

social
sociable

78 (1) He dedicated his life to _____ justice. 그는 사회 정의에 평생을 바쳤다.

(2) She's a _____ girl who enjoys meeting new people.
그녀는 새로운 사람들을 만나는 걸 즐기는 사교적인 소녀다.

spatial
spacious

79 (1) The room is _____ enough to seat 10 people.
그 방은 10명이 앉을 수 있을 만큼 널찍하다.

(2) This is designed to test children's _____ awareness.
이것은 아이들의 공간 인식 능력을 테스트하기 위해 고안되었다.

ANSWER

76. (1) momentous (2) momentary   **77.** (1) regrettable (2) regretful   **78.** (1) social (2) sociable   **79.** (1) spacious (2) spatial

80 successful : successive

successful	성공한[성공적인]	a _____ meeting	성공적인 모임
successive	연속적인	five _____ victories	5연승

81 temporary : contemporary

temporary	일시적인[임시의]	_____ work/accommodation	임시직/임시 숙소
contemporary	❶ 동시대[당시]의	_____ accounts	동시대[당시]의 기록
	❷ 현대의(=modern)	_____ music/art/fashion	현대 음악/미술/패션

82 terrific[awesome] : terrible[horrible/awful]

terrific [awesome]	멋진[아주 좋은]	a(n) _____ idea/sight	멋진 생각/광경
		to look/sound _____	멋진[아주 좋은] 것 같다
		to feel _____	기분이 아주 좋다
terrible [horrible/ awful]	끔찍한[아주 나쁜]	_____ weather/news	끔찍한 날씨/소식[뉴스]
		a(n) _____ accident	끔찍한 사고

83 varied : variable

varied	다양한(=various)	_____ opinions	다양한 의견들
variable	변하기 쉬운[가변적인]	_____ temperature	가변적인 온도

빈칸에 알맞은 단어 넣기

보기

successful
successive

80 (1) I was _____ in persuading my parents. 나는 부모님을 설득하는 데 성공했다.

(2) The industrial production fell for the fourth _____ month.
산업 생산이 네 달 연속 하락했다.

temporary
contemporary

81 (1) More than half the staff are _____. 반 이상의 직원들이 임시직[비정규직]이다.

(2) The old song has a _____ feel to it. 옛 노래는 그것과 동시대의 느낌을 지닌다.

terrific
[awesome]
terrible
[horrible/awful]

82 (1) What a(n) _____ accident! 끔찍한 사고구나!

(2) I hope you have a(n) _____ time. 멋진[아주 좋은] 시간을 보내기 바란다.

varied
variable

83 (1) He led a full and _____ life. 그는 충만하고 다양한 삶을 살았다.

(2) The weather is at its most _____ in the spring. 날씨는 봄에 가장 변하기 쉽다.

ANSWER

80. (1) successful (2) successive   81. (1) temporary (2) contemporary   82. (1) terrible[horrible/awful] (2) terrific[awesome]   83. (1) varied (2) variable

84 affect : effect : affection

affect	통 ❶ 영향을 미치다 ❷ (정서적) 충격을 주다	decisions which _____ our lives 우리 삶에 영향을 미치는 결정
effect	명 영향, 결과, 효과	to have a big _____ on you 너에게 큰 영향을 미치다
affection	명 애정	a deep _____ for children 아이들에 대한 깊은 애정

85 board : aboard : abroad

board	명 ❶ 판(게시판/칠판) ❷ 이사회 통 타다[탑승하다]	Passengers are waiting to _____. 승객들이 탑승하기를 기다리고 있다.
aboard	부 전 (배·비행기·열차를) 타고	to go _____ the plane 비행기를 타고 가다
abroad	부 외국에[으로]	to live/go _____ 외국에 살다/가다

86 cite : recite : site :sight

cite	통 예로 들다, 인용하다	to be _____d as an example 예로 들어지다
recite	통 암송하다, 열거하다	to _____ a poem 시를 암송하다
site	명 장소, 현장, 웹 사이트	a construction _____ 건설 현장
sight	명 시력, 광경	to lose/regain _____ 시력을 잃다/되찾다

빈칸에 알맞은 단어 넣기

보기
affect
effect
affection

84 (1) She has deep _____ for her parents. 그녀는 부모님에 대한 깊은 애정을 갖고 있다.

(2) The decision can _____ the lives of many people.
그 결정은 많은 사람들의 삶에 영향을 미칠 수 있다.

(3) Modern farming methods can have an adverse _____ on the environment.
현대 농사법은 환경에 부정적인 영향을 미칠 수 있다.

board
aboard
abroad

85 (1) We're supposed to _____ at 7:00. 우리는 7시에 탑승하기로 되어 있다.

(2) They are popular, both at home and _____. 그들은 국내와 해외 모두에서 인기가 있다.

(3) He climbed _____ just as the train was leaving.
그는 열차가 막 떠나고 있을 때 올라탔다.

cite
recite
site
sight

86 (1) The disease has affected his _____. 그 병이 그의 시력에 영향을 미쳤다.

(2) Each child had to _____ a poem to the class.
아이들 각자 반 아이들 앞에서 시를 암송해야 했다.

(3) Safety helmets must be worn on the construction _____.
건설 현장에서는 안전모를 써야 한다.

(4) The passage _____d above is from a William Wordsworth poem.
위에 인용된 구절은 윌리엄 워즈워스의 시에서 나온 것이다.

ANSWER

84. (1) affection (2) affect (3) effect   **85.** (1) board (2) abroad (3) aboard   **86.** (1) sight (2) recite (3) site (4) cite

87 immediate : mediate : meditate

immediate	형 즉각적인	an _____ response 즉각적인 반응
mediate	동 중재하다	to _____ between the hostile nations 적대국들 사이를 중재하다
meditate	동 ❶ 명상하다 ❷ (~ on) 숙고하다	to _____ on the day's events 하루의 일들에 대해 숙고하다

88 moral : morale : mortal

moral	형 도덕의 명 (-s) 도덕률, 교훈	_____ standards/values 도덕규범/도덕적 가치
morale	명 사기(士氣)	to boost[raise] _____ 사기를 북돋우다
mortal	형 영원히 살지 못하는, 치명적인	a _____ wound 치명상

89 object : objection : objective

object	명 ❶ 물건[물체] ❷ 목적 ❸ 대상 동 (~ to) 반대하다	an unidentified flying _____ [UFO] 미확인 비행 물체 an _____ of study/pity 연구/동정의 대상 to _____ to the proposal 제안에 반대하다
objection	명 반대	an _____ to the plan 계획에 대한 반대
objective	형 객관적인 (↔ subjective) 명 목표(=goal)	an _____ assessment 객관적인 평가 to achieve your _____s 목표를 성취하다

빈칸에 알맞은 단어 넣기

보기
immediate
mediate
meditate

87 (1) I spent hours _____ing on my future.
나는 나의 미래에 대해 숙고하느라 몇 시간을 보냈다.

(2) This overall crisis calls for _____ action.
이 총체적 위기는 즉각적인 조처를 필요로 한다.

(3) He has been appointed to _____ the dispute. 그는 분쟁을 중재하도록 임명되었다.

moral
morale
mortal

88 (1) The victory boosted the team's _____. 승리가 팀의 사기를 북돋우었다.

(2) I feel I have a _____ obligation to help the poor.
나는 가난한 사람들을 도울 도덕적 의무가 있다고 느낀다.

(3) Her father's death reminded her that she was _____.
그녀 아버지의 죽음이 그녀에게 영원히 살지 못한다는 걸 상기시켰다.

object
objection
objective

89 (1) Many people _____ to nuclear power plants. 많은 사람들이 원자력 발전소에 반대한다.

(2) It went ahead despite strong _____s from the public.
그것은 대중의 강한 반대에도 불구하고 추진되었다.

(3) An outsider can give a more _____ assessment than a friend.
외부인이 친구보다 더 객관적인 평가를 해 줄 수 있다.

ANSWER

87. (1) meditate (2) immediate (3) mediate **88.** (1) morale (2) moral (3) mortal **89.** (1) object (2) objection (3) objective

90 punctual : punctuality : punctuation : puncture

punctual	형 시간을 지키는	to be _____ for appointments 약속 시간을 지키다
punctuality	명 시간 엄수	_____ is imperative. 시간 엄수는 필수적이다.
punctuation	명 구두점	_____ marks 구두점
puncture	명 구멍[상처]	_____ wounds 찔린상처

91 saw : sew : sewer : sow

saw	명 톱 동 톱질하다	a thin _____ blade 얇은 톱날
sew	동 바느질하다[깁다]	to _____ clothes 옷을 바느질하다
sewer	명 하수관	_____ rats 하수관 쥐들
sow	동 (씨를) 뿌리다	to _____ the seeds 씨를 뿌리다

92 sequence : consequence : consequent : subsequent

sequence	명 순서, 일련	in a logical _____ 논리적 순서로 a _____ of events 일련의 사건들
consequence	명 결과, 중요함	serious _____s 심각한 결과
consequent	형 결과로 일어나는	the drought and _____ famine 가뭄과 그 결과 발생하는 기근
subsequent	형 그다음의	_____ generations 그다음 세대들

빈칸에 알맞은 단어 넣기

보기: punctual, punctuality, punctuation, puncture

90 (1) I place a high value on _____. 나는 시간 엄수에 높은 가치를 둔다.

(2) You have been reliable and _____. 너는 믿을 수 있고 시간도 지켜 왔다.

(3) Her messages are completely without _____. 그녀의 메시지는 완전히 구두점이 없다.

보기: saw, sew, sewer, sow

91 (1) Threats of war have _____ fear in the region.
전쟁의 위협이 그 지역에 공포의 씨를 뿌렸다.

(2) Surgeons were able to _____ the finger back on.
외과 의사들이 손가락을 다시 꿰매 붙일[봉합할] 수 있었다.

보기: sequence, consequence, consequent, subsequent

92 (1) The slightest error can have serious _____.
가장 사소한 실수가 심각한 결과를 가져올 수도 있다.

(2) Scenes of a film are often shot out of _____.
영화의 장면들은 흔히 순서가 뒤바뀌어 촬영된다.

(3) His work had a great influence on _____ generations.
그의 작품은 그다음 세대들에게 큰 영향을 미쳤다.

(4) Falling sales and a _____ loss of profits forced him to lay off workers.
판매 감소와 그 결과 발생한 수익 손실로 그는 노동자들을 해고하지 않을 수 없었다.

ANSWER
90. (1) punctuality (2) punctual (3) punctuation   91. (1) sown(←sow) (2) sew   92. (1) consequence (2) sequence (3) subsequent (4) consequent

307

93 refuge : refugee : refuse

refuge	몡 피난(처)	to take/seek _____ 피난하다
refugee	몡 난민	a _____ camp 난민 수용소
refuse	됭 거절하다	to _____ an offer 제안을 거절하다

94 sleep : asleep : sleepy

sleep	됭 자다 몡 잠[수면]	to _____ well/badly 잘/잘 못 자다
asleep	혱 (서술적) 자고 있는 [잠든]	to fall _____ 잠들다
sleepy	혱 졸리는	to feel _____ 졸리다

95 wake : awake

| wake | 됭 (~ up) 깨다[깨우다] (=waken, awake, awaken) | I usually _____ up early. 난 보통 일찍 깬다. |
| awake | 혱 (서술적) 깨어 있는 됭 (-awoke-awoken) 깨다[깨우다] | to be half/fully _____ 반쯤/완전히 깨어 있다 |

96 beside : besides

| beside | 젠 ~ 옆에 | He sat _____ her. 그는 그녀 옆에 앉았다. |
| besides | 뷧 게다가 젠 ~ 외에 | other reasons _____ money 돈 외에 다른 이유 |

빈칸에 알맞은 단어 넣기

보기	
refuge refugee refuse	**93** (1) Residents took _____ in a bomb shelter. 주민들은 방공호로 대피했다. (2) _____s were streaming across the border. 난민들이 국경을 건너서 줄줄이 이어졌다. (3) She _____d to accept that there was a problem. 그녀는 문제가 있다는 걸 받아들이기를 거부했다.
sleep asleep sleepy	**94** (1) I felt _____ and went to bed. 나는 졸려서 잠자리에 들었다. (2) Did you _____ soundly last night? 어젯밤에 푹 잤니? (3) I was so exhausted that I fell _____ at my desk. 나는 너무 기진맥진해서 책상에서 잠들었다.
wake awake	**95** (1) I was _____ during the operation on my leg. 나는 다리 수술 동안 깨어 있었다. (2) Don't hesitate to _____ me up if you need anything. 무엇이 필요하면 망설이지 말고 나를 깨워라.
beside besides	**96** (1) Nothing _____ a miracle could save them now. 기적 이외의 아무것도 지금 그들을 구조하지 못할 것이다. (2) Stand _____ the statue and I'll take your picture. 조각상 옆에 서면 네 사진을 찍어 줄게.

ANSWER

93. (1) refuge (2) Refugee (3) refuse   94. (1) sleepy (2) sleep (3) asleep   95. (1) awake (2) wake   96. (1) besides (2) beside

97 alternate : alternative

alternate	동 번갈아 하다	to _____ work with play 일과 놀이를 번갈아 하다
	형 번갈아 나오는	He works _____ days.
		그는 격일로 일한다.
alternative	형 대체[대안]의	_____ energy/medicine 대체 에너지/의학
	명 대안	

98 blink : brink

blink	동 (눈을/빛이) 깜박이다	He _____ed in the bright sunlight.
		그는 밝은 햇빛에 눈을 깜박였다.
brink	명 직전, (벼랑) 끝	on the _____ of collapse/death 붕괴/죽음 직전에

99 council : counsel

council	명 지방 의회, 회의	local _____ elections 지방 의회 선거
counsel	동 상담[조언]하다	to _____ alcoholics 알코올 중독자를 상담하다
	명 조언	

100 devote : devout

| devote | 동 바치다 | to _____ yourself to your career 직업에 헌신하다 |
| devout | 형 독실한 | a _____ Buddhist/Christian 독실한 불교/기독교 신자 |

빈칸에 알맞은 단어 넣기

보기
alternate
alternative

97 (1) Do you have an _____ solution? 너는 대안이 될 해결책이 있니?

(2) Her mood _____s between joy and despair.
그녀의 기분은 기쁨과 절망 사이를 번갈아 오간다.

blink
brink

98 (1) He _____ed her eyes when the light flashed. 그는 빛이 비치자 눈을 깜박였다.

(2) The crisis brought the two nations to the _____ of war.
그 위기는 두 나라를 전쟁 직전까지 몰고 갔다.

council
counsel

99 (1) Therapists were brought in to _____ the bereaved.
(심리) 치료사들이 유족들을 상담해 주도록 투입되었다.

(2) The local _____ has decided to allocate funds for the project.
지방 의회는 그 프로젝트에 자금을 배정하기로 결정했다.

devote
devout

100 (1) She is a _____ Buddhist/Christian/Muslim.
그녀는 독실한 불교/기독교/이슬람교 신자다.

(2) He has _____d his life to the care of homeless people.
그는 노숙자들을 돌보는 데 평생을 바쳤다.

ANSWER

97. (1) alternative (2) alternate 98. (1) blink (2) brink 99. (1) counsel (2) council 100. (1) devout (2) devote

101 except : excerpt

except	전 접 ~ 제외하고는 [외에는]	every day _____ Sundays 일요일을 제외하고 매일
excerpt	명 발췌	an _____ of the speech 연설의 발췌

102 facilitate : facility

facilitate	동 용이하게 하다 [촉진하다]	to _____ economic growth 경제 성장을 촉진하다
facility	명 ❶ 시설 ❷ 재능	leisure _____ies 레저 시설 an _____ for languages 언어에 대한 재능

103 famine : feminine

famine	명 기근	_____ relief in Africa 아프리카 기근 구호
feminine	형 여성의[여성스러운]	the traditional _____ role 전통적인 여성의 역할

104 flash : flesh

flash	동 번쩍이다 명 섬광	Lightning _____ed. 번개가 번쩍였다.
flesh	명 살	_____ and blood 혈육

빈칸에 알맞은 단어 넣기

보기

except excerpt	**101** (1) Not a sound was heard _____ the wind howling. 바람이 윙윙거리는 소리를 제외하고는 어떠한 소리도 들리지 않았다. (2) I've read only _____s of *Harry Potter*, never the whole book. 나는 '해리포터' 책 전체가 아니라 발췌 부분들만 읽었다.
facilitate facility	**102** (1) Structured teaching _____s learning. 조직화된 가르침은 학습을 용이하게 한다. (2) She has an amazing _____ for languages. 그녀는 언어에 대한 놀라운 재능이 있다. (3) The hotel has special _____ies for welcoming disabled people. 그 호텔은 장애인들을 맞이할 수 있는 특수 시설이 있다.
famine feminine	**103** (1) Widespread _____ triggered violent protests. 광범위한 기근이 폭력적인 시위를 촉발시켰다. (2) The film describes the experience from a _____ perspective. 그 영화는 여성의 관점에서 경험을 묘사한다.
flash flesh	**104** (1) Thunder rumbled and lightning _____ed. 천둥이 우르릉거리고 번개가 번쩍였다. (2) The thorn went deep into the _____ of my hand. 가시가 내 손의 살 속 깊이 박혔다.

ANSWER

101. (1) except (2) excerpt   102. (1) facilitate (2) facility (3) facility(facilities)   103. (1) famine (2) feminine   104. (1) flash (2) flesh

105 mean : means

mean	통 의미[의도]하다	What do you _____? 무슨 뜻이니?
	형 ❶ 못된[심술궂은]	The _____ of 7, 9 and 14 is 10.
	❷ 평균의	7과 9와 14의 평균은 10이다.
	명 평균, 중용	
means	명 ❶ 수단 ❷ 돈[수입]	a _____ of transportation 교통수단

106 outlook : overlook

outlook	명 ❶ 관점 ❷ 전망	a good _____ on life 훌륭한 인생관
overlook	통 ❶ 간과하다	to _____ one key fact 중요한 사실 하나를 간과하다
	❷ 내려다보다	The house _____s the river.
		그 집은 강을 내려다보고 있다.

107 pat : pet

pat	통 쓰다듬다[토닥거리다]	to _____ the dog on the head 개의 머리를 쓰다듬다
pet	명 애완동물	a _____ dog/cat 애완견/애완용 고양이
	통 어루만지다[애무하다]	to _____ the kitty 새끼 고양이를 어루만지다

108 personal : personnel

personal	형 개인의	_____ belongings 개인 소지품
personnel	명 ❶ 직원들[인원]	skilled _____ 숙련된 직원들
	❷ 인사 부서	

빈칸에 알맞은 단어 넣기

보기
mean
means

105 (1) Music is a powerful _____ of communication. 음악은 강력한 의사소통 수단이다.

(2) Try to find a golden _____ between doing too little and doing too much.
너무 적게 하는 것과 너무 많이 하는 것 사이의 중용을 찾도록 노력해라.

outlook
overlook

106 (1) I have a positive _____ on life. 나는 긍정적인 인생관을 갖고 있다.

(2) You seem to have _____ed one important fact.
너는 한 가지 중요한 사실을 간과한 것 같다.

(3) We had lunch at a restaurant _____ing the river.
우리는 강이 내려다보이는 식당에서 점심을 먹었다.

pat
pet

107 (1) A dog named Merry was our first family _____.
'메리'라고 이름 지어진 개가 우리 가족 최초의 애완동물이었다.

(2) She _____ted my back and told me everything would be fine.
그녀가 나의 등을 쓰다듬으며 모든 것이 잘될 거라고 말했다.

personal
personnel

108 (1) This is just my _____ opinion/preference.
이것은 단지 나 개인의 의견/선호일 뿐이다.

(2) They've reduced the number of _____ working on the project.
그들은 그 프로젝트에서 일하는 직원들의 수를 줄여 왔다.

ANSWER

105. (1) means (2) mean   106. (1) outlook (2) overlook (3) overlook   107. (1) pet (2) pat   108. (1) personal (2) personnel

109 pray : prey

| pray | 통 기도[기원]하다 | to _____ for peace 평화를 위해 기도하다 |
| prey | 명 먹잇감 | a tiger stalking its _____ 먹잇감을 뒤쫓는 호랑이 |

110 principal : principle

principal	형 주요한 명 교장	the _____ source of income 주요 수입원
		a high school _____ 고등학교 교장
principle	명 원칙[원리]	high moral _____s 높은 도덕적 원칙

111 scrap : scrape

scrap	명 조각, 조금, 남은 음식	to feed the dog on _____s 개에게 남은 음식을 주다
scrape	통 긁다[긁어내다]	to _____ the mud off your boots 부츠에서 진흙을 긁어내다
	명 긁힌 상처[찰과상]	cuts and _____s 베인 상처와 긁힌 상처

112 strip : stripe

| strip | 통 (옷을) 벗(기)다 | to _____ naked 발가벗다 |
| stripe | 명 줄무늬 | the Stars and S_____s 성조기 |

Q ┌ 보기 ┐

빈칸에 알맞은 단어 넣기

pray
prey

109 (1) We _____ she will recover from her illness.
우리는 그녀가 병에서 회복하기를 기원한다.

(2) Elderly people are often easy _____ for swindlers and other criminals.
노인들은 흔히 사기꾼들과 다른 범죄자들의 손쉬운 먹잇감이다.

principal
principle

110 (1) I won't lie about it; it's against my _____s.
나는 그것에 대해 거짓말하지 않겠다. 그것은 내 원칙에 위배된다.

(2) The _____ reason for changing the plan is lack of time and money.
계획을 바꾸는 주된 이유는 시간과 돈의 부족이다.

scrap
scrape

111 (1) I fell and _____d my knee. 나는 넘어져서 무릎이 긁혔다.

(2) After the scandal, she had no _____ of dignity left.
스캔들 후에 그녀는 조금의 위엄도 남아 있지 않았다.

strip
stripe

112 (1) The zebra is a wild horse with black and white _____s.
얼룩말은 흑백 줄무늬를 가진 야생마다.

(2) They were forced to _____ naked in freezing temperatures.
그들은 영하의 온도에 강제로 발가벗겨졌다.

ANSWER

109. (1) pray (2) prey   **110.** (1) principle (2) principal   **111.** (1) scrape (2) scrap   **112.** (1) stripe (2) strip

113 vague : vogue

| vague | 형 모호한[막연한/희미한] | a _____ description 모호한 묘사 |
| vogue | 명 유행(=fashion) | Short skirts are in _____. 짧은 치마가 유행이다. |

114 vain : vein

vain	형 ❶ 자만심이 강한	a _____ girl 자만심이 강한 소녀
	❷ 헛된	a _____ hope 헛된 희망
vein	명 정맥	to find a _____ in your arm 팔의 정맥을 찾다

115 sometime : sometimes

| sometime | 부 (미래·과거의) 언젠가 | _____ in September/around 1900 9월/1900년경 언젠가 |
| sometimes | 부 때때로[가끔] | I _____ have to work late. 난 때때로 늦게까지 일해야 한다. |

116 deep : deeply

deep	형 깊은	a _____ river/hole 깊은 강/구멍
	부 (표면 속·아래로) 깊이	to be buried/hidden _____ 깊이 묻히다/숨겨지다
deeply	부 (정도가) 깊이[매우]	to sleep/think _____ 깊이 자다/생각하다

빈칸에 알맞은 단어 넣기

보기
vague
vogue

113 (1) Social networking sites are in _____. 소셜 네트워킹 사이트들이 유행하고 있다.

(2) The politicians make _____ promises about the future.
정치가들은 미래에 대한 모호한 약속을 한다.

vain
vein

114 (1) She is _____ about her appearance. 그녀는 자신의 외모에 대해 자만심이 강하다.

(2) Many _____s are found just under the skin.
많은 정맥들이 피부 바로 아래에서 찾아진다.

sometime
sometimes

115 (1) It's likely to happen _____ soon. 그것은 언젠가 곧 일어날 것 같다.

(2) A moment's insight is _____ worth a life's experience.
한순간의 통찰력이 때때로 평생의 경험만큼 가치가 있다.

deep
deeply

116 (1) I was _____ moved by the movie. 나는 그 영화에 깊이 감동했다.

(2) The miners were trapped _____ underground. 광부들이 땅속 깊이 갇혔다.

ANSWER

113. (1) vogue (2) vague 114. (1) vain (2) vein 115. (1) sometime (2) sometimes 116. (1) deeply (2) deep

117 hard : hardly

hard	형 단단한, 어려운	a _____ chair/task 딱딱한 의자/어려운 일
	부 열심히	to concentrate _____ 열심히 집중하다
hardly	부 거의 ~ 않다	I can _____ believe it.
		난 그것을 거의 믿을 수 없다.

118 high : highly

high	형 높은 부 높이	_____ altitudes 높은 고도
		to jump/fly/kick _____ 높이 뛰다/날다/차다
highly	부 매우[고도로](=very)	_____ successful/trained 매우 성공적인/고도로 훈련된

119 late : lately

late	형 늦은 부 늦게	Sorry I'm _____.
		늦어서 미안해.
		to study _____ 늦게까지 공부하다
lately	부 최근에(=recently)	What have you been doing _____?
		최근에 어떻게 지냈니?

120 near : nearly

near	부 전 가까이	to live _____ the school 학교 가까이 살다
	형 가까운	in the _____ future 가까운 장래
nearly	부 거의(=almost)	Is the job _____ finished?
		일이 거의 끝났니?

빈칸에 알맞은 단어 넣기

보기	
hard	**117** (1) She has worked _____ all her life. 그녀는 평생 열심히 일해 왔다.
hardly	(2) I am so busy I _____ notice the days pass by.
	나는 너무 바빠서 세월이 지나가는지도 거의 알지 못하겠다.
high	**118** (1) This is a _____ sensitive matter. 이것은 매우 민감한 문제다.
highly	(2) My desk is piled _____ with books. 내 책상은 책들로 높이 쌓여 있다.
late	**119** (1) I have been feeling better _____. 나는 최근에 상태가 좋아지고 있다.
lately	(2) The package arrived _____, but better _____ than never!
	소포가 늦게 도착했지만, 안 온 것보다 늦게라도 온 게 더 낫지 않은가!
near	**120** (1) I _____ missed the train. 나는 열차를 거의 놓칠 뻔했다.
nearly	(2) We're getting _____er to the truth. 우리는 진실에 더 가까이 가고 있다.

ANSWER

117. (1) hard (2) hardly   118. (1) highly (2) high   119. (1) lately (2) late, late   120. (1) nearly (2) near

퀴즈 테스트
미니 영어 사전

부록

뜯어먹는 수능 1등급 주제별 영단어 **1800**

퀴즈 테스트

구성
일일 테스트(앞면): 당일 학습한 단어 30개의 뜻을 우리말로 씁니다.
누적 테스트(뒷면): 해당일 이전 3일 간 학습한 단어 중 30개가 쌓여 있습니다.
⑩ 누적 테스트 DAY 15 : DAY 12~14의 단어 테스트

사용법
1. 일단 해당 날짜의 테스트 용지를 뜯어냅니다.
2. 반으로 잘라 아래 부분은 내일을 위해 잘 보관해 둡니다.
3. 일일 테스트부터 시작합니다. (2분)
4. 뒷장을 넘겨 누적 테스트를 계속합니다. (2분)
5. 채점해 보고 틀린 것들을 골라내 다시 암기합니다. (3분)

▶총 소요 시간: 약 7분

정답 확인 방법
일일 테스트는 해당 날짜에 나와 있는 30개 단어를 참조하고,
누적 테스트는 부록 '미니 영어 사전'을 이용합니다.

미니 영어 사전

**이 사전은 고등학교 영어 교과서와 수능 단어 전부를 검색·분석해 실제로
자주 쓰이는 의미만 추려 실은 것입니다.**

– 알파벳순으로 정리되어 있습니다.
– 각 단어 뒤에 이 책에서의 페이지가 나와 있습니다.
– 늘 몸에 지니고 다니며 외우기도 하고 찾아보기도 할 수 있습니다.

일일 암기장

– 1일분 30개씩 60일분 1800개가 정리되어 있습니다.
– 영어와 우리말 사이를 접어 영어는 우리말로, 우리말은 영어로 각각 외울
  수 있습니다.
– 늘 몸에 지니고 다니면서 외울 수 있습니다.

01 ancestor
02 descendant
03 offspring
04 sibling
05 orphan
06 companion
07 acquaintance
08 infant
09 adolescent
10 juvenile
11 puberty
12 lifespan
13 pregnancy
14 abortion
15 embryo
16 fetus
17 cradle
18 gender
19 spouse
20 engagement
21 divorce
22 euthanasia
23 corpse
24 coffin
25 condolence
26 funeral
27 cremation
28 grave
29 cemetery
30 widow ↔ widower

01 beverage
02 refreshment
03 liquor
04 dairy
05 veal/mutton
06 vegetarian
07 gourmet
08 cuisine
09 ingredient
10 dough
11 spice
12 seasoning
13 flavor
14 appetite
15 leftover
16 nutrition
17 nourishment
18 carbohydrate
19 protein
20 intake
21 fiber
22 fabric
23 textile
24 garment
25 outfit
26 costume
27 cosmetic
28 gem
29 vogue
30 fad

1일째에는 누적 테스트가 없습니다.

01	orphan	16	divorce
02	infant	17	condolence
03	juvenile	18	companion
04	corpse	19	fetus
05	descendant	20	funeral
06	gender	21	cradle
07	sibling	22	cemetery
08	ancestor	23	acquaintance
09	embryo	24	coffin
10	offspring	25	abortion
11	engagement	26	puberty
12	pregnancy	27	cremation
13	grave	28	spouse
14	euthanasia	29	lifespan
15	adolescent	30	widow ↔ widower

01	shelter	16	attic
02	dwelling	17	cellar
03	residence	18	closet
04	real estate[realty]	19	ceiling
05	cottage	20	pillar
06	cabin	21	porch
07	hut	22	hearth
08	skyscraper	23	hedge
09	landlord/landlady	24	faucet
10	tenant	25	outlet
11	suburb	26	plumbing
12	outskirts	27	appliance
13	province	28	utensil
14	chamber	29	broom
15	suite	30	chore

01	organ	16	skull
02	forehead	17	spine
03	retina	18	rib
04	wrist	19	flesh
05	thumb	20	tissue
06	thigh	21	nerve
07	lap	22	vein
08	breast	23	artery
09	bosom	24	pulse
10	abdomen	25	circulation
11	belly	26	respiration
12	kidney	27	metabolism
13	liver	28	complexion
14	womb	29	mustache
15	skeleton	30	mole

01 orphan	16 beverage
02 infant	17 refreshment
03 juvenile	18 vegetarian
04 corpse	19 ingredient
05 descendant	20 spice
06 gender	21 protein
07 offspring	22 nutrition
08 ancestor	23 appetite
09 grave	24 flavor
10 pregnancy	25 nourishment
11 cradle	26 gem
12 divorce	27 cosmetic
13 adolescent	28 intake
14 funeral	29 fabric
15 puberty	30 costume

01 engagement	16 leftover
02 acquaintance	17 fiber
03 spouse	18 outfit
04 condolence	19 garment
05 lifespan	20 carbohydrate
06 fetus	21 shelter
07 companion	22 real estate[realty]
08 coffin	23 hut
09 sibling	24 tenant
10 cemetery	25 province
11 liquor	26 attic
12 dairy	27 ceiling
13 cuisine	28 hearth
14 dough	29 outlet
15 seasoning	30 utensil

01 ailment
02 disorder
03 disability
04 deformity
05 syndrome
06 infection
07 plague
08 epidemic
09 germ
10 immunity
11 measles
12 pneumonia
13 diabetes
14 arthritis
15 heatstroke/sunstroke

16 allergy
17 addiction
18 poisoning
19 symptom
20 diarrhea
21 fatigue
22 insomnia
23 itch
24 lump
25 blister
26 bruise
27 scratch
28 scar
29 coma
30 nearsightedness

01 remedy
02 therapy
03 first aid
04 physician
05 surgeon
06 surgery
07 checkup
08 diagnosis
09 acupuncture
10 acupressure
11 crutch
12 pharmacy
13 prescription
14 antibiotic
15 painkiller

16 pill[tablet]
17 dose[dosage]
18 psychiatry
19 psychoanalysis
20 subconscious
21 ego
22 narcissism
23 insanity
24 fitness
25 vigor
26 workout
27 strain
28 obesity
29 sanitation
30 hygiene

01	veal/mutton	16	cellar
02	gourmet	17	pillar
03	textile	18	hedge
04	vogue	19	plumbing
05	fad	20	broom
06	beverage	21	retina
07	ingredient	22	thigh
08	nutrition	23	bosom
09	nourishment	24	kidney
10	intake	25	skeleton
11	dwelling	26	rib
12	cottage	27	nerve
13	skyscraper	28	pulse
14	suburb	29	metabolism
15	chamber	30	mole

01	residence	16	skull
02	cabin	17	flesh
03	landlord/landlady	18	vein
04	outskirts	19	circulation
05	suite	20	complexion
06	closet	21	ailment
07	porch	22	deformity
08	faucet	23	plague
09	appliance	24	immunity
10	chore	25	diabetes
11	organ	26	allergy
12	wrist	27	symptom
13	lap	28	insomnia
14	abdomen	29	blister
15	liver	30	scar

01 sentiment
02 sensation
03 instinct
04 intuition
05 impulse
06 contentment
07 compassion
08 ecstasy
09 zeal
10 gratitude
11 solitude
12 nostalgia
13 suspense
14 indifference
15 hatred
16 contempt
17 disgrace
18 jealousy
19 heartbreak
20 melancholy
21 misery
22 panic
23 temper
24 rage
25 fury
26 wrath
27 agony
28 anguish
29 pang
30 woe

01 public/private school
02 kindergarten
03 coeducation
04 discipline
05 tuition
06 tutor
07 instructor
08 faculty
09 undergraduate
10 sophomore
11 diploma
12 degree
13 certificate
14 arts[humanities]
15 elective
16 admission
17 attendance
18 assignment
19 thesis
20 midterm/final
21 encyclopedia
22 atlas
23 dormitory
24 intellect
25 IQ
26 prodigy
27 creativity
28 self-improvement
29 self-directed learning
30 socialization

01 forehead
02 thumb
03 breast
04 belly
05 womb
06 spine
07 tissue
08 artery
09 respiration
10 mustache
11 disorder
12 syndrome
13 epidemic
14 measles
15 arthritis
16 addiction
17 diarrhea
18 itch
19 bruise
20 coma
21 remedy
22 physician
23 checkup
24 acupressure
25 prescription
26 pill[tablet]
27 psychoanalysis
28 narcissism
29 vigor
30 obesity

01 disability
02 infection
03 germ
04 pneumonia
05 heatstroke/sunstroke
06 poisoning
07 fatigue
08 lump
09 scratch
10 nearsightedness
11 therapy
12 surgeon
13 diagnosis
14 crutch
15 antibiotic
16 dose[dosage]
17 subconscious
18 insanity
19 workout
20 sanitation
21 sentiment
22 intuition
23 compassion
24 gratitude
25 suspense
26 indifference
27 disgrace
28 melancholy
29 temper
30 anguish

01	occupation	16	freelance(r)
02	vocation	17	recommendation
03	professionalism	18	promotion
04	livelihood	19	incentive
05	toil	20	flextime
06	workload	21	retirement
07	overtime	22	pension
08	overwork	23	unemployment
09	workforce	24	capability
10	personnel	25	competence
11	executive	26	craft
12	supervisor	27	expertise
13	consultant	28	proficiency
14	novice	29	efficiency
15	newbie	30	morale

일일 테스트 DAY **10** Score /30

01	carriage	16	honk
02	wagon	17	aviation
03	path	18	navigation
04	lane	19	altitude
05	alley	20	vessel
06	avenue	21	ferry(boat)
07	pavement	22	liner
08	highway	23	tanker
09	ramp	24	raft
10	intersection	25	port
11	milepost[milestone]	26	dock
12	commute	27	deck
13	freight	28	canal
14	burden	29	lighthouse
15	congestion	30	shipwreck

01 first aid
02 surgery
03 acupuncture
04 pharmacy
05 painkiller
06 psychiatry
07 ego
08 fitness
09 strain
10 hygiene
11 sensation
12 contentment
13 zeal
14 solitude
15 hatred

16 jealousy
17 misery
18 rage
19 wrath
20 pang
21 public/private school
22 discipline
23 instructor
24 sophomore
25 certificate
26 admission
27 thesis
28 atlas
29 IQ
30 self-improvement

01 instinct
02 impulse
03 ecstasy
04 nostalgia
05 contempt
06 heartbreak
07 panic
08 fury
09 agony
10 woe
11 kindergarten
12 tuition
13 faculty
14 diploma
15 arts[humanities]

16 attendance
17 midterm/final
18 dormitory
19 prodigy
20 self-directed learning
21 occupation
22 livelihood
23 overtime
24 personnel
25 consultant
26 freelance(r)
27 incentive
28 pension
29 competence
30 proficiency

01 amusement

02 relaxation

03 pastime

04 amateur

05 maniac

06 fanatic

07 archery

08 martial art

09 lottery

10 gambling

11 tourism

12 backpacking

13 voyage

14 cruise

15 expedition

16 excursion

17 outing

18 landscape

19 scenery

20 spectacle

21 attraction

22 monument

23 souvenir

24 accommodation

25 jet lag

26 feast

27 banquet

28 reception

29 reunion

30 hospitality

01 (a)esthetic

02 masterpiece

03 genre

04 avant-garde

05 parody

06 plot

07 climax

08 narrative

09 myth(ology)

10 verse

11 lyric

12 epic

13 prose

14 essay

15 biography/autobiography

16 oil painting/watercolor

17 portrait

18 mural

19 calligraphy

20 ceramic

21 pottery/porcelain

22 chorus

23 chord

24 tune

25 tempo

26 playwright

27 script

28 sequence

29 auditorium

30 intermission

01	coeducation	16	recommendation
02	tutor	17	flextime
03	undergraduate	18	unemployment
04	degree	19	craft
05	elective	20	efficiency
06	assignment	21	carriage
07	encyclopedia	22	lane
08	intellect	23	pavement
09	creativity	24	intersection
10	socialization	25	freight
11	vocation	26	honk
12	toil	27	altitude
13	overwork	28	liner
14	executive	29	port
15	novice	30	canal

01	professionalism	16	aviation
02	workload	17	vessel
03	workforce	18	tanker
04	supervisor	19	dock
05	newbie	20	lighthouse
06	promotion	21	amusement
07	retirement	22	amateur
08	capability	23	archery
09	expertise	24	gambling
10	morale	25	voyage
11	wagon	26	excursion
12	alley	27	scenery
13	highway	28	monument
14	milepost[milestone]	29	jet lag
15	burden	30	reception

01　linguistics
02　lingua franca
03　dialect
04　accent
05　intonation
06　slang
07　literacy ↔ illiteracy
08　bilingual
09　fluency
10　consonant/vowel
11　idiom
12　usage
13　maxim
14　quotation
15　excerpt

16　anecdote
17　rhetoric
18　metaphor
19　analogy
20　irony
21　paradox
22　satire
23　connotation
24　euphemism
25　session
26　agenda
27　controversy
28　consensus
29　discourse
30　forum

01　multimedia
02　newscast
03　channel
04　coverage
05　correspondent
06　anchor
07　journal
08　periodical
09　column
10　feature
11　headline
12　deadline
13　subscription
14　publicity
15　public relations[PR]

16　sponsor
17　copywriter
18　classified ad
19　leaflet
20　brochure
21　bulletin
22　publication
23　draft
24　manuscript
25　format
26　footnote
27　margin
28　copyright
29　pirate
30　censorship

01	path	16	outing
02	avenue	17	spectacle
03	ramp	18	souvenir
04	commute	19	feast
05	congestion	20	reunion
06	navigation	21	(a)esthetic
07	ferry(boat)	22	avant-garde
08	raft	23	climax
09	deck	24	verse
10	shipwreck	25	prose
11	relaxation	26	oil painting/watercolor
12	maniac	27	calligraphy
13	martial art	28	chorus
14	tourism	29	tempo
15	cruise	30	sequence

01	pastime	16	portrait
02	fanatic	17	ceramic
03	lottery	18	chord
04	backpacking	19	playwright
05	expedition	20	auditorium
06	landscape	21	linguistics
07	attraction	22	accent
08	accommodation	23	literacy ↔ illiteracy
09	banquet	24	idiom
10	hospitality	25	maxim
11	masterpiece	26	anecdote
12	parody	27	analogy
13	narrative	28	satire
14	lyric	29	session
15	essay	30	consensus

01	era	16	antique
02	archive	17	treasure
03	throne	18	mummy
04	majesty	19	anthropology
05	noble(wo)man	20	tribe
06	knight	21	kinship
07	commoner	22	folklore
08	slavery	23	heritage
09	feudalism	24	inheritance
10	imperialism	25	legacy
11	colony	26	convention
12	arch(a)eology	27	ritual
13	relic	28	morality
14	remains	29	virtue
15	artifact	30	vice

01	Christian	16	salvation
02	Muslim	17	sin
03	Buddhist	18	devil
04	Confucian	19	idol
05	monk/nun	20	superstition
06	shaman	21	taboo
07	hermit	22	fate
08	pilgrim	23	destiny
09	cathedral	24	misfortune[mischance]
10	monastery	25	outlook
11	shrine	26	perspective
12	altar	27	conscience
13	heaven ↔ hell	28	idealism
14	hymn	29	realism
15	mercy	30	materialism

01 genre
02 plot
03 myth(ology)
04 epic
05 biography/autobiography
06 mural
07 pottery/porcelain
08 tune
09 script
10 intermission
11 lingua franca
12 intonation
13 bilingual
14 consonant/vowel
15 quotation

16 rhetoric
17 irony
18 connotation
19 agenda
20 discourse
21 multimedia
22 coverage
23 journal
24 feature
25 subscription
26 sponsor
27 leaflet
28 publication
29 format
30 copyright

---

01 dialect
02 slang
03 fluency
04 usage
05 excerpt
06 metaphor
07 paradox
08 euphemism
09 controversy
10 forum
11 newscast
12 correspondent
13 periodical
14 headline
15 publicity

16 copywriter
17 brochure
18 draft
19 footnote
20 pirate
21 era
22 majesty
23 commoner
24 imperialism
25 relic
26 antique
27 anthropology
28 folklore
29 legacy
30 morality

Score   /30

01	sociology	16	discrimination
02	individualism	17	segregation
03	citizenship	18	racism
04	NGO	19	violence ↔ non-violence
05	framework	20	riot
06	infrastructure	21	turmoil
07	celebrity	22	overpopulation
08	prestige	23	density
09	privilege	24	slum
10	reputation	25	anonymity
11	equality ↔ inequality	26	activism
12	justice ↔ injustice	27	feminism
13	minority	28	boycott
14	bias	29	petition
15	stereotype	30	patron

Score   /30

01	constitution	16	arson
02	legislation	17	fraud
03	regulation	18	bribery
04	offense	19	jury
05	violation	20	defendant
06	delinquency	21	prosecutor
07	conspiracy	22	attorney
08	murder	23	alibi
09	robbery	24	oath
10	burglar	25	testimony
11	theft	26	guilt ↔ innocence
12	pickpocket	27	verdict
13	assault	28	penalty
14	kidnapping	29	punishment
15	hostage	30	confinement

01	channel	16	treasure
02	anchor	17	tribe
03	column	18	heritage
04	deadline	19	convention
05	public relations[PR]	20	virtue
06	classified ad	21	Christian
07	bulletin	22	Confucian
08	manuscript	23	hermit
09	margin	24	monastery
10	censorship	25	heaven ↔ hell
11	archive	26	salvation
12	noble(wo)man	27	idol
13	slavery	28	fate
14	colony	29	outlook
15	remains	30	idealism

01	throne	16	sin
02	knight	17	superstition
03	feudalism	18	destiny
04	arch(a)eology	19	perspective
05	artifact	20	realism
06	mummy	21	sociology
07	kinship	22	NGO
08	inheritance	23	celebrity
09	ritual	24	reputation
10	vice	25	minority
11	Muslim	26	discrimination
12	monk/nun	27	violence ↔ non-violence
13	pilgrim	28	overpopulation
14	shrine	29	anonymity
15	hymn	30	boycott

01 agriculture
02 peasant
03 orchard
04 plantation
05 fertilizer
06 manure
07 pesticide[insecticide]
08 shovel[spade]
09 plow
10 irrigation
11 reservoir
12 barn
13 livestock
14 shepherd
15 ranch
16 pasture
17 hay
18 fishery
19 mining
20 petroleum
21 lumber
22 manufacturing
23 mill
24 smokestack
25 automation
26 prefabrication
27 warehouse
28 productivity
29 competitiveness
30 patent

01 economics
02 supply ↔ demand
03 profit ↔ loss
04 revenue
05 expenditure
06 corporation
07 enterprise
08 monopoly
09 commerce
10 transaction
11 investment
12 retail
13 wholesale
14 vendor
15 merchandise
16 finance
17 budget
18 currency
19 property
20 asset
21 bond
22 depression
23 recession
24 bankruptcy
25 consumerism
26 trademark
27 warranty
28 frugality
29 extravagance
30 luxury

01 Buddhist
02 shaman
03 cathedral
04 altar
05 mercy
06 devil
07 taboo
08 misfortune[mischance]
09 conscience
10 materialism
11 individualism
12 framework
13 prestige
14 equality ↔ inequality
15 bias
16 segregation
17 riot
18 density
19 activism
20 petition
21 constitution
22 offense
23 conspiracy
24 burglar
25 assault
26 arson
27 jury
28 attorney
29 testimony
30 penalty

01 citizenship
02 infrastructure
03 privilege
04 justice ↔ injustice
05 stereotype
06 racism
07 turmoil
08 slum
09 feminism
10 patron
11 legislation
12 violation
13 murder
14 theft
15 kidnapping
16 fraud
17 defendant
18 alibi
19 guilt ↔ innocence
20 punishment
21 agriculture
22 plantation
23 pesticide[insecticide]
24 irrigation
25 livestock
26 pasture
27 mining
28 manufacturing
29 automation
30 productivity

01 statesman
02 self-reliance
03 autonomy
04 federation
05 sovereignty
06 monarchy
07 aristocracy
08 dictatorship
09 tyranny
10 regime
11 reign
12 administration
13 ministry
14 diplomacy
15 doctrine
16 ambassador
17 embassy
18 assembly
19 council
20 delegate
21 ballot
22 poll
23 referendum
24 capitalism
25 socialism
26 nationalism
27 fascism
28 liberalism
29 conservatism
30 radicalism

01 combat
02 clash
03 territory
04 frontier
05 fortress
06 foe
07 ally
08 troop
09 corps
10 warrior
11 veteran
12 captive
13 civilian
14 aggression
15 conquest
16 revenge
17 strategy
18 tactic
19 nuke
20 pistol
21 bullet
22 cannon
23 artillery
24 shell
25 submarine
26 spear ↔ shield
27 armor
28 disarmament
29 ceasefire[truce]
30 treaty

01 regulation
02 delinquency
03 robbery
04 pickpocket
05 hostage
06 bribery
07 prosecutor
08 oath
09 verdict
10 confinement
11 peasant
12 fertilizer
13 shovel[spade]
14 reservoir
15 shepherd

16 hay
17 petroleum
18 mill
19 prefabrication
20 competitiveness
21 economics
22 revenue
23 enterprise
24 transaction
25 wholesale
26 finance
27 property
28 depression
29 consumerism
30 frugality

01 orchard
02 manure
03 plow
04 barn
05 ranch
06 fishery
07 lumber
08 smokestack
09 warehouse
10 patent
11 supply ↔ demand
12 expenditure
13 monopoly
14 investment
15 vendor

16 budget
17 asset
18 recession
19 trademark
20 extravagance
21 statesman
22 federation
23 aristocracy
24 regime
25 ministry
26 ambassador
27 council
28 poll
29 socialism
30 liberalism

01	zoology/botany	16	beak
02	organism	17	fin
03	mammal	18	aquarium
04	primate	19	stable
05	reptile	20	hibernation
06	herbivore/carnivore	21	veterinarian
07	predator	22	stalk
08	prey	23	twig
09	caterpillar	24	thorn
10	herd	25	petal
11	flock	26	pollen
12	swarm	27	moss
13	claw	28	fungus
14	feather	29	photosynthesis
15	plume	30	hybrid

일일 테스트 DAY 24

Score /30

01	ecology	16	landfill
02	contamination	17	fallout
03	global warming	18	reuse
04	greenhouse gas	19	upcycling
05	fumes	20	conservation
06	emission	21	mound
07	acid rain	22	ridge
08	deforestation	23	meadow
09	ozone layer	24	wetland
10	extinction	25	swamp[marsh]
11	habitat	26	brook[creek]
12	sanctuary	27	strait
13	detergent	28	bay
14	sewage	29	glacier
15	disposable	30	iceberg

Score /30

01 profit ↔ loss
02 corporation
03 commerce
04 retail
05 merchandise
06 currency
07 bond
08 bankruptcy
09 warranty
10 luxury
11 self-reliance
12 sovereignty
13 dictatorship
14 reign
15 diplomacy
16 embassy
17 delegate
18 referendum
19 nationalism
20 conservatism
21 combat
22 frontier
23 ally
24 warrior
25 civilian
26 revenge
27 nuke
28 cannon
29 submarine
30 disarmament

Score /30

01 autonomy
02 monarchy
03 tyranny
04 administration
05 doctrine
06 assembly
07 ballot
08 capitalism
09 fascism
10 radicalism
11 clash
12 fortress
13 troop
14 veteran
15 aggression
16 strategy
17 pistol
18 artillery
19 spear ↔ shield
20 ceasefire[truce]
21 zoology/botany
22 primate
23 predator
24 herd
25 claw
26 beak
27 stable
28 stalk
29 petal
30 fungus

01 meteorology
02 precipitation
03 fog/mist
04 frost
05 drizzle
06 downpour
07 sleet
08 hail
09 blizzard
10 avalanche
11 gale/gust
12 blast
13 typhoon
14 thermometer/barometer
15 Celsius/Fahrenheit

16 humidity
17 moisture
18 catastrophe
19 hazard
20 eruption
21 lava
22 ash
23 tidal wave
24 tsunami
25 drought
26 famine
27 starvation
28 shortage
29 refugee
30 survivor

01 geography
02 Arctic/Antarctic
03 mainland/island
04 peninsula
05 coral reef
06 geology
07 crust
08 gravel
09 pebble
10 erosion
11 astronomy
12 cosmos
13 chaos
14 hemisphere
15 equator

16 latitude/longitude
17 orbit
18 axis
19 galaxy
20 constellation
21 sunspot
22 eclipse
23 Mercury/Venus/Mars/Jupiter
24 comet
25 spacecraft
26 probe
27 blast-off
28 aerospace
29 alien
30 extraterrestrial

01 territory
02 foe
03 corps
04 captive
05 conquest
06 tactic
07 bullet
08 shell
09 armor
10 treaty
11 organism
12 reptile
13 prey
14 flock
15 feather

16 fin
17 hibernation
18 twig
19 pollen
20 photosynthesis
21 ecology
22 greenhouse gas
23 acid rain
24 extinction
25 detergent
26 landfill
27 upcycling
28 ridge
29 swamp[marsh]
30 bay

01 mammal
02 herbivore/carnivore
03 caterpillar
04 swarm
05 plume
06 aquarium
07 veterinarian
08 thorn
09 moss
10 hybrid
11 contamination
12 fumes
13 deforestation
14 habitat
15 sewage

16 fallout
17 conservation
18 meadow
19 brook[creek]
20 glacier
21 meteorology
22 frost
23 sleet
24 avalanche
25 typhoon
26 humidity
27 hazard
28 ash
29 drought
30 shortage

01 phenomenon
02 specimen
03 hypothesis
04 formula
05 analysis
06 gene
07 chromosome
08 genome
09 blueprint
10 heredity
11 mutation
12 physiology
13 anatomy
14 fossil
15 oxygen/hydrogen
16 molecule
17 catalyst
18 physics
19 atom
20 nucleus
21 particle
22 radiation
23 friction
24 gravity/gravitation
25 optics
26 refraction
27 ultraviolet rays
28 wavelength
29 conduction
30 vapor

01 high tech
02 innovation
03 electronics
04 semiconductor
05 (micro)chip
06 circuit
07 electromagnetism
08 cellphone
09 tablet
10 input ↔ output
11 download ↔ upload
12 update
13 information superhighway
14 fiber optics
15 satellite
16 telecommunications
17 teleconference
18 telecommuting
19 e-commerce
20 GPS
21 AI
22 cybernetics
23 virtual reality
24 CAD/CAM
25 ergonomics
26 biotechnology
27 genetic engineering
28 clone
29 stem cell
30 test-tube baby

01 global warming	16 moisture
02 emission	17 eruption
03 ozone layer	18 tidal wave
04 sanctuary	19 famine
05 disposable	20 refugee
06 reuse	21 geography
07 mound	22 peninsula
08 wetland	23 crust
09 strait	24 erosion
10 iceberg	25 chaos
11 precipitation	26 latitude/longitude
12 drizzle	27 galaxy
13 hail	28 eclipse
14 gale/gust	29 spacecraft
15 thermometer/barometer	30 aerospace

01 fog/mist	16 orbit
02 downpour	17 constellation
03 blizzard	18 Mercury/Venus/Mars/Jupiter
04 blast	19 probe
05 Celsius/Fahrenheit	20 alien
06 catastrophe	21 phenomenon
07 lava	22 formula
08 tsunami	23 chromosome
09 starvation	24 heredity
10 survivor	25 anatomy
11 Arctic/Antarctic	26 molecule
12 coral reef	27 atom
13 gravel	28 radiation
14 astronomy	29 optics
15 hemisphere	30 wavelength

01 arithmetic
02 algebra
03 geometry
04 statistics
05 equation
06 numeral
07 fraction
08 decimal
09 dot
10 dimension
11 extent
12 ratio
13 proportion
14 percentage
15 probability
16 frequency
17 minimum ↔ maximum
18 multitude
19 abundance
20 excess
21 surplus
22 rectangle
23 polygon
24 cube
25 sphere
26 spiral
27 oval
28 cone
29 diameter/radius
30 symmetry

01 sundial/hourglass
02 phase
03 procedure
04 transition
05 scope
06 realm
07 hub
08 core
09 advent
10 outbreak
11 prospect
12 criterion
13 stance
14 outage
15 mechanism
16 equilibrium
17 pros and cons
18 drawback
19 flaw
20 shortcoming
21 adversity
22 pitfall
23 brink
24 fragment/segment
25 remnant
26 by-product
27 cluster
28 concept/conception
29 scrutiny
30 tribute

01	mainland/island	16	catalyst
02	geology	17	nucleus
03	pebble	18	friction
04	cosmos	19	refraction
05	equator	20	conduction
06	axis	21	high tech
07	sunspot	22	semiconductor
08	comet	23	electromagnetism
09	blast-off	24	input ↔ output
10	extraterrestrial	25	information superhighway
11	specimen	26	telecommunications
12	analysis	27	e-commerce
13	genome	28	cybernetics
14	mutation	29	ergonomics
15	fossil	30	clone

01	hypothesis	16	teleconference
02	gene	17	GPS
03	blueprint	18	virtual reality
04	physiology	19	biotechnology
05	oxygen/hydrogen	20	stem cell
06	physics	21	arithmetic
07	particle	22	statistics
08	gravity/gravitation	23	fraction
09	ultraviolet rays	24	dimension
10	vapor	25	proportion
11	innovation	26	frequency
12	(micro)chip	27	abundance
13	cellphone	28	rectangle
14	download ↔ upload	29	polygon
15	fiber optics	30	spiral

01 install

02 inject

03 insert

04 embed

05 enclose

06 cram

07 choke

08 smother

09 heap

10 dangle

11 dip

12 soak

13 scoop

14 splash

15 sprinkle

16 sow

17 scatter

18 disperse

19 dispatch

20 transport

21 transmit

22 transplant

23 shift

24 propel

25 thrust

26 drag

27 haul

28 heave

29 tug

30 jerk

01 grip

02 grab

03 pinch

04 retain

05 manipulate

06 imprison

07 pitch

08 fling

09 hurl

10 toss

11 flip

12 tickle

13 stroke

14 caress

15 pat

16 pound

17 punch

18 thump

19 slam

20 slap

21 spank

22 thrash

23 smash

24 collide

25 stab

26 poke

27 pierce

28 penetrate

29 slice

30 slash

01 electronics
02 circuit
03 tablet
04 update
05 satellite
06 telecommuting
07 AI
08 CAD/CAM
09 genetic engineering
10 test-tube baby
11 algebra
12 equation
13 decimal
14 extent
15 percentage

16 minimum ↔ maximum
17 excess
18 cube
19 oval
20 diameter/radius
21 sundial/hourglass
22 transition
23 hub
24 outbreak
25 stance
26 equilibrium
27 flaw
28 pitfall
29 by-product
30 cluster

01 geometry
02 numeral
03 dot
04 ratio
05 probability
06 multitude
07 surplus
08 sphere
09 cone
10 symmetry
11 phase
12 scope
13 core
14 prospect
15 outage

16 pros and cons
17 shortcoming
18 brink
19 remnant
20 concept/conception
21 install
22 embed
23 choke
24 dangle
25 scoop
26 sow
27 dispatch
28 transplant
29 thrust
30 heave

01	lean	16	dodge
02	crook	17	trace
03	crouch	18	trail
04	tilt	19	crawl
05	roam	20	creep
06	stroll	21	glide
07	stride	22	skid
08	shuffle	23	stumble
09	descend	24	tumble
10	bound	25	plunge
11	hop	26	rotate
12	dash	27	revolve
13	dart	28	spin
14	sprint	29	swirl
15	flee	30	whirl

01	blink	16	vomit
02	frown	17	suck
03	gaze	18	lick
04	glance/glimpse	19	devour
05	glare	20	nibble
06	peep[peek]	21	digest
07	overhear	22	shiver[quiver]
08	grin	23	wag
09	wail	24	flap[flutter]
10	sob	25	hug
11	exhale ↔ inhale	26	embrace
12	gasp	27	shrug
13	snore	28	sprain
14	hiccup	29	throb
15	burp[belch]	30	paralyze

Score　　/30

01	procedure	16	scatter
02	realm	17	transport
03	advent	18	shift
04	criterion	19	drag
05	mechanism	20	tug
06	drawback	21	grip
07	adversity	22	retain
08	fragment/segment	23	pitch
09	scrutiny	24	toss
10	tribute	25	stroke
11	inject	26	pound
12	enclose	27	slam
13	smother	28	thrash
14	dip	29	stab
15	splash	30	penetrate

Score　　/30

01	insert	16	punch
02	cram	17	slap
03	heap	18	smash
04	soak	19	poke
05	sprinkle	20	slice
06	disperse	21	lean
07	transmit	22	tilt
08	propel	23	stride
09	haul	24	bound
10	jerk	25	dart
11	grab	26	dodge
12	manipulate	27	crawl
13	fling	28	skid
14	flip	29	plunge
15	caress	30	spin

01 generate	16 weave
02 yield	17 synthesize
03 reproduce	18 improvise
04 breed	19 duplicate
05 mate	20 imitate
06 cultivate	21 mimic
07 consist	22 simulate
08 compose	23 disguise
09 comprise	24 adorn
10 constitute	25 illuminate
11 compile	26 illustrate
12 edit	27 scribble
13 devise	28 provoke
14 mold	29 spark
15 forge	30 trigger

01 abolish	16 withdraw
02 eliminate	17 omit
03 erase	18 abbreviate
04 delete	19 extract
05 deplete	20 pluck
06 deprive	21 uproot
07 discard	22 bleach
08 dispose	23 scrub
09 dispense	24 ruin
10 expend	25 demolish
11 exile	26 devastate
12 expel	27 ravage
13 banish	28 obliterate
14 displace	29 exterminate
15 dismiss	30 extinguish

Score   /30

01	pinch	16	trace
02	imprison	17	creep
03	hurl	18	stumble
04	tickle	19	rotate
05	pat	20	swirl
06	thump	21	blink
07	spank	22	glance/glimpse
08	collide	23	overhear
09	pierce	24	sob
10	slash	25	snore
11	crook	26	vomit
12	roam	27	devour
13	shuffle	28	shiver[quiver]
14	hop	29	hug
15	sprint	30	sprain

Score   /30

01	crouch	16	suck
02	stroll	17	nibble
03	descend	18	wag
04	dash	19	embrace
05	flee	20	throb
06	trail	21	generate
07	glide	22	breed
08	tumble	23	consist
09	revolve	24	constitute
10	whirl	25	devise
11	frown	26	weave
12	glare	27	duplicate
13	grin	28	simulate
14	exhale ↔ inhale	29	disguise
15	hiccup	30	illustrate

01 fuse
02 integrate
03 merge
04 blend
05 mingle
06 tangle
07 entangle
08 hook
09 correlate
10 incorporate
11 overlap
12 assemble
13 accumulate
14 adhere
15 cling

16 seal
17 sew
18 rip
19 undo
20 detach
21 isolate
22 segregate
23 alienate
24 exclude
25 distinguish
26 differentiate
27 discriminate
28 diverge
29 classify
30 categorize

01 equip
02 furnish
03 impart
04 render
05 bestow
06 endow
07 entitle
08 entrust
09 empower
10 authorize
11 allocate
12 assign
13 distribute
14 donate
15 dedicate

16 sacrifice
17 submit
18 succumb
19 surrender
20 forfeit
21 refund
22 restore
23 retrieve
24 inherit
25 lease
26 interchange
27 barter
28 substitute
29 utilize
30 harness

01	gaze	16	synthesize
02	peep[peek]	17	imitate
03	wail	18	adorn
04	gasp	19	scribble
05	burp[belch]	20	spark
06	lick	21	abolish
07	digest	22	delete
08	flap[flutter]	23	discard
09	shrug	24	expend
10	paralyze	25	banish
11	yield	26	withdraw
12	mate	27	extract
13	compose	28	bleach
14	compile	29	demolish
15	mold	30	obliterate

01	reproduce	16	omit
02	cultivate	17	pluck
03	comprise	18	scrub
04	edit	19	devastate
05	forge	20	exterminate
06	improvise	21	fuse
07	mimic	22	blend
08	illuminate	23	entangle
09	provoke	24	incorporate
10	trigger	25	accumulate
11	eliminate	26	seal
12	deplete	27	undo
13	dispose	28	segregate
14	exile	29	distinguish
15	displace	30	diverge

01	maintain	16	escort
02	sustain	17	steer
03	preserve	18	usher
04	conserve	19	complement
05	reserve	20	supplement
06	safeguard	21	subsidize
07	shield	22	rear
08	insulate	23	nurture
09	liberate	24	nourish
10	release	25	foster
11	rescue	26	educate
12	rid	27	facilitate
13	acquit	28	promote
14	spare	29	motivate
15	accompany	30	underpin

01	ban	16	deter
02	forbid	17	threaten
03	outlaw	18	menace
04	obstruct	19	bully
05	hinder	20	abuse
06	disrupt	21	exploit
07	intercept	22	persecute
08	interfere	23	torture
09	intrude	24	distort
10	invade	25	contaminate
11	impair	26	betray
12	confine	27	assassinate
13	restrain	28	execute
14	suppress	29	slaughter
15	withhold	30	strangle

01	erase	16	sew
02	deprive	17	detach
03	dispense	18	alienate
04	expel	19	differentiate
05	dismiss	20	classify
06	abbreviate	21	equip
07	uproot	22	render
08	ruin	23	entitle
09	ravage	24	authorize
10	extinguish	25	distribute
11	integrate	26	sacrifice
12	mingle	27	surrender
13	hook	28	restore
14	overlap	29	lease
15	adhere	30	substitute

01	merge	16	submit
02	tangle	17	forfeit
03	correlate	18	retrieve
04	assemble	19	interchange
05	cling	20	utilize
06	rip	21	maintain
07	isolate	22	conserve
08	exclude	23	shield
09	discriminate	24	release
10	categorize	25	acquit
11	furnish	26	escort
12	bestow	27	complement
13	entrust	28	rear
14	allocate	29	foster
15	donate	30	promote

01 cooperate
02 collaborate
03 contend
04 confront
05 cope
06 tackle
07 mediate
08 negotiate
09 compromise
10 reconcile
11 regulate
12 dominate
13 domesticate
14 tame
15 supervise
16 oversee
17 appoint
18 designate
19 nominate
20 recruit
21 undertake
22 comply
23 conform
24 assimilate
25 violate
26 disobey
27 defy
28 rebel
29 disregard
30 overlook

01 convey
02 correspond
03 converse
04 chatter
05 gossip
06 utter
07 pronounce
08 proclaim
09 convict
10 affirm
11 assert
12 narrate
13 depict
14 portray
15 characterize
16 clarify
17 specify
18 exemplify
19 certify
20 testify
21 demonstrate
22 manifest
23 disclose
24 signify
25 notify
26 foretell
27 prophesy
28 pledge
29 vow
30 insure

01	impart	16	steer
02	endow	17	supplement
03	empower	18	nurture
04	assign	19	educate
05	dedicate	20	motivate
06	succumb	21	ban
07	refund	22	obstruct
08	inherit	23	intercept
09	barter	24	impair
10	harness	25	suppress
11	sustain	26	threaten
12	reserve	27	abuse
13	insulate	28	torture
14	rescue	29	betray
15	spare	30	slaughter

01	preserve	16	withhold
02	safeguard	17	exploit
03	liberate	18	menace
04	rid	19	distort
05	accompany	20	assassinate
06	usher	21	cooperate
07	subsidize	22	confront
08	nourish	23	mediate
09	facilitate	24	reconcile
10	underpin	25	domesticate
11	forbid	26	oversee
12	hinder	27	nominate
13	interfere	28	comply
14	invade	29	violate
15	restrain	30	rebel

01 assent
02 consent
03 concur
04 accord
05 acknowledge
06 concede
07 confess
08 oppose
09 dissent
10 dispute
11 contradict
12 grumble
13 induce
14 enlist
15 urge
16 advocate
17 preach
18 caution
19 compel
20 enforce
21 oblige
22 exclaim
23 chant
24 mumble
25 stammer
26 brag
27 exaggerate
28 publicize
29 cite
30 quote

01 amuse
02 entertain
03 enchant
04 fascinate
05 captivate
06 dazzle
07 tempt
08 lure
09 arouse
10 evoke
11 inspire
12 stimulate
13 refresh
14 lull
15 soothe
16 sympathize
17 esteem
18 adore
19 worship
20 idolize
21 marvel
22 long
23 yearn
24 crave
25 aspire
26 detest
27 loathe
28 deplore
29 despise
30 scorn

Score /30

01 outlaw
02 disrupt
03 intrude
04 confine
05 deter
06 bully
07 persecute
08 contaminate
09 execute
10 strangle
11 collaborate
12 cope
13 negotiate
14 regulate
15 tame
16 appoint
17 recruit
18 conform
19 disobey
20 disregard
21 convey
22 chatter
23 pronounce
24 affirm
25 depict
26 clarify
27 certify
28 manifest
29 notify
30 pledge

Score /30

01 contend
02 tackle
03 compromise
04 dominate
05 supervise
06 designate
07 undertake
08 assimilate
09 defy
10 overlook
11 correspond
12 gossip
13 proclaim
14 assert
15 portray
16 specify
17 testify
18 disclose
19 foretell
20 vow
21 assent
22 accord
23 confess
24 dispute
25 induce
26 advocate
27 compel
28 exclaim
29 stammer
30 publicize

01	irritate	16	preoccupy
02	distress	17	beware
03	afflict	18	resent
04	harass	19	inflame
05	torment	20	startle
06	tease	21	astonish
07	disgust	22	astound
08	discourage	23	stun
09	dismay	24	horrify
10	distract	25	appall
11	perplex	26	dread
12	bewilder	27	exhaust
13	humiliate	28	grieve
14	overwhelm	29	mourn
15	obsess	30	lament

일일 테스트　　DAY **46**　　　Score _____ /30

01	revive	16	endure
02	situate	17	tolerate
03	dwell	18	surmount
04	reside	19	refrain
05	occupy	20	abstain
06	inhabit	21	contain
07	populate	22	strive
08	migrate	23	endeavor
09	lodge	24	exert
10	accommodate	25	pursue
11	linger	26	venture
12	lurk	27	incline
13	abound	28	accomplish
14	necessitate	29	attain
15	undergo	30	fulfill

01	converse	16	preach
02	utter	17	enforce
03	convict	18	chant
04	narrate	19	brag
05	characterize	20	cite
06	exemplify	21	amuse
07	demonstrate	22	fascinate
08	signify	23	tempt
09	prophesy	24	evoke
10	insure	25	refresh
11	consent	26	sympathize
12	acknowledge	27	worship
13	oppose	28	long
14	contradict	29	aspire
15	enlist	30	deplore

01	concur	16	esteem
02	concede	17	idolize
03	dissent	18	yearn
04	grumble	19	detest
05	urge	20	despise
06	caution	21	irritate
07	oblige	22	harass
08	mumble	23	disgust
09	exaggerate	24	distract
10	quote	25	humiliate
11	entertain	26	preoccupy
12	captivate	27	inflame
13	lure	28	astound
14	inspire	29	appall
15	lull	30	grieve

01	emerge	16	ensue
02	originate	17	evolve
03	derive	18	vanish
04	launch	19	perish
05	embark	20	fade
06	initiate	21	recede
07	commence	22	retreat
08	persist	23	resign
09	persevere	24	desert
10	erupt	25	suspend
11	recur	26	halt
12	alternate	27	adjourn
13	coincide	28	postpone
14	synchronize	29	expire
15	precede	30	terminate

01	emit	16	groan
02	discharge	17	shriek
03	glow	18	howl
04	glitter	19	roar
05	blaze	20	toll
06	bang	21	stink
07	boom	22	perspire
08	zoom	23	bleed
09	swish	24	shed
10	snap	25	spit
11	crack	26	drip
12	clatter	27	leak
13	rattle	28	seep
14	buzz	29	overflow
15	hum	30	sprout

01 enchant
02 dazzle
03 arouse
04 stimulate
05 soothe
06 adore
07 marvel
08 crave
09 loathe
10 scorn
11 distress
12 torment
13 discourage
14 perplex
15 overwhelm

16 beware
17 startle
18 stun
19 dread
20 mourn
21 revive
22 reside
23 populate
24 accommodate
25 abound
26 endure
27 refrain
28 strive
29 pursue
30 accomplish

01 afflict
02 tease
03 dismay
04 bewilder
05 obsess
06 resent
07 astonish
08 horrify
09 exhaust
10 lament
11 situate
12 occupy
13 migrate
14 linger
15 necessitate

16 tolerate
17 abstain
18 endeavor
19 venture
20 attain
21 emerge
22 launch
23 commence
24 erupt
25 coincide
26 ensue
27 perish
28 retreat
29 suspend
30 postpone

Score   /30

01 alter	16 magnify
02 convert	17 amplify
03 transform	18 diffuse
04 adjust	19 dignify
05 modify	20 enlighten
06 amend	21 ventilate
07 revise	22 purify
08 refine	23 dilute
09 reform	24 dehydrate
10 renew	25 evaporate
11 renovate	26 accelerate
12 innovate	27 falsify
13 reinforce	28 degenerate
14 enhance	29 deteriorate
15 intensify	30 dehumanize

Score   /30

01 flourish	16 rot
02 prosper	17 impoverish
03 thrive	18 compound
04 boost	19 degrade
05 soar	20 collapse
06 inflate	21 crumble
07 swell	22 crumple
08 diminish	23 shatter
09 dwindle	24 crush
10 wane	25 mash
11 shrink	26 dissolve
12 contract	27 thaw
13 compress	28 overturn
14 condense	29 capsize
15 wither	30 submerge

01 dwell	16 evolve
02 inhabit	17 fade
03 lodge	18 resign
04 lurk	19 halt
05 undergo	20 expire
06 surmount	21 emit
07 contain	22 glitter
08 exert	23 boom
09 incline	24 snap
10 fulfill	25 rattle
11 originate	26 groan
12 embark	27 roar
13 persist	28 perspire
14 recur	29 spit
15 synchronize	30 seep

01 derive	16 shriek
02 initiate	17 toll
03 persevere	18 bleed
04 alternate	19 drip
05 precede	20 overflow
06 vanish	21 alter
07 recede	22 adjust
08 desert	23 revise
09 adjourn	24 renew
10 terminate	25 reinforce
11 discharge	26 magnify
12 blaze	27 dignify
13 zoom	28 purify
14 crack	29 evaporate
15 buzz	30 degenerate

Score /30

01 ponder
02 deliberate
03 contemplate
04 meditate
05 suspect
06 visualize
07 conceive
08 daydream
09 associate
10 foresee
11 recollect
12 comprehend
13 perceive
14 discern
15 acquaint
16 investigate
17 inspect
18 inquire
19 browse
20 analyze
21 dissect
22 decode
23 diagnose
24 ascertain
25 verify
26 coordinate
27 infer
28 equate
29 formulate
30 resolve

일일 테스트 DAY 52

Score /30

01 evaluate
02 assess
03 appraise
04 estimate
05 appreciate
06 deem
07 attribute
08 cherish
09 compliment
10 flatter
11 commemorate
12 compensate
13 assume
14 presume
15 speculate
16 condemn
17 denounce
18 reproach
19 reprove
20 scold
21 curse
22 mock
23 sue
24 penalize
25 triumph
26 prevail
27 excel
28 exceed
29 surpass
30 transcend

01	glow	16	amplify
02	bang	17	enlighten
03	swish	18	dilute
04	clatter	19	accelerate
05	hum	20	deteriorate
06	howl	21	flourish
07	stink	22	boost
08	shed	23	swell
09	leak	24	wane
10	sprout	25	compress
11	convert	26	rot
12	modify	27	degrade
13	refine	28	crumple
14	renovate	29	mash
15	enhance	30	overturn

01	transform	16	impoverish
02	amend	17	collapse
03	reform	18	shatter
04	innovate	19	dissolve
05	intensify	20	capsize
06	diffuse	21	ponder
07	ventilate	22	meditate
08	dehydrate	23	conceive
09	falsify	24	foresee
10	dehumanize	25	perceive
11	prosper	26	investigate
12	soar	27	browse
13	diminish	28	decode
14	shrink	29	verify
15	condense	30	equate

01	prior	16	eternal
02	subsequent	17	continuous/continual
03	simultaneous	18	consecutive
04	immemorial	19	successive
05	initial	20	sustainable
06	ultimate	21	durable
07	timely	22	chronic
08	punctual	23	ongoing
09	abrupt	24	upcoming
10	prompt	25	annual/biannual
11	offhand	26	chronological
12	momentary	27	spatial
13	temporary	28	cramped
14	transient	29	halfway
15	perpetual	30	innermost

✂

01	numerous	16	intense
02	innumerable	17	intensive
03	multiple	18	drastic
04	infinite	19	moderate
05	immense	20	temperate
06	gigantic	21	fragile
07	vast	22	frail
08	extensive	23	vulnerable
09	massive	24	susceptible
10	substantial	25	prone
11	ample	26	mortal ↔ immortal
12	minute	27	fatal
13	mighty	28	destined
14	formidable	29	inevitable
15	potent	30	terminal

01 thrive
02 inflate
03 dwindle
04 contract
05 wither
06 compound
07 crumble
08 crush
09 thaw
10 submerge
11 deliberate
12 suspect
13 daydream
14 recollect
15 discern

16 inspect
17 analyze
18 diagnose
19 coordinate
20 formulate
21 evaluate
22 estimate
23 attribute
24 flatter
25 assume
26 condemn
27 reprove
28 mock
29 triumph
30 exceed

01 contemplate
02 visualize
03 associate
04 comprehend
05 acquaint
06 inquire
07 dissect
08 ascertain
09 infer
10 resolve
11 assess
12 appreciate
13 cherish
14 commemorate
15 presume

16 denounce
17 scold
18 sue
19 prevail
20 surpass
21 prior
22 immemorial
23 timely
24 prompt
25 temporary
26 eternal
27 successive
28 chronic
29 annual/biannual
30 cramped

01 optimistic ↔ pessimistic
02 extrovert ↔ introvert
03 sociable
04 courageous
05 ambitious
06 industrious
07 cowardly
08 timid
09 reserved
10 meek
11 courteous ↔ discourteous
12 considerate
13 earnest
14 discreet
15 prudent
16 altruistic
17 tolerant
18 stern
19 stubborn
20 arrogant
21 vain
22 inquisitive
23 candid
24 devout
25 skeptical
26 cynical
27 hostile
28 corrupt
29 cunning
30 wicked

01 slim
02 plump
03 stout
04 lame
05 dynamic ↔ static
06 brisk
07 intriguing
08 keen
09 blunt
10 spontaneous
11 reluctant
12 inert
13 monotonous
14 arduous
15 flexible
16 elastic
17 versatile
18 eloquent
19 transparent
20 superficial
21 fluffy
22 cozy
23 tidy
24 shabby
25 sticky
26 foul
27 vulgar
28 coarse
29 crude
30 obscene

01	appraise	16	continuous/continual
02	deem	17	sustainable
03	compliment	18	ongoing
04	compensate	19	chronological
05	speculate	20	halfway
06	reproach	21	numerous
07	curse	22	infinite
08	penalize	23	vast
09	excel	24	substantial
10	transcend	25	mighty
11	subsequent	26	intense
12	initial	27	moderate
13	punctual	28	frail
14	offhand	29	prone
15	transient	30	destined

01	simultaneous	16	intensive
02	ultimate	17	temperate
03	abrupt	18	mortal ↔ immortal
04	momentary	19	vulnerable
05	perpetual	20	inevitable
06	consecutive	21	optimistic ↔ pessimistic
07	durable	22	courageous
08	upcoming	23	cowardly
09	spatial	24	meek
10	innermost	25	earnest
11	innumerable	26	altruistic
12	immense	27	stubborn
13	extensive	28	inquisitive
14	ample	29	skeptical
15	formidable	30	corrupt

Score /30

01 objective ↔ subjective
02 rational
03 sensible
04 empirical
05 consistent
06 coherent
07 absurd
08 compatible
09 feasible
10 plausible
11 apt
12 liable
13 reliable
14 handy
15 functional

16 utilitarian
17 hands-on
18 authentic
19 sheer
20 thorough
21 intact
22 partial
23 apparent
24 evident
25 explicit
26 vivid
27 vague
28 ambiguous
29 subtle
30 fuzzy

Score /30

01 superb
02 supreme
03 foremost
04 prime
05 dominant ↔ recessive
06 fundamental
07 underlying
08 requisite
09 indispensable
10 imperative
11 compulsory
12 obligatory
13 mandatory
14 prominent
15 eminent

16 renowned
17 obscure
18 peripheral
19 trivial
20 splendid
21 magnificent
22 marvelous
23 fabulous
24 gorgeous
25 elegant
26 exquisite
27 clumsy
28 invaluable
29 worthy
30 state-of-the-art

01	multiple	16	tolerant
02	gigantic	17	arrogant
03	massive	18	candid
04	minute	19	cynical
05	potent	20	cunning
06	drastic	21	slim
07	fragile	22	lame
08	susceptible	23	intriguing
09	fatal	24	spontaneous
10	terminal	25	monotonous
11	extrovert ↔ introvert	26	elastic
12	ambitious	27	transparent
13	timid	28	cozy
14	courteous ↔ discourteous	29	sticky
15	discreet	30	coarse

01	sociable	16	versatile
02	industrious	17	superficial
03	reserved	18	tidy
04	considerate	19	foul
05	prudent	20	crude
06	stern	21	objective ↔ subjective
07	vain	22	empirical
08	devout	23	absurd
09	hostile	24	plausible
10	wicked	25	reliable
11	plump	26	utilitarian
12	dynamic ↔ static	27	sheer
13	keen	28	partial
14	reluctant	29	explicit
15	arduous	30	ambiguous

01 ordinary ↔ extraordinary
02 normal ↔ abnormal
03 abstract ↔ concrete
04 commonplace
05 equivalent
06 homogeneous
07 unanimous
08 sole
09 varied
10 diverse
11 distinct
12 distinctive
13 discrete
14 remarkable
15 striking
16 ingenious
17 inherent
18 intrinsic
19 innate
20 peculiar
21 weird
22 bizarre
23 freak
24 exotic
25 morbid
26 approximate
27 straightforward
28 elaborate
29 intricate
30 sophisticated

01 masculine ↔ feminine
02 maternal ↔ paternal
03 marital
04 eligible
05 monetary
06 preliminary
07 eco-friendly
08 renewable
09 medi(a)eval
10 divine
11 sacred
12 secular
13 verbal ↔ nonverbal
14 attentive
15 wholesome
16 stale
17 toxic
18 contagious
19 mobile
20 ubiquitous
21 aerial
22 hollow
23 vacant
24 dazed
25 somber
26 stricken
27 stranded
28 wretched
29 adverse
30 reverse/inverse

01	stout	16	hands-on
02	brisk	17	thorough
03	blunt	18	apparent
04	inert	19	vivid
05	flexible	20	subtle
06	eloquent	21	superb
07	fluffy	22	dominant ↔ recessive
08	shabby	23	fundamental
09	vulgar	24	indispensable
10	obscene	25	obligatory
11	rational	26	renowned
12	consistent	27	trivial
13	compatible	28	exquisite
14	apt	29	invaluable
15	handy	30	marvelous

01	sensible	16	eminent
02	coherent	17	requisite
03	feasible	18	magnificent
04	liable	19	clumsy
05	functional	20	worthy
06	authentic	21	ordinary ↔ extraordinary
07	intact	22	equivalent
08	evident	23	unanimous
09	vague	24	sole
10	fuzzy	25	distinct
11	supreme	26	distinctive
12	underlying	27	discrete
13	imperative	28	inherent
14	prominent	29	approximate
15	obscure	30	intricate

A

B

수능과 내신을 한 번에 잡는
프리미엄 고등 영어 **수프림** 시리즈

Supreme 고등영문법
쉽게 정리되는 고등 문법 / 최신 기출 문제 반영 /
문법 누적테스트

Supreme 수능 어법 기본
수능 어법 포인트 72개 / 내신 서술형 어법 대비 /
수능 어법 실전 테스트

Supreme 수능 어법 실전
수능 핵심 어법 포인트 정리 / 내신 빈출 어법 정리
어법 모의고사 12회

독해

Supreme 구문독해
독해를 위한 핵심 구문 68개 / 수능 유형 독해 /
내신·서술형 완벽 대비

Supreme 유형독해
수능 독해 유형별 풀이 전략 / 내신·서술형 완벽 대비 /
미니모의고사 3회

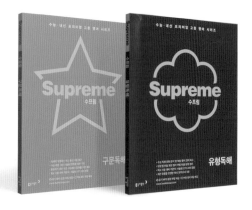

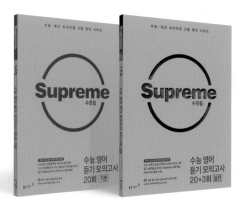

듣기

Supreme 수능 영어 듣기 모의고사 20회 기본
14개 듣기 유형별 분석 / 수능 영어 듣기 모의고사 20회 /
듣기 대본 받아쓰기

Supreme 수능 영어 듣기 모의고사 20+3회 실전
수능 영어 듣기 모의고사 20회+고난도 3회 /
듣기 대본 받아쓰기

뜯어먹는
수능 1등급
주제별 영단어 1800

김승영   연세대 영어영문학과 졸업
연세대 교육대학원 영어교육과 졸업
전 계성여고 교사
현 한국영어교재개발연구소 대표

저 서   뜯어먹는 중학 기본 영단어 1200
뜯어먹는 중학 영단어 1800
뜯어먹는 수능 1등급 기본 영단어 1800
뜯어먹는 수능 1등급 영숙어 1200

고지영   서강대 영어영문학과 졸업
서울대 사범대학원 영어교육과 졸업
현 한국영어교재개발연구소 연구실장

저 서   뜯어먹는 중학 기본 영단어 1200
뜯어먹는 중학 영단어 1800
뜯어먹는 수능 1등급 기본 영단어 1800
뜯어먹는 수능 1등급 영숙어 1200

뜯어먹는 수능 1등급 주제별 영단어 **1800**

발행일	2019년 07월 20일
인쇄일	2023년 11월 30일
펴낸곳	동아출판㈜
펴낸이	이욱상
등록번호	제300-1951-4호(1951. 9. 19)
개발총괄	장옥희
개발책임	이미경
개발	이윤임
영문교열	Andrew Finch
디자인책임	목진성
디자인	문조현
대표번호	1644-0600
주소	서울시 영등포구 은행로 30 (우 07242)